# Law, Religion and Love



Increasingly, the modern neo-liberal world marginalises any notion of religion or spirituality, leaving little or no room for the sacred in the public sphere. While this process advances, the conservative and harmful behaviours associated with some religions and their adherents exacerbate this marginalisation by driving out those who remain religious or spiritual. And all of this is seen through the lens of social science, which seems to agree that religion remains important, if not in a spiritual sense, at least as a source of folklore and a means of identification: religions remain rooted in the societies from which they emerged, and the legal systems of many of those societies emerged from religious sources, even if those societies remain unwilling to admit that fact. In the modern materialistic world of conformity, religion is less a source of guidance than a label of identification.

The world therefore faces two issues. First, the decreasing level of spirituality in the 'West' widens the gap between worshippers and those who have left their faith (eg agnostics and atheists, or those who look at religion as a matter of 'picking and choosing' from a range of options). And, second, the strong connections to religion which remain in many nations, but which are often misused in the secular public sphere (both in the West and internationally). In such divided worlds, both religious and secular forces tend to lock themselves into closed groupings of 'pure truth' and in so doing increase the level of disagreement, in turn producing radicalism. In short, the modern world is divided in two ways: between religious and non-religious (although some have argued that the non-religious secular is itself a form of civil religion), and between those subscribing to divergent understandings of the same religious tradition. While hyperbolic and histrionic, the term 'culture wars' nonetheless best captures what we see happening in the public sphere today.

The question emerges, then: how best to accommodate the democratic principle which posits that the majority should feel that it lives in a society of its own with the human rights principle, holding that it is necessary to ensure the full protection of the minority's rights? How to balance these seemingly opposed principles? We are very familiar with the differences that appear between secular and sacred in the modern world; yet, what of the similarities amongst scriptures and laws which seek to encourage mutual understanding, cooperation and even cohabitation? Because religion itself is a source of law, a set of exhortations or commands as much as a set of rights, every major religion offers an approach to encountering 'the Other' in a positive, constructive, affirming way; and it is here that religions reveal much that they have in common. This book draws together the work of scholars engaged in exploring the possibilities for a 'utopian' world in the sense fostered by St Thomas More. The essays explore those dimensions of religious and civil law where 'love' – however that is defined by relevant texts – fosters and encourages acceptance of 'the Other' and will offer perspectives on the ways in which religious or civil/state law command one to act in the spirit of 'love'.

**Paul Babie** holds a Personal Chair of Law and is Associate Dean of Law (International) in the Adelaide Law School, The University of Adelaide, Australia.

**Vanja-Ivan Savić** is Assistant Professor of Law in the Faculty of Law of the University of Zagreb, Croatia.

## Law and Religion

Series Editor: Professor Norman Doe

*Director of the Centre for Law and Religion, Cardiff University, UK*

The practice of religion by individuals and groups, the rise of religious diversity, and the fear of religious extremism, raise profound questions for the interaction between law and religion in society. The regulatory systems involved, the religious laws of secular government (national and international) and the religious laws of faith communities, are valuable tools for our understanding of the dynamics of mutual accommodation and the analysis and resolution of issues in such areas as: religious freedom; discrimination; the autonomy of religious organisations; doctrine, worship and religious symbols; the property and finances of religion; religion, education and public institutions; and religion, marriage and children. In this series, scholars at the forefront of law and religion contribute to the debates in this area. The books in the series are analytical with a key target audience of scholars and practitioners, including lawyers, religious leaders, and others with an interest in this rapidly developing discipline.

**Series Board**



For a full list of titles in this series, visit www.routledge.com/law/series/LAWRELIG

**Titles in this series include:**

**Law, Religion and Love**
Seeking Ecumenical Justice for the Other
*Paul Babie and Vanja-Ivan Savić*

**Religion, Law and the Constitution**
Balancing Beliefs in Britain
*Javier García Oliva and Helen Hall*

**Forthcoming titles in this series include:**

**State and Religion**
The Australian Story
*Renae Barker*

# Law, Religion and Love

## Seeking Ecumenical Justice for the Other

**Edited by**
**Paul Babie and Vanja-Ivan Savić**

Routledge
Taylor & Francis Group
LONDON AND NEW YORK

First published 2018 by Routledge

2 Park Square, Milton Park, Abingdon, Oxfordshire OX14 4RN
52 Vanderbilt Avenue, New York, NY 10017

*Routledge is an imprint of the Taylor & Francis Group, an informa business*

First issued in paperback 2019



*British Library Cataloguing-in-Publication Data*
A catalogue record for this book is available from the British Library

*Library of Congress Cataloging-in-Publication Data*
A catalog record for this book has been requested

ISBN: 978-1-138-68456-0 (hbk)
ISBN: 978-0-367-33677-6 (pbk)

Typeset in Galliard
by Apex CoVantage, LLC

**Cover Photo © Vanja-Ivan Savić, 2014 'Cemetery, Roermond, Netherlands'.** A small southern town, Roermond, Netherlands was historically divided between Catholics and Protestants. According to the law of the time, the cemetery in Roermond marked out separate Catholic and Protestant sections, with a wall dividing the two. Children of mixed marriages often bought two plots of land for their parents in the cemetery, one on the Catholic side and one on the Protestant, so that they could be close to one another in death. Separate memorial monuments were built for each parent on each side of the wall. The cover photo shows one particularly poignant example of these separate monuments, unique in this cemetery, and perhaps throughout Europe, for the fact that the two are joined by holding hands over the top of the dividing wall. This photo captures the motivating intention for this book: while the positive law divides, the law of love unites.

For Rachael and Iva

# Contents

# Contributors

**Ibrahim Haruna Hassan al-Wasewi** is Associate Professor of Islamic Studies, University of Jos, Nigeria. He holds degrees in Civil Engineering and Development, and a BA, MA and a PhD in Islamic Studies. His teaching and research focus on Islamic sciences as well as Islam in the modern world, with a specific focus on the intersection of Islamic and western thought. He has held collaborative researches at Birmingham University and the University of Arizona and a Fulbright visiting at Northwestern, Evanston IL.

**Paul Babie** holds a Personal Chair of Law in the Adelaide Law School and is Associate Dean of Law (International) and Associate Dean (International) of the Faculty of the Professions, The University of Adelaide. He holds a BA in sociology from the University of Calgary, a BThSt from Flinders University of South Australia, an LLB from the University of Alberta, an LLM from the University of Melbourne, and a DPhil in law from the University of Oxford. He is a Barrister and Solicitor (inactive) of the Court of Queen's Bench of Alberta (Canada), and an Associate Member of the Law Society of South Australia. His primary research interests include private law theory and property theory. He has published and spoken extensively in these fields. He teaches property law, property theory, law and religion, and Roman law.

**Robert Crotty** has studied Christian Theology, Biblical Studies, History and Education in Australia, Rome and Jerusalem. His current research involves religious ethics, ethical theory and the ethics of education. The majority of his working academic life has been spent at the University of South Australia where he was Professor of Religion and Education and the Dean of Research Degrees when he retired in 2001. He remains an Emeritus Professor at that University. In all, he has written some 35 academic books as well as professional journal articles and chapters in books.

**Raphael Dascalu** is an Adjunct Research Fellow at Monash University, Australia. He completed a MA in comparative religion at the Hebrew University of Jerusalem and a PhD in the history of Judaism at the University of Chicago. The primary focus of his research is medieval Jewish philosophy and scriptural interpretation, with a focus on the Judeo-Arabic tradition. His research interests include philosophical exegesis of the Hebrew Bible; intellectual currents in the Islamic world, particularly as they cross confessional boundaries; religious and philosophical ethics and psychology; and medieval Jewish engagement with Islamic philosophy and Sufism.

**Joseph E David** has held academic positions at the University of Pennsylvania, Rutgers University, New York University, the University of Oxford, the Hebrew University and the Interdisciplinary Centre Herzliya. He is currently Professor of Law and Religion at Sapir Academic College, Israel. He teaches and studies law and religion, comparative jurisprudence, legal theory and legal history. His publications focus on the morality of belonging in premodern intellectual history and on law and religious identity.

**Davor Derenčinović** is a Professor of Criminal Law, Head of Chair for Criminal Law, Vice-Dean, Faculty of Law, University of Zagreb, Croatia and President of the Croatian Academy of Legal Sciences. His research focuses on corporate and criminal law; he has published and lectured widely in these fields.

**Alessandra Gaetani** is a jurist, anthropologist of law, and Adjunct Professor in religious rights and community mediation in the University of Insubria, Como. She holds a PhD in the philosophy of law from the University of Milan. Her main research interests include law and religion, comparative religious rights, human rights, and interreligious dialogue.

**Hovhannes Hovhannisyan** received his BA in Theology from Yerevan State University, Faculty of Theology in 2000, and his MA in 2002. He is also a graduate of the Public Administration School of Armenia and the Diplomatic School of Armenia. He is currently Associate Professor, Department of the History of Religions, Faculty of Theology, Yerevan State University, and Associate Professor, American University of Armenia. The author of more than 40 scientific articles, his research focuses on dialogue and religious pluralism.

**Dubravka Hrabar** is Professor and Dean of Law, Faculty of Law, University of Zagreb, Croatia. The author of several books, textbooks, legal Acts, commentaries, and numerous scientific and professional papers, she is a member of the International Society of Family Law, the Association for Civil Law Sciences and Practice of Croatia and the Croatian Association for International Law.

**Slavica Jakelić** is Associate Professor of Humanities and Social Thought at the Honors Christ College, Valparaiso University. Her scholarly interests and publications center on religion and identity, the relationship of religious and secular humanisms, theories of religion and secularism, theories of modernity, interreligious dialogue and conflict resolution, and Christianity in global perspective.

**Joshua Neoh** is Senior Lecturer in Law, Australian National University, Australia, and PhD candidate, University of Cambridge. He holds an LLM from Yale

Law School and an LLB, with First Class Honours and the University Medal, from the Australian National University. He has held visiting research positions at the University of Oxford and the Harvard Law School. He writes in the areas of law, philosophy and theology.

**Steven H Resnicoff** is Professor, DePaul University College of Law and Director of its Center for Jewish Law & Judaic Studies (JLJS). His research involves bankruptcy, commercial paper, and professional responsibility, in which he has authored or co-authored four books, including a law school casebook, as well as numerous book chapters and articles. Perhaps his greatest scholarly contributions, however, have addressed Jewish law and the diverse ways in which it compares to and interrelates with other legal systems. Resnicoff has lectured extensively on Jewish law and antisemitism. He has served as Chair of the Jewish Law Association, an international organisation dedicated to promoting Jewish law scholarship, and Chair of the Association of American Law School's Section on Jewish Law.

**Vanja-Ivan Savić** is Assistant Professor and Head of the Legal Theory Department, Faculty of Law, University of Zagreb, Croatia. He is a graduate of the University of Zagreb Faculty of Law *cum laude*, where he obtained his First Law Degree, a Master of Science in Law Degree (Company Law and Criminal Law), and a PhD. His research involves legal theory, theory of law and state, law and religion, corporate criminal law and human rights. He has published in Croatian, English, and Vietnamese and has been a Visiting Professor at DePaul and Northwestern Universities and at the Universities of Adelaide and Vienna.

**Brett G Scharffs** is the Director of the International Center for Law and Religion Studies and the Rex E. Lee Chair and Professor of Law, Brigham Young University Law School. Together with his colleagues at the Center, he pursues the Center's mission of helping secure the blessing of freedom of religion and belief for all people. Professor Scharffs is a graduate of Georgetown University, where he received a BSBA in international business and an MA in philosophy. He was a Rhodes Scholar at Oxford University, where he earned a BPhil in philosophy. He received his JD from Yale Law School, where he was Senior Editor of the *Yale Law Journal*. He was a law clerk on the DC Circuit of the US Court of Appeals, and a legal assistant on the Iran–US Claim Tribunal in The Hague. Over the past decade he has helped organise advanced academic training programs on religion and the rule of law in China, Vietnam, and Myanmar, as well as programs on Islamic Sharia law and human rights at several universities in Indonesia. He has written more than 100 articles and book chapters, and has made over 300 scholarly presentations in 30 countries.

**Leonard Swidler** is Professor of Catholic Thought/Interreligious Dialogue, Temple University, USA. He holds a BA from St Norbert College, an MA from Marquette University, a PhD from the University of Wisconsin, a STL from Tübingen University. He has been a Visiting Professor at the Universities of Graz, Hamburg, Tübingen, Nankai, Fudan, Temple University Japan, Malaya, Hong Kong, and Azerbaijan. He has published over 200 articles and 75 books.

**Michael Trainor** is a Senior Lecturer in biblical studies, Australian Catholic University, and Adjunct Lecturer in the School of Theology, Flinders University of South Australia. A Catholic priest involved in inter-faith and inter-religious matters, he is Executive Board Member of the International Council of Christians and Jews, Chair of the Australian Council of Christians and Jews, Co-Chair of the South Australian Council of Christians and Jews, Co-Chair of the Uniting Church-Roman Catholic Dialogue of South Australia, and President of the Australian Catholic Biblical Association. His research interests concern the early Jesus movement in the Greco-Roman world and the relevance of religion and dialogue in society.

# Table of Cases

# Table of Legislation

## Italy



## Latvia



## Luxembourg



## Poland



## Portugal



## Russian Federation



## Slovakia



## Spain



## Sweden



## UN



## United Kingdom

## United States

# Acknowledgments

There is little doubt that we have incurred many debts in the course of producing this collection of essays. We attempt here to recognise each of the people that have helped us along the way, recognising, however, that we are likely to overlook some who made an important contribution. For that we apologise.

We begin with our contributors: each of the scholars who have joined this project did so enthusiastically. That made completing the book much easier. Thanks so much to each of you for your commitment to seeing this through to completion.

The Routledge team have been fantastic in their support throughout and their timely reminders. Thanks especially to our Editors, Katie Carpenter and Olivia Manley.

Sincere thanks to Brett Scharffs, Director, and his colleagues at the International Centre for Law and Religion Studies at BYU Law. As with so many of our projects with most of the contributors to this volume, Brett has been an invaluable resource and support in everything we have done. The global law and religion community is fortunate for the champion it has in Brett and ICLRS.

We are immensely grateful to Emily Carr (LLB, Adelaide, 2016) for research, editorial, and general assistance; without her amazing help we would not have been able to complete this book.

Finally, as one might expect in a book about love, we are indebted to our families. Without their kindness, generosity and patience we could not have done this.

Paul Babie and Vanja-Ivan Savić
Adelaide, Australia and Zagreb, Croatia
4 April 2017

# Introduction

## Law's love

*Paul Babie and Vanja-Ivan Savić*

### America 2017

At the time of writing this introductory essay, President Donald Trump had just issued an Executive Order temporarily banning travel from seven Muslim-majority countries. This resulted in the detention of people who had previously been approved to travel whereby they were subsequently detained either at their departure airports or at airports upon arrival in the United States.[1] This act, literally at the stroke of a pen, set off an international maelstrom of protests around the United States and, indeed, around the world, and raised a series of legal questions that quickly engulfed all branches of the US government, including the federal courts.[2] Political solutions were sought and mooted, leading to federal litigation initiated by a number of states and at least one city.[3] A temporary restraining order ('TRO') of execution of the ban was sought and granted in

1 The White House, Executive Order 13769, 'Protecting the Nation from Foreign Terrorist Entry into the United States', 27 January 2017, 82 Fed Reg 8,977, accessed on 10 February 2017, available at: <www.whitehouse.gov/the-press-office/2017/01/25/executive-order-border-security-and-immigration-enforcement-improvements>, promulgated pursuant to *The Immigration and Nationality Act of 1952*, Pub L 82–414, 66 Stat 163, enacted 27 June 1952, 8 USC ch 12, § 212(f).

2 See NPR, 'Trump's Executive Order On Immigration, Annotated', 31 January 2017, accessed on 10 February 2017, available at: <www.npr.org/2017/01/31/512439121/trumps-executive-order-on-immigration-annotated>.

3 Ibid. Massachusetts, New York, Virginia and Washington, as well as San Francisco sued the federal government, alleging violations of the United States Constitution's guarantees of religious freedom (more states were in the process of suing as we were writing): Scott Malone and Dan Levine, 'Challenges to Trump's immigration orders spread to more US states', *Reuters*, 31 January 2017, accessed on 10 February 2017, available at: <www.reuters.com/article/us-usa-trump-immigration-sanfrancisco-idUSKBN15F2B1>. See Andrew Liptak, 'In the last 24 hours, four federal courts have objected to Trump's actions: Here's where we stand', *The Verge*, 29 January 2017, accessed on 10 February 2017, available at: <www.theverge.com/2017/1/29/14430082/four-federal-courts-ruled-trump-immigration-ban>; NPR, 'Trump's Executive Order On Immigration, Annotated', 31 January 2017, accessed on 10 February 2017, available at: <www.npr.org/2017/01/31/512439121/trumps-executive-order-on-immigration-annotated>.

relation to the entire nation in one of those actions, *State of Washington v Trump*,[4] in which the TRO was ultimately upheld in a unanimous judgment of the United States Court of Appeals for the Ninth Circuit.[5]

President Trump argued in the *State of Washington* litigation that the Order was motivated by national security concerns. There is clearly no question that the President has the power to promulgate an Executive Order in the face of such concerns.[6] Indeed, President Trump acted pursuant to Congressional authority under section 212(f) of *The Immigration and Nationality Act of 1952*, which provides that:

> whenever the President finds that the entry of any aliens or of any class of aliens into the United States would be detrimental to the interests of the United States, he may by proclamation, and for such period as he shall deem necessary, suspend the entry of all aliens or any class of aliens as immigrants or nonimmigrants, or impose on the entry of aliens any restrictions he may deem to be appropriate.[7]

Moreover, every nation must certainly enjoy the right to so protect itself.

Yet, while we in no way question the legitimate authority of President Trump to act to protect the United States against possible terrorism threats, at least part of the motivation for the Executive Order – despite protestations by President Trump and his Administration to the contrary – seemed also to be related to the religion of people coming from the seven countries covered. It soon became apparent, based upon statements made by President Trump and some of his supporters, that what the Executive Order sought to achieve was not merely the barring of entry to citizens from those countries who might pose a national security risk, but rather the banning of Muslims from entering the United States. President Trump kept his word: he had promised as much throughout the Presidential election campaign of 2015–16.[8]

Since the 2016 US Presidential election, it has become axiomatic to say that that world is growing more, not less, divided. Commentators frequently make the

4 *State v Washington, et al, v Donald J Trump, et al* (United States District Court, Western District of Washington at Seattle, Robart J) (3 February 2017), C17-0141JLR.

5 *State of Washington, State of Minnesota v Donald J Trump, President of the United States; US Department of Homeland Security; Rex W Tillerson, Secretary of State; John F Kelly, Secretary of the Department of Homeland Security; United States of America* (United States Court of Appeals for the Ninth Circuit, Canby, Clifton, Friedland JJ) (9 February 2017), 17-35105.

6 Ibid, 13.

7 *The Immigration and Nationality Act of 1952*, Pub L 82–414, 66 Stat 163, enacted 27 June 1952, 8 USC ch 12, § 212(f)

8 *State of Washington, State of Minnesota v Donald J Trump, President of the United States; US Department of Homeland Security; Rex W Tillerson, Secretary of State; John F Kelly, Secretary of the Department of Homeland Security; United States of America* (United States Court of Appeals for the Ninth Circuit, Canby, Clifton, Friedland JJ) (9 February 2017), 17-35105, 24–26.

claim that the nadir of this divisiveness is in the United States itself.[9] Division and chaos appear to be spreading beyond the borders of those places traditionally associated with such disruption, to those in places long immune to the hostilities and atrocities to which many of the earth's inhabitants have become accustomed. Some claim that the origins of these conflicts are traceable to religious ideological differences, found in almost every corner of the globe. With the world in crisis, it might be easy to believe that no one is truly able to absorb and deeply understand the needs, pains and suffering of others. *The Brothers Karamazov* might capture this best when Dostoyevsky writes that man is not really ready to accept anyone else as a sufferer except him/herself.[10] And, indeed, while seemingly creating a climate favourable to some religions, on the one hand, President Trump's Executive Order might, at the very least, give one pause for concern about the possible treatment of those holding some religious beliefs on the other, and in this case, especially those who hold the Muslim faith. It might seem trite to say, but these recent events in the United States indicate that religion and law have a difficult and complex relationship to one another.

The contributors to this collection, each an internationally recognised scholar of law, religion, and theology, working from a wide diversity of backgrounds and disciplinary perspectives from a range of backgrounds, seek to demonstrate that despite the claims of some that religious ideological differences lie at the heart of global violence and harm, and that such conflict requires the use of secular/civil law to control the dangerous excesses of religious extremism; that religion does not cause conflict, and it may in fact offer opportunities to work together with law to control whatever excesses many be attributed to religion. Despite the increase and escalation of global religious conflicts between various countries, a consequence of the increased conflict has also simultaneously led to a greater sense of empathy, understanding and tolerance of religious differences. Detractors, President Trump and his Administration among them, name ethnicity and religion as a source of the differences in beliefs which can cause trouble, violence, and even war. Even when religion is not the major reason of the conflict, (and on most occasions it is not), once the roots of dissension have been sown and grown it is often given a religious garb so as to make it appear that religion serves only to cause suffering and spark conflict. President Trump's Executive Order is a case in point.

Another way of viewing the dispute over President Trump's Executive Order, though, might be to see it as one involving love. Are those who support it, and the underlying justification of national security proffered for it, acting out of concern for the 'Other' as achieved through the application of law? Put another

9 The Economist, 'What the visa ban shows about American foreign policy', *The Economist*, 4 February 2017, accessed on 10 February 2017, available at: <www.economist.com/news/briefing/21716079-divided-nation-seeks-divided-world-what-visa-ban-shows-about-american-foreign-policy>.

10 Fyodor Dostoyevsky, *The Brothers Karamazov* (Penguin, 2003 [1879–1880]), Book II, ch 4.

way, and at a higher level of generality going beyond this specific dispute, is there a place for love in the establishment and application of law? And is that present in the actions that have been taken by the Trump Administration. Of course, the Executive Order is the focus neither of this essay, nor this book, but it does serve to highlight the issues that we address. Is there any role at all for love in law? And, if so, what is that role? Does it require treating only fellow citizens according to its dictates? Or does it require treating all people that way, regardless of origin or religion? And what, exactly, are the dictates of love? This book is about the presence of love in law, whether that law is the secular/civil law of the state or of religion.

This debate is in fact nothing new. Nor are we the first to consider it.[11] At least as early as the 19th century, the role of love containing the power for society to achieve its aims has been mooted. Indeed, during that tumultuous century, during which Europe saw revolutions and counter-revolutions spread back and forth across the continent (and as nascent post-Westphalian nations experimented with the earliest forms of written constitutions, and the very existence of constitutional monarchies and democracies solidified from that earlier molten form in which republicanism and liberalism fought for supremacy. Along with forms of socialism and communism), two of the dominant personalities of the age staked their claims either to revolution or to love as the solution to the human condition as it existed within the selfish interests of the state. But while Karl Marx and his followers pinned their hopes to revolution and emancipation of the proletariat, some, notably Richard Wagner, chose the redeeming power of – perhaps surprisingly to some – love.[12] The potential of love to unite, then, is nothing new. Indeed, as we will see, its origins lie much earlier than the 19th century.

What is new, though, and what requires much more scholarship – international in its scope – than can be offered even in this or the few other books like it, is the fact that the debate over the place of love in law has taken on new meaning and urgency in the 21st century neo-liberal world. That urgency stems from the revival of religion as a source of meaning and values for many people.[13] Increasingly, though, the modern neo-liberal world marginalises any notion of religion or spirituality, leaving little or no room for the sacred in the public sphere. Conversely, what a minority portray as the conservative and harmful behaviours associated with some religions and their adherents only serves to exacerbate this marginalisation by driving out those who may consider themselves religious but who wish to avoid being labelled as extremists and, thus, targeted for public abuse and legal vituperation through legislative and judicial means. Examples abound, not least the

11 See, eg, Robert F Cochran and Zachary R Calo (eds), *Agape, Justice, and Law: How Might Christian Love Shape Law?* (Cambridge University Press, 2017).

12 Peter Bassett, 'Wagner: Lord of the Ring' (November 2013) *Limelight* 32.

13 See John Micklethwait and Adrian Wooldridge, *God is Back: How the Global Revival of Faith is Changing the World* (Penguin, 2010).

bans on foreign law recently popular in some US states, used as nothing more than thinly veiled racist efforts to discriminate against Muslims.[14]

When seen through the lens of social science, however, religion remains important, if not in a spiritual sense, at least as a source of folklore and a means of identification: religions remain rooted in those societies from which they emerged, and the legal systems of many of those societies emerged from religious sources.[15] In the modern neo-liberal, materialistic world of conformity, then, one finds a paradoxical stance on religion; in many cases, it is seen as a source of values necessary for that world, but in others, religion is seen less as a source of guidance than as a label of identification, and a negative one at that. And the paradox of religion plays itself out on the international stage in two ways. On the one hand, the decreasing level of spirituality in the 'West' widens the gap between worshippers and those who have left their faith (such as agnostics and atheists, or those who look at religion as a matter of 'picking and choosing' from a range of options).[16] But on the other, the strong connections to religion remain so in many nations, albeit often misused in the secular public sphere (both in the West and globally).[17]

In a divided world, both religious and secular forces seemingly lock themselves into closed groupings of 'pure truth' and in so doing increase the level of disagreement, in turn producing radicalism. In short, the modern world is divided in two ways: between religious and non-religious (although some have argued that the non-religious secular is itself a form of civil religion), and between those subscribing to divergent understandings of the same religious tradition. While hyperbolic and histrionic, the term 'culture wars' nonetheless best captures what we see happening in the public sphere today.

The question therefore arises: how best to accommodate, to balance, not only the democratic principle positing that the majority should feel that it lives in a society of its own, but also the principle of human rights holding that it is necessary to ensure the full protection of the minority's rights? While it is easy, familiar, for us to identify the differences that appear not only between, but also among the secular and the sacred, those of us writing in this book argue that our focus ought to be turned towards the similarities amongst scriptures and laws which seek to encourage mutual understanding, cooperation and even cohabitation. And they find the source of this joint activity in religion, itself a significant source of law with its own

14 See Faiza Patel, Matthew Duss, and Amos Toh, *Foreign Law Bans: Legal Uncertainties and Practical Problems* (Centre for American Progress; Brennan Centre for Justice at New York University School of Law, 2013), accessed on 10 February 2017, available at: <www.brennancenter.org/sites/default/files/publications/ForeignLawBans.pdf>.

15 See Gary D Bouma, *Australian Soul: Religion and Spirituality in the 21st Century* (Cambridge University Press, 2007); John Micklethwait and Adrian Wooldridge, *God is Back: How the Global Revival of Faith Is Changing the World* (Penguin, 2010).

16 See the magisterial work of Charles Taylor, *A Secular Age* (The Belknap Press of Harvard University Press, 2007).

17 See Paul Babie, 'Religion and Constitutionalism: Oscillations Along a Continuum' (2015) 39 *Journal of Religious History* 123.

distinctive requests and commands which, despite popular misconception, provides rules fostering mutual understanding and respect. Because religion itself is a source of law, a set of exhortations or commands as much as a set of rights, every major religion offers its own approach to encountering the Other in a positive, constructive, affirming way; and it is here that religions reveal that they share much in common with other religious and secular traditions.

The contributors to this volume feel that there is a deep need for serious academic research about these rules that guide the treatment of others with empathy, consideration, and tolerance. We seek here to understand how both secular/civil law and religion advances love for the Other. We do this through the pursuit of two themes. First, we explore the rules which particular religions have adopted about how to treat and interact with non-members of their faiths. And, second, we examine the methods by which secular state law can encourage and support the achievement of a standard of 'good mutual living' for all. In short, this book is a collaborative effort of scholars engaged in exploring the possibilities for a 'utopian' world in the sense fostered by St Thomas More.[18] And what we find is that, at the heart of religion, as at the heart of the issue surrounding President Trump's Executive Order, lies the question of love.

Our essays explore, then, those dimensions of religious and secular/civil law where 'love' – however that may be defined by the relevant texts of a tradition, whether it be religious or secular – fosters and encourages acceptance of the Other, in turn offering perspectives on the ways in which religious or civil/state law command one to act in the spirit of 'love'. We scrutinise the ways in which law, both religious and secular/civil, means love, and the ways in which the positive law of the state may divide while the inner heart of love found in 'religious law' may unite. We explore, in short, not only the ways in which law, in the absence of love, may offer an opportunity for growth and understanding of the Other, but also, and much more importantly, how law animated by love may foster that understanding and lead to unity.

## Themes of love

The scholars whose work is brought together in this volume come from every corner of the globe, representing diverse religious, ethnic and cultural backgrounds. Our approach takes both religious and secular stances, with the essays coalescing around three principal themes: religious perspectives on love, legal perspectives on love, and the synthesis of law and love.

### *Religious*

The first part of the book will consider religious perspectives on love for the Other and how those perspectives speak to a contemporary global world, with representation from each of the three monotheistic perspectives. These chapters explore

18 St Thomas More, *Utopia* (Penguin, 2003 [1516]).

perspectives found in religion that we may not have considered before, and which might remain hidden from view due to their religious orientation. The first contribution, for instance, written by Brett Scharffs, explores the boundaries of love and the way in which it can be understood from economic, psychological, evolutionary biological, and neuroscientific perspectives, revealing that whether one considers this either with or without the presence of God, religion has something to say about our lives.

The remaining four chapters in this part of the book each take a specific aspect of religious thought, uncovering important aspects of love for the modern world. Joshua Neoh considers the Old Testament Garden of Eden story, common to each of the monotheistic faiths, contrasting the meta-narratives of law (the Hobbesian narrative) and love (the Edenic narrative). From this foundation, Neoh considers the potential for the reconciliation of those two paradigms in contemporary society. Steven Resnicoff's chapter examines the relationship between free will, responsibility and hope within Jewish thought. Resnicoff argues that, contrary to popular belief, free will plays an essential part in establishing a religious duty to practise justice and love towards others. Michael Trainor's contribution offers an exegesis of controversial passages found in the New Testament which suggests that these apparent inconsistencies may in fact provide rules for the treatment of the non-religious Other. Trainor argues for a normative reading of these passages which supports tolerance and understanding of non-religious persons. Finally, Ibrahim Haruna Hassan al-Wasewi's chapter explores the relationship between Islamic law (Shari'a) and external political influences, and how that connection shapes Shari'a's understanding of the Other. Each of these perspectives provides insight into contemporary life, and what religious understandings of love might mean for international coexistence, peace, and security.

### *Legal*

The second theme emerging from the contributions to this book concerns the perspectives taken by secular/civil law on love. Taking a broader view of the meaning of 'law' and 'legal', these authors consider how law contains a core conception of love with its source in the personal private sphere, which in turn manifests itself in the public sphere through its relationship to the law and politics of the nation-state and the global order. Thus, as concerns the personal private sphere, Slavica Jakelić looks at emerging global patterns of secularism and the increasing conflict of that concept with law and solidarity, as law attempts to embody the power of the secular and its interplay with what is perceived to be the private personal domain of religion. And Joseph David considers the influence of legalism in an economy of religious differences, demonstrating how freedom of religion can be accommodated in a world of expanding and conflicting personal religious differences.

At the level of the nation-state, the broader public sphere is also considered. Hovhannes Hovhannisyan looks at the role of religion and identity in light of the Armenian Genocide and the 'de-victimisation' of Armenian society. This chapter considers the potential for reconciliation with Turkey through the canonisation of Armenian Genocide victims.

And two authors examine legal perspectives on love in the wider global order from a broader trans-national perspective. Leonard Swidler undertakes a consideration of the meaning of global ethics and global law; in an increasingly secular society, this necessitates a review of the efficacy of a universal declaration of global ethics in global law. Davor Derenčinović provides an in-depth comparison of the European freedom of expression and legal protections of religious feelings under the European Convention on Human Rights and Fundamental Freedoms. This involves a close examination of historical developments in European case law and legislation.

### *Synthesis*

The third part of the book contains three chapters, each of which seek a synthesis of the way love is understood in both secular/civil law and in religion. Alessandra Gaetani, in the first essay, explores the role of the International Forum on Religious Democracy ('FIDR') in an ever-secular world as a pathway for civic mediation. The expansion of Islam in Italy offers a primary case study of this role. Robert Crotty, compares the boundaries between various religions, ethics and the given law of a state, arguing that there is a potential for the reconciliation of these seemingly competing sources of secular and religious ethics. Raphael Dascalu continues this theme by exploring the theory of religious law espoused by Maimonides' *imago* and *imitation*, being the perfection of the individual and society, with specific reference to the Jewish faithful as the embodiment of the divine attributes of justice and compassion. Finally, Dubravka Hrabar examines the universal commandment of love as the overarching and prevailing guiding principle of global family law.

## Reflecting on the future

In *Lautsi v Italy*,[19] Professor Joseph Weiler argued before the Grand Chamber of the European Court of Human Rights that there can be no one solution in matters of tolerance; rather, different localities must take into account different social and political realities.[20] Put another way, we might say this: while there are two traditions (religious and secular), two approaches, two systems of rules, there is but one system of values: *human values*. And whether a state is secular or religious, as a matter of human values, it ought to strive to find space for the Other in a spirit of cooperation. The contributors to this book argue that finding that space involves an exploration of two seemingly competing principles of modern life: the democratic principle, on the one hand, which posits that the majority

19 *Lautsi v Italy*, App No 30814/06, 2011 Eur Ct HR (GC).

20 Joseph Weiler, 'Oral Submission on Behalf of Armenia, Bulgaria, Cyprus, Greece, Lithuania, Malta, The Russian Federation, and San Marino – Third Party Intervening States in the Lautsi Case Before the Grand Chamber of the European Court of Human Rights', accessed on 10 February 2017, available at: <www.ilsussidiario.net/News/Politics-Society/2010/7/1/EXCLUSIVE-Oral-Submission-by-Professor-Joseph-Weiler-before-the-Grand-Chamber-of-the-European-Court-of-Human-Rights/6/96909/> [28].

should live in a society of its own choosing, and, on the other hand, the human rights principle, which seeks to protect minority rights, particularly those who are threatened and in danger. And as with those instances of persecution, examples of this balancing abound in law, such as those instances in which the European Court of Human Rights employs the margin of appreciation to give priority to the unique culture of European member states.[21]

We argue in this book that the seeking of that space of cooperation achieves three objectives. First, and perhaps above all, we hope to demonstrate that both law and religion have at their core the need to encounter others in positive ways. In other words, both religion and law are, at their core, the mediation of relationships, within which the neo-liberal individual encounters the other. And it is our contention that this role as mediator, whether found in secular/civil law or in religion, has as its fundamental attribute a conception of love common to both.

Of course, as we learn from Weiler, this exercise is not one that admits of easy, ready-made, neatly packaged answers. Rather, what we present in this volume reveals that rather than answers, exploring the nature and content of relationship in religion and law produces many more questions than answers. This is no relativistic, post-modern cop-out. Rather, it expresses the truth that both law and religion are attempts, very different attempts, true, but attempts nonetheless, to grapple with the mystery of existence.

Yet the way in which our materialistic neo-liberal world presents this reality to us seems to be more a challenge to 'fix' the problems which it bequeaths us: inequality, global environmental crises, shrinking food supplies, poverty, religious conflict, and the list goes on. But no one approach can answer all of the questions, meet all of the demands, fix all of the problems that continue to beset us. The scholars who have written in this book took up this challenge in the spirit of seeking the core and essence of the possibility to reconcile the various inconsistent perceptions over which different cultures and religions seem increasingly to clash.

With this in mind, some contributors have written about the possibility for a different way in which to conceive of religion. As we noted above, it is sometimes argued that state can yield no space to the Other; instead, the argument goes, a state has room only for its own nationalist-secular creed, which acts as an absolute rule in determining the nature and extent of toleration and respect for the rights of others who do not share that secular faith as their own. In the face of such restrictiveness, though, what we all agree on in this volume is this: we must retain our curiosity about the essence of religious law itself and about the roots of legal systems which prioritises the notion of a search for the common universal source of rights which all nations, religions, cultures and ethnicities share. This is an important message in a world riven by strife. Our conclusion is that there are basic

21 See *Otto Preminger v Austria* [1994] ECHR 26 (20 September 1994), *Sahin v Turkey* [2005] ECHR 819 (10 November 2005), *Dhalab v Switzerland* [2001] ECHR 899 (15 February 2001), *SAS v France* [2014] ECHR 695 (1 July 2014), *Eweida v UK* [2013] ECHR 37 (15 January 2013).

norms associated with living together, mutual respect and cohabitation found just as much in the Hebrew Scriptures, the Bible, the Qur'an, and major scriptures from other religious traditions, as they are found in secular legal texts, from the Magna Carta to the European Convention on Human Rights. These norms find expression in one of three ways: respect for the Other who is weak; respect for the dominant culture within the context of preserving concern for the weak; and accommodation of both groups to the maximum extent possible.

Our second goal involves seeking out positive examples of the ways in which law and religion might coexist through their common core of love, not only now, but also prospectively into the future. The contributors to this book draw upon secular/civil and religious texts in existence for centuries. As we have seen from our short visit to the United States of 2017, typically, law and religion are seen as separate phenomena, at loggerheads with one another. While it is true that they are separate phenomena, what the contributors to this volume reveal is that they need not be, indeed are not, at loggerheads with one another. Rather, both share the common core of love. The ways in which secular and sacred texts are utilised here are thus novel, seeking a sensitive and cooperative approach to the ways in which different religious groups, including the secular, cohabit both nationally and globally.

And if we allow ourselves the space to see both law and religion as sharing this common core, as the chapters in this volume suggest and demonstrate, then our work here stands as a testament to the potential to draw together and unify a vast range of divergent approaches, both religious and legal, to the meditation of relationships between individuals. In this way, religion becomes a part of public life and in most every jurisdiction it becomes possible for those of different legal cultures found in religious and secular law to seek, together, a peaceful cohabitation. Both secular/civil law and religion are capable, together, of achieving such outcomes. And this allows this conversation to occur even in societies where the population might predominantly identify as having no religion, in a world becoming increasingly secular.[22]

From these two objectives, we draw one final conclusion: it is possible to find in secular/civil law and in religion the potential for cohabitation, coexistence and respect. And that we find in a core of love, common to both secular civil law and religion. We do not pretend that this contribution to the debate now raging in places like the United States can reverse some of the populist tendencies we find. But we do believe that our work, and that of others, can encourage scholars, practitioners, and all people of good will to develop alternative approaches to thinking about the relationship between law and religion. We suggest here that it is in the heart of both that one finds love and its offer to the Other.

22 Michael Lipka, 'Religious "nones" are not only growing, they're becoming more secular', *Pew Report on Religion*, Pew Research Center, 11 November 2015, accessed on 10 February 2017, available at: <www.pewresearch.org/fact-tank/2015/11/11/religious-nones-are-not-only-growing-theyre-becoming-more-secular/?utm_source=Pew+Research+Center&utm_campaign=7bbbb7536a-Religion_Weekly_Nov_12_2015&utm_medium=email&utm_term=0_3e953b9b70–7bbbb7536a-399949201>.

## References

Babie, Paul, 'Religion and Constitutionalism: Oscillations Along a Continuum' (2015) 39 *Journal of Religious History* 123

Bassett, Peter, 'Wagner: Lord of the Ring' (November 2013) *Limelight* 32

Bouma, Gary D, *Australian Soul: Religion and Spirituality in the 21st Century* (Cambridge University Press, 2007)

Cochran, Robert F and Zachary R Calo (eds), *Agape, Justice, and Law: How Might Christian Love Shape Law?* (Cambridge University Press, 2017)

*Dhalab v Switzerland* [2001] ECHR 899 (15 February 2001)

Dostoyevsky, Fyodor, *The Brothers Karamazov* (Penguin, 2003 [1879–1880])

*Eweida v UK* [2013] ECHR 37 (15 January 2013)

*Lautsi v Italy*, App No 30814/06, 2011 Eur Ct HR (GC)

Lipka, Michael, 'Religious "nones" are not only growing, they're becoming more secular', *Pew Report on Religion*, Pew Research Center, November 11 2015, accessed on 10 February 2017, available at: <www.pewresearch.org/fact-tank/2015/11/11/religious-nones-are-not-only-growing-theyre-becoming-more-secular/?utm_source=Pew+Research+Center&utm_campaign=7bbbb7536a-Religion_Weekly_Nov_12_2015&utm_medium=email&utm_term=0_3e953b9b70–7bbbb7536a-399949201>

Liptak, Andrew, 'In the last 24 hours, four federal courts have objected to Trump's actions: Here's where we stand', *The Verge*, 29 January 2017, accessed on 10 February 2017, available at: <www.theverge.com/2017/1/29/14430082/four-federal-courts-ruled-trump-immigration-ban>

Malone, Scott and Dan Levine, 'Challenges to Trump's immigration orders spread to more US states', *Reuters*, 31 January 2017, accessed on 10 February 2017, available at: <www.reuters.com/article/us-usa-trump-immigration-sanfrancisco-idUSKBN15F2B1>

Micklethwait, John and Adrian Wooldridge, *God is Back: How the Global Revival of Faith is Changing the World* (Penguin, 2010)

NPR, 'Trump's Executive Order On Immigration, Annotated', 31 January 2017, accessed on 10 February 2017, available at: <www.npr.org/2017/01/31/512439121/trumps-executive-order-on-immigration-annotated>

*Otto Preminger v Austria* [1994] ECHR 26 (20 September 1994)

Patel, Faiza, Matthew Duss, and Amos Toh, *Foreign Law Bans: Legal Uncertainties and Practical Problems* (Centre for American Progress; Brennan Centre for Justice at New York University School of Law, 2013), accessed on 10 February 2017, available at: <www.brennancenter.org/sites/default/files/publications/ForeignLawBans.pdf>

*Sahin v Turkey* [2005] ECHR 819 (10 November 2005)

*SAS v France* [2014] ECHR 695 (July 1 2014)

St Thomas More, *Utopia* (Penguin, 2003 [1516])

*State v Washington, et al, v Donald J Trump, et al* (United States District Court, Western District of Washington at Seattle, Robart J) (3 February 2017), C17 0141JLR

*State of Washington, State of Minnesota v Donald J Trump, President of the United States; US Department of Homeland Security; Rex W Tillerson, Secretary of State; John F Kelly, Secretary of the Department of Homeland Security; United States of America* (United States Court of Appeals for the Ninth Circuit, Canby, Clifton, Friedland JJ) (9 February 2017) 17–35105

Taylor, Charles, *A Secular Age* (The Belknap Press of Harvard University Press, 2007)

The Economist, 'What the visa ban shows about American foreign policy', *The Economist*, 4 February 2017, accessed on 10 February 2017, available at: <www.economist.com/news/briefing/21716079-divided-nation-seeks-divided-world-what-visa-ban-shows-about-american-foreign-policy>

*The Immigration and Nationality Act of 1952*, Pub L 82–414, 66 Stat 163, enacted 27 June 1952, 8 USC

The White House, Executive Order 13769, 'Protecting the Nation from Foreign Terrorist Entry into the United States', 27 January 2017, 82 Fed Reg 8,977, accessed on 10 February 2017, available at: <www.whitehouse.gov/the-press-office/2017/01/25/executive-order-border-security-and-immigration-enforcement-improvements>

Weiler, Joseph, 'Oral Submission on Behalf of Armenia, Bulgaria, Cyprus, Greece, Lithuania, Malta, The Russian Federation, and San Marino – Third Party Intervening States in the Lautsi Case Before the Grand Chamber of the European Court of Human Rights', accessed on 10 February 2017, available at: <www.ilsussidiario.net/News/Politics-Society/2010/7/1/EXCLUSIVE-Oral-Submission-by-Professor-Joseph-Weiler-before-the-Grand-Chamber-of-the-European-Court-of-Human-Rights/6/96909/>

# Part I

# Religious perspectives

# 1 Understanding love

## With and without God

*Brett G Scharffs*

## Introduction

The question animating this inquiry is whether love as an idea makes sense without God. And how we as human beings are to understand the experience of love, both with and without God. When a person experiences genuine love, that person begins to understand something about the profound power of selflessly regarding another. Scientific and other secular disciplines struggle and often fail to account for this genuine other-regard in a satisfying way. Scientific approaches to love tend to break down the selfless experience of love into various species of self-regard, and such explanations focus on the self rather than the other in their quest to understand love. In sharp contrast, religious perspectives – specifically Christianity – endeavour to understand love as genuinely other-regarding, based upon an effort to understand God and His character. My query, therefore, is whether it even makes sense for us to claim to believe in the possibility of love if we insist upon the non-existence of God. My claim, tentative but confident, is that the very idea of love, as we commonly experience and understand it, may make no sense at all in the absence of God.

This chapter will proceed as follows. After some introductory housekeeping, I will note briefly the approach to love that we find in the humanities such as literature and poetry. The primary focus will then be to explore how love is explained in four scientific disciplines – economics, psychology, evolutionary biology, and neuroscience. I will then note the striking similarities between how these scientific approaches understand God, and how they parallel their understanding of love. Finally, I will contrast how religious perspectives, specifically Christianity, explain the experience and purpose of love.

## Setting the stage

### *Definitions*

First, there is the important matter of definitions. I will talk about love in the usual way, noting different types of love and utilising familiar classifications, but the basic definitional essence of love is a genuine and real regard of a 'self' for an 'other'.[1] Love, thus, is in some genuine sense 'self-less' and something other than 'self-ish'.[2] For 'love' to be genuine, this 'other-regard' must not be something more than covert selfishness, an impulse or strategy for survival or self-perpetuation, or a mechanism for meeting one's own ends or needs. Genuine love also must not be a compulsion, a mechanistic response to stimuli, a mistake, or an illusion. In other words, love must at least in part be chosen and intended, perhaps involving 'self-sacrifice', but at least involving genuine 'other-regard'. Love, as I'm using the term, really is about the 'other' rather than just the 'self.'

## *Early philosophical accounts of love*

Early philosophical accounts of love assert the reality of a genuine other-regarding experience. Additionally, these accounts also tend to posit the existence of some kind of God. Early Greek philosophy separates love into three separate categories: *eros*, or passionate/romantic love; *philia*, or friendship/brotherly love; and *agape*, or God-like love/charity. Later, philosophers also began identifying a fourth category: *storge*, or familial love.

*Eros* is largely described as romantic or passionate love and is sometimes considered equivalent to sexual desire. One of the earliest discussions of *eros* is offered by Plato. At the heart of Plato's account is the metaphor of love (*eros*) as a ladder by which a person can ascend towards philosophy.[3] At the base of the 'ladder of love' is a more carnal, sexual form of love: a desire for the beauty of another person's body.[4] However, by ascending the ladder, a person moves from *eros* towards a single person to *eros* towards all beautiful bodies. From there, the person develops *eros* towards all beauty and eventually for the divine form of beauty itself, a more philosophical type

1 Harry Frankfurt argues that love 'consists most basically in a disinterested concern for the well-being or flourishing of the person who is loved. It is not driven by any ulterior purpose but seeks the good of the beloved . . . for its own sake'. Harry Frankfurt, *The Reasons of Love* (Princeton University Press, 2004) 29. St Thomas Aquinas claimed: 'To love is to wish good to someone'. St Thomas Aquinas, *Summa Theologica* (Fathers of the English Dominican Province trans, 1920, Vol 2.2) question 23, article I. The *Oxford English Dictionary* defines love as '[a] feeling or disposition of deep affection or fondness for someone . . . manifesting itself in concern for the other's welfare and pleasure in his or her presence.' See 'Love, N.1', *Oxford English Dictionary*, accessed 28 June 2016, available at: <www.oed.com/viewdictionaryentry/entry/110566>. Webster's dictionary also states 'unselfish loyal and benevolent concern for the good of another' as a definition of love. See 'Love', *Merriam-Webster Online*, accessed 28 June 2016, available at: <www.merriam-webster.com/dictionary/love>.

2 By 'self-less' I do not mean a complete disregard of self, but rather something less strenuous, the regard for something other than self.

3 See Plato, *Symposium* (Harold Fowler trans, Harvard University Press, 1925) 210d.

4 See ibid 210a ('In the first place . . . he must be in love with one particular body'). This first form of *eros*, for Plato, is 'an egocentric love: it tends toward conquering and possessing the object that represents a value for man'. John Paul II, *Man and Woman He Created Them: A Theology of the Body* (Michael Waldstein trans, Pauline Books & Media, 2006) 315, note 56.

of love.[5] Hence, a person who correctly experiences *eros* will be led toward the divine.[6] Plato's account of love, of course, assumes the existence of God.[7] Together, reason and love ('rational love') incline us towards truth and towards God.

*Philia*, on the other hand, is an appreciation, fondness, or loyalty to certain others. The concept of *philia* was largely first explored by Aristotle, who described this kind of love as a type of 'excess of feeling' based on the virtues present in the other.[8] As this kind of love becomes more mature it becomes more about the well-being of the other.[9] Only lesser kinds of *philia* are based on obtaining selfish utility out of the relationship, and these tend to end when utility ends.[10] According to Aristotle, characteristics present in relationships of true *philia* include such things as shared dispositions, similar goals, quick forgiveness, mutual temperance, justice, etc.[11] Interestingly, Aristotle considered virtues to be objective characteristics tied to rationality. Therefore, the more rational an individual is, then the more worthy and capable of *philia* he or she becomes.

5 See Plato, above n 3, 210a – 211d. In the *Symposium*, Plato describes the process that occurs when one 'has learned to see the beautiful in due order and succession' as progressing:

> from one [beautiful body] to two, and from two to all beautiful bodies; and from beautiful bodies to beautiful institutions, from beautiful institutions to beautiful learning, . . . and finally from learning to that particular learning which is no other than that of beauty itself; so that finally one comes to know the very essence of beauty. This . . . is that life above all others which man should live, in the contemplation of beauty absolute.

Ibid 211c3 – d1.

6 Ibid 211c – e.

7 Apart from the traditional pantheon of Greek gods and goddesses, Plato's *Timaeus* describes a Creator: 'He [the Creator] was good, and in him that is good no envy ariseth ever concerning anything; and being devoid of envy He desired that all should be, so far as possible, like unto Himself'. Plato, *Timaeus* (Benjamin Jowett trans, Echo Library, 2006) 27c – 34a. In addition to creating the earth, the Creator was responsible for creating the souls of mortal men. Ibid 41d – 44d.

8 Aristotle, *Nicomachean Ethics* (W D Ross trans, Digireads.com, 2005) book viii. 'Perfect friendship is the friendship of men who are good, and alike in virtue; for these wish well alike to each other qua good, and they are good themselves'.

9 Aristotle discussed *philia* in his *Rhetoric*: 'Let "loving" [ie, *philia*] be wishing for someone the things that he deems good, for the sake of that person and not oneself, and the accomplishment of these things to the best of one's ability. A friend is one who loves and is loved in return'. Aristotle, *Rhetoric* (W Rhys Roberts trans, Dover Publications, 2004) book II, part 4. Aristotle continues, '[t]hings that cause friendship are: doing kindnesses; doing them unasked; and not proclaiming the fact when they are done, which shows that they were done for our own sake and not for some other reason'. Ibid.

10 Aristotle, above n 8, book vii, part 3:

> Therefore those who love for the sake of utility love for the sake of what is good for themselves . . . and not in so far as the other is the person loved but in so far as he is useful or pleasant. And these friendships are only incidental; for it is not as being the man he is that the loved person is loved, but as providing some good or pleasure. Such friendships, then, are easily dissolved.

11 Aristotle, above n 9, book II, part 4.

*Agape* largely means the love of God for man and the extension of that love man feels for his fellow being. Such love draws on elements of other kinds of love and seeks a perfect form of transcendent other-regard. *Agape* does not depend upon reciprocity, and is often regarded as unconditional.[12] Interestingly, ideas of *agape* have developed primarily through Christian traditions, and the earliest writings about *agape*, or charity as it is sometimes translated, are primarily found in the Bible.[13] Additionally, it is sometimes argued that *agape* cannot be understood through reason alone.[14]

*Storge* has been more recently developed to mean familial love.[15] Anciently, the familial ties described by *storge* seemed to be considered a second kind of *philia* instead of a concept of their own.[16] In modern times, however, *storge* used to describe the affection that a parent has toward offspring or vice versa. It can also exist wherever the relationship between two individuals becomes exceptionally strong.

These four categories of love have arguably become the most influential catalogue of love in the Western world.[17] While there is much more that could be said about them, the important point is this: all of these accounts of love are based upon and understanding of love as being a genuine regard about the 'other'. Love is not viewed as a mechanism for vindicating the interests of needs of the self. This is not to say that the self does not get anything from love, but that the basic experience, meaning, depth, and character of love revolve around the other.

### *Love in poetry, music, and literature*

The other-regard of love is also the preeminent theme of accounts of love in poetry, music, and literature.[18] It is one of the fundamental themes of the humanities worldwide and has largely shaped some of the world's most predominant cultures.[19]

12 *Agape* is a 'spontaneous and unmotivated' type of love that concludes God loves us, not because we deserve it, but because that is His nature. Instead of Him loving us for some value we have, value is created by His love. Anders Nygren, 'Agape and Eros', in Alan Soble (ed), *Eros Agape, and Philia: Readings in the Philosophy of Love* (Paragon House, 1989) 85–95.

13 See, eg, 1 John 4: 10, which states: 'Herein is love, not that we loved God, but that he loved us'.

14 See, eg, Alan Soble, *The Structure of Love* (Yale University Press, 1990) 5. *Agape* is considered 'incomprehensible' as opposed to reasonable.

15 The Liddell-Scott-Jones Greek-English Lexicon defines *storge* as: 'love, affection, esp. of parents and children.' See '*Storge*', The Liddel-Scott-Jones Greek-English Lexicon, accessed 28 June 2016, available at: <http://stephanus.tlg.uci.edu/lsj/#eid=99866&context=lsj&action=from-search>.

16 Gerasimos Santas in *Plato and Freud* stated: 'In Ancient Greek, and certainly in Plato and Aristotle, *philia* was standardly used to signify two kinds of love: familial love, whether parental, filial, or sibling, and the love of friendship.' He cites Phaedrus in Plato's *Symposium* as an example of *philia* being discussed as family love. Gerasimos Santas, *Plato and Freud: Two Theories of Love* (Basil Blackwell Inc, 1988) 8.

17 See, eg, C S Lewis, *The Four Loves* (Harcourt Publishing, 1960) discussed at length in 'C S Lewis – The Four Loves' section of this paper.

18 See, eg, Denis de Rougement, *Love in the Western World* (Princeton University Press, 1983) (discussing love as a theme of western culture, including literature, poetry, and song); see also Ted Gioia, *Love Songs* (Oxford University Press, 2015) (discussing the history and development of the 'love song').

19 See eg, William R Jankowiak and Edward F Fischer, 'A cross-cultural perspective on romantic love' (1992) 31 *Ethnology* 149–55, which concludes love is a universal constant across all world

For present purposes, the point is in the humanities, love – understood as something involving genuine and real regard of a 'self' for an 'other' – is usually presumed and rarely questioned.[20]

Consider, for example, common and classical literature. For centuries, authors have depicted love as a powerful and other-focused experience. Jane Austen wrote in *Northanger Abbey*: 'There is nothing I would not do for those who are really my friends. I have no notion of loving people by halves; it is not my nature.'[21] Charles Dickens wrote in *Barnaby Rudge*: 'she better liked to see him free and happy, even than to have him near her, because she loved him better than herself.'[22] Thomas Hardy wrote in Jude the Obscure: 'the highest form of affection is based on full sincerity on both sides.'[23] Emily Bronte in *Wuthering Heights* wrote: 'he's more myself than I am. Whatever our souls are made of, his and mine are the same'.[24] Charlotte Bronte in *Jane Eyre* wrote: 'Every atom of your flesh is as dear to me as my own: in pain and sickness it would still be dear.'[25] George Orwell wrote in *Nineteen Eighty-Four*: 'If you loved someone, you loved him, and when you had nothing else to give, you still gave him love.'[26] Examples could easily be multiplied.

The power of other-regarding love is no less present in poetry. 'The Clod and the Pebble' by William Blake asserts that 'Love seeketh not itself to please, Nor for itself hath any care; But for another gives its ease, And builds a Heaven in Hell's despair.' William Douglas's 'Annie Laurie' states: 'Her voice is low and sweet, And she's all the world to me, And for bonnie Annie Laurie, I'd lay me down and die.' Thomas Ford also expresses a profound regard for another in his poem, 'There is a Lady Sweet and Kind': 'Her gesture, motion, and her smiles, Her wit, her voice my heart beguiles, Beguiles my heart, I know not why, And yet, I'll love her till I die.' And William Shakespeare described love's feeling for the other as boundless in *Romeo and Juliet*: 'My bounty is as boundless as the sea, my love as deep; the more I give to thee, the more I have, for both are infinite.' It is clear to see a recurring theme across literature and poetry: love is an experience of powerful and genuine other-regard.

It is also important to note the consequences of excessive self-love. This is illustrated by the well-known ancient Greek myth of Narcissus. Narcissus, an

---

cultures; Wayne Cristuado, *A Philosophical History of Love* (Transaction Publishers, 2012) which argues that one would be hard pressed to understand western culture without first understanding the power of love; and Simon May, *Love: A History* (Yale University Press, 2011) which asserts that society has somewhat shifted from the idea that God is love to the idea that love is God.

20 'Our stories of gods and God and, for the most part, of life are love stories, attempts to make sense of love as the ground and/or end of life. Of course, there have been other grounds and ends, but, in the Western world at least, no attempt to give a meaning to life has been quite as compelling.' Cristaudo, above n 19, 1. 'The evolution of the West is, inter alia, a synthesis of three main loves: love of wisdom (philosophy), love of God (the church), and romantic love, which eventually becomes . . . the source of endless "entertainment."' Ibid 9.

21 Jane Austen, *Northanger Abbey* (Little, Brown, & Company, 1903) 39.

22 Charles Dickens, *Barnaby Rudge* (Chapman and Hall, 1841) 74.

23 Thomas Hardy, *Jude the Obscure* (Harper & Brothers, 1895) 307.

24 Emily Bronte, *Wuthering Heights* (Harper & Brothers, 1858) 71.

25 Charlotte Bronte, *Jane Eyre* (JM Dent & Sons Ltd, 1922) 301.

26 George Orwell, *Nineteen Eighty-Four* (Houghton Mifflin Harcourt, 1949) 358.

especially beautiful person, fell in love with himself when he saw his reflection in the river. He eventually took his own life when he realised that he could never obtain his heart's desire. Similar types of extreme selfishness and self-obsession are also currently regarded as forms of mental illness.[27]

### *Scientific perspectives*

These perspectives on love from philosophy and literature stand in stark contrast with the most influential scientific conceptions of love. These scientific conceptions of love understand love primarily, if not exclusively, as something that serves the 'self' rather than the 'other.' In this chapter I will focus on four scientific perspectives of love: economics (which looks at external human behaviour and understands love primarily as a mechanism for pursuing and realising one's own self-interest), psychology (which looks inwards at human motivations and understands love primarily as a way of fulfilling our own physical and emotional needs), evolutionary biology (which looks backwards at human evolution and understands love primarily in terms of its adaptive value or our genes acting selfishly to maximise their own chance for perpetuation), and neuroscience (which looks into our brains and explains love in mechanistic terms as a chemical process involving various stimuli and response).

The following chart summarises the primary orientation and focus of these disciplines, as well as the key concepts they employ to understand love.

*Table 1.1* Summary chart of the four disciplines and their associated orientation, primary focus and key concepts

| *Discipline* | *Primary orientation* | *Primary focus* | *Key concepts* |
|---|---|---|---|
| Economics | Looks externally | Behaviour | Self-interest<br>Utility maximisation |
| Psychology | Looks inward | Mental states/ emotional needs, motives | Needs<br>Healthy development<br>Prioritise goals based on needs<br>Emotions are mechanisms to motivate us to action |
| Evolutionary biology | Looks backwards | Evolution and survival | Survival<br>Perpetuating our DNA<br>Judging reproductive fitness |
| Neuroscience | Brain and chemical processes | Brain function | Sub-rational processes<br>Chemical processes involving stimuli and response |

27 American Psychiatric Association, *Diagnostic and statistical manual of mental disorders: DSM-IV-TR*, (Washington, DC: American Psychiatric Association, 2000).

As different as they are, what these scientific approaches to understanding love have in common is striking: they all explain love in terms of the self rather than the other. Indeed, the other, to the extent he or she matters at all, is a mechanism for achieving the interests of the self. All of these approaches to understanding love view it as being fundamentally selfish, and each discount, indeed, go to great lengths to explain away, the possibility of genuine self-lessness. Love, understood as real and genuine other-regard, is treated almost as an impossibility or an absurdity – or at least as irrational, self-defeating, an illusion, a suboptimal genetic flaw, or a chemical reaction triggered by certain stimuli.

## Four scientific approaches to love: economic, psychological, evolutionary biology, neuroscience

### *Economics*

From an economic perspective, love can be explained as a strategy for maximising self-interest.[28] Economic man, or what is sometimes called *homo economicus*,[29] is based upon a view of human nature that posits human beings as being basically rational self-regarding utility maximisers.[30] Our behaviour can be explained

28 Paul Frijters and Foster Gigi discuss love as being willing to care for someone or something even if there is no visible reward. This willingness comes because loving someone or something else produces in the lover an 'internal warmth.' Ultimately, however, the love is still promoting one's own self-interest: 'someone who loves has effectively redefined the other as part of himself, and therefore feels rewarded when the object of his love is nurtured, as if he himself is being nurtured.' Paul Frijters and Foster Gigi, *Economic Theory of Greed, Love, Groups, and Networks* (Cambridge University Press, 2013) 74.

29 Joseph Persky, 'Retrospectives: The Ethology of Homo Economicus' (1995) 9 *Journal of Economic Perspectives* 221–231:

> ('While John Stuart Mill is generally identified as the creator of the economic man, he never actually used this designation in his own writings. But the term did emerge in reaction to Mill's work. In its first appearances in the late nineteenth century, "economic man" carried a pejorative connotation reflecting the widespread hostility of the historical school toward Mill's theoretical abstractions. Economic man also raised the indignation of Victorian moralists shocked at the postulation of such blatant selfishness.')

The earliest use of the term that Persky identifies is in John Kells Ingram's *A History of Political Economy* (Cambridge University Press, 2013 [1888]). 'Ingram . . . took considerable pains to disparage John Stuart Mill's political economy, which "dealt not with real but with imaginary men "economic men" . . . conceived as simply "money-making animals."' Ibid.

30 '[T]he economic man is one who judges the comparative efficacy of means to obtain wealth, as well as one who seeks to maximize pleasure.' Irene C L Ng and Lu-Ming Tseng, 'Learning to Be Sociable: The Evolution of Homo Economicus' (2008) 67 *American Journal of Economics & Sociology* 265–86, 266. In its most basic, neutral form, 'economic man is usually assumed to be perfectly rational. He (the economic man) is able to predict every possible

primarily as reflecting our efforts to maximise our own welfare.[31] Indeed, rationality is defined in terms of utility maximisation, and cognitive biases or mistakes of cognition are viewed as defects that prevent us from being fully rational in this economic sense.[32]

Economics typically begins with a key assumption about human beings – that they are self-interested rational utility maximisers.[33] With this assumption in hand, economics goes about explaining or accounting for apparently other-regarding activities, including love, as covert strategies for self-regarding utility maximisation. Love, on this view, is just another mechanism or strategy for maximising self-interest. Generosity or kindness, 'agapic expressiveness', is a way of feeling good about ourselves when we give to others.[34] Friendship, like other types of love, is based upon the idea of reciprocity, giving in order to get in return, ultimately satisfying selfish impulses.[35] Romantic love is a strategy for fulfilling one's

---

outcome for all his choices, and *his decision will be the one that will maximize his utility.*' Ibid 268 (citations omitted) (emphasis added).

31 'The model of rational judgment used by decision scientists is one in which a person chooses options based on the option which has the largest expected utility.' Keith E Stanovich, Maggie E Toplak and Richard F West, 'The Development of Rational Thought: A Taxonomy of Heuristics and Biases', in Robert V Kail (ed), *Advances in Child Behavior and Development* (Elsevier, Vol 36, 2008) 251–85, 252. See also Ramon Febrero and Pedro S Schwartz (eds), *The Essence of Becker* (Hoover Institution Press Publication, 1995). ('[T]he ultimate goal of economic activity [is] the maximization of utility by consumers.') xxi.

32 'Degrees of rationality can be assessed in terms of the number and severity of . . . cognitive biases that individuals display. Failure to display a bias becomes a measure of rational thought.' Keith E Stanovich, *Rationality & The Reflective Mind* (Oxford University Press, 2011) 7.

33 Howard Margolis, *Selfishness, Altruism, and Rationality: A Theory of Social Choice* (Cambridge University Press, 1984) 6:

> At the heart of economic theory is an abstract model of rational choice. Highly idealized actors (consumers and producers; households and firms) operate in a highly idealized setting (perfectly efficient markets) exchanging highly idealized objects (pure private goods). Each actor seeks to maximize an index known as a utility function, whose value depends on the vector (list) of goods possessed by that actor. Rationality, in the model, implies very little beyond a certain consistency of choice: If I prefer A to B and B to C, then I Prefer A to C.

See also JL Baxter, *Social and Psychological Foundations of Economic Analysis* (Harvester and Wheatsheaf, 1988) 2 ('Consumers, we assume, are motivated by the goal of utility-maximization.').

34 See Frijters and Gigi, above n 28.

35 Aristotle apparently believed that most friendships are of this type, and that 'true' friendships are rare because true friendship exists only between virtuous people, and 'such men are few.' See Aristotle, above n 8, 220. Aristotle described the majority of 'friendships' this way:

> when the motive of the affection [ie, the 'love,' or *philia*] is usefulness, the partners do not feel affection for one another *per se* but in terms of the good accruing to each from the other. The same is also true of those whose friendship is based on pleasure: we love witty people not for what they are, but for the pleasure they bring us.

Ibid 218.

own desires,[36] and even a parent's love for a child is understood as doing what one values, and a rational investment that will hopefully yield positive returns on the investment.[37]

The economic theories of cost–benefit analysis and revealed preferences explain love as selfish and predictable. Economic theory will consider love to be irrational unless the costs outweigh the benefits.[38] Revealed preferences theory will assume that future love can be predicted by the revealed preference of past decisions to love.[39]

Economic theory can rationalise every category of love as covert vindication of self-interest.

### *Storge*

For example, *storge*, or natural empathy of affection is handily dispatched. Thus, an economist explains the everyday generosity of giving a dollar to a panhandler as not being motivated by concern for the other, but as a way of making the giver feel better about themselves.[40] Garden variety altruism,[41] it turns out from an

36 Paul Frijters and Foster Gigi explain that feelings of romantic love, both 'love at first sight and the love that grows between partners over time' are essentially the result of satisfying the individual's desires. However, in love partnerships, 'the love of both requires the two individuals to submit mutually to the power of the other.' Frijters and Gigi, above n 28, 88.

37 Ramon Febrero and Pedro Schwartz summarised some of the views of Nobel Prize-winning economist Gary Becker as follows:

> for parents . . . children are seen as consumer durables, similar to cars or washing machines, who provide parents with a flow of valuable services (psychic and monetary in nature) over time . . . [a]ll this makes having children (procreating or adopting them) an economic decision (to be more accurate, an investment decision) . . . Becker's approach to fertility allows us to relate family size to economic variables so that optimal family size can be expressed as the outcome of a utility maximization program.
>
> Febrero and Schwartz, above n 31, xxvii–xxviii.

Bryan Caplan further explains that having and loving children could also be viewed as a self-interested act on a societal level: 'Fertility is . . . vital to our retirement systems. Programs like Social Security and Medicare are pyramid schemes: As long as there are a lot of young workers for every retiree, low taxes can fund high benefits.' Bryan Caplan, *Selfish Reasons to Have More Kids: Why Being a Great Parent Is Less Work and More Fun Than You Think* (Basic Books, 2011) 8.

38 For example, the 'economic man' might ask himself, 'is the time and money I spend to take care of my child worth the benefits I receive?' Or, 'It's nice to have a romantic partner to spend time with, but do the benefits outweigh the cost of lost autonomy?'

39 For example, if a woman has only dated men that are taller than 6 feet and have brown hair, then an economist might assume that the next person the woman dates will also be a man that is taller than 6 feet and has brown hair.

40 Elliot Sober and David Sloan Wilson claim that 'all altruistic acts can always be explained by the "internal rewards" that are received by those who act altruistically, such as the avoidance of guilt or the warm feeling that such actions may give a person.' Randy Hodson, 'Altruism', in *International Encyclopedia of Economic Sociology* (Routledge, 2016) 10–11, 10 (citing JS Brunero, 'Evolution, Altruism, and "Internal Reward" Explanations' (2002) 33 *The Philosophical Forum* 413–24).

41 Much of the research in economics and psychology refers to altruism, rather than love. From my point of view, altruism is the overarching term referring to genuine selflessness and love is a subcategory of altruism.

economic perspective, is actually motivated by self-regard. Giving is neither better nor worse than not giving; each reflects a different set of utility preferences. Indeed, giving may be worse, since it likely fosters a kind of self-deception, the false idea that we are thinking of others when we are actually only trying to feel better about ourselves.[42]

### *Philia*

Friendship, *philia*, is understood in terms of reciprocity. We give in order to get; we are a friend in order to have a friend. When friendships are no longer satisfying to us, we seek new friendships. Friendship-love may seem other-regarding, but it is really a tool of reciprocity that has a goal of maximising one's own utility.[43] Social exchange theory posits that friendship can be explained and predicted much like a marketplace; friendships will not continue unless both friends feel that the friendship provides more benefits than costs.[44]

Parental relationships involve parents making a calculation that having and rearing children is in their self-interest, because of the satisfaction it will give them now, and the protection it will afford them later in life. The decision to have or adopt children is viewed as essentially an investment choice for the parents, one in which they weigh the costs associated with having children – in terms of time, money, etc – against the potential future benefit they will receive from their children.[45] Having an optimally sized family is seen as an act in maximising utility.[46]

### *Eros*

Economic rationality finds romantic love easy to understand. *Eros* will motivate a romantic economist to find an outlet for his or her sexual needs. According to classic economic accounts, men might be attracted to a woman based upon her physical attractiveness, while a woman might be attracted to a man based upon his earning capacity and social status.[47] Each feels 'love', but that love is based

42 Video Interview with Paul Bloom, 'Against Empathy', *The Atlantic*, 21 March 2016 (discussing a book to be published until December of 2016), accessed 24 June 2016, available at: <www.theatlantic.com/video/index/474588/why-empathy-is-a-bad-thing/>.

43 Mark Searle, 'Testing the reciprocity norm in a recreation management setting' (1989) 11 *Leisure Sciences* 353–65 ('relations made stable through the provision of mutually satisfying gratification will be self-perpetuating.')

44 'Social exchange theory suggest[s] that people will continue to interact when there is an exchange of rewards, but if the exchange is costly to one or more of the exchanging parties, it is less likely to continue.' Christopher Auld and Alan Case, 'Social exchange processes in leisure and non-leisure settings: A review and exploratory investigation' (1997) 29 *Journal of Leisure Research* 183–200.

45 See Febrero and Schwartz, above n 31.

46 Ibid.

47 See Glen H Elder Jr, 'Appearance and Education in Marriage Mobility' (1969) 34 *American Sociological Review* 519–33 (finding, among other things, that attractive women tended to

upon what gives them self-satisfaction. Marriage is viewed as an investment, successful if it actually generates the expected return.[48]

### *Agape and self-sacrifice*

But might not a rational utility maximiser be acting for the good of a group, rather than just himself or herself? That group might be a couple or a family, or a clan or nation. The rational economist responds that even acting on behalf a group can be accounted for without giving up on basic economic assumptions.[49] The idea is that people who act on behalf of a group do so because it provides for their basic needs (physical protection, food, shelter), and also gives them personal satisfaction, which is also a utility function. In other words, the 'self' is compensated for being 'group-minded'. This compensation might take the form of having a selection advantage,[50] being paid, or in psychic income, having one's reputation enhanced among the group, or simply the self-regard of doing something you like, or feeling better about yourself as a person. Thus, what looks like acting to serve the greater good is actually a mechanism for maximising self-interest.

Even extreme acts of self-sacrifice are viewed from an economic perspective as self-regarding utility maximisation. If you were to sacrifice your life for a 'greater cause', this is understood as the result of cost–benefit calculation. For example, when a soldier gives her life in defence of the nation, this is viewed not as an exception to the rule of self-interest, rather that she is simply fulfilling her self-interests. She is simply acting to vindicate what she values most.[51]

### *Conclusion*

Thus, from the perspective of economics, love is yet another strategy or mechanism for utility maximisation. When someone 'loves' another, they are doing something

---

settle down with less attractive but wealthier men). Although this finding has since been questioned, the research has not been conclusively discredited.

48 See Gary Becker, 'A Theory of Marriage: Part I' (1973) 81 *Journal Politics & Economics* 813–46 in Febrero and Schwartz, above n 31, 274: 'since marriage is practically always voluntary, either by the persons marrying or their parents . . . persons marrying (or their parents) can be assumed to *expect to raise their utility level* above what it would be were they to remain single' (emphasis added). Some of the 'commodities' which determine the 'utility' of a marriage include 'the quality of meals, the quality and quantity of children, prestige, recreation, companionship, love, and health status.' Ibid 276.

49 '[I]f we clearly understand that the group-utility the individual seeks to maximize is *his own perception of group-interest*, and by no means necessarily identical to someone else's perception, then the individual is using any resources allocated to group interest to maximize *his own* group-interested utility function', Margolis, above n 33, 2 (emphasis added). Margolis later states: 'without departing in any radical way from what Kuhn has taught us to call the economist's "paradigm", a good deal of *social* motivation can be allowed for.' Ibid 7.

50 Ibid 26.

51 Because the soldier is maximizing group-utility, the soldier would really be maximizing her own interest. See Margolis, above n 33, 2.

that will, if their calculations are correct, make themselves happy. From the perspective of *homo economicus*, love is rational under certain circumstances, when the balance of costs and benefits to oneself associated with loving create a positive ledger, and one with a larger balance than other ways of living.

There is, of course, something rather circular about this economic logic. How do we know that someone loves another out of self-interest rather than other-regard? Because we 'know' they are self-interested utility maximisers, thus, we conclude confidently, acting 'as if' they love another is 'actually' a course of action that maximises their utility.

## Psychology

The prevailing viewpoint in the discipline of psychology is that love is a mechanism for fulfilling human needs, most fundamentally survival and reproduction.[52] Douglas T Kenrick is representative of how many psychologists view love. He explains that, 'love is at base a set of evolved decision biases'.[53] On this view, the mind 'is composed of a set of innate biases that affect what we pay attention to, how we interpret events, what we retrieve from memory, and how we make decisions. Those biases are designed to promote behaviours that, on average, would have served to enhance reproduction'.[54] On this view, social bonds including love 'were essential to our ancestors' survival and reproduction', and so 'decision biases designed to facilitate those bonds would have been highly adaptive.'[55]

Psychology also tends to view love as involving interrelated behavioural and motivational systems. Although the accounts vary, these systems include attachment, caregiving, sex, affiliation, and exploration, among others.[56] These innate motivational systems have 'evolved over thousands of years because they increase the likelihood that infants would survive to reproductive age and be likely to contribute their genes to the next generation'.[57]

52 In spite of the general trend, there are psychologists that reject both evolutionary psychology and gratification of personal needs as sufficient to explain love. See Marissa Beyers and Jeffrey Reber, 'The illusion of intimacy: A Levinasian critique of evolutionary psychology' (1998) 18 *Journal of Theoretical and Philosophical Psychology* 176.

53 Douglas T Kenrick, 'A Dynamical Evolutionary View of Love' in Robert J Sternberg and Karen Weis (eds), *The New Psychology of Love* (Yale University Press, 2006) 16.

54 Ibid.

55 Ibid.

56 See Phillip R Shaver and Mario Mikulincer, 'A Behavior Systems Approach to Romantic Love Relationships: Attachment, Caregiving, and Sex' in Sternberg and Weis, above n 53, 35, 64, 35. Sternberg proposes a 'triangle theory of love', where different types of love reflect different combinations of responses to the psychological needs for intimacy, commitment, and passion. See Robert J Sternberg, 'Triangulating Love' in Sternberg and Weis above n 53, 119–38. John Lee suggests six classifications of love: *eros* (passionate love), ludus (game playing, uncommitted love), *storge* (friendship love), pragma (calculating love), *agape* (altruistic love), and mania (obsessional love). Karen Weis, 'Introduction' in Sternberg and Weis, above n 53, 1–11, 7 (internal citations omitted).

57 Shaver and Mikulincer, above n 56, 35.

Different types of love will involve different decision biases. While each may have 'the surface similarity of serving to promote social bonds', from a functional perspective, each may involve motivations that are 'as distinct and specialised as those distinguishing hunger, thirst, or fear.'[58] These dynamics will be dynamic, since they involve social interactions, and will reflect different cultural norms. Love is viewed as a set of behavioral systems that each involve the attainment of a specific goal and a set of evolutionary strategies for attaining those goals, which are triggered automatically, or 'activated' by certain stimuli.[59]

The basic psychological precursor to love is 'attachment', which is an innate system that is rooted in evolutionary history and the need of infants to stay close to their primary protector.[60] Much of the psychological literature about love focuses on the needs of infants, and of love as a mechanism that allows the infant to 'attach' to an adult, often the mother, in a way that enables the child to develop into a healthy human being. This need for attachment is essential 'from the cradle to the grave'.[61] Love is attachment, feeling a secure attachment either with one's partner or one's parent is a foundation for a well-adapted and fully functioning adult. It is when children are not loved, but instead abused or neglected, or when adults are in negative or harmful relationships, that some of the most intense and damaging mental health issues frequently arise.[62]

One influential account of love from the field of psychology begins by studying the infant's relationship to 'attachment figures' who provide protection and security to children. Bowlby viewed human infants as naturally relationship-seeking, naturally oriented to what Harlow called 'contact comfort,' and naturally inclined to seek proximity to comforting figures in times of need. On this basis, Bowlby reasoned that the formation of an infant's emotional tie to its primary caregiver depends on this natural tendency to seek proximity, on the caregiver's responsiveness to the infant's bids for proximity, and on the caregiver's ability to provide protection and comfort in times of need.[63]

### *Storge*

From the perspective of evolutionary psychology, compassionate love, or concern for the welfare of others, is a 'part of the human biological heritage'.[64] The vulnerability of human infants made such systems of attachment and care necessary from an evolutionary point of view.

> If it is true that all humans are born with an unlearned caregiving system that results in responding to distress calls made by other members of the species

58 Ibid.
59 Ibid 40.
60 See Ellen Berscheid, 'Searching for the Meaning of "Love"', in Sternberg and Weis, above n 53, 171–83, 176.
61 Shaver and Mikulincer, above n 56, 35.
62 Susan Johnson, *Hold Me Tight* (Little, Brown and Company Hachette Book Group, 2008) 40.
63 Shaver and Mikulincer, above n 56, 37
64 Berscheid, above n 60, 176.

> then, as is true of the attachment system, the causal conditions for activation of the caregiving system do *not* follow reward-punishment principles.[65]

However, other psychologists say that a mother's love for her child is understood largely as a mother acting in a way that fills the mother with happiness and other positive emotions, which encourages her to continue to care for and love the baby.[66]

### *Philia*

Psychology tends to view friendship or companionate love as firmly rooted in reward–punishment principles – 'that is, it is well established that we feel positive affect for – "like" – those who reward us, and we dislike those who punish us.' This is a result of our 'evolutionary heritage' and the 'pain–pleasure principle that has served as the basic motivating principle underlying almost all psychological theories of behavior'.[67] Thus, social psychology 101 teaches that 'we like people who are familiar (as opposed to unfamiliar), who are similar (as opposed to dissimilar), who like us (as opposed to dislike us), and who are physically attractive (as opposed to unattractive)'.[68] These characteristics of the 'target' (or the other) 'tend to make our interactions with him or her rewarding, at least more rewarding than interactions with persons who do not possess those characteristics'.[69] Thus, friendship is understood as a system that rewards the self, rather than a system that is genuinely oriented toward the other.

### *Eros*

One influential psychologist, Helen Fisher explains that romantic love can also be understood by our evolutionary history. Fisher says, '[p]sychological studies indicate that romantic love is associated with a discrete constellation of emotions, motivations, and behaviors'.[70] Perhaps most notably, 'romantic love is involuntary, difficult to control, and impermanent'.[71] As Fisher describes, 'the sex drive (libido or lust) is characterised by the craving for sexual gratification; it is often directed toward many partners'.[72] According to Fisher:

> the sex drive evolved to motivate our ancestors to seek coitus with a *range* of appropriate partners. Attraction (and its developed human form, romantic

65 Ibid 177.
66 Johnson, above n 62, 35.
67 Berscheid, above n 60, 177.
68 Ibid.
69 Ibid.
70 Helen Fisher, 'The Drive to Love: The Neural Mechanism for Mate Selection' in Sternberg and Weis, above n 53, 87–115, 88.
71 Ibid 88.
72 Ibid 89.

> love) evolved to motivate individuals to select among potential mates, *prefer* a particular individual, and *focus* courtship attention on this favored mating partner, thereby conserving courtship time and energy. Attachment evolved primarily to motivate individuals to sustain an affiliative connection with this reproductive partner at least long enough to complete species-specific parental duties.[73]

Kenrick adds: 'Because ancestral males and females contributed different resources to their offspring, the two sexes are presumed to use slightly different criteria to select mates'.[74]

### *Love and marriage*

Long-term marital bonds are viewed as a problem of mate retention, and 'because human offspring are helpless at birth and require substantial resources to survive, modern humans are the descendants of ancestral pairs in which males cooperated with females'.[75] On this view, '[t]he ultimate function of human parental bonds is offspring care'.[76] Thus, love, marriage, and childrearing, are all understood as functional mechanisms for enhancing the human need for survival, successfully mating, and having children survive into adulthood.

Other psychologists, taking their cue from both economics and evolutionary biology, view long-term romantic love as 'an evolved solution to the problem of commitment'. David M Buss explains, 'if a partner chooses you for rational reasons, he or she might leave you for the same rational reasons; finding someone slightly more desirable on all of the "rational" criteria.' This creates a commitment problem, since there is no guarantee a partner will stay with you, as:

> If your partner is blinded by an uncontrollable love that cannot be helped and cannot be chosen, a love for only you and no other, then commitment will not waver when you are in sickness rather than in health, when you are poorer rather than richer. Love overrides rationality. It is the emotion that ensures that you will not leave when someone more desirable comes along. Love, in short, may be a solution to the commitment problem, providing a signal to the partner of strong long-term intent and resolve.[77]

73 Ibid 90.

74 Douglas Kenrick, 'A Dynamical Evolutionary View of Love', citing Norman P Li, J Michael Bailey, Douglas T Kenrick and Joan A Linsenmeier, 'The necessities and luxuries of mate preferences: testing the trade-offs' (2002) 82 *Journal of Personality and Social Psychology* 947–55.

75 Douglas T Kenrick in Li et al, above n 74, citing David C Geary, *Male, Female: The Evolution of Human Sex Differences* (American Psychological Association, 1998) 20.

76 Ibid.

77 David M Buss, 'The Evolution of Love' in Sternberg and Weis, above n 53, 65, 86, 71.

The causal connection may also run in the other direction: 'Love may be the psychological reward we experience when the problem of commitment is successfully being solved'.[78]

Maternal love is also understood as a matrix of complex psychological and physiological processes:

> The picture emerging for humans is of mothers for whom cognitive processes play a more important role, although physiological changes in the mother during pregnancy and the birth process clearly prime mothers for responding maternally, and after-birth cues from the infant play a role in sustaining maternal commitment as do psychological processes linked to lactation.[79]

### *Agape*

*Agape*, or unconditional love, is noticeably absent from psychological taxonomies and accounts of love.[80] It is sometimes described as a willingness to come to the aid of someone in distress, which is more usually described as a feature of *storge*, the least demanding type of love.[81] One psychological study found that *agapic* love was more characteristic of women from Asian societies than western, 'suggesting that psychological collectivism promotes the development of a caring network of close relationships'.[82] It is almost as if conceptualising love so thoroughly from the perspective of satisfying the needs of the self, a thorough and real regard for the other is outside the field of enquiry.

### *Conclusion*

The 'dynamic evolutionary model of love presumes that powerful bonds serve several distinct functions for human beings'.[83] Psychology understands love primarily as a mechanism for satisfying both the most basic and the most complex needs of human beings. Love provides an assurance that one is protected from harm, will be taken care of when one is in need, and that there is meaning in one's life and worth in one's self.[84] Psychology tends to view emotions, such as love, as

78 Ibid.

79 James F Leckman, Sarah B Hardy, Eric B Keverne, and C Sue Carter, 'A Behavioral Model of Attachment and Bonding' in Sternberg and Weis, above n 53, 116, 145, 119 (internal citations omitted.)

80 Robert Sternberg identifies three different psychological systems involved in love – intimacy, passion, and commitment – and labels as 'consummate love' the love that is a full combination of all three components. See Robert J Sternberg, 'A Duplex Theory of Love' in Sternberg and Weis, above n 53, 184–99, 187.

81 See, eg, Shaver and Mikulincer, above n 56, 46.

82 See Karen K Dion and Kenneth L Dion, 'Individualism, Collectivism, and the Psychology of Love' in Sternberg and Weis, above n 53, 298–312, 306.

83 Kenrick, above n 53, 30.

84 See Johnson, above n 62, 24.

useful features of human psyche that motivate us to action. Some branches of psychology focus primarily on behaviour, while other branches try to understand motivations and other states of mind through more direct inquiries into emotions and therapeutic discussion.

Love is understood largely in terms of the benefits it provides to the subject – a sense of assurance and security, an ability to accomplish one's goals. This view of love is expanded to understand it as a mechanism for realising a broader set of emotional needs. The study of love in psychology has recently moved beyond examining love as an emotional need to focus on the physiological changes that take place in a brain while a person is feeling love. These physiological bases for love will be developed further in our discussion of neuroscience.

Psychology, for all of its depth and nuance, primarily endeavours to understand love from the perspective what love does for the self. For example, David P Schmitt says that love can give meaning to our lives and give us a greater sense of fulfillment and feelings of happiness. 'This drive to emotionally attach – to find someone to whom we can turn and say "hold me tight" – is wired into our genes and our bodies. We need emotional attachments . . . to be physically and mentally healthy – to survive.'[85] Notice the systematic and structural emphasis on the self rather than the other; love is a 'drive' to emotionally attach, to find someone to 'hold *me* tight', a 'need' that is a component of our own physical and mental health.[86]

Love, in short, can be understood as a phenomenon based upon what it does for me.

## Evolutionary biology

Evolutionary biology is explicit about understanding love as the result of selfishness, not a selfishness of the rational pursuit of self-interest (as in economics), or based on the fulfillment of basic human needs (as in psychology), but rather a selfishness that exists at a deep genetic level. This is captured most dramatically in the title of Richard Dawkins' field-defining book about evolutionary biology, *The Selfish Gene*.[87]

Whereas evolutionary psychologists focus on the evolutionary development of people and groups, evolutionary biology accounts for the phenomena of love as

85 See David P Schmitt, 'Evolutionary and Cross-cultural Perspectives on Love: The Influence of Gender, Personality, and Local Economy on Emotional Investment in Romantic Relationships' in Sternberg and Weis, above n 53, 251.

86 Ibid (emphasis added).

87 Richard Dawkins, *The Selfish Gene* (Oxford University Press, 1989). Dawkins notes that an important debate in evolutionary biology is about the unit at which natural selection occurs – the group, the individual, or the gene? Dawkins urges the view that natural selection takes place among genes, hence the title of his book. In explanation of this title, Dawkins states, 'We are survival machines – robot vehicles blindly programmed to preserve the selfish molecules known as genes.' Ibid xxi.

an evolutionary response to the 'desire' of genes to replicate and perpetuate themselves.[88] At the level of human organisms, this is done by finding suitable sexual partners with whom to mate, which will maximise the number of surviving children. Even practising family planning can be explained as a genetic maximising strategy. Dawkins explains that parents practise family planning 'to maximise the number of surviving children that they have, and this means having neither too many babies nor too few.'[89] Thus, Dawkins maintains, evolution is a process of natural selection at the level of 'genes', where genes can be personified as behaving 'selfishly'.[90]

### *Storge*

In terms of familial love, or *storge*, evolutionary biologists see protection of children as a direct result of genes attempting to ensure offspring will live to reproductive maturity in order to continue perpetuating genes. Robin Allott provides a representative summary of the view of love advanced by evolutionary biology. In her article, 'Evolutionary Aspects of Love and Empathy', Allott maintains that 'human love evolved on the basis of the mother/infant relation', and that there are 'survival benefits' that arise from the development of empathy, attachment, language, self-awareness, and consciousness. 'The genetic complex leading to the advance of each of the separate components, which then interacted to constitute love, would not need a separate genetic basis for love.'[91] The same genetic advantages that flowed from the mother/infant relationship also resulted in additional survival benefits for those 'in whom the complex operated most effectively'.[92]

88 Although evolutionary psychology and evolutionary biology are still related fields based on similar precepts. For example, David Buss, notes, 'The basic idea is that acts of love occur primarily in the context of mating relationships, parent–child relationships, and other kin relationships . . . these relationships are crucial for reproducing. Thus, acts that fall in the category of "love" are hypothesized to have evolved to . . . achieve goals that are linked with reproductive success.' David M Buss, 'Love Acts: Evolutionary Biology of Love' in Sternberg and Weis, above n 53, 100.

89 Dawkins, above n 87, 122. According to Dawkins, this family planning is a result of selfish genes motivating parents to only bear the children they have the resources to raise to maturity. He states, 'Genes that make an individual have too many babies tend not to persist in the gene pool, because children containing such genes tend not to survive to adulthood.'

90 Dawkins cites W D Hamilton for an explanation of the purpose of this 'personification' of genes. Says Hamilton, 'We are going to be concerned with genes supposed to affect the social behavior of their bearers, so let us try to make the argument more vivid by attributing to the genes, temporarily, intelligence and a certain freedom of choice.' Ibid xi.

91 Robin Allott, 'Evolutionary Aspects of Love and Empathy' (1992) 15 *Journal of Social and Evolutionary Systems* 353, 360.

92 As Alott explains:

> human love evolved on the basis of the mother/infant relation, dependent on empathy as a mode of perception of the infant's state and needs, with the primitive attachment manifested in many species of animals deepening into interpersonal love as, with the growth of self-awareness dependent in its turn on language, perception extended more

Thus, families with stronger familial ties became more likely to survive and subsequently reproduce, thereby perpetuating the family-oriented gene.

## *Eros*

An evolutionary biologist's view of romantic love focuses on love 'not simply [as] an internal state of feelings, drives and thoughts', but rather focuses on actions. According to biologist David Buss, 'Love has tangible manifestations in everyday conduct, and those manifestations have clear goals and ultimate reproductive consequences'.[93] Buss focuses attention on actions that reflect what we label 'love', and notes that, '[a]cts of love exist in the present because in the past they have served several proximate goals in the generation of offspring who will in turn be reproductively successful'.[94] Thus, romantic love is the result of the species learning which acts would be more likely to perpetuate the selfish gene.

## *Love and marriage*

Additionally, biologist Sydney Mellen accounts for love and marriage from the perspective of evolutionary biology as follows:

> The sexual interaction of protohuman males and females had evolved towards durable attachments of an emotional character, the beginnings of love. This . . . was strongly favoured by natural selection because it increased the chances that the exceptionally vulnerable and long-dependent young would survive until reproductive age . . . [t]he average human being of today inherits tendencies to love others . . . because in the evolutionary past such tendencies were as a general rule highly advantageous to individual protohumans possessing them and to their children and incidentally to their groups. And the

---

and more profoundly into the self of the other. The survival value, the "fitness" function of the mother/infant relation for altricial creatures is already generally accepted – and the question then is what evolutionary mechanism made the deepening of this relation additionally valuable. Of course, if love consists of interaction between empathy, mother/infant attachment, language, self-awareness, and consciousness, all advancing together under the impulse of the survival benefits each offers, then there would not be any need for a separate benefit flowing from love as such. The genetic complex leading to the advance of each of the separate components, which then interacted to constitute love, would not need a separate genetic basis for love. But there is no reason why the advantages flowing from this capacity for love manifested first in the mother/infant relation should not have generated additional survival benefits increasing even further the fitness of those in whom the complex operated most effectively.

Ibid 359–60.

93 Buss, above n 88, 109.

94 Ibid 101. Buss identifies a number of what he considers to be the overt actions of love and shows how each of them primarily furthers the central goals of mate selection and having children. These actions include: resource display, fidelity and guarding, commitment and marriage, sexual intimacy, reproduction, resource sharing, and parental investment. Ibid.

> general advantage to those individuals, in terms of reproductive success, was on average so great that it outweighed the costs to them, even though a few of them were lost through rare acts of self-sacrifice. Putting it very crudely, what I suggest is not a gene for altruism – but a gene for love or, slightly less crudely, a complex of many genes for various kinds and degrees of human affection.[95]

Love, therefore, is viewed as a genetic inheritance resulting from human evolution favouring parents who would enter into 'durable attachments' that would survive until 'reproductive age', which would lead to further 'reproductive success', that outweighed the costs associated with loving.

### *Philia*

Evolutionary biologists do not have a direct explanation for friendship-type love, but *The Selfish Gene* does make room for something similar. It should not come as a surprise, Dawkins says, to 'find individual organisms behaving altruistically "for the good of the genes", for example by feeding and protecting kin who are likely to share copies of the same genes.'[96] This kind of altruism covers more than simply direct parent–child relationships – it extends to any who might be associated with one's genetic heritage. Kin altruism of this sort is one of the ways that 'gene selfishness can translate itself into individual altruism'.[97]

### *Agape*

Dawkins makes sense of species-wide altruism by distinguishing between the gene and the individual and expressing that the individual can overcome the gene. Dawkins does not posit that selfish genes imply that at the level of an individual organism altruism is impossible. Dawkins does not advocate basing human morality 'on the gene's law of universal ruthless selfishness'. Rather, if a moral is to be extracted from the book, Dawkins says, let it be a warning: 'Be warned that if you wish, as I do, to build a society in which individuals cooperate generously and unselfishly towards a common good, you can expect little help from biological nature. Let us try to *teach* generosity and altruism, because we are born selfish.'[98] Dawkins

95 Sydney L W Mellen, *The Evolution of Love* (W H Freeman, 1981) 278.

96 Dawkins, above n 87, viii. Dawkins further explains, '[R]elatives are a substantial proportion of [an individual's] genes. Each selfish gene therefore has its loyalties divided between different bodies.' Ibid.

97 Ibid.

98 Ibid 3. Dawkins further observes that we, as developed humans, 'can even discuss ways of cultivating and nurturing pure, disinterested altruism, something that has no place in nature, something that has never existed before in the history of the world.' Ibid 179. Dawkins clarifies later that the selfishness he is talking about is a characteristic of genes (the unit of replication), rather than the organism (the unit in the sense of vehicle): 'It was not until 1978 I began

maintains that learning such altruism would not result as something explainable by evolutionary biology, but instead by overcoming our biological history.[99]

### *Conclusion*

In essence, evolutionary biology explains love as the direct result of our selfish genes attempting to meet their own goals and ends through successful reproduction. This is true in familial love, romantic love, and even friendship. While evolutionary biology does attempt to leave room for sincere altruism, it does so by explaining one must overcome genetic history, for genetics cannot explain altruism itself.

## Neuroscience

The neuroscience approach to love focuses on studying various brain regions and associated neurochemical processes that correlate with different experiences of love. While neurology is a relatively young science, there have been a number of studies conducted on the processes behind experiences such as empathy and altruism (something like *agape*); ingroup love (something like *philia*); sexual urges, romantic love, and mate attachment (*eros*); and parent–child type attachment (*storge*). While neuroscience can only observe the brain's physical processes, researchers have attempted explanations as to why the processes function as they do and what that means for the human experience.[100] Almost always, these explanations focus on the

---

to think clearly about the distinction between "vehicles" and the "replicators" that ride inside them. . . . [t]here are two kinds of unit of natural selection, and there is no dispute between them. The gene is the unit in the sense of replicator. The organism is the unit in the sense of vehicle.' According to Dawkins, it is the gene, not the organism, that is selfish. Ibid ix.

99 '[I]t is a fallacy – incidentally a very common one – to suppose that genetically inherited traits are by definition fixed and unmodifiable. Our genes may instruct us to be selfish, but we are not necessarily compelled to obey them all our lives.' Ibid 3. The effect of selfish genes, Dawkins notes, is not a prohibition of altruism, but that 'it may just be more difficult to learn altruism than it would be if we were genetically programmed to be altruistic.' Dawkins does, however, leave room for an alternative theory of altruism that is explainable by evolutionary biology. In the introduction to the 30th anniversary edition of *The Selfish Gene*, he writes that if he were to write the book again he 'should also give some space to Amotz Zahavi's idea that altruistic donation might be a "Potlatch" style of dominance signal: see how superior to you I am, I can afford to make a donation to you!' Ibid viii.

100 It should be noted that some neurologists have pointed out the danger in making these kinds of inferences. They point out that results can often differ from study to study and researchers can only make guesses as to why. Additionally, some neurologists contend that parts of the brain cannot be correlated to experiences of the mind, but can only be observed as a whole system. Thus, they contend, neuro-studies cannot explain human experience, only how the brain experiences them. See Nikos K Logothetis, 'What We Can & What We Can't Do with fMRI' (2008) 453 *Nature* 869, 869–78 and Paolo Fusar-Poli and M R Broome, 'Love & Brain: From Mereological Fallacy to "Folk" Neuroimaging' (2007) 154 *Psychiatry Research: Neuroimaging* 154, 285–6.

evolution of the mammal brain, the dopaminergic reward system, and the species' need to reproduce.

### *Agape*

Thus far, neuroscience has yet to conduct in-depth analysis on what kinds of neurochemical processes correlate with the traditional notion of *agape* in its fullness. Neurologists have, however, explored the processes behind empathy and various altruistic actions. One seminal work by Jorge Moll and others conducted Functional Magnetic Resonance Imaging ('fMRI') on various individuals in the process of choosing to donate money to charity or keep it for themselves.[101] The study results indicated that some brain areas, specifically those associated with the mesolimbic reward system, activated in both decisions.[102] The authors postulated this correlation suggests charitable acts activate 'the same ancient parts of the brain activated in response to food, sex, and material gains, suggesting altruism is a hardwired pleasure in the brain'.[103] The study also noted a few areas of the brain that activated specifically with decisions to give to charities or other broader social causes. Such areas were associated with the 'more primitive mechanisms of social attachment and aversion'.[104]

Ultimately, the findings of the study led the authors to speculate any human affinity to commit to the broader social good is a result of a similar gene evolution as those suggested in reciprocity theories – ie, people learned to give in expectancy that others will eventually give back.[105] According to the authors, this provides evidence that 'human altruism draws on the general mammalian neural system of reward, social attachment, and aversion'.[106]

101 Jorge Moll, Frank Krueger, Roland Zahn, Matteo Pardini, Ricardo de Oliveira-Souza and Jordan Grafman, 'Human Fronto-Mesolimbic Networks Guide Decisions About Charitable Donation' (2006) 103 *Proceedings of the National Academy of Science* 15623–8.

102 'We show that the mesolimbic reward system is engaged by donations in the same way as when monetary rewards are obtained.' Ibid 15623.

103 'The importance of these fronto-limbic networks for human altruism concurs with their key roles in more basic social motivational mechanisms. The mesolimbic system regulates overall reward reinforcement and prediction and is activated by a host of stimuli, including food, sex, drugs, and money.' Ibid.

104 These areas include the medial orbitofrontal-subgenual and lateral orbitofrontal areas. Ibid.

105

> We speculate that our capacity to feel attachment or aversion to societal causes might have emerged through similar gene culture coevolution mechanisms as those proposed by the strong reciprocity theory. This premise would allow primitive reward, social attachment, and aversion neural systems to operate beyond the immediate sphere of kinship, thus enabling humans to directly link motivational value to abstract collective causes, principles, and ideologies.

Ibid 15626.

106 The authors also note, however, that when the decision to be altruistic also includes moral beliefs the decision 'relies on the uniquely developed anterior prefrontal cortex.' A section of the brain associated with 'altruistic punishment, moral judgment, assessment of abstract future rewards, and long-term goals.' Ibid 15626.

### *Philia*

Neuroscience has also explored the foundations for experiences similar to *philia*, or friendship-type love with similar individuals. One study conducted by Vani A Mathur and others describes this phenomenon as ingroup love.[107] The study attempts to observe differences in neural processes between people empathising with pain experienced by other humans in general and pain experienced by those in a similar life situation as their own (eg race). Mathur and the others ultimately found that 'empathy for ingroup members is neurally distinct from empathy for humankind, more generally'.[108] Upon further explanation, the empathy felt for humans in general tended to be more associated with emotional processes while empathy for ingroup members recognised a kind of self-identity that engaged more cognitive processes.[109] In attempting to determine why this distinction might exist, the authors postulate a number of explanations, but identify two as likely. The first is reciprocal altruism, 'whereby people tend to help family members, or those they expect to return the favor'.[110] The second is that individuals regard similar persons in a way related to how they regard themselves.[111]

### *Eros*

Neurology posits that what humans experience as romantic love developed from the dopaminergic reward pathways that commonly govern mammalian brains. Researchers tested this hypothesis by conducting fMRI scans on individuals viewing photographs of romantic partners.[112] The study yielded a number of conclusions.

107 Vani A Mathur, Tokiko Harada, Trixie Lipke, and Joan Y Chiao, 'Neural Basis of Extraordinary Empathy and Altruistic Motivation' (2010) 51 *NeuroImage* 1468.

108 People showed greater response within anterior cingulate cortex and bilateral insula when observing the suffering of others, but African American individuals additionally recruit medial prefrontal cortex when observing the suffering of members of their own social group. Ibid.

109

> [N]eural activity within medial prefrontal cortex in response to pain expressed by ingroup relative to outgroup members predicated greater empathy and altruistic motivation for one's ingroup, suggesting that neurocognitive processes associated with self-identity underlie extraordinary empathy and altruistic motivation for members of one's own social group.

Ibid.

110 Ibid 1472. 'Importantly, effective cooperative living sometimes entails belonging to smaller social groups and limiting resource sharing to members of that group so that individual costs and risks associated with non-reciprocated altruism are reduced.' Ibid 1474.

111 '[I]nclusion of other group members in one's self concept underlies intergroup and inter individual differences in extraordinary empathy and altruistic motivation. Prior social psychological research has shown that inclusion of another person in the self leads to enhanced empathy and altruistic motivation.' Ibid 1473 (citation omitted).

112 Helen E Fisher, Arthur Aron and Lucy L Brown, 'Romantic love: a mammalian brain system for mate choice' (2006) 361 *Philos Trans R Soc Lond B Biol Sci* 2173–86. See also Helen Fisher, Lucy Brown and Arthur Aron, 'Romantic Love: an fMRI study of a neural mechanism

Initially, researchers noted activation of several areas of the brain associated with the dopaminergic reward system, and so concluded the original hypothesis was accurate, and romantic love is motivated by the dopaminergic reward systems in our brains.[113] Furthermore, researchers also noted that the brain activated areas associated with anger, obsessive/compulsive tendencies, and high-stakes gambling – much like addiction.[114]

Additionally, researchers compared their results with results of other studies and determined romantic love can be separated into at least three separate neural processes: sex drive, romantic attraction, and mate attachment. All of these, according to study conclusions, work in different but overlapping neural systems in order to achieve one common goal: reproduction. The sex drive 'enables individuals to initiate courtship and mating with a range of partners',[115] romantic attraction 'motivates them to focus their mating energy on specific individuals, thereby conserving time and metabolic energy',[116] and mate attachment 'evolved primarily to motivate mating partners to sustain an affiliative connection long enough to complete species-specific parental duties'.[117]

---

for mate choice' (2005) 493 *The Journal of Comparative Neurology* 58–62 and Arthur Aron, Helen Fisher, Debra J Mashek, Greg Strong, Haifang Li, and Lucy L Brown, 'Reward, Motivation, & Emotion Systems Associated With Early & Stage Intense Romantic Love' (2005) 94 *Journal of Neurophysiology* 327–37.

113 Researchers primarily noted activation of the right ventral tegmental area (VTA) and the right postero-dorsal body of the caudate nucleus. The VTA is a central system to brain rewards, and the caudate nucleus also processes goals, expectations, and rewards. Fisher et al, 'Romantic love', above n 112.

114 Ibid. See also Helen E Fisher, Lucy L Brown, Arthur Aron, Greg Strong, and Debra Mashek, 'Reward, Addiction, & Emotion Regulation Systems Associated With Rejection in Love' (2010) 104 *Journal of Neurophysiology* 51, stating:

> reward, addiction, and emotion regulation systems associated with rejection in love, which states 'Forebrain activations associated with motivational relevance, gain/loss, cocaine craving, addiction, and emotion regulation suggest that higher-order systems subject to experience and learning may also mediate the [reaction when one's love is rejected] . . . Activation of areas involved with cocaine addiction may help explain the obsessive behaviors associated with rejection in love.

115 Fisher et al, 'Romantic love', above n 112. It is well established that the sex drive is associated with neurochemicals like testosterone and other androgens/estrogens. Researchers note that these chemicals do not tend to cause people to fall in love. For example, taking these chemicals artificially may arouse an individual sexually, but it does not cause romantic love. Ibid 2176–7.

116 Ibid 2173. 'Several lines of investigation indicate that the sex drive and the courtship attraction/romantic love are distinct neural systems, designed to orchestrate different aspects of the reproductive process. The sex drive enables individuals to initiate courtship and mating with a range of partners; courtship attraction/romantic love motivates them to focus their mating energy on specific individuals, thereby conserving time and metabolic energy.' Ibid 2177.

117 Ibid 2178. Comparing the results of their own study to results of others, the authors noticed a difference in brain system activation between short-term and long-term relationships. They postulated that these differences represented a difference between early romantic passion and long-term attachment to one's mate. 'Partner attachment, or pairbonding, in birds and mammals is characterized by mutual territory defense and/or nest building, mutual feeding and

Interestingly, authors also indicate that the study provides evidence for the theory that romantic love is not primarily an emotion, but a 'motivation system designed to enable suitors to build and maintain intimate relationships with a preferred mating partner'.[118] Romantic love, as neurology reports, is, therefore, a result of reward-seeking behaviours evolved from mammalian precursors to enable individuals to 'respond to sexually selected courtship traits and motivate individuals to make a mate choice'.[119]

### *Storge*

For neurology, familial love is a subset of or variation on mate attachment. For example, part of the Fisher study's explanation of mate attachment reads as follows: 'primates have evolved an innate attachment system designed to motivate infants to seek comfort and safety from their primary caregiver, generally their mother'. Researchers have emphasised that this attachment system remains active throughout their life and serves as a foundation for attachments between spouses as they raise children.[120] Additionally, maternal love activates specific regions in the brain that differ from other types of love but are similar to mate attachment.[121] This type of love, however, is also based on the dopaminergic rewards system and supposedly evolved as part of our reproductive strategy.[122]

### *Conclusion*

In the end, neuroscience attempts to explain love in similar ways to other scientific disciplines. Whether it is altruism/empathy, ingroup love, romantic love, or familial attachment, neuroscience tends to postulate that humans engage in love as a way of activating the mammalian rewards system or to seek perpetuation of the species.

---

grooming, maintenance of close proximity, separation anxiety, and shared parental chores and affiliative behaviors.' Such behaviours have been associated with activity of the neuropeptides, oxytocin in the nucleus accumbens, the opioid system, and other neural processes. Ibid.

118 Ibid 2181. See also Fisher et al, 'Romantic love', above n 112, 61, which states 'several results support our hypothesis that early-stage, intense romantic love is importantly influenced by subcortical reward regions that are dopamine-rich; that romantic love is primarily a neural system associated with motivation to acquire a reward, rather than a specific emotion; that this brain system is distinct, yet overlapping with the sex drive; that this brain system is derived from mammalian precursors; and that it evolved as a mechanism to enable individuals to respond to sexually selected courtship traits and motivate individuals to make a mate choice'.

119 Ibid. 'This brain system has inspired love songs, love poems, love magic, myths and legends about love, and suicide and homicide cross culturally. Romantic love is most likely a primary aspect of our complex reproductive strategy.' Ibid (citations omitted).

120 See Fisher et al, 'Romantic Love', above n 112.

121 Ibid 2179. See also Andreas Bartels and Semir Zeki, 'The Neural Correlates of Maternal and Romantic Love' (2004) 21 *NeuroImage* 1155.

122 Bartels and Zeki describe maternal affection as a different kind of social attachment that activates the same reward system, but also activates different regions compared to those in partner attachment. Ibid.

## Summary

Thinking about the approaches to love employed by these scientific disciplines, one gets the distinct impression that the phenomena of other-regarding love are threatening to these scientific worldviews. If love involves genuine other-regard, then the economic hypothesis about the nature of man as being essentially selfish is called into question. If love really involves genuine regard for the feelings of others, then the theory of our psychological makeup as beings that satisfy our own emotional needs is undermined. If love is self-less, then the hypothesis that the key to understanding human beings is to understand 'the selfish gene' is weakened.[123] If other-regarding love is real, then the mechanistic explanations that reduce love to selfishly-oriented chemical reactions will be insufficient to truly understand the phenomena.

All of these disciplines' attempts to understand love in terms of the self are deeply ironic, since the essence of love, desiring and willing the good of another, is the antinomy of self-based understandings of human nature. It is not that we are not selfish; as all of us know all too well, we are selfish. The question, love posits, is whether we are capable of being something other than entirely selfish. Love – genuine other-regarding love – says, yes.

## Scientific approaches to God

As a side observation, it is interesting to note that it is not just love that science seeks to understand from the perspective of the 'self' rather than taking seriously the reality and importance of the 'other'. Scientific accounts of God – in economics, psychology, evolutionary biology, and neuroscience – all tend to treat inquiries about the nature and existence of God in ways that are very similar to their treatment of the nature and existence of love.

Economics is mostly silent on the question of God, but the classic economist Adam Smith argued that there is an 'invisible hand' guiding the economic decisions of all that will ultimately lead to the benefit of society.[124] One religious economist claims that the 'invisible hand' is God,[125] whereas the 'invisible hand' is generally understood as an explanation of 'how rational self-interest in a free-market economy leads to economic well-being'.[126] However, economists typically only discuss God when measuring how the religiosity of individuals impacts economic growth.[127]

123 Even overcoming our selfish natures for utilitarian purposes can still be considered self-serving. See Dawkins, above n 87, 3.

124 Adam Smith, *An Inquiry into the Nature and Causes of the Wealth of Nations*, (Edwin Cannan, ed, 1904) Library of Economics and Liberty, IV.2.9 23, accessed 23 June 2016, available at: <www.econlib.org/library/Smith/smWN13.html>.

125 Jerry Bowyer, *God And The Economists*, Forbes opinion, 17 August 2011, accessed 23 June 2016, available at: <www.econlib.org/library/Enc/bios/Smith.html>.

126 Adam Smith, *The Concise Encyclopedia of Economics*, accessed on 23 June 2016, available at: <www.econlib.org/library/Enc/bios/Smith.html>.

127 A recent economic study about religion determined that believing in an afterlife (especially hell) increased economic growth, but that church attendance decreases economic growth.

Psychology tends to view God as a creation of the mind of man, rather than man as a creation of God.[128] Freud, for example, is famously dismissive of belief in God as reflecting childish projections of the 'all-powerful father' to an unseen 'all-powerful' God. Growing up and being mature involves overcoming this childish illusion of father's power. As we as a species become mature, Freud asserts confidently, in *The Future of An Illusion*, mankind will overcome its collective childish notion of an all-powerful God.

Evolutionary biology also views God as nonsensical. For example, in his classic book on evolutionary biology, *The Selfish Gene*, Richard Dawkins asserts that faith 'is capable of driving people to such dangerous folly that faith seems to me to qualify as a kind of mental illness'.[129] Dawkins has of course added a book-length polemic against the rationality of believing in God, with a title that gives away its thesis, *The God Delusion*.[130] If belief in God is a delusion, and God is defined as love, it is no surprise that Dawkins treats love as a kind of delusion as well.

Neuroscience approaches the question of the existence of God in a very similar vein. The focus is on the brain, and its chemical and biological reactions while believers report to be having spiritual experiences.[131] The neuroscience literature often ignores the possibility that the spiritual experiences might be genuine encounters with the divine and assume that evolutionary heritage and ritualistic behaviours have combined to induce spiritual feelings in our brains.[132] Although, spiritual experience is 'real' in a neurobiological sense, most neuroscientists would dismiss the possibility of God because, '[s]cience concerns itself with that which

---

Robert Barro and Rachel McCleary, *Religion and Economic Growth, NBER Working Paper Series* (National Bureau of Economic Research, 2003).

128 However, some religious psychologists disagree with the current paradigm and urge that psychologists acknowledge religious phenomena in order to better understand the psychology of religion: 'Recent thinking suggests that the time is right for a reconsideration of the interface between psychology and religion. We argue that most accounts of religion in contemporary psychology (especially as typified by evolutionary theory) have been toxic to the phenomena of religious experience.' Edward Gantt and Richard Williams, 'Explaining Religion to Death: Reductionism, Evolution, and the Psychology of Religion' (2008) 32 *Issues in Religion and Psychotherapy* 3–13, 3.

129 Dawkins, above n 87, 198. Dawkins defines faith as 'a state of mind that leads people to believe something – it doesn't matter what – in the total absence of supporting evidence. If there were good supporting evidence then faith would be superfluous, for the evidence would compel us to believe it anyway.' Ibid.

130 'The God of the Old Testament is arguably the most unpleasant character in all fiction: jealous and proud of it; a petty, unjust, unforgiving control-freak; a vindictive, bloodthirsty ethnic cleanser; a misogynistic, homophobic, racist, infanticidal, genocidal, filicidal, pestilential, megalomaniacal, sadomasochistic, capriciously malevolent bully. Those of us schooled from infancy in his ways can become desensitized to their horror.' Richard Dawkins, *The God Delusion* (Houghton Mifflin Company, 2006) 31.

131 See Andrew Newberg and Eugene D'Aquili, *Why God Won't Go Away: Brain Science and the Biology of Belief* (Random House Publishing, 2011) 1–7.

132 Ibid 8.

can be weighed, counted, calculated, and measured – anything that can't be verified by objective observation simply can't be called scientific'.[133]

Scientific accounts of God are not universally hostile to the idea of God, but the prevailing tendency in current scientific disciplines is to argue, or more frequently assume, that God does not exist, or that He or It is a human creation.[134]

## Religious (and in particular) Christian perspectives of love

### *Biblical perspective of love*

From most religious perspectives, love is (or is at least among) the most important and powerful force and reality in the universe.

#### *Love from a Christian perspective*

Here, I will speak primarily of the Christian conception of love, although love plays a similar and perhaps equally central role in many other religious traditions, including the other Abrahamic faiths (Judaism[135] and Islam[136]), as well as the other major world religions, including Hinduism[137] and Buddhism,[138] among others.

From a religious perspective love is a powerful force. John 3:16 declares, '[f]or God so loved the world, that he gave his only begotten Son, that whosoever believeth in him should not perish, but have everlasting life'. And so, for example, in the New Testament, John the Revelator says, '[h]e that loveth not knoweth not God; for God

133 Newberg and D'Aquili, above n 131, 2.

134 A recent Pew Research Center Poll found that only 51% of scientists believe in God or in a universal spirit or higher power whereas 95% of the general public does. Pew Research Center, 'Scientists and Belief' (5 November 2009), accessed 23 June 2016, available at: <www.pewforum.org/2009/11/05/scientists-and-belief/>.

135 'Thou shalt love thy neighbor as thyself.' (Lev. 19:18) (All Biblical quotations unless otherwise indicated are from the King James version). 'Thou shalt love the Lord thy God with all thine heart.' (Deut. 6:5). 'Love ye . . . the stranger.' (Deut. 10:19). 'Love joyfully with the wife whom thou lovest.' (Eccl. 9:9).

136 'And of His signs, another one is that He created for you mates from among yourselves that you may find comfort with them, and *He planted love and kindness in your hearts*' (Qur'an 30:21) (emphasis added).

137 Love is central to Hindu perception of God. Swami Vivekananda, an influential 19th-century Hindu monk, said, 'Who becomes learned? He who can feel even one drop of love. God is love, and love is God. And God is everywhere.' 'Divine Love' in Swami Vivekananda (trans), *Complete Works of Swami Vivekananda* (Vol 6, Lectures and Discourses, 1984). 'Love is the firstborn, loftier than the gods, the Fathers and men. You, O Love, are the eldest of all, altogether mighty. To you we pay homage!' *Atharva Veda* 9.2.19–20, 25.

138 'O good man! Compassion acts as parent to all beings. The parent is compassion. Know that compassion is the Tathagata.' *Mahaparinirvana Sutra* 259, World Scripture, accessed on June 28 2016, available at: <www.unification.net/ws/theme010.htm#18>. 'The Great Compassionate Heart is the essence of Buddhahood.' *Gandavyuha Sutra*. Ibid.

is love'. (1 John 4:8). This love is not some highly abstract or theoretical concept; rather it is manifested in the atoning sacrifice of Jesus Christ. John continues:

> In this was manifested the love of God toward us, because that God sent his only begotten Son into the world, that we might live through him. Herein is love, not that we loved God, but that he loved us, and sent his Son to be the propitiation for our Sins. Beloved, if God so loved us, we ought also to love one another.
> (1 John 4: 9–11).[139]

Indeed, love is seen as the most important and most powerful force in the universe. Paul waxes poetic, declaring, '[f]or I am persuaded, that neither death, nor life, nor angels, nor principalities, nor powers, nor things present, nor things to come, Nor height, nor depth, nor any other creature, shall be able to separate us from the love of God, which is in Christ Jesus our Lord' (Romans 8:38–39). Paul also wrote in 1 Corinthians 2:9: 'But as it is written, Eye hath not seen, nor ear heard, neither have entered into the heart of man, the things which God hath prepared for them that love him'.

Paul's prayer in Ephesians 3, includes the plea:

> That Christ may dwell in your hearts by faith; that ye, being rooted and grounded in love, May be able to comprehend with all saints what is the breadth, and length, and depth, and height, And to know the love of Christ, which passeth knowledge, that ye might be filled with all the fullness of God.
> (Ephesians 3:17–19).

Note the four-dimensional character of Christ's love, stretching both forwards and backwards and side to side (breadth and length), as well as both up and down (depth and height).

*Love as a commandment*

But from a Christian perspective, not only is God's love the first and most important reality, our responsibility to love – both God and others – is our most important mandate. When a lawyer enquired of Jesus, which is the first commandment, Jesus answered:

> Thou shalt love the Lord thy God with all thy heart, and with all thy soul, and with all thy mind, and with all thy strength: this is the first commandment. And the second is like, namely this, Thou shalt love thy neighbor as thyself. There is none other commandment greater than these.[140]

139 See also 1 John 4:16 ('And we have known and believed the love that God hath to us. God is love; and he that dwelleth in love dwelleth in God, and God in him.').

140 Mark 12:30–31; Matthew 22:37–39 (similar account of the first and second commandments); Luke 10:25–27 (similar account with the lawyer citing to Jesus the two first

Following this exchange comes the question, 'who is my neighbor?', which Jesus answers with the parable of the Good Samaritan, a story that illustrates selfless care of someone who is a stranger or even an enemy.[141]

God commands us to love, because love is His essence, and He wants us to become like Him. 1 John 3:2: 'Beloved, now are we the sons of God, and it doth not yet appear what we shall be: but we know that, when he shall appear, we shall be like him; for we shall see him as he is'. John continues in 1 John 5:2–3: 'By this we know that we love the children of God, when we love God, and keep his commandments. For this is the love of God, that we keep his commandments: and his commandments are not grievous'.

### *Relationship between first two commandments*

The linkage of the first two commandments suggests that it is not possible to genuinely love God without also loving others. As John the Revelator explains, '[i]f a man say, I love God, and hateth his brother, he is a liar: for he that loveth not his brother whom he hath seen, how can he love God whom he hath not seen, (1 John 4:20).

### *Love as selflessness*

God's love for the world, in sending His Son, and Christ's love, in dying to atone for the sins of the world, is the very incarnation and manifestation of love as selflessness. No doubt, a self-regarding account of Christ's love is possible to imagine, but it would be a distortion, indeed a falsification and misrepresentation of the meaning of the love so rendered.

Biblical accounts of the love expected of us also emphasise the importance of love as genuine regard for the other. For example, 1 John 3:17, asks, '[b]ut who so hath this world's god, and seeth his brother have need, and shutteth up his bowels of compassion from him, how dwelleth the love of God in him?' Then the injunction, '[m]y little children, let us not love in word, neither in tongue; but in

---

commandments). See also Leviticus 19:18 ('thou shalt love thy neighbor as thyself: I am the Lord'); Matthew 5:43–45 ('Ye have heard that it hath been said, Thou shalt love thy neighbor, and hate thine enemy. But I say unto you, Love your enemies, bless them that curse you, do good to them that hate you, and pray for them which despitefully use you and persecute you; That ye may be the children of your Father which is in heaven: for he maketh his sun to rise on the evil and on the good, and sendeth rain on the just and the unjust.'); Romans 13:9–10 ('Thou shalt love thy neighbor as thyself. Love worketh no ill to his neighbour: therefore love is the fulfilling of the law.'); Galatians 5:14 ('For all the law is fulfilled in one word, even in this; Thou shalt love thy neighbor as thyself.'); James 2:8 ('If ye fulfil the royal law according to the scripture, Thou shalt love thy neighbor as thyself, ye do well').

141 Luke 10: 29–37. In some interpretations of this story, it is Jesus Christ who is symbolised by the Good Samaritan, and who is a model for how we should behave as human beings. See Hugh Nibley, 'Since Cumorah' in *Collected Works of Hugh Nibley* (Deseret Books Company, 1988) 100.

deed and in truth'. (1 John 3:18). The book of Colossians also speaks of the hearts of saints 'being knit together in love,' (Colossians 2:2).

### *Love as a gift of and from God*

This is not to say that love is easy; in Romans, the Apostle Paul suggests that to love, we need God's help: '[t]he love of God,' Paul says, 'is shed abroad in our hearts by the Holy Ghost which is given unto us' (Romans 5:5). The point is not that a religious point of view posits a human nature that is selfless, while most scientific approaches posit a human nature that is selfish. The religious point of view sees man as naturally selfish as well, thus the label 'natural man', which is the Biblical term that describes man's ordinary, fallen state. What God's love does is raise the possibility that we can rise above the natural man, with God's help, and become saints, new creatures that are imbued with a disposition to love, with a disposition towards selflessness rather than selfishness. God holds out the possibility that selfishness is not the entire story.

## *C S Lewis – the four loves*

One of the most popular Christian articulations of the four types of love is C S Lewis's account in his brief book, *The Four Loves.* Note how differently his account of these categories of love is in comparison with the scientific accounts described above.

### *Affection – storge – empathy bonds*

C S Lewis maintains that *storge* (which he refers to as 'affection'), includes both 'Need-love' and 'Gift-love'.[142] Lewis describes 'Need-love' as the selfish desire that compels us to seek out the company of others in order to satisfy our social needs.[143] 'Gift-love' is the selfless affection that we give to others when we care for them, the love that parents give to children, or the love that Jesus showed by giving his life for humanity.[144] Although it is natural to give affection for selfish reasons, (eg, because we simply 'need to be needed'),[145] it is a symptom of 'Being a Fallen Man', and maybe even a sin.[146] True affection is 'responsible for nine-tenths of whatever solid and durable happiness there is in our natural lives',[147] and it is usually combined with one of the other types of love.[148]

142 C S Lewis, above n 17, 53.
143 Ibid.
144 Ibid 81.
145 Ibid 78.
146 Ibid 80.
147 Ibid 80.
148 Ibid 57.

### *Friendship – philia – friend bonds*

Lewis says, 'without Eros none of us would have been begotten and without Affection none of us would have been reared; but we can live and breed without Friendship'.[149] Although friendship may have had evolutionary survival value,[150] it is free from biological instinct or any sense of duty.[151] Although there is a reciprocal nature of friendship, reciprocity is far from being the purpose of friendship.[152] Friendship is distinct from romantic love, but true friendship can easily 'pass into erotic love' and 'erotic love may lead to Friendship'.[153] Friendship must 'invoke the divine protection if it hopes to remain sweet',[154] and avoid becoming proud and experiencing 'the degrading pleasure of exclusiveness'.[155] Friendships are not formed by chance, but are divinely influenced; Christ could say to a group of Christian friends, '[y]ou have not chosen one another but I have chosen you for one another'.[156]

### *Romantic – eros – erotic bonds*

Lewis defines *eros* as 'being in love', acknowledging that sex can occur without *eros* and that *eros* can occur without sex.[157] *Eros* begins with 'simply a delighted pre-occupation with the Beloved a general, unspecified pre-occupation with her in her totality . . . [t]he fact that she is a woman is far less important than the fact that she is herself. He is full of desire, but the desire may not be sexually toned'.[158] In *eros*, 'the lover desires the Beloved herself, not the pleasure she can give. No lover in the world ever sought the embraces of the woman he loved as the result of a calculation, however unconscious, that they would be more pleasurable than those of any other woman'.[159] Lewis continues, 'without *Eros* sexual desire, like

149 Ibid 88.
150 Ibid 94.
151 Ibid 111.
152 'We are sorry that any gift or loan or night-watching should have been necessary and now, for heaven's sake, let us forget all about it and go back to the things we really want to do or talk of together.' Ibid 102.
153 Ibid 98–9. Lewis contrasts friendship from *eros* like this: 'Lovers are always talking to one another about their love; Friends hardly ever about their Friendship. Lovers are normally face to face, absorbed in each other; Friends, side by side, absorbed in some common interest.' Ibid 91.
154 Ibid 124.
155 Ibid 122.
156 Ibid 126.
157 Ibid 131–2. Lewis doubts that it is common for a man who has 'first felt mere sexual appetite for a woman and then gone on at a later stage to "fall in love with her."'
158 Ibid 133. 'Sexual desire, without Eros, wants it, the thing in itself; Eros wants the Beloved.' Ibid 134.
159 Ibid 135. 'If we had not all experienced this, if we were mere logicians, we might boggle at the conception of desiring a human being, as distinct from desiring any pleasure, comfort, or service that human being can give.' Ibid 136.

every other desire, is a fact about ourselves. Within *Eros* it is rather about the Beloved'.[160] Lewis did not believe that *eros* could be explained solely by an evolutionary perspective that love is designed to perpetuate and improve the human race.[161] *Eros* 'toss[es] personal happiness aside as a triviality and plant[s] the interests of another in the centre of our being'.[162]

### *Charity – agape – unconditional godlike love*

Lewis claims that *storge*, friendship, and *eros* in themselves are not enough to be 'kept sweet' without the 'Christian life', which is charity, *agape*, or the love of the God.[163] God never taught us to be calculating in our love so that we can maximise our self-interest, we were taught to love unconditionally.[164] God gives us charity, which is a love for our 'fellow-men'.[165] Although 'there is something in each of us that cannot be naturally loved', the love of God helps others to love us in spite of our flaws.[166] God is the inventor of all of the different types of love.[167] Indeed, if we were not made in the image of God, we never could have truly loved here on earth.[168]

## Conclusion

Science strives strenuously to understand love from the perspective of the self – in terms of self-interest, realisation of one's own needs, an evolutionary strategy of projecting one's DNA into the future, and as bodily mechanisms that can be understood as complex chemical processes. Since love is so closely associated with God – His existence and essence – it is interesting, and perhaps not surprising, that science's approach to understanding God, and the human belief in God, follows a very similar pattern – an understanding rooted in self-interest, realising one's own needs, an evolutionary strategy of meaning-making, and as a manifestation of chemical processes in the brain. The implications for law are interesting to contemplate. To the extent we think of law from the perspective of science, our conceptions of love and of God will follow the same, predictable scientific pattern.

160 Ibid.

161 Ibid 153. Lewis says, referring to the motivation behind evolution as the 'Life Force': 'And what on earth was the Life Force doing through all those countless generations when the begetting of children depended very little on mutual Eros and very much on arranged marriages, slavery, and rape? Has it only just thought of this bright idea for improving the species?'

162 Ibid 158.

163 Ibid 163. 'The loves prove that they are unworthy to take the place of God by the fact that they cannot even remain themselves and do what they promise to do without God's help.' Ibid 166.

164 'If I am sure of anything I am sure that His teaching was never meant to confirm my congenital preference for safe investments and limited liabilities.' Ibid 168.

165 Ibid 179.

166 Ibid 183.

167 Ibid 176.

168 Ibid 190.

## References

Allott, Robin, 'Evolutionary Aspects of Love and Empathy' (1992) 15 *Journal of Social and Evolutionary Systems* 353

American Psychiatric Association, *Diagnostic and statistical manual of mental disorders: DSM-IV-TR*, (Washington, DC: American Psychiatric Association, 2000)

Aristotle, *Nicomachean Ethics* (W D Ross trans, Digireads.com, 2005)

Aristotle, *Rhetoric* (W Rhys Roberts trans, Dover Publications, 2004)

Aron, Arthur, Helen Fisher, Debra J Mashek, Greg Strong, Haifang Li and Lucy L Brown, 'Reward, Motivation, & Emotion Systems Associated With Early & Stage Intense Romantic Love' (2005) 94 *Journal of Neurophysiology* 327

Auld, Christopher and Alan Case, 'Social exchange processes in leisure and non-leisure settings: A review and exploratory investigation' (1997) 29 *Journal of Leisure Research* 183

Austen, Jane, *Northanger Abbey* (Little, Brown & Company, 1903)

Barro, Robert and Rachel McCleary, *Religion and Economic Growth, NBER Working Paper Series* (National Bureau of Economic Research, 2003)

Bartels, Andreas and Semir Zeki, 'The Neural Correlates of Maternal and Romantic Love' (2004) 21 *NeuroImage* 1155

Baxter, JL, *Social and Psychological Foundations of Economic Analysis* (Harvester and Wheatsheaf, 1988)

Becker, Gary, 'A Theory of Marriage: Part I' (1973) 81 *Journal Politics & Economics* 81

Beyers, Marissa and Jeffrey Reber, 'The illusion of intimacy: A Levinasian critique of evolutionary psychology' (1998) 18 *Journal of Theoretical and Philosophical Psychology* 176

Bloom, Paul, 'Against Empathy', *The Atlantic*, 21 March 2016, accessed 24 June 2016, available at: <www.theatlantic.com/video/index/474588/why-empathy-is-a-bad-thing/>.

Bowyer, Jerry, *God And The Economists*, Forbes opinion, 17 August 2011, accessed 23 June 2016, available at: <www.econlib.org/library/Enc/bios/Smith.html>.

Bronte, Charlotte, *Jane Eyre* (JM Dent & Sons Ltd, 1922)

Bronte, Emily, *Wuthering Heights* (Harper & Brothers, 1858)

Brunero, JS, 'Evolution, Altruism, and "Internal Reward" Explanations' (2002) 33 *The Philosophical Forum* 413

Caplan, Bryan, *Selfish Reasons to Have More Kids: Why Being a Great Parent Is Less Work and More Fun Than You Think* (Basic Books, 2011)

Cristuado, Wayne, *A Philosophical History of Love* (Transaction Publishers, 2012)

Dawkins, Richard, *The God Delusion* (Houghton Mifflin Company, 2006)

Dawkins, Richard, *The Selfish Gene* (Oxford University Press, 1989)

De Rougement, Denis, *Love in the Western World* (Princeton University Press, 1983)

Dickens, Charles, *Barnaby Rudge* (Chapman and Hall, 1841)

Elder Jr, Glen H, 'Appearance and Education in Marriage Mobility' (1969) 34 *American Sociological Review* 519

Febrero, Ramon and Pedro S Schwartz (eds), *The Essence of Becker* (Hoover Institution Press Publication, 1995)

Fisher, Helen E, Arthur Aron and Lucy L Brown, 'Romantic love: a mammalian brain system for mate choice' (2006) 361 *Philos Trans R Soc Lond B Biol Sci* 2173

Fisher, Helen E, Lucy L Brown, Arthur Aron, Greg Strong and Debra Mashek, 'Reward, Addiction, & Emotion Regulation Systems Associated With Rejection in Love' (2010) 104 *Journal of Neurophysiology* 51

Fisher, Helen, Lucy Brown and Arthur Aron, 'Romantic Love: an fMRI study of a neural mechanism for mate choice' (2005) 493 *The Journal of Comparative Neurology* 58

Frankfurt, Harry, *The Reasons of Love* (Princeton University Press, 2004)

Frijters, Paul and Foster Gigi, *Economic Theory of Greed, Love, Groups, and Networks* (Cambridge University Press, 2013)

Fusar-Poli, Paolo and M R Broome, 'Love & Brain: From Mereological Fallacy to "Folk" Neuroimaging' (2007) 154 *Psychiatry Research: Neuroimaging* 154

Gantt, Edward and Richard Williams, 'Explaining Religion to Death: Reductionism, Evolution, and the Psychology of Religion' (2008) 32 *Issues in Religion and Psychotherapy* 3

Geary, David C, *Male, Female: The Evolution of Human Sex Differences* (American Psychological Association, 1998)

Gioia, Ted, *Love Songs* (Oxford University Press, 2015)

Hardy, Thomas, *Jude the Obscure* (Harper & Brothers, 1895)

Ingram, John Kells, *A History of Political Economy* (Cambridge University Press, 2013 [1888])

*International Encyclopedia of Economic Sociology* (Routledge, 2016)

Jankowiak, William R and Edward F Fischer, 'A cross-cultural perspective on romantic love' (1992) 31 *Ethnology* 149

John Paul II, *Man and Woman He Created Them: A Theology of the Body* (Michael Waldstein trans, Pauline Books & Media, 2006)

Johnson, Susan, *Hold Me Tight* (Little, Brown and Company Hachette Book Group, 2008)

Kail, Robert V (ed), *Advances in Child Behavior and Development* (Elsevier, Vol 36, 2008)

Lewis, C S, *The Four Loves* (Harcourt Publishing, 1960)

Li, Norman P, J Michael Bailey, Douglas T Kenrick and Joan A Linsenmeier, 'The necessities and luxuries of mate preferences: testing the trade-offs' (2002) 82 *Journal of Personality and Social Psychology* 947

Logothetis, Nikos K, 'What We Can & What We Can't Do with fMRI' (2008) 453 *Nature* 869

Mahaparinirvana Sutra 259, World Scripture, accessed on 28 June 2016, available at: <www.unification.net/ws/theme010.htm#18>.

Margolis, Howard, *Selfishness, Altruism, and Rationality: A Theory of Social Choice* (Cambridge University Press, 1984)

Mathur, Vani A, Tokiko Harada, Trixie Lipke and Joan Y Chiao, 'Neural Basis of Extraordinary Empathy and Altruistic Motivation' (2010) 51 *NeuroImage* 1468

May, Simon, *Love: A History* (Yale University Press, 2011)

Mellen, Sydney L W, *The Evolution of Love* (W H Freeman, 1981)

Moll, Jorge, Frank Krueger, Roland Zahn, Matteo Pardini, Ricardo de Oliveira-Souza and Jordan Grafman, 'Human Fronto-Mesolimbic Networks Guide Decisions About Charitable Donation' (2006) 103 *Proceedings of the National Academy of Science* 15623

Newberg, Andrew and Eugene D'Aquili, *Why God Won't Go Away: Brain Science and the Biology of Belief* (Random House Publishing, 2011)

Ng, Irene C L and Lu-Ming Tseng, 'Learning to Be Sociable: The Evolution of Homo Economicus' (2008) 67 *American Journal of Economics & Sociology* 265

Nibley, Hugh, *Collected Works of Hugh Nibley* (Deseret Books Company, 1988)

Orwell, George, *Nineteen Eighty-Four* (Houghton Mifflin Harcourt, 1949)

Persky, Joseph, 'Retrospectives: The Ethology of Homo Economicus' (1995) 9 *Journal of Economic Perspectives* 221

Pew Research Center, 'Scientists and Belief' (5 November 2009), accessed 23 June 2016, available at: <www.pewforum.org/2009/11/05/scientists-and-belief/>

Plato, *Symposium* (Harold Fowler trans, Harvard University Press, 1925)

Plato, *Timaeus* (Benjamin Jowett trans, Echo Library, 2006)

Santas, Gerasimos, *Plato and Freud: Two Theories of Love* (Basil Blackwell Inc, 1988)

Searle, Mark, 'Testing the reciprocity norm in a recreation management setting' (1989) 11 *Leisure Sciences* 353–65

Smith, Adam, *An Inquiry into the Nature and Causes of the Wealth of Nations*, (Edwin Cannan, ed, 1904) Library of Economics and Liberty, IV.2.9 23, accessed 23 June 2016, available at: <www.econlib.org/library/Smith/smWN13.html>

Smith, Adam, *The Concise Encyclopedia of Economics*, accessed on 23 June 2016, available at: <www.econlib.org/library/Enc/bios/Smith.html>

Soble, Alan (ed), *Eros Agape, and Philia: Readings in the Philosophy of Love* (Paragon House, 1989)

Soble, Alan, *The Structure of Love* (Yale University Press, 1990)

St Thomas Aquinas, *Summa Theologica* (Father of the English Dominican Province trans, 1920, Vol 2.2)

Stanovich, Keith E, *Rationality & The Reflective Mind* (Oxford University Press, 2011)

Sternberg, Robert J and Karen Weis (eds), *The New Psychology of Love* (Yale University Press, 2006)

The Liddel-Scott-Jones Greek-English Lexicon, accessed June 28 2016, available at: <http://stephanus.tlg.uci.edu/lsj/#eid=99866&context=lsj&action=from-search>

Vivekananda, Swami (trans), *Complete Works of Swami Vivekananda* (Vol 6, Lectures and Discourses, 1984)

# 2 Law and love in Eden

*Joshua Neoh*

What founds a community[1] – law or love? There are *at least* two metanarratives that could be told to answer the question of what binds a political community: one is the metanarrative of law and the other is the metanarrative of love. The metanarrative of law tells a Hobbesian story. In the Hobbesian picture, law is needed to regulate and mediate our relationships because of the egoistic nature of humankind. Without law, life would be unliveable. Law founds a political community, invests it with normative authority, and creates its trans-temporality. On the other hand, the metanarrative of love tells an Edenic story. In the Edenic picture, before the law – before the Fall – there was love. That which ultimately sustains a political community and connects an individual to that community is love, not law. In contemporary legal and political discourse, the Hobbesian narrative has been the dominant paradigm with which we view our legal and political world. This paper wants to explore the dormant paradigm of the Edenic narrative, which remains part of our intellectual tradition and provides an alternative vision to the Hobbesian one. This paper will track the existence of love and the emergence of law in the Garden of Eden. In this paper, the Hobbesian and the Edenic paradigms are heuristic devices that are deployed to elucidate the taxonomy of law and love in our 'social imaginary'.[2]

Law and love provide us with two different modes of relating to the world. In the Garden of Eden, the first emergence of law shatters the primordial state of love. The subsequent fall from grace is traceable beyond the transgression to the prohibition, which marks the emergence of law and the concomitant loss of love. To mount that argument, this paper will engage in a thematic analysis of the Edenic narrative as presented in the Book of Genesis (Part II). The Edenic analysis will form the basis for Part III, which compares and contrasts the Edenic account with the Hobbesian account. Hobbes posits that, in our primordial state, life is nasty, brutish and short; law then becomes the solution to our problematic

1 In the words of Gillian Rose, 'we have given up communism – only to fall more deeply in love with the idea of "the community"': Gillian Rose, 'Athens and Jerusalem: A Tale of Three Cities' (1994) 3 *Social and Legal Studies* 333, 333.

2 Charles Taylor, 'Modern Social Imaginaries' (2002) 14 *Public Culture* 91.

primordial state – in the Hobbesian worldview, law is necessary for love. In contrast, the Book of Genesis conceives of our primordial prelapsarian state as paradisiacal, in which we live a life of love; law is not the solution, but the cause and source of our problem – in the Edenic worldview, law destroys love. Our attitude towards law is both Edenic and Hobbesian – we hold both of these competing conceptions in tension. Both are part of our intellectual inheritance. Our political community is founded on both the need for law and the desire for love because we are driven by the Hobbesian nightmare of war inasmuch as we are drawn to the Edenic dream of paradise on earth. Faced with this dilemma, we hedge our bets: while we live under law, we dream of love.

## Methodology and choice of text

The methodology of this paper draws on the biblical narrative of Eden to better understand the place of law in our social imaginary. It treats biblical narratives as works of literature, in the same way that Shakespearean plays are works of literature. For many, biblical narratives are not just works of literature. Historians may use biblical narratives as clues to reconstruct the ancient Near East; linguists may use biblical narratives for philological ends; and theologians may use biblical narratives to understand the will of God. However, they all have to grapple with the genre of the Bible, for the Bible consists of narratives told in the form of prose and poetry. To study the Bible is to be immersed in stories of yore. Whatever other functions and purposes the narratives of the Bible may serve, they are works of literature, and this project will treat them as such. The interpretation of narratives 'has always required that the reader actively and imaginatively engage the texts'; 'through the process of interpretation, the reader's living experience comes to be woven into ancient texts, so that what was "dead letter" again comes to life'.[3] In turning, or returning, to biblical narratives, the goal is not to establish their true meaning exegetically or historically; rather, the goal is to invite readers to engage in an interpretive exercise that draws on those narratives but presses toward an understanding of our contemporary predicament.[4] In this interpretive project, orthodoxy and tradition certainly has 'a vote but not a veto'.[5]

In the course of the past two millennia, biblical narratives have been etched onto our collective cultural consciousness (and sub-consciousness). Patterns of thought arising out of biblical mythologies, alongside Greco-Roman mythologies, still underlie much of our moral and metaphysical discourses. Geertz defines culture as 'an historically transmitted pattern of meanings embodied in symbols, a system of inherited conceptions expressed in symbolic forms by means of which men [and women] communicate, perpetuate, and develop their knowledge

3 Elaine Pagels, *Adam, Eve and the Serpent* (Random House, 1988) xxvii–xxviii.

4 Paul Kahn, *Out of Eden: Adam and Eve and the Problem of Evil* (Princeton University Press, 2006) 12.

5 Alan Dershowitz, *The Genesis of Justice* (Warner Books, 2000) 18.

about and their attitudes toward life'.[6] For centuries, many thinkers in the West 'saw their own situations, their sufferings and their hopes mirrored in the story of the creation and the fall'; they 'read the story of Adam and Eve, and often projected themselves into it.'[7] The myth contains, 'not scientific accounts of actual events, but theological statements about human identity'; 'as in most creation stories, the main point of the tale was to tell them about who they were and how they fitted into the broader cosmos'.[8] Their 'conceptions of perfection and experiences of imperfection' were 'explicated in terms of the Genesis story'.[9] This paper aims to explicate the dichotomy between perfection and imperfection, fall and redemption, in terms of law and love; and, in so doing, construct a legal theory from within 'this puzzling, question-raising and meaning-overloaded text'.[10] The methodological approach of this paper aligns with a trajectory of legal scholarship that seeks to understand legal themes and legal theory from within narrative frameworks.

The Garden of Eden may not be immediately recognisable as a site of law; indeed, the word 'law' is not mentioned there at all. It is not difficult to find other passages in the Bible in which law takes centre stage. The immediate examples that come to mind include the handing down of the law on Mount Sinai in the Book of Exodus, the legal codification in the Books of Leviticus and Deuteronomy, the expounding of the law by Jesus in the Sermon on the Mount,[11] or the purported transcendence of the law in Paul's Letter to the Romans.[12] Nonetheless, the Garden of Eden is where the very first law is given – that of not eating from the tree of knowledge of good and evil. Here, then, is the seed of law, the place from which all further law springs. While it is the eating of this fruit – the transgression – that is traditionally seen as the cause of the Fall, this paper will explore what role the issuing of the law itself – the prohibition – plays in fracturing the divine–human relationship which leads to the Fall. The Edenic narrative is the origin of the recurrent trope of 'fall and redemption' that is so pervasive in Western literature and philosophy.[13] If our redemption lies in recovering Eden, then our first task must surely be to identify what went wrong in Eden.

6 Clifford Geertz, 'Religion as a Cultural System' in *The Interpretation of Cultures* (Basic Books, 1973) 87, 89.

7 Pagels, *Adam, Eve and the Serpent*, above n 3, xx–xxi.

8 David Carr, *Erotic Word: Sexuality, Spirituality and the Bible* (Oxford University Press, 2005) 36, 29.

9 Paul Morris, 'A Walk in the Garden: Images of Eden' in Paul Morris and Deborah Sawyer (eds), *A Walk in the Garden: Biblical, Iconographical, and Literary Images of Eden* (Sheffield Academic Press, 1992) 21, 21.

10 Ibid 21.

11 See Joshua Neoh, 'The Rhetoric of Precedent and Fulfillment in the Sermon on the Mount and the Common Law' (2016) 12 *Law, Culture and the Humanities* 419.

12 See Joshua Neoh, 'Jurisprudence of Love in Paul's Letter to the Romans' (2015) 33 *Law in Context* 7.

13 Stephen Mulhall, *Philosophical Myths of the Fall* (Princeton University Press, 2007).

## Thematic analysis of the Edenic narrative

### *The creation story: from blessings to curses*

At this point, this paper will take a narrative turn. The narrative to which we are turning has a chronological plot, which, as I shall argue, charts the emergence of law and the loss of love in the Garden of Eden. I tell the chronological story in order to advance the structural, specifically taxonomical, thesis about the tension between law and love. The story of the Garden of Eden is a creation story, which consists of two accounts of creation. The first account runs from Genesis 1:1 to 2:3. The second account runs from Genesis 2:4 to 3. Although the text of the narrative – the two accounts – may have been redacted from multiple sources, the crucial starting point for this paper is that it has been received as a single text for generations. The challenge then is to understand it as a *single* unified text.

In the first account of creation, God says, 'Let us make man in our image, after our likeness' (Gen 1:26). 'God created man in his own image, in the image of God he created him, male and female he created them' (Gen 1:27). The act of creation is accomplished through his words: God speaks humans into existence, and creates male and female together. At that point, God moves from solitude to society: a community of three – God, man and woman – comes into existence. Then God says, in verse 28, 'Be fruitful and multiply'. This statement is not so much a commandment, but a statement of ontological fact. The nature of human beings is to be fruitful and multiply. That is the very nature of being human. Humans share this creative and procreative nature with the earth and other beings on the earth: verses earlier, the creatures of the seas are similarly called to 'be fruitful and multiply and fill the waters in the seas' (Gen 1:22) and the earth is called to 'put forth vegetation' (Gen 1:11) and 'bring forth living creatures' (Gen 1:24).[14] Even if one were to read this statement as a commandment, it is an affirmative commandment with no punishment attached, which is radically different from the commandment that we will encounter in the second creation account.

In verse 29, God says, 'Behold, I have given you every plant . . . and every tree.' Note the word *every*. The gift by God is given in abundance, and indeed in superabundance. The earth is lavish and plentiful for human dwelling. In verse 31, the final verse of the chapter, 'God saw everything that he had made, and behold, it was very good.' It is not just good, but very good. The image is one of goodness, overwhelming and overflowing goodness.

On the seventh day, God rested. But while God rested, in chapter 2 verse 3, something happened. We do not know what happened, but we know that in the next verse, in verse 4, God has to recreate the world. In the second account, God has to exert some physical force to form man out of dust or clay. In contrast to the first account, man is not created with woman. Woman is created later, out of the ribs of man.

14 Mark Brett, *Genesis: Procreation and the Politics of Identity* (Routledge, 2000) 27.

In the first account, God says, 'Behold, I have given you every plant . . . and every tree.' In the second account, there is no such plenary grant. In verses 16–17, 'the Lord God commanded the man, saying, 'You may freely eat of every tree of the garden; but of the tree of the knowledge of good and evil you shall not eat, for in the day that you eat of it you shall die.' This commandment is very significant, because in this statement lies the emergence of law in the Garden of Eden. The phrasing of the command consists of two clauses: the first clause ('you may freely eat of every tree of the garden') suggests that everything is permitted – only to, a moment later, take it back in the same breath with the second clause ('but of the tree of the knowledge of good and evil you shall not eat'). One's mind is teasingly brought to imagine total freedom only to be encaged immediately by the prohibition. The resulting image is not one of plenitude, but rather it is one of limitation. This prohibition is backed by the threat of punishment, capital punishment: 'in the day that you eat of it you shall die.' This is the first law in the Bible, the first of many.[15]

The story then proceeds to the famed transgression. The serpent confronts Eve to ask her to clarify God's command. The serpent is like a typical lawyer who is obsessed with clarifying the boundaries of the rule. Eve's reply is found in chapter 3 verses 2–3: 'And the woman said to the serpent, "We may eat of the fruit of the trees of the garden, but God said, you shall not eat of the fruit of the tree which is in the midst of the garden, neither shall you touch it, lest you die."' Eve's restatement of the rule is not entirely accurate. The prohibition is limited to the eating of the fruit. Eve has extended the prohibition to cover, not only the eating of the fruit, but also the touching of it. The serpent responds by saying, 'You will not die.' God's threat is that, *on the day* humans eat of the fruit, they shall die. However, as it turns out, after eating the fruit, Adam and Eve did not die. The threat did not materialise. It is often said that the cunning serpent tricked Adam and Eve into eating the fruit, but did it really? The serpent is, strictly-speaking, truthful: Adam and Eve did not die upon eating the fruit.[16] In fact, Adam will continue to live for another 930 years! One could only speculate as to why God did not carry out his threat. My own speculation is that he wants to continue to have a relationship with humans.[17] He wants to love and be loved by humans – he cannot love them if he kills them; they cannot love him if they are dead.[18]

15 'The Book of Genesis tells the story of the developing legal system' – the elaborate legal regime that is set out in the Books of Exodus, Leviticus, Numbers and Deuteronomy is the culmination of a process begun in the opening narrative of the Bible in the Garden of Eden: Dershowitz, above n 5, 245.

16 Gnostic Christians 'turned the story upside down and told it, in effect, from the serpent's point of view: some said he was wiser than all the other animals and so tried desperately to persuade Adam and Eve to partake of the tree of knowledge, defying their jealous and hostile creator; this wise serpent, some dared say, was a manifestation of Christ himself!': Pagels, *Adam, Eve and the Serpent*, above n 3, xxiv.

17 This is, actually, Robert Burt's speculation which I have made my own: see Robert Burt, *In the Whirlwind: God and Humanity in Conflict* (Harvard University Press, 2012).

18 One could rebut this hypothesis by positing a life after death: one could claim that God can continue to love humans even after death in the hereafter. Sometimes we console the bereaved

Eve eats the fruit and gives it to Adam, who also eats it. The first thing that they realise after they eat the fruit and gain the knowledge of good and evil is that they are naked. So, they sew fig leaves to cover themselves. Up till this point, they were naked before God and they were not ashamed; they were in an intimate relationship with God, in which shame had no place. This linkage between nakedness and shame is a sign that the divine–human relationship is no longer the same. Adam and Eve then hear the sound of God 'walking in the garden in the cool of the day', as if taking an evening stroll. God the Almighty is looking for his human companion, whom he has just created. God calls, 'Where are you?' Despite his great power and might, God nonetheless longs for human company. This longing by God for human company only arises after the giving of the command,[19] which suggests that the giving of the command has resulted in a kind of separation, or at least a feeling of separateness, between God and humankind. But Adam and Eve are in hiding. In the words of Adam, 'I was afraid . . . and I hid' (Gen 3:10). Fear, particularly the fear of authority, has entered the Garden: Adam and Eve are now conscious, indeed acutely conscious, of the power differential between them and God. They are now aware of their vulnerability in the face of this overwhelming power.[20]

When Adam's wrongdoing is discovered, he does what generations of man after him are fond of doing – blaming it on the woman! In verse 12, the man says, 'The woman whom thou gavest to be with me, she gave me the fruit of the tree, and I ate.' More than blaming the woman, who is Adam actually blaming? God! And who does Eve blame? In verse 13, 'the woman says, 'The serpent beguiled me, and I ate.' After witnessing the world's first blame game, God curses Adam, Eve and the serpent, and expels humans from the Garden of Eden.[21] A story that begins with blessings in abundance ends with curses.

---

with the thought that God loves the deceased so much more that he has brought the deceased back to himself. The problem with this interpretation is that the Hebrew Bible 'never mentions the hereafter'. On the contrary, God tells Adam quite directly that 'you are dust and to dust you shall return': Dershowitz, above n 5, 33.

19 At this stage in the narrative, all that God knows is that he has given humans a command. God has not yet found out about the breach of the command. One could rebut this reading of the text by positing that God is omniscient, but that would be reading (or forcing) omniscience into the text. There is no indication in the text that God is omniscient. On the contrary, the text suggests that God is not all-knowing: why, for example, would God be calling out to humans and asking them where they are if he already knows where they are? To reconcile this narrative detail with God's omniscience, one would have to impute to God some kind of double-speak, which gives rise to more puzzles than it solves. And it makes the story far less interesting.

20 Jonathan Magonet, 'The Themes of Genesis 2–3' in Paul Morris and Deborah Sawyer, above n 9, 39, 44.

21 The story not only contains 'the first breach of the law', but also 'the first criminal prosecution' and 'the first sentencing decision': Richard Fox, 'Sentencing in the Garden of Eden' (2006) 32 *Monash University Law Review* 4, 4. See also Timothy Lytton, 'Due Process and Legal Authority in the Garden of Eden: Jurisprudence in Aggadic Midrash' (2006) 16 *Jewish Law Annual* 185.

## *Before the law: blessings*

Notwithstanding the tragic end to the story, in our imagination, we still think of the Garden of Eden as paradise on earth, as a place of perfect harmony between God, humankind and nature, as a place of abundance and everlasting life. Prior to the Fall, in the Garden of Eden, man and woman are in paradise. There is neither scarcity nor competition in Eden – instead, it is a site of boundless, self-renewing fecundity that satisfies and nurtures all forms of life.[22] Not only is there no scarcity and competition, prior to the giving of the command, there is also no notion of obedience to authority. It is only with the giving of the command that obedience, or disobedience, to God's authority becomes a distinct and comprehensible possibility.[23] Prior to that, there is nothing to obey or disobey – indeed, the very concept of obedience to an external authority would have been unintelligible in the absence of any assertion of authority.

In the first creation account, man and woman live in a state of union and oneness with each other and with God: they are created together, and together they are the image and likeness of God. In the second creation account, God creates man in an intensely physical, even erotic, manner when God moulds man from clay and breathes into man's nostrils the breath of life. Woman, in turn, is created out of the ribs of man – man and woman are of 'one flesh' (Gen 2:24), and they carry within them the breath of God. The Edenic picture that emerges is one of union and oneness, that is, of love.[24] The Garden of Eden is not only where we find the first law, but it is also where we find the first love – for before the law, there was love. Out of Eden, love for God is replaced by obedience to God, but 'obedience is not love'.[25] We continue to long for a return to Eden because we long for love – we long to be one and to be whole again. Tillich defines love as 'the drive towards the unity of the separated' and the reunion of that 'which belongs essentially together'; love presupposes 'an original unity' and 'ultimate belongingness' – hence, the ontology of love is not 'the union of the strange but the reunion of the estranged'.[26] Love seeks a relationship of union: a communion in community.

The ontology of love that this paper presents in the context of Eden is similar to the Aristophanes idea of love. The Aristophanes myth of love tells us that each of us is separated from our other half, 'and when one of them meets with his other half, the actual half of himself . . . the pair are lost in an amazement of love'. 'Human nature was originally one and we were a whole, and the desire and pursuit

22 Burt, above n 17, 13.
23 Burt, above n 17, 28.
24 The English language combines a great variety of experiences under the term of 'love' – 'the advantage of this linguistic reduction consists in the implicit acknowledgement of the deeper connection between all forms and expressions of love': Werner Jeanrond, *A Theology of Love* (T&T Clark, 2010) 30.
25 Paul Tillich, *Love, Power, and Justice* (Oxford University Press, 1954) 31.
26 Ibid 25.

of the whole is called love'; love is 'this meeting and melting into one another, this becoming one instead of two'. Love leads us back 'to our own nature', 'restore us to our original state', and make us whole again.[27] Aristophanes tells us the story of what happens when we fall in love with a person. However, we could, sometimes, love a more abstract entity than a person. We could, for example, love nature, a people, or even a nation. In the latter cases, the effect of love is oceanic. Freud defines the oceanic feeling as 'the sensation of "eternity", a feeling as of something limitless, unbounded'; 'a feeling of an indissoluble bond, of being one with the external world as a whole.'[28] Like the Aristophanes myth, Freud's oceanic feeling appeals to a sense of love as ultimate union. According to Freud, 'at the height of being in love, the boundary between ego and object threatens to melt away; against all the evidence of his senses, a man who is in love declares that "I" and "you" are one, and is prepared to behave as if it were a fact.'[29] In psychoanalytic terms, 'originally the ego includes everything [before] it separates off an external world from itself; our present ego-feeling is, therefore, only a shrunken residue of a much more inclusive – indeed, an all-embracing – feeling which corresponded to a more intimate bond between the ego and the world about it.'[30] We continue episodically to experience remnants of the original ego-feeling and, through love, we seek to recapture that oceanic feeling.[31]

In their primordial state in Eden, Adam and Eve are one with each other and with God. More than merely being in the presence of God, they are in the image and likeness of God. To be in the image and likeness of God is to identify with God – and, as Aristophanes reminds us, 'identity beyond difference' is the ultimate result of love.[32] Their every desire is satisfied in the universe that they find themselves in, like a foetus in the mother's womb.[33] They exist in a state of 'love', in both the Aristophanesian and Freudian sense. In love, the lovers – God, Adam and Eve – are complete in themselves: to experience love is 'to experience this

27 Aristophanes' Speech from Plato, *Plato's Symposium: Collected Works of Plato* (Benjamin Jowett trans, 4th ed, Oxford University Press, 1953) 520–5, <www.anselm.edu/homepage/dbanach/sym.htm>.

28 Sigmund Freud, *Civilisation and Its Discontent* (James Strachey trans, WW Norton, 1962) 11–12.

29 Ibid 13.

30 Ibid 15.

31 The frustration here is that this kind of love is insatiable. The drive for the dissolution of difference in a unitary state of being eliminates individuality. When this drive is frustrated – that is, when the object of one's love asserts individuality and exerts a degree of separateness – love could easily turn into hate. Love is dangerous, for heaven has no rage like love to hatred turned. The dream of love is potentially explosive.

32 See Paul Kahn's analysis of the Aristophanes' myth in Paul Kahn, *Finding Ourselves at the Movies: Philosophy for a New Generation* (Columbia University Press, 2013) 141.

33 The idea of 'the Garden as a womb' is often linked to a psychoanalytical – in particular, a Jungian – reading of the story, in which the initial state of the Garden represents 'the ego's original oneness with nature and deity': Adrian Cunningham, 'Type and Archetype in the Eden Story' in Paul Morris and Deborah Sawyer, above n 9, 292.

sense of completion – it is to lack nothing.'[34] Or in the words of Beatles, 'all you need is love'. Out of Eden, they, and we, yearn for a return to that Edenic love: we pine for what Tillich calls the reunion of the estranged or what Freud calls the oceanic feeling. However, where 'love collapses distinctions',[35] law creates distinctions, and therein lies the source of the tragedy in Eden which turns blessings into curses.

## *After the law: curses*

The expulsion of Adam and Eve from the Garden of Eden symbolises our fallen state, what Milton calls our 'Paradise Lost'. When exactly did we lose our original harmony with God and nature? The contention of this paper is that we lost that original organic harmony, not at the point of transgression, but at the prior point of prohibition, when God pronounced the world's first law. This law fractures the original organic union between God and humanity. It creates a power hierarchy in their relationship. It differentiates between the ruler and the ruled. The law gives rise to a relationship of power between God and humanity, eventually and inevitably leading to a power struggle between them. The serpent tempts humanity to eat the forbidden fruit by holding forth the promise that, by eating the forbidden fruit, humans will become like God: 'For God knows that when you eat of it your eyes will be opened, and you will be like God' (Gen 3:5). The temptation is not just about the fruit; more than the fruit, the temptation is about the desire of the ruled to be the ruler.

While the eating of the fruit is generally seen as the cause of the Fall, the prohibition on the eating of the fruit is a precondition for the transgression – when the prohibition is issued, the transgression is fated to follow. From that point in the narrative, we, the readers, are merely waiting for the inevitable – the transgression – to happen. Throughout the Hebrew Bible, we see a continuous proliferation of the dialectic of law and its transgression, from singular acts of divine judicial intervention to the codified rules of the Ten Commandments, culminating in the Book of Leviticus which contains an elaborate legal regime. We need law because of our fallen state. But in our original state of perfect harmony with God and nature in the Garden of Eden, there is no law. The state of perfect harmony – of perfect love – is also a state of lawlessness, in its literal sense.

Love in Eden is disrupted by the law of God. The commandment ruptures the undifferentiated state of union which existed prior to it – there is no longer a sense of equality or unity in the Garden; there is now a sovereign and a subject. Prior to the first law, there may have been a difference between the creator and the created, but it is a difference that binds, not one that divides. The created is bound to the creator in the act of creation. However, as soon as the law is issued, Adam becomes a distinct legal subject – subject to the sovereignty of God. When God chooses to

34 Paul Kahn, *Putting Liberalism in Its Place* (Princeton University Press, 2008) 214.
35 Kahn, above n 32, 141.

adopt the language of law, the result is that there is a changed relationship between the creator and the created.[36] Law, insofar as it requires hierarchy, necessarily disrupts love, understood as undifferentiated union. The hierarchy between God and Adam is later replicated in the hierarchy between Adam and Eve. After the eating of the fruit, God says to the woman that, henceforth, the man 'shall rule over' her (Gen 3:16). The hierarchy is also replicated in the relationship between humans and nature. At the start of the story, 'Adam assumes authority over the animals by innocently naming them'; at the end of the story, 'he is described as brutally stamping on the head of the serpent' and 'he is destined to have an almost intolerable struggle with nature'.[37] John Chrysostom, writing in the fourth century, saw this hierarchisation as the turning point in which 'fear and coercion infected the whole structure of human relationships, from family to city and nation'.[38]

Not only does the introduction of law necessitate the division between sovereign and subject, it also creates the circumstances for its transgression. This applies not only in a logical sense – for a rule to be transgressed, it must first exist – but also in a *psychological* way. As the saying goes, the forbidden fruit is the sweetest – a popular idiom which is derived from the Edenic narrative. Prohibition increases desire and stimulates transgression. As Paul points out in his Letter to the Romans, law 'makes all the more desirable the very thing it prohibits.'[39] 'By naming and individuating particular transgressions, the law actually puts them before our minds in a way that heightens their appeal to us.'[40] The forbidden fruit looks particularly tempting, not only because it is juicy and tasty, but because the eating of it represents the human desire to be free from the constraints of God's law: 'Only with the coming of the Law does man's [desire] take on the character of open rebellion.'[41] Law exposes 'the deliberateness of human disobedience.'[42] It becomes the 'primary source of human alienation' from God.[43] In hindsight, we can see that Eden could not continue once law had been introduced. This is

36 Magonet, above n 20, 42. God *chose* to adopt the language of law in issuing the prohibition at a specific point in the narrative, thereby transforming forever the nature of the divine-human relationship. Why did God do that? Only God knows.

37 John Sawyer, 'The Image of God, the Wisdom of Serpents and the Knowledge of Good and Evil' in Paul Morris and Deborah Sawyer, above n 9, 66, 69.

38 Elaine Pagels, 'The Politics of Paradise: Augustine's Exegesis of Genesis 1–3 versus that of John Chrysostom' (1985) 78 *Harvard Theological Review* 67, 71. Fear and coercion are often, though not always, the basis of law. Austin, for example, makes a big deal out of them in his theory of law. In the Hebrew Bible, God grounds his demand for obedience to his law on multiple bases: paternity, superior power, services rendered (especially after he delivered the Israelites out of slavery in Egypt) and, of course, fear and coercion.

39 Craig Hill, 'Romans' in John Muddiman and John Barton (eds), *The Oxford Bible Commentary* (Oxford University Press, 2007) 1096.

40 Jeremy Waldron, 'Dead to the Law: Paul's Antinomianism' (2006) 28 *Cardozo Law Review* 301, 313.

41 W D Davies, 'Paul and the Law: Reflections on Pitfalls in Interpretation' (1978) 29 *Hastings Law Journal* 1459, 1480.

42 Hill, above n 39, 1094.

43 Ibid 1086.

because the prelapsarian state of divine–human harmony is, literally, lawless. If any law were to be introduced, it could no longer be the same. 'With the law, the [human] subject has definitively exited from unity, and from innocence.'[44] Law's prohibition awakens human pride. Instead of saving Adam and Eve from death, God's prohibition in the Garden lures them to their death.[45] In the words of Paul, 'I was once alive apart from the law, but when the commandment came, sin revived and I died.'[46] 'The law is no longer just an inadequate solution to the problem of sin; the law itself is the problem.'[47]

Grant Gilmore famously said that: 'The better the society, the less law there will be. In Heaven, there will be no law, and the lion will lie down with the lamb, [while] in Hell there will be nothing but law, and due process will be meticulously observed.'[48] The Edenic narrative alerts us to the destructive consequences of the intrusion of law into relationships, by showing us how the language of law creates hierarchical distinctions, and ultimately, alienation.[49] God chose to use the language of law in his relationship with humans. That choice has certain consequences, the most significant of which is that it switches the mode of their relationship. The moral pedagogy of the Hebrew Bible is to teach about perfection through examples of imperfection: hence, 'the characters in the [Hebrew] Bible – even its heroes – are all flawed.'[50] Even God has his flaws. If we accept this premise – a premise which most pious readings of the narrative would not accept – one can begin to see how the prior prohibition by God as much as the subsequent transgression by humans might be responsible for the eventual Fall. Even a slight fracture ruins perfection, and a fracture is all that is required for such a situation to deteriorate. The serpent is ever ready to exploit this crack in the divine–human relationship after the issuing of the prohibition: give the devil an inch and he will take a mile.

## Hobbesian or Edenic, law or love

### *Law in the Hobbesian narrative*

Both the Edenic and the Hobbesian narratives explore the pre-legal nature of humanity: they both provide an account of humanity in its original state. That is where their similarity ends. The Hobbesian narrative has a fundamentally different

44 Alan Badiou, *Saint Paul: The Foundation of Universalism* (Stanford University Press, 2003) 82.
45 Hill, above n 39, 1097.
46 Romans 7:9.
47 Hill, above n 39, 1096.
48 Grant Gilmore, *The Ages of American Law* (Yale University Press, 1977) 111.
49 The law organises itself around multiple sets of opposition categories, and creates a world of hierarchical distinctions. 'If a tort or crime is committed, or a contract breached, a hierarchical relationship comes into force, between the promisee on the contract and the right-holder and the duty-holder, between the victim of the tort or crime and the perpetrator': George Fletcher, 'The Jurisprudence of Genesis' (2003) 56 *Current Legal Problems* 41, 53
50 Dershowitz, above n 5, 2.

starting point about human nature in its primordial state from the Edenic narrative. Hobbes begins his narrative by asking us to imagine a state of nature in which there are three principal causes of quarrel arising out of 'the nature of man': competition, diffidence and glory – 'the first maketh men invade for gain; the second, for safety; and the third, for reputation.'[51] The state of nature is a state of war, 'where every man is enemy to every man'.[52] 'To this war of every man against every man . . . nothing can be unjust': 'where there is no common power, there is no law; where no law, no injustice.' There is only force and fraud.

To attain peace, we need to get out of the state of nature – but how? Hobbes' solution is that we enter into a social contract among ourselves to set up a common, coercive, compelling power – in short, the Leviathan – to instil fear in us and keep us in awe. As Hobbes says, 'the passion to be reckoned upon is fear'.[53] There needs to be a sense of 'terror' among the subjects, for 'covenants, without the sword, are but words'.[54] Those who refuse to enter the state of civil society would be 'left in the condition of war he was in before; wherein he might without injustice be destroyed by any man whatsoever.'[55] Hobbes applies the same logic to the divine–human relationship: 'To those therefore whose power is irresistible, the dominion of all men adhereth naturally by their excellence of power; and consequently it is from that power that the kingdom over men, and the right of afflicting men at his pleasure, belongeth naturally to God Almighty; not as Creator and gracious, but as omnipotent.'[56] In Hobbes' theory, 'we don't find an obligation to God based on either God's creation or our gratitude, but simply on God's irresistible power'.[57]

For Hobbes, unlike Adam and Eve in Eden, and unlike 'bees and ants',[58] there is no natural unity among humankind. The only form of unity that can be achieved among a multitude of humankind is artificial unity through the artificial person of the sovereign: 'A multitude of men are made one person when they are by one man, or one person, represented . . . for it is the unity of the representer, not the unity of the represented, that maketh the person one'.[59] A group of persons become 'a people' through the ***artificial*** unity of the sovereign. Hobbes has a legalist view of sovereignty: 'a sovereign is by definition one who governs through law', and who is able to have its commands 'recognised as law'.[60] On Dyzenhaus' reading, Hobbes is best read as 'an early member of the rule of law

51 Thomas Hobbes, *Leviathan* (1651) ch 13.
52 Ibid ch 13.
53 Ibid ch 14.
54 Ibid ch 17.
55 Ibid ch 18. Like Cain, who exclaims after being exiled for murdering Abel: 'I shall be a fugitive and a wanderer on the earth, and whoever finds me will slay me' (Genesis 4:14).
56 Hobbes, above n 51, ch 31.
57 John Rawls, *Lectures on the History of Political Philosophy* (Harvard University Press, 2009) 44.
58 Hobbes, above n 51, ch 17.
59 Hobbes, above n 51, ch 16.
60 David Dyzenhaus, 'Hobbes and the Legitimacy of Law (2001) 20 *Law and Philosophy* 461, 464, 483.

tradition, whose members hold that the ultimate constitution of political order is legal.'[61] Within this order, 'the relationship between sovereign and subject is mediated by law'.[62] While Hobbes recognises that there are two sets of laws – natural unwritten laws and civil enacted laws – he qualifies it by saying that natural laws are really just dictates of reason: 'they [natural laws] are but conclusions or theorems concerning what conduceth to the conservation and defence of themselves; whereas law, properly, is the word of him that by right hath command over others.'[63] Hence, natural laws 'achieve effective force only when they are enforced by the sovereign through incorporation into the civil law'.[64]

If the state of civil society is a state of legal order, then conversely, the state of nature is a state of lawlessness. In contrast to Eden where the state of lawlessness could be read as the site of love, in the Hobbesian account, the state of lawlessness is persistently portrayed as the site of anarchy, chaos and violence. While lawlessness merely denotes, in a literal sense, a state of being without law, in the context of the Hobbesian narrative, it connotes tumult and turmoil. The more negative the lawlessness in the state of nature is, the more positive the legal order in the state of civil society will look. Hobbes tries to convince us that 'an effective sovereign is over all, over everything else, a desirable thing to have'.[65] He does that by trying to show that 'however bad some sovereigns may be, the state of war [in the state of nature] is still worse'; therefore, 'so far as people are rational, then, they will want to avoid having things collapse back into a state of nature'.[66] Without law, we would be left in the state of nature, where no humane relationships could ever survive, let alone relationships of love.

### *Hobbesian law versus Edenic love*

The Book of Genesis conceives of our primordial state as harmonious, in which we live a life of love. In Eden, law destroys love. Hobbes, on the other hand, conceives of our primordial state as a state of war, in which life is nasty, brutish and short. In the Hobbesian worldview, law does not destroy love; on the contrary, law is necessary for love. Our attitude towards law is both Edenic and Hobbesian – we hold both of these competing conceptions in tension.

If the Edenic state of nature is paradise on earth, the Hobbesian state of nature is the direct opposite – it is hell on earth. While we dream of returning to Eden, the Hobbesian state of nature is so deplorable that no one would seek to return to it. Anything is an improvement on the Hobbesian natural condition. Where

61 David Dyzenhaus, 'Hobbes's Constitutional Theory' in Ian Shapiro (ed), *Hobbes: Leviathan* (Yale University Press, 2010) 453, 456.
62 Ibid 453.
63 Hobbes, above n 51, ch 15.
64 Larry May, *Limiting Leviathan: Hobbes on Law and International Affairs* (Oxford University Press, 2013) 38.
65 Rawls, above n 57, 48
66 Ibid 51, 73.

there is no security or order at all in the state of nature, any law is better than none.[67] Originating from the chaotic and anarchic, dog-eat-dog, Hobbesian state of nature, it is unsurprising that the Hobbesian state of civil society requires a Leviathan. Coming from the Hobbesian state of nature, law is the solution to our problem; however, coming from the Edenic paradise, law is not the solution but the cause of our problem – law is a compromise on paradise, a lessening of paradise.

Having been expelled from Eden, Adam and Eve may have fallen into something like the Hobbesian state of nature, where life is indeed nasty, brutish and short. One could chronologise the Edenic state and the Hobbesian state of nature by sequencing the latter as following from the loss of the former: the Fall is a fall from the Edenic state into the Hobbesian state of nature. Out of Eden, one son, Cain, kills another, Abel; and humankind is pitted against God and nature in the Great Flood. In the former case, God has to intervene as a judge to make a ruling against homicide. In the latter case, God again has to intervene, but this time, it is to make a constitutional ruling to bind himself from ever destroying the world by flood again – God's covenant with Noah is then sealed through the sign of the rainbow. In Eden, law is the problem. Out of Eden, law becomes the solution to the problem. To phrase the *aporia* more sharply, out of Eden, law becomes the solution to the problem which law creates in Eden. Law is a paradox: it is simultaneously a tragedy and a triumph, a blessing and a bane. Out of Eden, life loses its simplicity and love loses its innocence: the desire for love now has to compete with the need for law.[68] Nonetheless, the Edenic myth invites us to dream of a different world, that is, to imagine a world without law. It invites us to cast our mind back to the prelapsarian state of innocent love, in which we exist in union with God and nature.

Life in Eden and life out of Eden present us with different ontological states. Out of Eden, the loss of communal love was compensated by the gain of individual freedom. Individual freedom was impossible – or, more accurately, non-existent – in the state of undifferentiated union that characterised life in Eden. Law inaugurates the condition for individual freedom. After the giving of the law, humans have a choice: they could either obey or disobey the law, that is, they could live either within or without the norm. Individual freedom could, of course, quickly lead to anarchy, which is the problem in the Hobbesian state of nature. Law is then called upon to constrain this freedom and halt the slide from freedom

67 Maurizio Viroli, *Jean-Jacques Rousseau and the Well-Ordered Society* (Cambridge University Press, 2003).

68 One could read the Edenic story psychoanalytically as a 'maturation' myth: 'the expulsion from Paradise is just as necessary, and just as painful, as a child's maturation and subsequent socialisation through the Oedipal stage': Kim Parker, 'Mirror, Mirror on the Wall, Must We Leave Eden, Once and for All? A Lacanian Pleasure Trip through the Garden' (1999) 24 *Journal for the Study of the Old Testament* 19, 20. We have to grow up. 'We are out of the garden forever, and nothing will be simple again . . . the enchantment of childlike existence in the garden is past': Carr, above n 8, 46.

to anarchy. Again, here, law appears as a paradox: law both enables and delimits freedom.

This linkage between law, love and freedom segues into another tension between the Edenic and Hobbesian accounts. The individuals in the state of nature in the Hobbesian account reason their way into the social contract. They decide rationally based on an analysis of costs and benefits, of advantages and disadvantages, of – in a word – *value*, to form the social contract. Adam and Eve's choice is made, on the other hand, without knowledge of good and evil. How are they to make value judgements, weighing advantages and disadvantages, without the concepts of *good* and *evil*? Even if Adam and Eve had rational capacities prior to eating the forbidden fruit from the tree of knowledge,[69] they could not have evaluated the situation in the same way that Hobbes' person in the state of nature does – for Adam and Eve had no notion of normative value. They lack the notion of good and evil, so they are not able to say what would be good or not. They do not choose the serpent's way through reasoned deliberation – 'there is not yet knowledge by which to judge the serpent's speech.'[70] Adam and Eve had to choose between good and evil before they had knowledge of good and evil.

Love is, however, beyond reason, beyond right and wrong or good and evil, which may be why Adam and Eve are not created with such knowledge already imbued and why the tree of knowledge is forbidden in Eden. To respond out of love, one does not require the fruit of knowledge of good and evil. Knowledge of good and evil is irrelevant. To love someone unconditionally is to love them regardless of whether they are good or evil. In pursuit of love, one often overlooks reason and morality – hence, the idioms 'love is blind' and 'all's fair in love and war'. What is at stake in the prohibition and the subsequent transgression is love. What is being tested is love. Before the prohibition and transgression, there is nothing else but love.

After imbibing the knowledge of good and evil, the first thing that Adam and Eve do is to cover their nakedness. Why is nakedness evil or shameful? God never commanded them to be clothed; God has thus far given only one commandment – the prohibition on the fruit of knowledge. Indeed, God created them in a naked state – therefore, nakedness is good, insofar as all that the Lord has made is 'very good'. One explanation may be that the knowledge of good and evil has interrupted the love that is manifested in the intimacy of unashamed nakedness. Before the Fall, 'they are not aware of being distinct beings, neither distinct from each other or from God'; after the Fall, they become aware, not only of their nakedness, but also of their separateness: the man and the woman begin to see that they are 'separate and different' from each other and from God.[71] 'The final realisation of separation and difference comes when God enters the Garden and Adam and Eve hide because they do not know how to respond to God as a totally separate

69 Maimonides, quoted in Dershowitz, above n 5, 38.
70 Kahn, above n 4, 40.
71 George Fletcher, 'Thinking about Eden' (2003) 22 *Quinnipiac Law Review* 1, 18.

being.'[72] The addition of a layer over the bare body – clothing the body – can be seen as a metaphor for a layer between the divine and the fallen. The antagonist in the Edenic narrative, the serpent, is forever shedding layers, but never getting rid of the final cloak – so many layers sit between it and the divine. In love as union, there are no clothes, no layers of separation.

## From law to lawlessness: between the nightmare and the noble dream

How we orient ourselves towards the law affects how we imagine the alternative state of lawlessness. Lawlessness is, at bottom, the absence of law.[73] Unlawfulness has to be distinguished from lawlessness: the unlawful is not the lawless. Crime, for example, is unlawful in that it contravenes the law. But crime, though unlawful, is part and parcel of the order and logic of law. In contrast, lawlessness is to step outside the order and logic of law entirely. Lawlessness could either be an ascent into love or a descent into hate; we could either rise up to heaven or fall into hell; lawlessness could either be utopian or dystopian. In short, lawlessness could either be Edenic or Hobbesian. Hence, law is caught between the nightmare and the noble dream. We feel that law is inadequate – hence, we dream of love beyond law – but we are fearful that, if we move beyond law, we may end up, not in the dreamland of love, but in the nightmare of war. Instead of recovering Eden, we may end up in the Hobbesian state of nature, where we may find ourselves killing one another and worshipping the Lord of the Flies. This paper began with the question of what founds a community – law or love? Unsurprisingly for an academic paper, the answer is both! While we live under law, we dream of love. While we juridicise our relationships, we lament the loss of love in those relationships. We think of ourselves as being committed to law but we imagine ourselves as capable of love.

We can perceive this tension most clearly in how we imagine the place of the family in our polity. On the one hand, we think of life inside the home as an escape from the public world of law into the private realm of love. The 'glorification of private life and the family' represents the flip side of our perception of the public world as 'alien, impersonal, remote and abstract'; hence, 'deprivations experienced in the public world have to be compensated in the realm of privacy.'[74] We imagine 'the family' to be 'the last refuge of love', as a haven in a heartless world.[75] We feel uneasy about importing law into the home and juridicising familial relationships because we are concerned that, if were to pry open the family to the public world of law, the family would no longer be the last refuge of love, but

72 Ibid 20.

73 Or 'the negation of law': Roberta Kevelson, 'The New Realism and Lawlessness in Kaleidoscope' in Roberta Kevelson (ed), *Law and Semiotics*, Vol 2 (Plenum Press, 1988) 189, 194.

74 Christopher Lasch, *Haven in a Heartless World: The Family Besieged* (Basic Books, 1977) 8.

75 Ibid xiii.

broken 'shells of detached and competing individuals'.[76] We have an Edenic vision of the family. On the other hand, we are equally concerned that without law in the home – that is, if we allow the home to be lawless – the brute within us will emerge. Without law, the home may not be the refuge of love, but the site of domestic violence – it may be the site of brutality and monstrosity. Law is needed to control and subdue the inner brute in the public as well as the private sphere. We are caught between the Edenic dream and the Hobbesian nightmare.

There is a long tradition in political philosophy which sees the family as a microcosm of the polity, or, inversely, the polity as an extension of the family – the familial and the political are two ends along the same continuum. The same tension between law and love in the private sphere of the family is replicated in the public sphere of the polity. On the one hand, the rule of law today constitutes our highest political ideal. No event, actor or claim escapes the rule of law.[77] Most law journal articles today follow a predictable paradigm: an article typically begins with the identification of a social or political problem. The problem is then traced to a lack of regulation or legal enforcement in that area. The article then ends with a proposed solution which produces more law. This phenomenon is most pronounced in the field of international human rights law. With the proliferation of noticeable human rights violations, we see a proliferation of human rights treaties and monitoring bodies. We need to fill the void of lawlessness with more law, because lawlessness is where bad things happen, both in public and in private. On the other hand, we are equally concerned about this trend towards the increasing juridification of our public and political space. Charles Taylor calls this modern obsession with law 'rule fetishism' or 'nomolatry'.[78] In coining the neologism 'nomolatry', Taylor alerts us to the risk that 'codes, even the best codes, can become idolatrous traps'.[79] We react, often strongly, against legalism in our public discourse.[80] This reaction is sometimes manifested in terms of a critique of rights talk as an impoverishment of political discourse.[81] The underlying intuition seems to be that there is, or should be, a deeper bond between us as a community of persons – as a people – than the one provided by the law.[82] Rephrased in terms of the taxonomy of this paper, one could say that we lament the absence of love in

76 Daniel Rodgers, 'Oedipus Deposed' (1978) 6 *Reviews in American History* 293, 294.

77 Paul Kahn, *Law and Love: The Trials of King Lear* (Yale University Press, 2000) xvi.

78 Charles Taylor, 'Perils of Moralism' in Charles Taylor (ed), *Dilemmas and Connections: Selected Essays* (Harvard University Press, 2011) 347–66.

79 Charles Taylor, *A Secular Age* (Harvard University Press, 2007) 743.

80 Judith Shklar, *Legalism* (Harvard University Press, 1986); Zenon Bankowski, 'Law, Love and Legality' (2001) 14 *International Journal for the Semiotics of Law* 199; Jay Michaelson, 'Hating the Law for Christian Reasons: The Religious Roots of American Antinomianism' in Ari Mermelstein et al (eds), *Jews and the Law* (Quid Pro Books, 2014) 207.

81 Mary Ann Glendon, *Rights Talk: The Impoverishment of Political Discourse* (The Free Press, 1991).

82 Vivian Liska, 'A Lawless Legacy: Hannah Arendt and Giorgio Agamben' in Marco Goldoni and Christopher McCorkindale (eds), *Hannah Arendt and the Law* (Hart Publishing, 2012) 89, 96.

our public life. With the Black Eyed Peas, we ask, 'Where is the Love?' In our moments of ecstasy, we have the eschatological vision of 'transform[ing] this world through love'.[83] We want more law in as much as we want more love: we are driven by the Hobbesian nightmare in as much as we are drawn to the Edenic dream.[84]

Law operates on the logic of distrust:[85] we distrust each other; hence we create the state to constrain each other; we distrust the state; hence we create the judiciary to constrain the state; we distrust the judiciary; hence we create constitutional theories to constrain the judiciary. In the absence of trust, we turn to law. Law is our compromise solution. Between war and law, we choose law. But between law and love, we long for love. However, love is utopian. Where love is impossible, we resort to law. Where law is impossible, we resort to war. Law is our mode of damage control, in which our task is 'less about attaining the best than avoiding the worst'.[86] Law may help us to avoid our worst fears, but it is love that defines our best hopes. In love, we hope for cohesion without coercion: we hope 'for a collective life without inner or outer boundaries, without obstacles or occlusions [and] without the perennial work which constantly legitimates and delegitimates the transformation of power into authority of different kinds.'[87] That is the 'pathos of redeeming love', in which we fantasise a life of perfect communion in community: 'a life of unbounded mutuality, a life without separation'.[88]

Our orientation towards law is beset by two extremes, the Hobbesian nightmare and the Edenic dream – like any other nightmare or dream, these may be flights of fancy, but 'they have much of value to teach the jurist in [our] waking

83 Jeanrond, above n 24, 228.

84 This reaction against legalism has a very long intellectual history in the Judeo-Christian tradition: one could trace it back to Pauline antinomianism, which in turn tapped into an even longer tradition of Jewish messianic antinomianism. The antinomian reaction against legalism in the theological context relies on the soteriological story of Jesus as the new Adam. Paul presents Jesus as the new Adam, who suspends the law, restores our brokenness and makes us whole again. Jesus is supposed to fulfil our Edenic dream and lead us back to Edenic paradise. The messianic age is supposed to herald a return to paradise where no external law will be required: the law 'belongs to the age of the first Adam', but 'through the advent of the messiah, there would be no need for the law' – with the abrogation of the law, 'life in the *new* Garden of Eden would encounter no such problems as had befallen the first paradise': Deborah Sawyer, 'The New Adam in the Theology of St Paul' in Paul Morris and Deborah Sawyer above n 9, 105, 114. If Schmidt is correct that 'all significant concepts of the modern theory of the state are secularized theological concepts', one should not be surprised to find there is a secular manifestation of Pauline antinomianism in contemporary political discourse: Carl Schmidt, *Political Theology: Four Chapters on the Concept of Sovereignty* (George Schwab trans, MIT Press, 1985) 37.

85 Russell Hardin, 'Liberal Distrust' (2002) 10 *European Review* 73. See also Judith Shklar, 'The Liberalism of Fear' in Nancy Rosenblum (ed), *Liberalism and the Moral Life* (Harvard University Press, 1989) 21.

86 Martin Krygier, 'Ethical Positivism and the Liberalism of Fear' (1999) 24 *Australian Journal of Legal Philosophy* 65, 67.

87 Rose, above n 1, 334.

88 Ibid 337, 339.

hours'.[89] Law could save us from the Hobbesian state of nature, but we need love to bring us back to Edenic paradise. Having begun with a Judeo-Christian text, let me end with Nietzsche, who wrote that 'all great things bring about their own destruction through an act of self-overcoming.'[90] If Nietzsche is right, then letus hope that law is truly great.

## References


Badiou, Alan, *Saint Paul: The Foundation of Universalism* (Stanford University Press, 2003)

Bankowski, Zenon, 'Law, Love and Legality' (2001) 14 *International Journal for the Semiotics of Law* 199

Brett, Mark, *Genesis: Procreation and the Politics of Identity* (Routledge, 2000)

Burt, Robert, *In the Whirlwind: God and Humanity in Conflict* (Harvard University Press, 2012)

Carr, David, *Erotic Word: Sexuality, Spirituality and the Bible* (Oxford University Press, 2005)

Davies, W D, 'Paul and the Law: Reflections on Pitfalls in Interpretation' (1978) 29 *Hastings Law Journal* 1459

Dershowitz, Alan, *The Genesis of Justice* (Warner Books, 2000)

Dyzenhaus, David, 'Hobbes and the Legitimacy of Law (2001) 20 *Law and Philosophy* 461

Fletcher, George, 'The Jurisprudence of Genesis' (2003) 56 *Current Legal Problems* 41

Fletcher, George, 'Thinking about Eden' (2003) 22 *Quinnipiac Law Review* 1

Fox, Richard, 'Sentencing in the Garden of Eden' (2006) 32 *Monash University Law Review* 4

Freud, Sigmund, *Civilisation and Its Discontent* (James Strachey trans, WW Norton, 1962)

Geertz, Clifford, *The Interpretation of Cultures* (Basic Books, 1973)

Gilmore, Grant, *The Ages of American Law* (Yale University Press, 1977)

Glendon, Mary Ann, *Rights Talk: The Impoverishment of Political Discourse* (The Free Press, 1991)

Goldoni, Marco and Christopher McCorkindale (eds), *Hannah Arendt and the Law* (Hart Publishing, 2012)

Hardin, Russell 'Liberal Distrust' (2002) 10 *European Review* 73

Hart, HLA, 'American Jurisprudence through English Eyes: The Nightmare and the Noble Dream' (1977) 11 *Georgia Law Review* 969

Hobbes, Thomas, *Leviathan* (1651)

Jeanrond, Werner, *A Theology of Love* (T&T Clark, 2010)

Kahn, Paul, *Finding Ourselves at the Movies: Philosophy for a New Generation* (Columbia University Press, 2013)

Kahn, Paul, *Law and Love: The Trials of King Lear* (Yale University Press, 2000)


89 HLA Hart, 'American Jurisprudence through English Eyes: The Nightmare and the Noble Dream' (1977) 11 *Georgia Law Review* 969, 989.

90 Friedrich Nietzsche, *On the Genealogy of Morals*, Essay III §27, in Walter Kaufmann (ed), *Basic Writings of Nietzsche* (Modern Library, 1968) 597.

Kahn, Paul, *Out of Eden: Adam and Eve and the Problem of Evil* (Princeton University Press, 2006)
Kahn, Paul, *Putting Liberalism in Its Place* (Princeton University Press, 2008)
Kaufmann, Walter (ed), *Basic Writings of Nietzsche* (Modern Library, 1968)
Kevelson, Roberta (ed), *Law and Semiotics*, Vol 2 (Plenum Press, 1988)
Krygier, Martin, 'Ethical Positivism and the Liberalism of Fear' (1999) 24 *Australian Journal of Legal Philosophy* 65
Lasch, Christopher, *Haven in a Heartless World: The Family Besieged* (Basic Books, 1977)
Lytton, Timothy, 'Due Process and Legal Authority in the Garden of Eden: Jurisprudence in Aggadic Midrash' (2006) 16 *Jewish Law Annual* 185
May, Larry, *Limiting Leviathan: Hobbes on Law and International Affairs* (Oxford University Press, 2013)
Mermelstein, Ari et al (eds), *Jews and the Law* (Quid Pro Books, 2014)
Morris, Paul and Deborah Sawyer (eds), *A Walk in the Garden: Biblical, Iconographical, and Literary Images of Eden* (Sheffield Academic Press, 1992)
Muddiman, John and John Barton (eds), *The Oxford Bible Commentary* (Oxford University Press, 2007)
Mulhall, Stephen, *Philosophical Myths of the Fall* (Princeton University Press, 2007)
Neoh, Joshua, 'Jurisprudence of Love in Paul's Letter to the Romans' (2015) 33 *Law in Context* 7
Neoh, Joshua, 'The Rhetoric of Precedent and Fulfillment in the Sermon on the Mount and the Common Law' (2016) 12 *Law, Culture and the Humanities* 419
Pagels, Elaine, 'The Politics of Paradise: Augustine's Exegesis of Genesis 1–3 versus that of John Chrysostom' (1985) 78 *Harvard Theological Review* 67
Pagels, Elaine, *Adam, Eve and the Serpent* (Random House, 1988)
Parker, Kim, 'Mirror, Mirror on the Wall, Must We Leave Eden, Once and for All? A Lacanian Pleasure Trip through the Garden' (1999) 24 *Journal for the Study of the Old Testament* 19
Plato, *Plato's Symposium: Collected Works of Plato* (Benjamin Jowett trans, 4th ed, Oxford University Press, 1953)
Rawls, John, *Lectures on the History of Political Philosophy* (Harvard University Press, 2009)
Rodgers, Daniel, 'Oedipus Deposed' (1978) 6 *Reviews in American History* 293
Rose, Gillian, 'Athens and Jerusalem: A Tale of Three Cities' (1994) 3 *Social and Legal Studies* 333
Rosenblum, Nancy (ed), *Liberalism and the Moral Life* (Harvard University Press, 1989)
Schmidt, Carl, *Political Theology: Four Chapters on the Concept of Sovereignty* (George Schwab trans, MIT Press, 1985)
Shapiro, Ian (ed), *Hobbes: Leviathan* (Yale University Press, 2010)
Shklar, Judith, *Legalism* (Harvard University Press, 1986)
Taylor, Charles, 'Modern Social Imaginaries' (2002) 14 *Public Culture* 91
Taylor, Charles, *A Secular Age* (Harvard University Press, 2007)
Taylor, Charles (ed), *Dilemmas and Connections: Selected Essays* (Harvard University Press, 2011)
Tillich, Paul, *Love, Power, and Justice* (Oxford University Press, 1954)
Viroli, Maurizio, *Jean-Jacques Rousseau and the Well-Ordered Society* (Cambridge University Press, 2003)
Waldron, Jeremy, 'Dead to the Law: Paul's Antinomianism' (2006) 28 *Cardozo Law Review* 301

# 3 Freedom, responsibility, and hope in Jewish thought

*Steven H Resnicoff*

## Introduction

The concepts of freedom, hope and responsibility are integrally intertwined in Jewish thought. Rather than regarding freedom and responsibility as opposites, a powerful, mainstream current in Jewish philosophy perceives a person's freedom – the divine blessing of free will – as the predicate for moral responsibility. Events are not predetermined. A person possesses the power to control his actions and, thereby, to improve himself and to contribute to the improvement of others, of the community, and of the world. This inherent ability produces an ever present opportunity for us to achieve spiritual enlightenment, justice and love. In turn, this potentiality implies a moral duty to act responsibly so as to realise these aspirations.

## Freedom

Let us examine a few of the many ways in which free will is fundamental to Judaism. God is not only the Creator, but also 'our Father and our King.'[1] As a Father, God loves each of us and provides ethical guidance regarding the path to perfecting our characters and repairing and improving the world. As a King, God goes beyond offering advice. He issues specific commands,[2] including some that have metaphysical purposes which we cannot fully fathom.[3]

1 The liturgical piece, 'Our Father, Our King,' plays an especially important role in the prayers of the High Holy Days and fasts. See, eg, 'Avinu Malkenu' in Michael Berenbaum and Fred Skolnik (eds), *Encyclopaedia Judaica* (Macmillan Reference USA, 2nd ed, 2007) 739–40. See Barbara Streisand's rendition of this prayer, with an English translation of the lyrics: 'Avinu Malkeinu Hebrew Lyrics – Hebrew English, *YouTube,* 5 December 2013, available at: <www.youtube.com/watch?v=3zHKsnZSFMg>.

2 See, eg, 'Duty' as defined in Michael Berenbaum and Fred Skolnik, above n 2, 72–3.

3 See, eg, Alexander Altmann, Scholem Gershom and Gerald Y Blidstein, '*Commandments, Reasons for*' in Michael Berenbaum and Fred Skolnik, above n 2, 85–90.

Commandments play a central role in Judaism. Some are regarded as having been communicated directly from God, while others are perceived as arising indirectly, from the biblical commandment to obey certain rabbinical authorities.[4] Some prescriptions are perceived as 'affirmative' or 'active,' while others are characterised as 'negative' or 'passive.'[5] These typological distinctions, which are subject to extensive scholarly debate, produce significant consequences under Jewish law, which exceed our present scope.

However, the very concept of a commandment (as well as of guidance, for that matter) presupposes that a person possesses the power – the freedom – to choose whether or not to obey. If a person's actions were predetermined, what purpose would a commandment play?

Traditional Jewish sources encourage and exalt the study of Jewish law, in part because such study 'brings a person to proper actions.'[6] But if actions were in fact predetermined, what point would there be to encourage study? A person would either study or not study. And whether a person studied would have no influence on how the person acted. The person would act or not act as was preordained.

A person's *ability* to affect his or her conduct by *choosing* is clearly inferred from the fact that God expressly directs us to choose wisely:

> See, I have set before thee this day life and good, and death and evil, in that I command thee this day to love the Lord thy God, to walk in His ways, and to keep His commandments and His statutes and His ordinances; then thou shalt live and multiply, and the Lord thy God shall bless thee in the land whither thou goest in to possess it. But if thy heart turn away, and thou wilt not hear, but shalt be drawn away and worship other gods, and serve them; I declare unto you this day, that you shall surely perish; ye shall not prolong your days upon the land, whither thou passest over the Jordan to go in to possess it. I call heaven and earth to witness against you this day that I have set before thee life and death, the blessing and the curse; therefore choose life.[7]

Moreover, in this passage, and in many others, God promises to reward people for fulfilling the commandments[8] and to punish those who flout them. Would this make sense if we could not determine our actions?[9] If one were unable to

4 Steven H Resnicoff, *Understanding Jewish Law* (LexisNexis, 2012) 36–8.

5 Ibid 39–41.

6 *The Babylonian Talmud*, *Kiddushin* 40b.

7 This translation is from The Soncino Chumash: Abraham Cohen (ed), *The Soncino Chumash: The Five Books of Moses with Haphtaroth* (Soncino Press, 1956) Deut. 30:15–19, 1143–4.

8 Ibid Exodus 15:26.

9 See Yitzchak Arama, *Akeidat Yitzchak* (Eliyahu Munk, trans, Lambda Publishers, 2001) 162: 'Why would the Torah make rainfall dependent on our conduct, (Leviticus 26, 1–5) if our behaviour were not free? The idea of receiving a reward for decisions made under duress would be difficult to swallow.' See also Moshe Chaim Luzzatto, *The Way of God* (Aryeh Kaplan, trans, Feldheim Publisher, 1981) 79.

control one's conduct, such a system of reward and punishment, which is a core Jewish tenet, would seem to be utterly inconsistent with any notion of justice or morality. As tenth century sage Rav Saadia Gaon wrote:

> if men acted out of compulsion, the believer and the infidel would alike have to be rewarded, since each would be doing what is requested of him, just as any intelligent person, if he employed two workingmen, the first to build and the other to tear down, would be obliged to pay each of them his wage.[10]

The proposition that the Divine doctrine of reward and punishment could be morally incoherent is heretical. As twentieth-century commentator Rabbi Walter Wurzburger explains, Judaism's affirmation of God's moral perfection was perhaps its greatest theological innovation:

> Jewish monotheism represents a radically different approach to religion. Its novelty consisted not primarily in the substitution of the belief in one God for the plurality of gods worshipped in polytheism. What was even more revolutionary in the Jewish conception of monotheism was, as against the pagan emphasis upon divine power, the attribution of moral perfection to God.[11]

Consequently, Jewish scholars agree that the doctrine of reward and punishment must be *morally* sound. Although they proffer diverse explanations for the apparently anomalous results witnessed in this world, virtually none explains these anomalies by positing a general lack of free will.[12] Instead, it is declared that, 'the Creator, magnified be His majesty, does not in any way interfere with the actions of men and . . . He does not exercise any force upon them either to obey or disobey Him.'[13]

Furthermore, free will is enjoyed by all humankind, not only by Jews, as is evidenced by some of the earliest biblical passages. God entrusts the very first person, Adam, a non-Jew, with but a single commandment – ie, not to eat from the tree of good and evil, yet Adam exercises his free will to disobey. Similarly, before Cain became the world's first murderer, God informs Cain that he possesses the power to vanquish the temptation to do evil.[14] Cain misuses his free will and commits fratricide. According to Judaism, even after the Sinaitic revelation, all non-Jews (known as the 'children of Noach') remain bound by a number of commandments

10 Saadia Gaon, *The Book of Beliefs & Opinions* (Samuel Rosenblatt, trans, Yale University Press, 1976) 189.

11 Walter S Wurzburger, *Ethics of Responsibility: Pluralistic Approaches to Covenantal Ethics* (The Jewish Publication Society, 1994) 4.

12 See, eg, Louis Isaac Rabinowitz, Alvin J Reines and Richard L Rubinstein, 'Reward and Punishment' in Berenbaum, Michael, Skolnik, Fred, above n 2, 269–72.

13 Gaon, above n 11, 188.

14 Cohen, above n 8, Genesis 4:7.

(the 'Noachide laws'),[15] and the doctrine of reward and punishment continues to apply. In making this point, the Jerusalem Talmud[16] cites Job (37:23): 'with Justice and an abundance of kindness, He does not deal harshly', and comments, 'God does not withhold reward from gentiles who perform His commandments.'[17] Similarly, the Babylonian Talmud states that righteous gentiles will have a place in the world to come.[18]

Of course, many Jewish authorities acknowledge that there may be a few isolated instances in which God may interfere with a person's exercise of his free will, but these are but minor exceptions.[19]

## Responsibility

The fact that a person's exercise of free will has real world consequences is illuminated in the Bible's discussion of the events immediately preceding the sale of Joseph. All of Joseph's brothers, except for Benjamin, are shepherding flocks in the countryside. Jacob sends Joseph to check on their welfare. Most of the brothers (for reasons too complex to explore here) express a desire to execute Joseph. One brother, Reuben, persuades the others to place Joseph into a pit instead. Based on this deed, the biblical text states that Reuben 'rescued him [Joseph] from their hands [ie, from his brothers].'[20]

This is an enigmatic accolade, given that Jewish tradition states that the pit, while empty of water, was full of poisonous snakes and scorpions.[21] How could putting Joseph into such a pit be characterised as a 'rescue'? The early-eighteenth

15 See, generally, Steven S Schwarzschild, Saul Berman and Menachem Elon, 'Noachide Laws' in Berenbaum, Michael, Skolnik, Fred, above n 2, 284–7. See also Nahum Rakover, 'Jewish Law and the Noahide Obligation to Preserve Social Order' (1991) 12 *Cardozo Law Review* 1073; Suzanne Last Stone, 'Sinaitic and Noahide Law: Legal Pluralism in Jewish Law' (1991) 12 *Cardozo Law Review* 1157; Resnicoff, above n 5, 41. There are communities of non-Jews who, even today, abide by the Noachide laws. See Ilana E Strauss, 'The Gentiles Who Act Like Jews' *Tablet*, 31 January 2016, available at: <www.tabletmag.com/jewish-life-and-religion/196588/the-gentiles-who-act-like-Jews?utm_source=tabletmagazinelist&utm_campaign=b61a718779-Sunday_January_31_20161_29_2016&utm_medium=email&utm_term=0_c308bf8edb-b61a718779-207151269>.

16 For a discussion of the differences between the Jerusalem Talmud and the Babylonian Talmud, see Resnicoff, above n 5, 67–70.

17 *The Jerusalem Talmud, Peah* 1:1.

18 *Babylonian Talmud, Sanhedrin* 105a. See also Moses ben Maimon (Maimonides; 1135–204), *Mishneh Torah*, 'Laws of Repentence' 3:4.

19 For example, there is considerable debate regarding Scripture's intent pertaining to the hardening of Pharaoh's heart. There is general agreement, however, that Pharaoh could have at least initially repented and that Pharaoh was punished for failing to use his free will to act properly. See, eg, Isaiah Horowitz, *Shnei Luchot HaBrit* (Eliyahu Munk, trans, Lambda Publishers, 1999) 430; Jacob Culi, *The Torah Anthology*, IV *Exodus* (Aryeh Kaplan, trans, Maznaim Publishing Company, 1977–1987) 85.

20 Cohen, above n 8, Genesis 37:21.

21 *Babylonian Talmud, Sabbath* 22a.

century Moroccan scholar, Rabbi Chayim ben Attar, provides an answer. He explains that because Joseph's brothers possessed free will, they could have killed Joseph even if, as was the fact, he did not 'deserve' death. In other words, it was not preordained whether or not Joseph would die at this point in history. By dissuading the brothers from this course of action, Reuben saved Joseph's life.

In contrast to human beings, animals lack free will.[22] Because Joseph was innocent, the snakes and scorpions in the pit could not kill him. Therefore, Reuben's quick action saved the innocent Joseph from execution by his brothers and placed him in a 'safe' pit from which Reuben planned to later release him.[23]

The ability of man's free will to innovatively alter the world is reflected in the Jewish belief that humankind was created to serve as a partner with God in perfecting the world. Humans are made in God's image[24] and are commanded to emulate God's 'traits.'[25] Thus, as God is creative, humans are to creatively use their knowledge and skill to 'subdue the world.'[26] As Rabbi J David Bleich writes, '[Judaism] rejects the notion that man may not harness nature or that man may not intervene and manipulate the laws of nature for the betterment of the human condition.'[27] From a Jewish perspective, doing so is not a presumptuous impingement on the purview of the Almighty. On the contrary, it is a fulfillment of human potential.

When Jews usher in the Sabbath, they recite a prayer known as 'Kiddush' ('Sanctification'). Its last sentence reads, 'God blessed the Seventh Day and hallowed it, because on it He had abstained from all His work which God created to make.'[28] The last two words, 'to make,'[29] seem superfluous. However, Jewish scholars explain that God's creation was not yet complete. As twentieth-century sage Rabbi Joseph B Soloveitchik writes:

> When God created the world, He provided an opportunity for the work of His hands – man – to participate in His creation. The Creator, as it were, impaired reality in order that mortal man could repair its flaws and perfect it.[30]

22 Chayim Ben Attar, *Or Hachayim: Commentary on the Torah* (Eliyahu Munk, trans, Lambda Publications, 1999) 310.
23 Ibid.
24 Cohen, above n 8, Genesis 1:27.
25 See, eg, Lev 19:2 ('You shall be holy, for holy am I, HaShem [ie, the Lord], your God'); Deut 13:5 ('HaShem [ie, the Lord], your God, shall you follow'). The translations are from Nosson Scherman (ed), *The Chumash: The Stone Edition* (Mesorah Publications Ltd, 1993). See also Warren Zev Harvey, 'Holiness: A Command to Imitatio Dei' (1977) 16 *Tradition* 7.
26 Scherman, above n 26, Genesis 1:26. See also Moses ben Nachman (Nachmanides: 1194–1270), Charles Chavel (ed), *Commentary on the Torah, Genesis* (Shilo Publishing House, 1971) 53, 55.
27 David Bleich, *Bioethical Dilemmas* (KTAV Publishing House, 1998) (stating that '[i]n rabbinic thought dispensation for such intervention is derived from Genesis 1:28') 206.
28 Dovid Weinberger (ed), *Ohel Sarah Women's Siddur* (Mesorah Publications Ltd, 2005) 345.
29 Ibid. (translating the Hebrew infinitive, la'asot, as 'to make').
30 Joseph B Soloveitchik, *Halakhic Man* (Jewish Publication Society of America, 1983) 101. See also Luzzatto, above n 10, 'God'.

As Jonathan Sacks, former Chief Rabbi of the United Kingdom, repeatedly and poignantly explains, in stark contrast to Karl Marx's epigram that religion is the 'opium of the people,'[31] Judaism is a religion of 'protest.'[32] Marx believed that religion reconciles people to the status quo, ie, 'to their poverty, their disease and death, their "station in life", their subjection to tyrannical rulers, the sheer bleakness of existence for most people most of the time.'[33] It tells people that all of these tragedies are 'the will of God' and should not be changed.[34]

But Judaism tells us to reject the status quo and to employ the resources God gives us to '[l]earn to do good, seek justice, aid the oppressed, uphold the rights of the orphan, defend the cause of the widow.'[35] Judaism requires that we 'seek justice,'[36] not that we accept the current state of affairs just because it is the 'will of God.' When God tells Abraham that He intends to destroy Sodom and Gomorrah, Abraham challenges this expression of God's will as itself unjust: 'That be far from Thee to do after this manner, to slay the righteous with the wicked, that so the righteous should be as the wicked; that be far from Thee; shall not the Judge of all the earth do justly?'[37]

We are taught not to regard the destitute as undeserving or their impoverished condition as God's will. Judaism's perspective is illustrated in the following discussion, recorded in the Talmud, between Rabbi Akiva and Tinus Rufus, the Roman governor of Israel:

*Tinus Rufus:* asked Rabbi Akiva, 'If your God loves the poor, why does He not provide for them?'

*Rabbi Akiva:* replied, 'So that we may be saved through them from the punishment of Gehenna [ie, charity atones].'

*Rufus:* said, 'On the contrary, it is this that will condemn you to Gehenna. I will make my point clear by a parable. A king of flesh and blood became angry with his slave, put him in prison and ordered that he be given neither food nor drink. A certain man went [to the prison] and gave him food and drink. When the king hears what the man did, will he not be angry with him? And after all you are no more than God's slaves, as it is written, "For to Me the children of Israel are slaves"

(Lev. 25–55).'

31 Karl Marx, 'A Contribution to the Critique of Hegel's Philosophy of Right', *Deutsch-Französische Jahrbücher*, as published in Paris on the 7 and 10 February 1844, available at: <www.marxists.org/archive/marx/works/1843/critique-hpr/intro.htm>.

32 Jonathan Sacks, *To Heal a Fractured World* (Schocken Books, 2005) 14.

33 Ibid 17.

34 Ibid.

35 Scherman, above n 26, Isaiah 1:17.

36 Ibid Deut. 16:20.

37 Ibid Genesis 18:25.

*Rabbi Akiva:* replied, 'I will prove my point with another parable. A king of flesh and blood became angry with his child, put him in prison, and ordered that he be given neither food nor drink. A certain man went [to the prison] and gave him food and drink. When the king hears what the man did, will he not reward him? And after all we are called [God's] children, as it is written, 'You are children of the Lord your God' (Deut. 14:1).[38]

Rather than teaching us to accept another's state of need as God's will, Judaism commands us not only to support their immediate material needs, but also – by training, employing, or financing them – to enable them to support themselves.[39] Through the latter, we can contribute to a lasting change in their standard of living, and the people so assisted can enjoy the spiritual satisfaction that arises upon their independence from direct financial subsidies.

Judaism similarly teaches a proactive approach to healing. The Midrash makes this point through a story involving the rabbis and a sick, but unlearned man:

> Rabbi Ishmael and Rabbi Akiva were walking through the streets of Jerusalem and met a sick man who asked them: 'How can I be cured?' They answered: 'Do thus and so until you are cured.' He said to them: 'But who afflicted me?' 'The Holy One, blessed be He,' they answered. 'So how can you interfere in a matter which is not your concern? God afflicted me and you wish to heal?' The rabbis then asked: 'What is your vocation?' 'I am a tiller of the soil. Here is the vine-cutter in my hand.' They asked: 'But who created the vineyard?' 'The Holy One, blessed be He.' 'Well, you interfered in the vineyard which is not yours. He created it and you cut away its fruits?' they asked. 'But were I not to plow and till and fertilize and weed, the vineyard would not produce any fruit,' he explained. 'So,' they responded, 'From your own work have you not learned what is written (Ps. 103:15): "As for man, his days are as grass." Just as the tree, if not weeded, fertilized, and plowed, will not grow and bring forth its fruits, so with the human body. The fertilizer is the medicine and the means of healing, and the tiller of the earth is the physician.'[40]

The biblical source for the license to heal is discerned from a verse directing a person who has injured another to 'surely cure' (or 'thoroughly cure') the person

38 *Babylonian Talmud*, *Baba Batra* 10a.

39 Maimonides states: 'The greatest level [of charity], above which there is no greater, is to support a fellow Jew by endowing him with a gift or loan, or entering into a partnership with him, or finding employment for him, in order to strengthen his hand until he need no longer be dependent upon others'. See Maimonides, *Mishneh Torah*, 'Laws of Charity' 10:7.

40 'Midrash Temurah' in JD Eisenstein, *Otzar Midrashim* (Heb), translated in David M Feldman, *Health and Medicine in the Jewish Tradition* (The Crossroad Publishing Company, 1986) 15–16.

who was injured.[41] The Talmud explains that this means that he must pay for his victim's medical expenses. In turn, this verse serves as the source that permits doctors to treat, rather than requiring them to leave the matter solely to prayer.[42] Some Jewish authorities believe that 'it was the prerogative and duty of man to harness his intellect and the resources of nature in his conquest of disease as in his striving for prosperity.'[43] Others, while acknowledging that illness may be a divine judgment, nevertheless affirm the biblical license to cure afflictions through medical treatment.[44] The sixteenth-century Code of Jewish Law,[45] which together with centuries of subsequent glosses upon it remains the most authoritative Jewish law codex, declares that, 'One who withholds medical treatment is a spiller of blood [ie, a murderer].'[46]

Consequently, throughout Jewish history, technological advances in medical treatment – from simple surgeries to modern organ transplants – have been approved by Jewish law authorities. Similarly, modern technology has been widely permitted for diagnostic and preventative purposes.

For example, within the Orthodox Jewish community, it is routine for high school seniors to be tested to determine if they are carriers of genetic disorders. The testing is done under the aegis of an organisation known as the Dor Yeshorim, which translates to the 'Upright Generation'. Each student is given an anonymous number and is not told of the results of the test. Instead, Dor Yeshorim keeps records of the tests. If an Orthodox man and woman are dating and think that the relationship might lead to marriage, they exchange their anonymous numbers and each calls Dor Yeshorim, giving it their two numbers. Dor Yeshorim checks the two test results and ascertains the statistical likelihood that the two people's progeny might be genetically afflicted. It then calls each of the two people and informs them regarding this likelihood.

When this genetic screening process first began, Rabbi Moses Feinstein, the leading Jewish law authority in the United States, was asked whether it might be better for a person to trust in God rather than to try to predict what might happen. The question was based on the verse, 'do not attempt to discern the future; rather, accept wholeheartedly whatever befalls you.'[47] Feinstein held the verse inapplicable to this situation. He endorsed the screening process, declaring that

41 Scherman, above n 26, Exodus 21:19.

42 Although some small Jewish sects believed that, at least as to illnesses, one should only resort to prayer, this was never a mainstream Jewish view. See Immanuel Jakobovits, *Jewish Medical Ethics* (Bloch Publishing Company, 1975) 2 (describing this approach as appealing to a few small Jewish sects).

43 Ibid (stating that this was the view of some Talmudists and that it also seemed to be the view of Maimonides).

44 Ibid.

45 See Resnicoff, above n 5, at 72–3, 277 (describing the place of the Shulhan Arukh among Jewish law literature).

46 *Shulhan Arukh, Yoreh Deah* 336:1.

47 Scherman, above n 26, Deut 18:13.

the failure to undergo this simple and available test would be tantamount to 'closing [one's] eyes to what it is possible to see.'[48]

## Hope

Jonathan Sacks crisply contrasts the Greek and Jewish perspectives:

> The great literary genre of ancient Greece was tragedy, and tragedy is born in the idea that there is a fate (*moira*) that is inexorable. Man struggles against it and is always doomed to failure. Tragedy in the Greek sense is a concept that simply cannot be translated into biblical Hebrew. Not only is there no such word; there could not be, for in Judaism there is no fate that is inevitable. The very concept of prophecy is the warning of a future that will happen unless – unless there is a change of heart. Israel had prophets; Greece had oracles. The difference between them is that an oracle predicts the future, while a prophet warns against it. If the foretold future comes to pass, the oracle has succeeded, but the prophet has failed. Judaism is therefore the systematic rejection of tragedy in the name of hope.[49]

Even more important than the ability to repair that which is external to us and to alter our future, we are given the ability to improve ourselves and the present. Although Judaism tells us that we are each born with particular natural predilections, it also assures us that we possess the capacity to change or sublimate them.[50] We are commanded to love our fellow man as we love ourselves.[51] To accomplish this, we must overcome many emotional challenges, such as spite, envy, temper, and conceit. Yet God does not command that which we lack the ability to accomplish.[52] In addition, He surely wants all His beloved children to achieve peace and harmony amongst each other and will enable us to do so. Indeed, He promises us that this will occur.[53] This is the ultimate source of our hope.

## References

Arama, Yitzchak, *Akeidat Yitzchak* (Eliyahu Munk, trans, Lambda Publishers, 2001)

Attar, Chayim Ben, *Or Hachayim: Commentary on the Torah* (Eliyahu Munk, trans, Lambda Publications, 1999)

Berenbaum, Michael and Fred Skolnik (eds), *Encyclopaedia Judaica* (Macmillan Reference USA, 2nd ed, 2007)

48 Moses Feinstein, IV *Iggerot Moshe*, Even HaEzer, No 10 (1985) (Hebrew).

49 Jonathan Sacks, *A Letter in the Scroll* (Free Press, 2000) 102. Kalman Kaplan contrasts the Greek and Jewish views regarding predetermination and the roles of oracles and prophets in his play, Kalman J Kaplan, *Oedipus in Jerusalem* (Resource Publications, 2015).

50 Arama, above n 10, 161–2.

51 Scherman, above n 26, Levit 19:18.

52 David J Bleich, *With Perfect Faith* (KTAV Publishing House Inc, 1983) 6.

53 Scherman, above n 26, Zachariah 14:9.

Bleich, David, *Bioethical Dilemmas* (KTAV Publishing House, 1998)

Bleich, David J, *With Perfect Faith* (KTAV Publishing House Inc, 1983)

Chavel, Charles (ed), *Commentary on the Torah, Genesis* (Shilo Publishing House, 1971)

Cohen, Abraham (ed), *The Soncino Chumash: The Five Books of Moses with Haphtaroth* (Soncino Press, 1956)

Culi, Jacob, *The Torah Anthology*, IV *Exodus* (Aryeh Kaplan, trans, Maznaim Publishing Company, 1977–1987)

Feinstein, Moses, IV *Iggerot Moshe*, Even HaEzer, No 10 (1985)

Feldman, David M, *Health and Medicine in the Jewish Tradition* (The Crossroad Publishing Company, 1986)

Gaon, Saadia, *The Book of Beliefs & Opinions* (Samuel Rosenblatt, trans, Yale University Press, 1976)

Harvey, Warren Zev, 'Holiness: A Command to Imitatio Dei' (1977) 16 *Tradition* 7

Horowitz, Isaiah, *Shnei Luchot HaBrit* (Eliyahu Munk, trans, Lambda Publishers, 1999)

Ilana E Strauss, 'Gentiles Who Act Like Jews' *Tablet*, 31 January 2016, available at: <www.tabletmag.com/jewish-life-and-religion/196588/the-gentiles-who-act-like-Jews?utm_source=tabletmagazinelist&utm_campaign=b61a718779-Sunday_January_31_20161_29_2016&utm_medium=email&utm_term=0_c308bf8edb-b61a718779-207151269>

Jakobovits, Immanuel, *Jewish Medical Ethics* (Bloch Publishing Company, 1975)

Kaplan, Kalman J, *Oedipus in Jerusalem* (Resource Publications, 2015)

Last Stone, Suzanne, 'Sinaitic and Noahide Law: Legal Pluralism in Jewish Law' (1991) 12 *Cardozo Law Review* 1157

Luzzatto, Moshe Chaim, *The Way of God* (Aryeh Kaplan, trans, Feldheim Publisher, 1981)

Marx, Karl, 'A Contribution to the Critique of Hegel's Philosophy of Right', *Deutsch-Französische Jahrbücher*, as published in Paris on the 7 and 10 February 1844, available at: <www.marxists.org/archive/marx/works/1843/critique-hpr/intro.htm>.

Rakover, Nahum, 'Jewish Law and the Noahide Obligation to Preserve Social Order' (1991) 12 *Cardozo Law Review* 1073

Resnicoff, Steven H, *Understanding Jewish Law* (LexisNexis, 2012)

Sacks, Jonathan, *A Letter in the Scroll* (Free Press, 2000)

Sacks, Jonathan, *To Heal a Fractured World* (Schocken Books, 2005)

Scherman, Nosson (ed), *The Chumash: The Stone Edition* (Mesorah Publications Ltd, 1993)

Soloveitchik, Joseph B, *Halakhic Man* (Jewish Publication Society of America, 1983)

Streisand, Barbara, 'Avinu Malkeinu Hebrew Lyrics – Hebrew English, *YouTube*, 5 December 2013, available at: <www.youtube.com/watch?v=3zHKsnZSFMg>

Weinberger, Dovid (ed), *Ohel Sarah Women's Siddur* (Mesorah Publications Ltd, 2005)

Wurzburger, Walter S, *Ethics of Responsibility: Pluralistic Approaches to Covenantal Ethics* (The Jewish Publication Society, 1994)

# 4 Texts of terror in the New Testament

## Encountering or hating the 'other'?

*Michael Trainor*

I am in a hotel foyer in Denizli, a city of just half a million people, in south west Turkey. It is morning and I am with six students and a colleague from my university. Having enjoyed a fulsome breakfast, we prepare to venture to archaeological sites in the area of the Lycus Valley.

A man, younger than me, comes through the doors of the hotel, looks at the two receptionists behind the desk. He begins to shout at them in English in what sounds like a North American accent:

> 'You must accept Christ as your saviour in order to be saved! You nailed him to the cross! You must repent of your sins and become his follower!'

As I take in the scene, hear his loud voice, the meaning of his address and its implications, as I notice the look of bewilderment on the faces of the receptionists and the quick disappearance of my Australian companions, especially my colleague, I know that I must do something.

I am not sure what, though.

I approach him and he spots me, directing his message now in my direction.

As I move towards him I think of the implications of this person's message, the manner of its delivery and the lack of meaning it would have for the receptionists in this hotel in a country that is 98 percent mainly Sunni Muslim.

As I draw closer to him I introduce myself and hold out my hand. He continues to shout and slowly shakes it.

The more he talks, the softer I speak.

The softer I speak, the quieter he becomes, until we are talking to each other at a conversational level.

'Are you Christian?' he asks. I tell him that I am.

'Have you been saved?' I assure him I have been.

'Do you believe in Jesus?' 'Of course'.

Our conversation seems to rob him of any desire to continue his evangelical tirade. He asks if I know of other Christians in the area. I suggest their presence some 30 kilometres out of the city, down the road to the south. He happily swings around on his heel and heads off.

I am amazed and embarrassed.

## Religion and violence

There are several things about this experience that stays with me: the young man's evangelising fervour; the imposition of his version of religious truth without respect for others; his unwillingness to engage in any form of dialogue; the presumption that the verbalising of his religious message was all that was needed; the lack of sensitivity of any possible religious convictions of his addressees; the potential for misunderstanding; and, in a different context, the possibility of violence that might result. Most of all, I remember my embarrassment at his version of Christianity that was very different from my own.

I witnessed in this hotel lobby in Turkey a form of religious fervour bordering on violence, with no awareness of the 'other' and no willingness to engage in respectful dialogue. I have not witnessed personally other extreme expressions of religious intolerance and violence but I know about them. One is most prominent: the 'terrorism' from Da'ish, the jihadist militant Wahhabi-Salafi Islamic State in Iran, Syria, Libya, Egypt, Algeria, Saudi Arabia, Yemen and France and the violence it has brought to religious and ethnic minorities.[1] Other acts of violence have been perpetrated under the name of religion or with the support of those who hold religious views. Without attempting to give an historical summary of such tragic acts, mention can be made of the Crusades in the Middle Ages, the Jewish holocaust in the 20th century, and the sexual abuse acts perpetrated by church leaders in the 20th and 21st centuries.[2]

Religion has been used to justify inquisitions, slavery, the just war, racism, sexism, anti-Semitism and capital punishment. Violence and religion seem to be intricately linked, a judgement not lost on a few social commentators. One social commentator analysing the 2005 London bombings wrote:

> it has never been clearer that there is only one place to lay the blame and it has ever been thus. The cause of all this misery, mayhem, violence, terror and ignorance is of course religion itself, and it seems ludicrous to have to state

1 For a critique of the language of 'terrorism', see Rakhamim Emanuilov and Andrey Tshlavsky, *Terror in the Name of Faith: Religion and Political Violence* (Academic Studies Press, 2011) 7–22. They define 'terrorism' as the 'use of premeditated, politically and ideologically motivated violence, or the threat of using such violence; this type of violence can only be committed by a non-state actor, and it is committed in the absence of a state of war (especially in the absence of conventional warfare)' 14.

2 See also the discussion of more contemporary expressions of the 'culture' of religious violence witnessed in abortion clinic bombings, the Catholic–Protestant conflict in Belfast, the assassination of Yitzhak Rabin, the World Trade Center bombing, Hamas suicide missions, assassinations in India and Buddhist violence, in Mark Juergensmeyer, *Terror in the Mind of God: The Global Rise of Religious Violence* (University of California Press, 2000) 19–118.

> such an obvious reality, the fact is that the government and the media are doing a pretty good job of pretending that it isn't so.[3]

As the scale of violence in our world seems to increase each year, the perception of an inextricable link between religion and violence becomes more common.[4] Some consider that all religious traditions have a violent and dark side. Others, that this side is not a legitimate expression of genuine religious belief and practice. Analyses of popular misinterpretations of religious texts, symbols and theologies become more pressing for identifying the causes of violence that perpetually rejects the religious or cultural 'other.' Common to all religious traditions is the desire to address the common human quest for happiness, physical, emotional and spiritual well-being. At this basic level of human existence, every religion, culture, ethnicity and language background is similar.[5]

Mark Juergensmeyer argues that the monotheistic conviction amongst some religious adherents – that death is not the last word in human existence, that there is an afterlife – leads ultimately to the 'denial of death'. They consider this conviction as a remedy to the human experience of mortality, frailty and corruption. Juergensmeyer believes that it is a distraction from the human inevitability of death. It emboldens some fundamentalist religionists with a means of control over destruction and disorder who are prone to express this theological tenet in religious violence. In this viewpoint, religious warfare becomes the 'cosmological re-enactment of the primacy of order over chaos . . . [b]ut in order to portray a state of harmony convincingly, religion has had to emphasise disharmony and its ability to contain it.'[6]

Religion then becomes the means of restoring order out of chaos and corruption. Some religious adherents further believe that the best mode of this restoration is through conversion of the 'other' and an imposition of control over the disorders

3 Muriel Gray, 'Religion itself is the fount of most evil', *Sunday Herald* (Glasgow), 24 July 2005. A similar view is held by Richard Dawkins in commentating on the 'dark side' of religious absolutism, *The God Delusion* (Bantam Press, 2008), 317–48.

4 A helpful balanced report on the current global situation with regard to peace and violence is the Institute for Economics & Peace, '2015 Global Peace Index: Measuring Peace, its Causes and its Economic Value', *Institute for Economics and Peace* (2015), (Sydney, New York and Mexico City), available at: <http://economicsandpeace.org/wp-content/uploads/2015/06/Global-Peace-Index-Report-2015_0.pdf>.

5 Bstan-'dzin-rgya-mtsho [Dalai Lama XIV] in Dalai Lama XIV, *Toward a True Kinship of Faiths: How the World's Religions Can Come Together* (Doubleday Religion, 2010) at 180 wrote:

> Whether one is rich or poor, educated or illiterate, religious or nonbelieving, man or woman, black, white, or brown, we are all the same. Physically, emotionally, and mentally, we are all equal. We all share basic needs for food, shelter, safety, and love. We all aspire to happiness and we all shun suffering. Each of us has hopes, worries, fears, and dreams. Each of us wants the best for our family and loved ones. We all experience pain when we suffer loss and joy when we achieve what we seek. On this fundamental level, religion, ethnicity, culture, and language make no difference.

6 Juergensmeyer, above n 2, 159.

which people experience. This control takes many forms, even ones that border on violence.

### *Christian 'warfare'*

Some Christians find the biblical and theological foundation for the imposition of this control in Christ's victory over death. Tortured and victimised through abusive death, he rises from the grave and conquers death forever. He becomes the symbol of the restoration of order. In the wake of this, some have proscribed the value of enduring suffering and violence, like Christ, as the means to overcoming evil and restoring order in the world – a point to which I shall return towards the latter part of this essay as I consider Jesus' injunction to 'offer the other cheek' (Luke 6.28).[7] In this very particular perspective, violence is inevitable. It must be endured in order for it to be suppressed and defeated. Taken to another extreme, for this view of religion to 'work', chaos must also be defeated in the same vein as Christ exorcised evil and overcame the evil spirits.

Some Christians believe that they are in a spiritual 'warfare' against evil, heresy and other demonic forces that reside in other (usually non-Christian) religions.[8] This battle will assure the ultimate victory. Pentecostal and evangelical Christians and 'Third Wave Movement' revivalists justify this warfare principally, though not exclusively, with seven New Testament texts.[9] I consider these 'texts of terror' below:[10]

- 2 Corinthians 10.3–4
- Ephesians 4.27
- Ephesians 6.10–17
- Mark 3.20–27
- Luke 12.51–53
- Luke 14.26
- Luke 22.35–38

A fundamentalist mindset would see these New Testament passages as supportive of a militant antagonistic stance towards the non-Christian world. They would very much appeal to my Denizli evangelist.

7 Juergensmeyer, above n 2,159.

8 There is a wide-ranging selection of writings on spiritual warfare. A key proponent of spiritual warfare and representative of the 'Third Wave' neo-Pentecostal revivalism is Charles Peter Wagner. His three key books are, *Engaging the Enemy: How to Fight and Defeat Territorial Spirits* (Gospel Light Publications, 1995), *Confronting the Powers: How the New Testament Church Experienced the Power of Strategic-Level Spiritual Warfare* (Regal Books, 1996) and *Hard-Core Idolatry: Facing the Facts* (Wagner Institute Publications, 1999). Clinton E Arnold, writing in a more moderate key, explores the key biblical passages that undergird spiritual warfare, in *Three Crucial Questions about Spiritual Warfare* (Baker, 1997). See also E Janet Warren, '"Spiritual Warfare": A Dead Metaphor?' 2 *Journal of Pentecostal Theology* (2012) 278–97.

9 See, eg, Arnold, above n 8, 22–3, who offers 26 other New Testament texts for consideration.

10 To borrow here from the expression used by Phyllis Trible in *Texts of Terror: Literary-Feminist Readings of Biblical Narratives* (Fortress Press, 1984).

### *Texts of 'terror'*

In what follows I shall summarise these texts in the way a particular evangelical literalist interpreter might understand them. This will lead me to consider the nature of biblical texts in general and the 1st century CE Mediterranean worldview of evil spirits in particular. Before concluding this essay and underscoring what I consider the principle hermeneutic principle essential for religious dialogue, I want to turn to one final New Testament pericope, Luke 6.27–36 (with a parallel in Matthew 5.39–47). This is an important and often quoted text. It is concerned with enemy love and counterbalances the perceived negativity and violence implied in the other scripture passages above. I will suggest that this passage can also become a potential 'text of terror', not in the manner of the abovementioned passages for the non-believer or atheist, but for the Christian believer herself.

1 In 2 Corinthians 10.3–4 the language of warfare seems explicit:

> [v3]Indeed, we live as human beings, but we do not wage war according to human standards;[v4] for the weapons of our warfare are not merely human, but they have divine power to destroy strongholds.[11]

The letter's writer, Paul, envisions that the struggle in which Jesus followers are engaged occurs within the lived reality of their lives that reflect the cosmic battle waged between good and evil.

2 In Ephesians 4.27, the author encourages the letter's addressees 'not to give an opportunity to the devil.' The verse affirms the presence and influence of a diabolic being looking for opportunities to bring about evil. The follower of Jesus must be on guard, as though ready for battle.

3 In Ephesians 6.10–17, the same author of the Letter to the Ephesians again animates Jesus' followers to be ready for combat against the devil. Using metaphors derived from military clothing, they are encouraged to:

> [v10]be strong in the Lord and in the strength of his power.[v11] Put on the whole armour of God, so that you may be able to stand against the wiles of the devil.[v12] For our struggle is not against enemies of blood and flesh, but against the rulers, against the authorities, against the cosmic powers of this present darkness, against the spiritual forces of evil in the heavenly places.[v13] Therefore take up the whole armour of God, so that you may be able to withstand on that evil day, and having done everything, to stand firm.[v14] Stand therefore, and fasten the belt of truth around your waist, and put on the breastplate of righteousness.[v15] As shoes for your feet put on whatever will make you ready to proclaim the gospel of peace.[v16] With all of these, take the

11 Unless otherwise indicated, the English translation of biblical texts is from the *New Revised Standard Version of the Bible* (Thomas Nelson Publishers, 1991) 2 Cor 10:3–4.

> shield of faith, with which you will be able to quench all the flaming arrows of the evil one.[v17] Take the helmet of salvation, and the sword of the Spirit, which is the word of God.[12]

The struggle of good and evil here in Ephesians takes on more cosmic, universal proportions. These are the unseen 'principalities' and 'powers', cosmic dark forces mirrored in tribal and military conflicts experienced in the Greco-Roman world and imposed by Rome's military might. Defence against such forces must be spiritual. Metaphors derived from battle armour provide the writer with the kind of spiritual resistance needed.

4 Mark 3.20–27 (with parallels in Matthew 12.24–29 and Luke 11.15–22) is a gospel story in which Jesus is accused of being possessed by Beelzebul, 'the prince of demons' (Mk 3.22) because he exorcises evil spirits. As is stated:

> [v22]And the scribes who came down from Jerusalem said, 'He has Beelzebul, and by the ruler of the demons he casts out demons.'[v23] And he called them to him, and spoke to them in parables, 'How can satan cast out satan?[v24] If a kingdom is divided against itself, that kingdom cannot stand.[v25] And if a house is divided against itself, that house will not be able to stand.[v26] And if satan has risen up against himself and is divided, he cannot stand, but his end has come.[v27] But no one can enter a strong man's house and plunder his property without first tying up the strong man; then indeed the house can be plundered.[13]

Jesus' response raises the obvious flaw in the argument of his aggressors: if he is casting out demons, which they acknowledge, then how will the kingdom of satan remain? It is at war within itself. It is being undermined and will come to an end (Mark 3.26). The imagery of contestation and combat is clearly present.

5 In another gospel, the Gospel according to Luke, Jesus instructs his disciples. He rhetorically asks them:

> [v51]'Do you think that I have come to bring peace to the earth? No, I tell you, but rather division![v52] From now on five in one household will be divided, three against two and two against three;[v53] they will be divided: father against son and son against father, mother against daughter and daughter against mother, mother-in-law against her daughter-in-law and daughter-in-law against mother-in-law.'[14]

It appears that Jesus is explicitly describing his world-wide mission in terms of bringing about division rather than peace. This will split up families and exacerbate tensions between household members caught up in an evil that permeates their world.

12 Ibid Ephesians 6.10–17.

13 Ibid Mark 3.22–27.

14 Ibid Luke 12:51–53.

6 In the same gospel in another passage several chapters later, in Luke 14.26, Jesus uses the language of 'hate' to describe the attitude which disciples must have towards members of their own family: 'Whoever comes to me and does not *hate* father and mother, wife and children, brothers and sisters, yes, and even life itself, cannot be my disciple.'

7 Later in Luke's Gospel, Jesus prepares his disciples for the traumatic events that are about to unfold in the gospel's dénouement in his suffering and death. He asks them:

> 'When I sent you out without a purse, bag, or sandals, did you lack anything?' They said, 'No, not a thing.'v36 He said to them, 'But now, the one who has a purse must take it, and likewise a bag. And the one who has no sword must sell his cloak and buy one.v37 For I tell you, this scripture must be fulfilled in me, "And he was counted among the lawless"; and indeed what is written about me is being fulfilled.'v38 They said, 'Lord, look, here are two swords.' He replied, 'It is enough.'[15]

Here Jesus seems to condone violence. He encourages his disciples to become armed with swords, steadying themselves for the battle that is about to be waged against the forces of evil arraigned against him and his entourage.

A literal reading of all three texts from Luke's Gospel portrays Jesus in a manner that contradicts his usual portrait as loving and peace-making. They reinforce the convictions of those Christians who consider the world locked in a cosmic struggle over good and evil, a conviction held by the author of Ephesians. These Christians see themselves as participants in a divine battle in which they must combat evil powers wherever these appear. Luke's Jesus seems to condone violence and encourage these Christians to be ready and armed for conflict, even prepared to 'hate' members of their own families.

All the above texts are fodder for Christians with a militant attitude in a non-Christian world. The seven New Testament passages provide them with the biblical foundation to reject the religious 'other', even members of their own family who do not subscribe to their particular Christian values. When these are cherry picked out of their original context they can contribute to an overall negative and combative picture endorsed by those who read and interpret the Bible from fundamentalist and literalist perspectives.

When these passages are further placed alongside the stories of Israel's war and victory against its enemies in the Old Testament (for example, in Joshua 6–10), Jesus' antagonism against his religious opponents in the gospels and the *oi iudaoi* in the Gospel of John (unhelpfully translated in English Bibles, without explanation or historical context, as 'the Jews'), his numerous exorcisms expelling demonic spirits from human beings, wind and water, and other Jesus sayings that seem to encourage violence – then it is possible that a particular picture could

15 Ibid Luke 22:35–38.

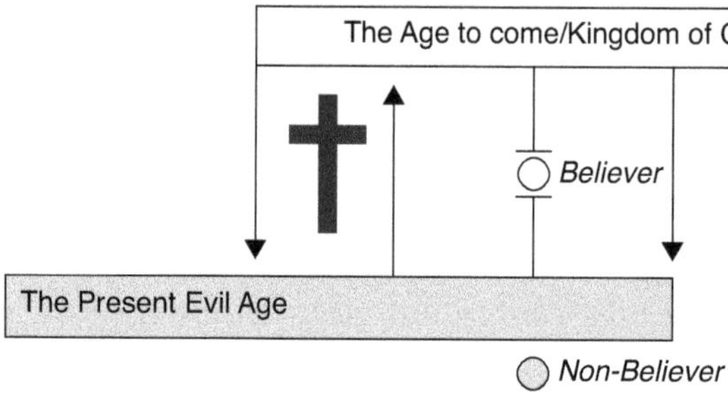


*Figure 4.1* Arnold's 'Two Ages'[16]

emerge. It might seem that the Bible affirms violence, revealed most explicitly in Jesus' deeds and words, in which Christians will be similarly engaged. This biblical snapshot would easily provide enthusiastic Christians with the kind of ammunition to wage 'war' against people who do not share their point of view and are judged evil or ambassadors for satan. There is simply no room for the 'other', including social, theological and cultural difference.

Arnold's figure of the 'Two Ages' (Figure 4.1) clearly sums up these insights:

There is more in Arnold's figure than meets the eye. It is theologically informative and illustrates the tension that exists between the present world, regarded as evil, and a future age to come. This is considered when the 'Kingdom of God' will be present and fully revealed. Two things stand out: Arnold's understanding of 'The Age to Come /Kingdom of God' and 'The Present Evil Age'.

Mainstream theologians would consider this language of 'kingdom' points to the reality of the human experience of God within the present cultural, environmental and historical situation.[17] They usually posit a 'now' but 'not yet' approach. They consider that God's 'Kingdom' (or 'Reign') is present now, but not fully revealed. It awaits its complete revelation at the end of time (the 'eschaton'). Evangelicals, on the other hand, look completely to the future.

Arnold reflects the more evangelical Christian perspective. His theological viewpoint is dualistic. It splits the heavenly from the earthly into two realms, divorced from each other with present-day Christians caught between the two.

16 Arnold, above n 8, 21.

17 Illustrative of a mainstream theological perspectives on 'Kingdom' theology are Ben Witherington, *Imminent Domain: The Story of the Kingdom of God and Its Celebration* (WB Eerdmans Publishing, 2009), Mary Ann Beavis, *Jesus & Utopia: Looking for the Kingdom of God in the Roman World* (Fortress Press, 2006), Elliott C Maloney, *Jesus' Urgent Message for Today: The Kingdom of God in Mark's Gospel* (Continuum, 2004), Richard A Horsley, *Jesus and Empire: The Kingdom of God and the New World Disorder* (Fortress Press, 2003) and Albert Schweitzer, *The Kingdom of God and Primitive Christianity* (Adam & Charles Black, 1968).

The 'Kingdom of God' is totally aligned with 'The Age to Come'. It is purely future oriented and apparently absent in the present. This interpretation of the cosmic drama is one of ongoing tension – which could be interpreted as 'warfare' – illustrated by the arrows that point in both directions, down and up. Two come down from 'The Age to Come', which will dominate and succeed eventually, over 'The Present Evil Age'. This only has one arrow moving upwards. The believer is caught in this in-between time, between the two movements.

The layer representing 'The Present Evil Age' deserves special comment. It is made up of bricks and contrasts to the lighter (whiter) upper realm with which it is in tension. This is the stratum of dross, earthliness, materialism and evil. Most significant is the identification of this earthly level with the 'Non-Believer'. This is not an inclusive term implying all those who have no religious faith, irrespective of whether they are Christian or non-Christian. Arnold's 'Non-Believer' are all those who are not *Christian* believers. Thus all those from other monotheistic traditions (Islam and Judaism) and other religious traditions are not connected with God's Kingdom. These 'non-believers' are yet to possess Christian faith to move into the upper heavenly realm. Dualism and Christocentrism dominate this interpretation of the cosmos. There is no room for the 'other' in this defined world. Those who do not hold Christian faith are 'other' and belong to the lower realm distinctly separate from the 'Age to Come'. Arnold's diagram clearly makes an exclusivist Christocentricism the essential feature of evangelical theology.

## *The nature of biblical texts*

Christian fundamentalists and some Evangelicals regard biblical texts a blue-print for contemporary living. In their view the Bible considers Christianity, anthropology and cosmology simply and easily applicable to the challenges of modern life without the need for critical interpretation. Their approach is monochromatic. They view biblical texts monolithically, that is, without any need for literary, cultural or historical criticism. In their view, the texts speak plainly; they require no interpretation. For them, the Bible offers trans-cultural and trans-temporal universal truth; it addresses local and contemporary issues without the need for any of the critical approaches developed by biblical scholars. This blue-print approach affects the way they view the 'other' and stands in contrast to a dialogical, critical approach taken by the majority of biblical scholars and theologians.

Christians from more mainstream theological contexts regard their Scriptures (the 'Old Testament' and the 'New Testament') as normative for living. They consider that the Scriptures are the written reflections of monotheistic believers' experience of God revealed in the story of Israel (the 'Old Testament') and the words and deeds of Jesus (the 'New Testament'). The biblical writings are not CCTV recordings of what actually took place, when it immediately happened – as some believe. One generation passed on to the next the memory of this divine encounter in oral form through story, song, fable, poetry, wisdom sayings and sagas. In some instances (in the final written formation of the Old Testament and the gathering of the different strands of tribal and family memory) this took place over hundreds of years. In the New Testament, this happened over several generations of Jesus followers. They remembered and spoke about his teachings and actions, but reflected upon them in the light of their present local and cultural situations, sometimes decades and thousands of kilometres removed from the historical and cultural context of the Galilean Jesus of Nazareth. They formulated for their day what biblical scholars today would call 'a hermeneutic'. We need to engage the story of Jesus and his teaching for our day.

An appreciation of these three aspects of the biblical traditioning process – from event, to oral–aural expression, to a final written form – is key for assisting a helpful and balanced understanding of the texts discussed above. This moves us away from the literalist approach adopted by Christians who interpret the world in militant, dualistic and exclusive Christocentric terms. An appreciation of biblical texts, as with any text and especially ancient texts, needs to take into consideration 'three worlds': the world *of* the text itself, the world *behind* the text and the world *in front of* the text.

- A consideration of the world *of* the text is a literary study of the writing itself: its literary structure and form, position in the overall work, themes and philological characteristics of the original language (in the case of the Bible, its Hebrew and Greek).
- Recognition of the world *behind* the text enables the interpreter to be sensitive to the cultural, historical and social matrix in which the text was written. This approach recognises that the biblical text is not a 21st century literary product, nor trans-cultural and trans-historical. The text is particular to time and place, with limited scientific, cosmological, cultural, patriarchal and androcentric perspectives.
- Affirming the importance of the world *in front of* the text allows ancient texts that come from a different time and place to speak to the present situation in which the interpreter finds herself. This means that there is not a 1:1 correspondence between the world and social concerns of biblical writers and our own. The theological insights drawn out of a different time and culture can critically address our own world. Our questions, the contemporary situations about which we are concerned – our environmental crisis, poverty, terrorism, the global movement of peoples seeking asylum – are the issues we bring to our engagement with the biblical text. This does not mean that these ancient authors had the same issues and concerns. Rather, the manner in which their faith in a God in whom they believed was revealing and active in their world enabled them to respond faithfully and authentically to what was happening in their world. It led them to profound insights into God, humanity and ethical conduct. These theological truths, gleaned from these ancient sacred writings, can illuminate the contemporary interpreter in her quest for religious meaning. The illumination occurs through a dialogical hermeneutic, in a backwards-forwards movement as the interpreter moves between her world and the Bible's (see Figure 4.2). In this way, greater clarity emerges to guide the conduct of the believer.

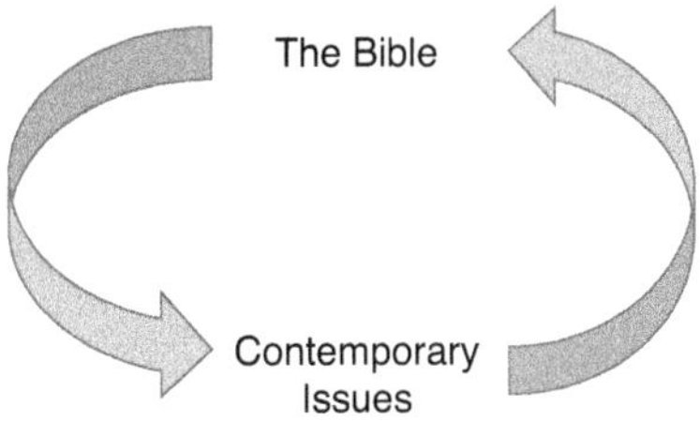


*Figure 4.2* The Dialogical Hermeneutic

For Christians who believe that the Bible is normative this dialogical dynamic is critical. As with all dialogue, the interpreter 'listens' deeply and respectfully to the world *of* and *behind* a text that comes out of an ancient Mediterranean context very different from her own. In the process the interpreter listens to and receives from this 'other', from the biblical text itself. What emerges in this 'listening' engages the interpreter's life and world in a dialogical inter-textual process. One text, the biblical text, engages the other 'text' – the personal, social, historical context of the interpreter's world. This expands the meaning of 'text' beyond writing. It is the comprehensive realities and culture, the 'weavings' (Latin, '*textere*' = 'to weave') of an individual and her community. Society and culture become the inter-texts in this dynamic that allows meaning to surface through engaging the various dimensions that have shaped us.[18]

The interpreter does not presume that the text's world matches her own. Dialogue is a two-way process. The interpreter brings her world into dialogue with the value-laden world of the text's authors. Through a backwards–forwards dynamic, insight emerges for the interpreter who believes that this insight has important, formative meaning for present human existence. This is, it is believed, the nature of sacred texts. They offer norms for human existence and touch into the core of the religious fabric of humans in their quest for happiness and communion. In our engagement with these sacred texts, we touch into the faith convictions of those who formulated them out of an oral tradition handed down from one generation to the next until the need arose to encapsulate these convictions and truths into written form. The time-conditioned, culturally limited human expression of these convictions is what the North American biblical scholar Sandra Schneiders calls the 'Word of God.' She describes it this way:

> 'Word of God' . . . is a metaphor for the totality of divine revelation, especially as it is expressed in Jesus. The Bible is a witness to the human experience of

18 On the influence of ancient texts and cultures on biblical texts see Loveday C Alexander, 'The Relevance of Greco-Roman Literature and Culture to New Testament Study' in Joel B Green (ed), *Hearing the New Testament: Strategies for Interpretation* (W B Eerdmans Publishing, 2010) 85–101.

> divine revelation. In other words, it is a limited, biased, human testimony to a limited experience of God's self-gift. The Bible is not divine revelation nor does it contain divine revelation. It contains the necessarily inadequate, sometimes even erroneous, verbal expression of the experience of divine revelation of those who are privileged subjects of that gift of God . . . The Bible is literally the word of human beings about their experience of God.[19]

### *Evil spirits in the ancient Mediterranean world*

An appreciation of the nature of biblical texts and their three worlds provides the context to reflect critically on those texts above which have been used as support for Christian warfare and a rejection of the religious and cultural 'other'. At the heart of the issue is a particular worldview which the biblical writers hold. This is the world *behind* the texts. To forget this world leads to a superimposition of an ancient anthropology on to our own.

The writers of these texts lived in a 1st century CE Greco-Roman Mediterranean cultural context. They believed in the existence of good and bad spirits which permeated the total cosmos. The Old Testament presents satan as a member of the heavenly court and supernatural accuser or adversary (as in Zechariah 3.1–10, Job 1–2 and 1 Chronicles 21.1). Later, those living around the Greco-Roman Mediterranean basin absorbed a cosmic mythology that influenced the New Testament writers, in which a cosmic battle waged between good and evil. Satan now became independent of the heavenly court exercising autonomous demonic power. The dualism of Persian Avestan Zoroastrianism and other ancient near eastern mythologies formulated during the inter-testamental period (between the time of the completion of the Old Testament and before the beginning of the New) was the catalyst for this development of an individual ruler of a demonic kingdom – the devil or satan. This being with other evil spirits caused sickness, disease and ethnic conflicts.[20] The task of the magician, holy person or prophet was to release the person from these spirits.

In the biblical texts we are considering, this ancient Mediterranean anthropology and pre-enlightened world view was prominent. Their authors presumed the presence of the devil or satan. Like those who lived around them in the circum-Mediterranean basin without the benefits of modern medicine and psychiatry, Jesus followers assumed that the struggles, suffering, maladies and any form of social marginalisation that they experienced were the result of evil spirits.

Jesus, too, was a person of his own time and culture. He believed similarly in the presence of satan and malevolent spirits. He also knew himself as a healer with power over these spirits to restore all humanity and creation to their divinely

19 Sandra Schneiders, *Beyond Patching: Faith and Feminism in the Catholic Church* (Paulist Press, 1991) 50.

20 Duane F Watson, 'Devil,' *Anchor Bible Dictionary*, volume 2 (Doubleday, 1992), 183 (article, 183–184).

intended wholeness. The gospel writers affirmed the ancient biblical vision of *shalom*, of peace, revealed in Jesus' act of restoration through his deeds of power and exorcisms. Here was God's 'reign' made visible as Jesus overcame chaos and the evil that caused it. 'For people in Israel, as for people everywhere in antiquity,' writes Gerhard Lohfink:

> chaos threatened on all sides. It revealed itself in a variety of illnesses, in lameness, in disfigurement, in wounds, in social isolation, in the powers of nature, and above all in death . . . In Jesus' time people were convinced that demonic powers were a constant danger. The most horrible power of all was death – and it too was occupied by demons. Hebrews 2.14 says that the devil has the power of death. When Jesus heals sick people, drives out demons, calms the waters, and raises the dead, the basic happening is the same in all cases: he confronts the powers of chaos, conquers demons, heals the damaged and distorted world, so that the reign of God may become visible and creation attain to the integrity and beauty God intends for it.[21]

The New Testament passages considered earlier reflect this world view. They acknowledge the presence of demons and the human struggle for *shalom*. For 1st century CE Jesus followers addressed by these writings, Jesus reveals God's power to overcome the demonic particularised in the devil or satan. The critique levelled at Jesus from his antagonists in Mark 3.20–27 affirms this. They label him as 'the prince of demons' because of his ability to exorcise evil spirits and dethrone satan. His success in this ministry attracts criticism from religious leaders who want to control his healing largesse. They consider him 'prince of demons'.

The writers of 2 Corinthians and Ephesians also come out of this pre-scientific worldview. They see a cosmic interconnectivity between the heavenly and earthly spheres. What occurs amongst human beings on earth's stage is a microcosm of the cosmos. The conflict which Jesus has with evil (symbolised in his conflict with satan) plays itself out celestially. These are 'the authorities . . . the cosmic powers of this present darkness . . . the spiritual forces of evil in the heavenly places' identified in Ephesians 6.12. Against these, the Ephesians writer suggests, Jesus followers have to defend themselves by putting on the armour of faith.

The author of Ephesians identifies existential and cosmic conflict as the power against which Jesus followers must protect themselves. Contemporary theologians would identify a similar reality. This is the fracture that occurs within human beings and mirrored in the wider culture. We know the pain (or debilitating 'power') that comes from this deep social crisis. Lohfink suggests that this crisis comes:

> from guilt, namely, from the self-betrayal, lies, egoisms, recklessness, meanness, and heartlessness of society. These things not only happen again and again; they settle themselves in the world in the form of a damaged and

21 Gerhard Lohfink, *Jesus of Nazareth: What He Wanted, Who He Was* (Liturgical Press, 2012) 134.

> distorted state of things that no individual can overcome . . . [e]vil in history and society can gather itself to a 'potency,' and it very often takes hold precisely of the weakest and objectifies itself in them in the symptoms that are common to a particular society. The illnesses thus produced can be so powerful that the sick persons require help from outside themselves – possibly through a word of power that transposes them into a new situation.[22]

This desire for a transposing power that brings security leads to a consideration of the three passages from Luke's Gospel, Luke 12.51–53; 14.26; and 22.35–38, concerned with 'division', 'hatred' and purchasing 'a sword'. Their proper interpretation must take into account the setting of the Jesus household envisaged by Luke's Gospel (the world *behind* the text), the literary context in which these pericopes occur (the world *of* the text) and the original intention behind the evangelist's use of certain expressions, like 'hate', (world *of* the text) that seem shocking to us today.

### *Luke's Greco-Roman world*

Luke's Greco-Roman late 1st century CE audience seeks to be reassured. The evangelist affirms that their chronological separation from the time of Jesus of Nazareth and its cultural location distant from Galilee (perhaps Syrian Antioch or Macedonia) do not compromise authentic discipleship. They seek reassurance that their lives, in a different time and place, are gospel expressions faithful to the spirit of Jesus of Nazareth. This desire for theological affirmation is reflected in Luke's opening lines, in Luke 1.4. Several times in the gospel Jesus encourages their alertness to God's presence in their day-to-day lives. This is the emphasis in Luke 12 where Jesus also highlights the realities with which they are dealing. This comes in the form of a warning and is the focus of Luke 12.51–53.

Viewed from this perspective, these words are not direct quotations from the historical Jesus of Nazareth accurately scripted and remembered word-for-word for Luke's later gospel audience. They are the evangelist's reflections drawn faithfully from the originating spirit of Jesus of Galilee. These words from Luke's Jesus reflect the tensions that will emerge in a household that does not conform to the socially prescribed lines of Greco-Roman domestic hierarchy. The gospel seeks to reconfigure the autocratic and patrilineal conventions that reinforce social divisions. Those who belong to Luke's renewed Jesus household would experience rejection and division, especially in those households where its members were not all Jesus followers. In this sense, Jesus brings division rather than peace. Division is not the *intention* of Jesus' mission; it is a *consequence* of what happens to those who are faithful to his vision of social inclusivity.

Fidelity to Jesus is what is being asked of the disciple, in the midst of conflict and the temptation to compromise the expected demands of status and honour

22 Ibid 144.

reflected in household relationships. When Jesus tells his disciples in the second Lukan text, Luke 14.26, that they are to *hate* their natural family and even their own lives, the language is deliberately strong and evocative. It demands critical reflection on what Jesus is actually telling his disciples, especially in the light of other contradictory sayings about enemy love, discussed below. What is at stake here is not emotional rejection or psychological abnegation of family members or one's being, but the commitment in loyalty to Jesus. As Johnson observes, '[t]he point is not how one feels towards parents and family but one's effective attitude when it comes to a choice for the kingdom.'[23]

The third Lukan text that we considered, Luke 22:35–38, has Jesus order his disciples to arm themselves, purchase a sword and prepare for battle. The context in which this passage occurs anticipates Jesus' arrest in the next scene, his trials and eventual execution. At the heart of this is Luke's theology about a God who cares for all, especially in times of trial. This is a consistent theme through the gospel: disciples are invited to commune with this God rather than rely on their own inventiveness, material possessions and a spirit of wealth that offers false security and ephemeral refuge. They are encouraged to trust in God. They will never need a sword!

Luke's Jesus reminds his disciples about this God whom they are constantly invited to trust: 'When I sent you out without a purse, bag, or sandals, did you lack anything?' They said, 'No, not a thing' (Luke 22.35). In light of this, the verses that follow (especially, 'the one who has no sword must sell his cloak and buy one' – Luke 22.36) must cohere with Luke's consistent theological teaching up to this point. Jesus is not offering literal encouragement to purchase a sword, but prepares his disciples and Luke's attentive audience for what will happen. The metaphor 'sword' anticipates the conflict for which Jesus followers must ready themselves. As one Lukan commentator says about this saying:

> the hyperbole of the statement should be obvious. Selling one's outer garment for a sword was not a literal but a symbolic point: they are entering a state of testing in which they will be without external resources and in danger.[24]

Jesus' words echo Luke's realistic awareness of the time of testing for all disciples throughout history engaged in difficult social situations. This interpretation also aligns with Jesus' instruction earlier in the gospel about enemy love, in Luke 6.27–36, a teaching to which we now turn.

### *Love of enemy (Luke 6.27–36)*

As flagged earlier, this teaching can also be a 'text of terror', but not from the point of view of encouraging aggressive behaviour or Christian warfare, as the

23 Luke Timothy Johnson, *The Gospel of Luke* (Liturgical Press, 1991) 229–30.
24 Ibid 347.

above seven passages have been interpreted. Luke 6.27–36 is 'text of terror' from another perspective. It could be interpreted as promoting a self-deprecating attitude that encourages physical abuse and poverty: when the aggressor strikes the cheek of the disciple she is encouraged to offer the other also! The text then becomes terror-producing for the Christian disciple who interprets the passage literally:

> [v27]But I say to you who hear, love your enemies, do good to those who hate you,[v28] bless those who curse you, pray for those who abuse you.[v29] To the one who strikes you on the cheek, offer the other also; and from the one who takes away your coat do not withhold even your shirt.[v30] Give to everyone who begs you, and of the one who takes away your possessions do not ask them again . . .[v35] [b]ut love your enemies, and do good, and lend expecting nothing in return, and your reward will be much, and you will be children of the most high who is kind (*chrestos*) to the ungrateful (*acharistoi*) and evil.[v36] Be compassionate (*oiktirmos*) as your father is compassionate.[25]

At first glance, Jesus seems to encourage the impossible – a positive emotional response of communion and affection from the wronged one towards the wrongdoer. The abused seem expected to dismiss the hurt put on them by their enemy and welcome more suffering and humiliation as they 'offer the other cheek'. This, however, is not Luke's intended meaning.

The evangelist offers practical wisdom in a world of violence and agonistic relationships in which people are hurt and viciously treated. Gospel householders would well know this experience. Jesus' teaching recommends a proactive response that subverts the aggressor and moves those aggrieved into the support of a community that will act on their behalf. As one Lukan commentator suggests, Jesus 'is asking people to accept an inversion of the world order, to agree with him that the world order has been inverted, and to act accordingly'.[26]

Eight noteworthy features about this teaching frequently escape the notice of those who take Jesus' injunctions literally and formulate them into a 'doormat' form of privatised spirituality. These features concern a realistic unsentimental appreciation of 'enemy love', the agential role of the gospel community in non-violent conduct and the mode of exposing the enemy to God's presence:

1 Luke's Jesus is not asking disciples to 'love the enemy' with an unrealistic affection that overlooks their need for well-being and dismisses the harm done to them. This is not about having naive feelings of warmth for their adversary.
2 The teaching is not advocating a form of ethical action which the abused disciple is expected to conduct privately. The plural form of address that

25 My translation of Luke 6.27–30, 35–36.
26 Joel Green, *The Gospel of Luke* (WB Eerdmans Publishing Co, 1997) 272.

permeates the teaching, the plural 'you' in the Greek text, locates the response to the enemy within the household of Jesus followers. The kinship network that operates in this ancient Greco-Roman household environment means that the response comes from the full community of disciples, affected by the hurt suffered by one of their number. The communal response becomes the response of the aggrieved disciple.[27]

3 Jesus householders are encouraged to act in a proactive, agential manner that surprises the enemy. Their pre-emptive action breaks the cycle of challenge-riposte as the expected conventional mode of interaction when people are dishonoured. The response subverts and disarms the possibility of ongoing violence. The enemy experiences deeds of love and goodness, rather than reciprocal actions of hatred socially prescribed and meted out by the representatives of the aggrieved party. Instead they are commanded to 'love your enemies, do good to those who hate you' (Luke 6.27). This is a directive, not a request.

4 The injunctions, 'bless those who curse you, pray for those who abuse you' (Luke 6.28), brings God into the interaction. The actions of 'blessing' and 'praying' are theologically intentional and explicit. The act of converting enemies and moving them to reconciliation becomes God's act. It not the total responsibility of the wounded household. Its conduct and response are the means by which God acts.

5 The most misinterpreted imperative follows next: 'To the one who strikes you on the cheek, offer the other also'. This could be inferred as encouraging ongoing victim abuse. However, the act of offering the other cheek is a culturally surprising act of non-violent retaliation and passive resistance that would have the potential to disarm the enemy. The 'other cheek' is the side of the face that is most protected. When this cheek is offered in an act of non-violent assertiveness the assailant is unable to attack it directly. Violence deescalates and aggression diffused.

6 The active response to violent aggression through 'offering the other cheek' is further reinforced by the way disciples are encouraged to let go of clothing and other possessions demanded by their opponents. These acts of radical non-retaliatory relinquishment, 'expecting nothing in return', further disarm and disrupt the conventional expectations of the enemy. It deliberately breaks the 'tit-for-tat' socially predictable response that would spiral into violence.

7 Luke's play on Greek in Luke 6.35, of *chrestos* ('kindness') and *acharistoi* ('lack of kindness'), subtly hints at the presence of the *Christos* ('Christ')

27 Within the contemporary context and the growing recognition of the prevalence of domestic violence, this is important teaching from Luke. Let me make it clear. Luke is *not* advocating that the victim continues to allow herself to remain a victim, or that the onus of action remains with the one abused. The primary responsibility for conversion and reconciliation remains with the aggressor called to conversion and reconciliation. Luke's teaching encourages the agency of the faith community to initiate this change in the abuser through the various strategies it employs outlined by the evangelist in this part of the gospel.

in the deeds of kindness which disciples perform in the face of opposition and aggression.

8 The final imperative in Luke's teaching on enemy love encourages disciples to act with a spirit of compassion – *oiktirmos* (Greek): 'Be compassionate (*oiktirmos*) as your father is compassionate' (Luke 6.36). *Oiktirmos* and Luke's other word for acting with compassion or mercy (*splagnizomai* – in 7.13; 10.33; and 15.20) reflect the Hebrew word for 'womb' (*rachem*). In other words, Jesus' disciples are invited to act with a womb-like sense of communion for those who struggle and suffer, including those who act with violence. They are to mirror the reaction that God has for all creation and humanity, good and bad alike, typified by mercy and compassion. *Oiktirmos* reveals the nature of God.

This brief exegesis of Luke 6.27–36 completes a study of some of key 'texts of terror' frequently misunderstood by Christians.

## Conclusion

As I have argued, the literal interpretation of these passages support an approach that rejects engagement with the non-Christian 'other' but seeks to bring about a conversion to Christ through aggressive missionary encounters that, in some instances, have led to violence. Without careful interpretation, the last text, Luke 6.27–36, can also become a text of terror that encourages a passive acceptance of physical abuse and violence. In public discourse, as commentators reflect on the cause of violence and terrorism, religion is frequently blamed. My reflections have focussed explicitly and exclusively on Christian biblical interpretations that present the Bible literally. Adherents of this form of biblical fundamentalism superimpose an ancient world view on to our era of post-Enlightenment without discrimination or critical understanding. They presume the Bible's anthropology and cosmology to be universal divine revealed truths applicable to every time and culture.

Most Christians understand the Bible as 'normative' for living. They take biblical teaching and the words of Jesus in the gospels of Mark, Matthew and Luke as important sources of existential wisdom. The manner in which these teachings and words are interpreted today from the various hermeneutical stances adopted by different Christian groups shape the pragmatics of relationships and the validity of religious dialogue.

My focus has been on some of the most provocative, abused and misunderstood texts of the New Testament. In these difficult texts or 'hard' sayings Jesus seems to encourage 'warfare', division, 'hatred' and rejection of the 'other'. Other sayings concern themselves with enemy love. Both groups of sayings, taken out of context and given a particular literalist slant, could reinforce an unequivocal stance by which Christians engage in self-harm through 'turning the other cheek,' hatred of members of their own family who disagree with their religious position and rejection of non-Christians. They would support a sectarian form of religious protectionism that considers that the only mode of engagement is one of forced conversion and aggressive proselytism.

The negative and potentially destructive stereotypes of the religious 'other' derived from a particular biblical interpretation can be addressed through the methods and insights derived from contemporary critical biblical scholars. Their voice needs to be heard. They would suggest a number of counterbalancing propositions:

- *Appreciate the original setting of sacred texts*: In interpreting religious texts, and for the Christian this means the Bible, understanding the originating social and cultural context of their writing is important. An appreciation of the world *behind* the text enables the contemporary interpreter to realise that her world circumscribed by particular values is not the same world out of which sacred texts emerge. This leads to an attitude of humility in the interpreter and the recognition that she is not the possessor of the fullness of knowledge. There is more to learn. Humility then becomes the foundation that can lead to genuine dialogue with the 'other' who may not share the same culture, religious disposition or even chronology.
- *Recognise the human conditioning of religious texts.* Biblical texts are not 'ready-made' receptacles of divine truth that drop from the heavens and require no effort in their interpretation. Sacred texts, as Schnieders has indicated, reflect the experience of human beings in their encounter with God. These texts are human expressions of divine encounter. This means that they are culturally, historically, scientifically and anthropologically limited expressions conditioned by a particular worldview. The different worldviews need to be respected.
- *Understand different worldviews.* This ancient worldview does not share with us the same understanding of the causes of sickness and other maladies that inflict human beings. For the ancients, as we saw, malevolent spirits were the cause. In our post-enlightened age, bio-medical research brings a different frame of reference for understanding sickness and disease. This difference means that the ancient understanding of evil spirits and the accompanied belief in the existence of the devil cannot be monolithically and literally transferred to our contemporary situation. This requires careful interpretation coherent with contemporary psychiatric and medical practice.
- *Affirm the search for wholeness.* Behind the 'texts of terror' that I have focussed upon lay the need to understand the causes of evil and sickness. The dualism of an ancient cosmology, the internecine battles conducted by the gods and the conflict between good and bad spirits helped biblical audiences understand their struggle to live good lives and the destructive forces that seem present in their world. They assumed 'possession' which explained why many of them were pushed to the social margins. In the gospels, Jesus exorcised human beings possessed by evil spirits. His actions affirmed that human beings were not, by nature, demonic. He released them from this possession to realise their divinely intended wholeness expressed through social inclusivity.

- *Develop a contemporary hermeneutic of evil.* The gospels' portrait of Jesus' healing ministry offers a key for developing a contemporary hermeneutic on suffering and evil. Our understanding for the causes of human maladies and social unrest may differ from the ancient Mediterraneans. The same underlying social issues, though, exist. We live in a chaotic world that suffers, in which people know distress and addictions. We all desire to be released of our demons and for our world to be restored to beauty. The need for a contemporary form of exorcism is ever present in which people recognise their communion with God who offers release and ultimate happiness.

Lohfink's earlier insights, in reflecting on social crisis that manifest itself in guilt and distortions and create the 'potency' of evil, suggest a contemporary understanding of what ancients would have seen as evil in terms of demonic possession. In both worldviews, ancient and modern, those 'possessed' seek a healing word that releases them and brings them to a new situation in which they feel included and healed. This appreciation of the power of the word returns us to the scenario where this essay began. The evangelising monological word of my Denizli preacher stands in contrast to the kind of word and dialogical process envisaged in diffusing the violent potential of the 'texts of terror' upon which I have focussed.

In conclusion, the clear hermeneutic principle implied in all this underscores the value of dialogue. This lies at the heart of human meaning and personal discovery. The capacity to move backwards and forwards between my world and that of an ancient text, between myself and the religious or cultural 'other', means that I become open to a truth of which I am not its exclusive guardian. For contemporary Jesus followers, the 'other' is not the one who needs Christian conversion. Every human being remains authentically religious and a potential revealer of the sacred presence, even without the Christian 'stamp of approval'. The truth of this can be slowly revealed through a conversation engaged within a spirit of openness and humility. Such a spirit is needed in an age when social upheaval and global fear seem dominant and sacred texts are marshalled to support expressions of religious terrorism and hatred.

## References

Arnold, Clinton E, *Three Crucial Questions about Spiritual Warfare* (Baker, 1997)

Beavis, Mary Ann, *Jesus & Utopia: Looking for the Kingdom of God in the Roman World* (Fortress Press, 2006)

Dalai Lama XIV, *Toward a True Kinship of Faiths: How the World's Religions Can Come Together* (Doubleday Religion, 2010)

Dawkins, Richard, *The God Delusion* (Bantam Press, 2008)

Emanuilov, Rakhamim and Andrey Tshlavsky, *Terror in the Name of Faith: Religion and Political Violence* (Academic Studies Press, 2011)

Gray, Muriel, 'Religion itself is the fount of most evil', *Sunday Herald* (Glasgow), 24 July 2005

Green, Joel B (ed), *Hearing the New Testament: Strategies for Interpretation* (WB Eerdmans Publishing, 2010)

Green, Joel *The Gospel of Luke* (WB Eerdmans Publishing Co, 1997)
Horsley, Richard A, *Jesus and Empire: The Kingdom of God and the New World Disorder* (Fortress Press, 2003)
Institute for Economics & Peace, '2015 Global Peace Index: Measuring Peace, its Causes and its Economic Value', *Institute for Economics and Peace* (2015), (Sydney, New York and Mexico City), available at: <http://economicsandpeace.org/wp-content/uploads/2015/06/Global-Peace-Index-Report-2015_0.pdf>.
Johnson, Luke Timothy, *The Gospel of Luke* (Liturgical Press, 1991)
Juergensmeyer, Mark, *Terror in the Mind of God: The Global Rise of Religious Violence* (University of California Press, 2000)
Lohfink, Gerhard, *Jesus of Nazareth: What He Wanted, Who He Was* (Liturgical Press, 2012)
Maloney, Elliott C, *Jesus' Urgent Message for Today: The Kingdom of God in Mark's Gospel* (Continuum, 2004)
*New Revised Standard Version of the Bible* (Thomas Nelson Publishers, 1991)
Schneiders, Sandra, *Beyond Patching: Faith and Feminism in the Catholic Church* (Paulist Press, 1991)
Schweitzer, Albert, *The Kingdom of God and Primitive Christianity* (Adam & Charles Black, 1968)
Trible, Phyllis, *Texts of Terror: Literary-Feminist Readings of Biblical Narratives* (Fortress Press, 1984)
Wagner, Peter Charles, *Confronting the Powers: How the New Testament Church Experienced the Power of Strategic-Level Spiritual Warfare* (Regal Books, 1996)
Wagner, Peter Charles, *Engaging the Enemy: How to Fight and Defeat Territorial Spirits* (Gospel Light Publications, 1995)
Wagner, Peter Charles, *Hard-Core Idolatry: Facing the Facts* (Wagner Institute Publications, 1999)
Warren, E Janet, '"Spiritual Warfare": A Dead Metaphor?' 2 *Journal of Pentecostal Theology* (2012) 278
Watson, Duane F, 'Devil,' *Anchor Bible Dictionary*, volume 2 (Doubleday, 1992)
Witherington, Ben, *Imminent Domain: The Story of the Kingdom of God and Its Celebration* (WB Eerdmans Publishing, 2009)

# 5 Weathering the storm

## Shari'a in Nigeria from the earliest times to the present

*Ibrahim Haruna Hassan al-Wasewi*

### Introduction

In 2010, Pew researchers ranked Nigeria as the first, and in 2015 as the second, most religious country in the world; which Nigerians themselves believe is easily evident if religious identities and religious conflicts are the key issues of consideration. Many writers have identified the struggle for the implementation of Shari'a in Nigeria in the struggle for religious identity and as a main factor of religious conflict and insurgency in the country.[1] Lacking any official census figures, the Muslim percentage of the country's population is contested in particular by the Christian population who believe it should at best be fairly divided between the two faiths. However, an American Professor of Political Science who has written much on Islam and Muslims of northern Nigeria rightly noted that, 'Nigeria remains a predominantly Muslim country, but with a recognition of the importance of pluralism'.[2] The Politburo Report, authored by Nigeria's elite class of Muslims and Christians recognise Islam as 'a major political force for many of its adherents'.[3] The Politburo also found that many contributors to the debate (of 1979) on a new social order for the country 'claimed that Muslims constitute a majority of the population of the country.'[4] According to the botched 1983 Census, Nigeria is predominantly a Muslim country. The contesting claim of population superiority also mirrors the contest, albeit much more fierce, for the implementation of Shari'a in some parts of the country and at some levels of the judicial system of the country. There is also a strong argument that Shari'a is the most provocative and divisive dispute in Nigeria's attempts to weld its pluralism into a democratic unified federal republic.

1 See National Institute, *Research Reports on Conflict and Integration in Nigeria*, Kuru-Nigeria (National Institute for Policy and Strategic Studies, 2003); Eghosa Osaghe and Rotimi Seberu, *A History of Identity and Violence in Nigeria*, CRISE Working Paper No 6 (Queen Elizabeth House, 2005); Hakeem Onapajo, 'Politics for God: religion and conflict in democratic Nigeria' (2012) 4 *The Journal of Pan African Studies* 42, 42–66.

2 John N Paden, *Ahmadu Bello Sardauna of Sokoto: Values and Leadership in Nigeria* (Al Hudahuda Publishing Co Ltd, 1986).

3 Political Bureau Report, *Abuja: The Directorate of Social Mobilisation* (Politburo, 1987) 20.

4 Ibid 51.

This chapter addresses the historical development of Shari'a in Nigeria beginning from 16th century empires colonised by the British at the beginning of the 20th century, woven into the Federal Republic of Nigeria by mid-20th century to the present.

## State of the art

Shari'a is one aspect of Islam that has arguably received the most attention, yet also the most biased approach and presentation, and therefore remains the most misunderstood and most controversial. Muslims write with the strong passion of believers while non-Muslims fail to divest themselves of preconceived stereotypes and earlier readings of Orientalism. For instance, Abdulmalik Bappa Mahmud in 1988 demonstrates the believer's passionate approach when claiming to write *A brief history of Shari'a in the defunct Northern Nigeria*, he concentrates on perverse treatment of the Shari'a by the British colonial rulers.[5] He suggests the colonialists were not sincere in their application of the treaty of indirect rule which, according to Mahmud, was a 'treaty of non-interference with religion and Shari'a.'[6] Mahmud claims that, the British found Islam and the Shari'a 'well entrenched in the lives and affairs of the inhabitants' of Northern Nigeria.[7]

In fact, Mahmud continued:

> in all the areas colonized by the British, nowhere was Islam being observed as thoroughly as was the case in Northern Nigeria, except perhaps in some parts of the Arab world . . . the Emir's courts were filled with learned and pious Jurists whose decisions were always based on authorities from the Quran, Hadith or other Islamic law books . . . [d]espite the political wranglings (*sic*) and discord amongsts (*sic*) the Emirs which were brought about by the weakness of the central government at Sokoto, the administration of Sharia continued unabated and the piety of the Judges unaffected.[8]

Mahmud cited court cases to show how the colonialists considered some rulings based on the Sharia as contrary to natural justice while other rulings of customary courts were upheld even though they appeared more absurd.[9]

Mahmud was apparently dissatisfied that the British allowed only the indirect administration of Northern Nigeria 'and the continuance of the then existing

5 Abdulmalik Bappa Mahmud, *A Brief history of Shari'a in the defunct Northern Nigeria* (Jos University Press, 1988).
6 Ibid 2.
7 Ibid 1.
8 Ibid 1–2.
9 Ibid 15–22.

courts of the Shari'a' while other colonies did not enjoy 'such freedom'.[10] Mahmud claims that, the Shari'a was banned in Southern Nigeria, adulterated with English Law in Kenya and 'in Tunisia, Morocco or Algeria, it was the colonial masters who used to sit and administer the Sharia with the Qadis sitting only as advisers . . .'[11] Mahmud further claims that among Muslims, the British 'used to adopt their style of propaganda by separating religion from politics'[12] and that:

> even before the ink with which Lord Lugard signed his promise of none interference with our judicial system dried, he made an announcement for withdrawing their recognition of courts of Sharia . . . when it became impossible for the British to abrogate Sharia by an express provision [they] resorted to making use of their courts which were given unlimited jurisdiction on all matters and persons, and the ambiguous repugnancy clause, to negate Sharia to the extent that even if it was in existence it would be weakened.[13]

Mahmud cited several cases to support his thesis of gradual colonial elimination of the Shari'a. Shari'a in Southwest Nigeria is especially addressed by Muslims from that part of the country such as: Abdul-Fatah Kola Makinde, Ishaq Lakin Akintola, Dawud O S Noibi, Titilola Euba, Murtala Okunola. Philip Ostien, the versatile US expert on Shari'a in Nigeria also addressed the issue in two papers with Abdul-Fatah Kola Makinde.[14] The issues include: the existence of Shari'a in pre-colonial Southern Nigeria, the concern for the colonial government's expunge of Shari'a in that part of the country and the agitation for government implementation of Shari'a as well as private initiatives in its implementation following government failure. Abdul-Fatah Kola Makinde and Philip Ostien demonstrate 'another example of British hostility to Islam, often held to be responsible for the failure of Islamic law to thrive in the predominantly Yoruba southwest . . .'[15] Their paper, they claim, 'is an attempt to restore the context, and thus perhaps to help improve the analysis of the fate of Islamic law in Nigeria's southwest'.[16] Some of the authors also capture this idea.

10 Ibid 2.
11 Ibid 2.
12 Ibid 5.
13 Ibid 9–10.
14 Abdul-Fatah Kola Makinde and Philip Ostien, 'The Independent Sharia Panel of Lagos State' (2011) 25 *Emory International Law Review* 921–44, accessed 30 May 2015, available at: <http://papers.ssrn.com/sol3/papers.cfm?abstract_id=1973946>; Abdul-Fatah Kola Makinde and Philip Ostien, *Legal Pluralism in Colonial Lagos: The 1894 Petition of the Lagos Muslims to Their British Colonial Masters* (Leiden, 2012); Ishaq Lakin Akintola, 'The Implementation of the Sharīah in Nigeria: The Impact on the common folks' in Zakariyau I Oseni (ed), *A Digest on Islamic Law and Jurisprudence in Nigeria* (Darun-Nur, 2003); Dawud O S Noibi, 'Shari'ah in the South West', a paper at the 4th *National Conference of Shari'ah Implementing States*, Kano (December, 2009) and Titilola Euba, 'Muhammad Shitta Bey and the Lagos Muslim Community' (1850–1895)' (1979) 2 *Journal of Islam* 7.
15 Makinde and Ostien, above n 14, 1.
16 Ibid 1.

Sulaiman Kumo represents the few Muslim Northern Nigerian scholars who argued that the British found the Shari'a in the Sokoto Caliphate only a pale imitation of its original self and that indeed the absence of Shari'a eased the British conquest and they in turn helped the Shari'a.[17] Kumo wrote:

> By the mid-eighteen fifties the original zeal and commitment to the truly Islamic system of government had waned; and of the system [. . . of Shari'a] itself only the shell had remained. By that time most of the rulers (who were descendants of the Jihad leaders) had become as corrupt as the erstwhile Habe rulers overthrown by the Jihad. By the time the British forces started their Northern Nigerian campaign in earnest, there was not any 'system' to talk about other than the personal rule of the chiefly circles and warlords in the whole of today's Northern Nigeria. And this situation helped to make Northern Nigeria an easy target for the invading British forces. And in point of fact, the British arrived everywhere virtually as liberators of the masses.
>
> With the advent of the British colonial rule in Nigeria, things changed very much for the better for the Sharia and ironically, the sharia obtained a new lease of life, as a result of the colonial administration's decision to leave what they found on the ground well alone, under the Indirect Rule System . . . the British confined themselves to supervisory role . . . the first enactment on the judicial system by the British, (the Native Courts Proclamation of 1900) was expressly stated to be for the purpose of making provisions 'for the better regulation and control of the native courts.'[18]

Kumo's view is in the minority but seemingly most objective and right. While the British do not believe in the divinity, letter and wisdom of the Shari'a, they actually helped the Shari'a in terms of ensuring better procedures and structures of the judiciary.

Yadudu, a Nigerian Muslim Professor of Constitutional Law, represents Nigerian Muslims who locate Shari'a in Nigeria as a political imperative and a constitutional right. He writes that (i): 'it has become politically incorrect for any leader, in office or aspiring to be, to ignore the unceasing loud clamor for the Shari'a'; (ii) there are evidences of 'an unquenchable desire and determination to submit to the Will of Allah (ie the Shari'a) in private as well as in political spheres'; and (iii) 'it is obvious that the Shari'a implementation in Nigeria is: 'a result of intense public agitation and struggle'.[19] The professor went on to prove the place of the

17 Sulaiman Kumo, 'The Shari'a Issue: Politics and Legal Technicalities' *Abuja: Workshop on Implementation of the Shari'a in a Democracy The Nigerian Experience*, 7–9 July 2004. (See edited and published version of the same paper in H Bobboyi and Mahmood Yakubu (eds), *The Sokoto Caliphate: History and Legacies, 1804–2004* (Arewa House, 2006) 285–96.

18 Bobboyi and Yakubu, above n 17, 286.

19 Auwala Hamisu Yadudu, 'Benefits of Shari'a and Challenges of Reclaiming a Heritage', *International Conference on the Restoration of Shariah in Nigeria*, London, 14 April 2001, 5.

Shari'a in the Nigerian legal system, its legal and constitutional basis and its accord with the democratic process.[20]

Expectedly the approach of Western writers to Shari'a suggests intolerance of the views, beliefs and tradition of the 'other' but at times so hostile as to diminish any sense of the Western claim to understanding and rationality. With regards to Shari'a 21st century Western scholarship fails to divest itself from the doom representation of Islam or indeed of Orientalism as articulated by Edward Said.[21] The Western stereotypes and other encumbrances in fair presentation of the Shari'a issue transcends to non-Muslim writers in Nigeria.

Ricardo Rene Laremont represents those who desire Shari'a to be viewed with the lenses of other law traditions neglecting the Muslims' understanding of Shari'a as not merely a legal system.[22] Thus he examines *Islamic Law and Politics in Northern Nigeria*, through comparative analysis of the meaning of justice in Islamic, Jewish and Continental European and Anglo-American law and by contrasting Nigerian experience with Iran, Saudi Arabia, Indonesia, Malaysia and Sudan.

In the academic realm, Rotimi Suberu is a good representative of Nigerian writers' adverse and unwarranted attacks on Northern Muslims and Shari'a as well as the misrepresentation of Shari'a in Nigeria and the role of northern Muslims' in Nigerian politics. My attention was drawn to Suberu's three papers addressing Shari'a in Nigeria when a graduate student at a leading American university described to her professor Suberu's texts as 'absurd intellectual failure to read through'. The professor who gave them Suberu's papers as reading text for his course apologised. The papers relied too much on church newsletters and market prints for data presented in arguments lacking the simplest demands of academic presentation.

Paul M Lubeck's, 'Nigeria Mapping a Shari'a Restorationist movement' represents recent international publications that demonstrate western writers writing on Shari'a with the real agenda to depict Muslims as the bad guys of an otherwise perfect world.[23] All depict a clever usage of academic objectivity in their writings about Shari'a. Lubeck in his work 'Mapping a Shari'a Restorationist Movement' devoted the first quarter of his paper in a tirade that could have passed for a Nigerian Pentacostal prophet's sermon seeking for bloody strikes at the neck of Muslims in his neighborhood. Writing in 2011, long after Obasanjo had sunk deep into the waters of corruption, Lubeck presents 'Olusegun Obasanjo, a born-again Christian . . . as the democratically elected president of Nigeria's Fourth Republic' set to rescue the country from 'northern generals' and 'Muslim political elites'

20 Ibid 7–11.

21 Edward Said, *Orientalism* (Routledge, 1978).

22 Ricardo Rene Laremont. *Islamic Law and Politics in Northern Nigeria* (Africa World Press; 1st ed, 2011).

23 Paul M Lubeck, 'Nigeria: Mapping a Shari'a Restoration Movement' in Robert W Hefner (ed), *Shari'a Politics Islamic Law and Society in the Modern World* (Indiana University Press, 2011).

who had Nigeria fall 'to pariah status within the international community'.[24] Again writing long after the 1979 elections were contested and won or lost, Lubeck put words into the mouth of 'informed observers to claim that "playing the Shari'a card" . . . "was a radical departure from . . . constructing multi-ethnic coalitions to hold federal power and control the distribution of petro-rents"'.[25] Lubeck let loose ancient hatreds in writing about Muslims in the Nigerian political economy rather than about Shari'a restoration.

Of course regarding Shari'a, the West is not without objective academics who give the Shari'a problem deserved attention such that ensures peaceful co-existence. Other Nigerian authors reject Shari'a simply because it infringes on non-Muslims' rights to sell intoxicants and to practise prostitution amongst Muslims. For example, Mohammed Bolaji, a Muslim from Southwestern Nigeria asserts that, '[a]s a result of the ban on alcohol, lottery, and prostitution, many beer and disco parlors, lottery shops, and other businesses that Christians of southern origins largely run in the north, have been closed down'.[26] While Muslims mostly only report the news (Sodiq, Yushau),[27] Christians including their clerics create horrifying scenarios or construct harm to the southern Christian beer sellers and prostitutes.[28]

Philip Ostien represents one of the few western writers that seek to present the case of Shari'a simply as it is with a tinge of understanding. Ostien argues that as a matter of fact the criminal law of the Shari'a was in use in many parts of northern Nigeria. Ostien wrote massive five massive volumes, *Sharia Implementation in Northern Nigeria 1999–2006: A Sourcebook*.[29] The first volume, *Historical Background* documents the Shari'a reforms of 1958, 1960 and 1962. He describes the 1960 *Northern Nigerian Penal Code* as a 'settlement' accepted by northern Nigerian politicians, ostensibly for the necessary co-existence of the north–south parts of the country;[30] volume two documents Shari'a implementation reports of 1999 to 2006; volume three discusses the aims of the Shari'a states in suppressing social vices; volume four documents the Shari'a penal codes of 1960 and of 2000 and volume five documents the proceedings and judgement according to Shari'a of two famous cases of adultery in 2001–2003.

Danny McCain, an American who spent more than two decades in Nigeria working as a university professor as well as a Christian evangelist yet offers a 'live

24 Ibid 244.
25 Ibid 245.
26 Mohammed H A Bolaji, 'Between Democracy and Federalism: Shari'ah in northern Nigeria and the paradox of Institutional Impetuses' (2013) 59 *Africa Today* 93.
27 Yushau Sodiq, 'Can Muslims and Christians Live Together Peacefully in Nigeria?' (2009) 99 *The Muslim World* 646, 646–688.
28 Matthew Hassan Kukah, *Religion, Power and Politics in Northern Nigeria* (Spectrum Books, 1993).
29 Philip Ostien (ed), *Sharia Implementation in Northern Nigeria 1999–2006: A Sourcebook* (5 Vols, Spectrum Books, 2007).
30 Ibid vol 1:3.

and let's live' approach.[31] He argues that the non-compulsion tenet of the Christian faith demands that where Christians are in the majority, non-Christians should be given 'the right to practice their religion to the extent that it does not infringe upon the rights of others'.[32] Where Christians are in the minority particularly where there is a Muslim majority, McCain argues further, 'Christians should attempt to live at peace with every one (Romans 12:18) and respect not only the laws of the land but the cultural traditions of that society.'[33]

Another Western scholar, Haar objectively overviews the role of religion in general in human life. He submits that: Religion provides people with a life orientation and a moral point of reference; it is also a cultural anchor that provides them with a social identity and places them in a social framework that becomes a safety net if and when the need arises. A core problem in the relations between believers and non-believers, or religionists and secularists, is the lack of understanding among secularists of what religion means to believers and the power – spiritual power – they derive from it.[34]

Parrinder, a British orientalist reflecting on the Nigerian case noted, 'political and religious history have been closely entwined in Islam'.[35]

## The meaning and conceptions of Shari'a

Fitz Herbert Ruxton for example notes that the Islamic law is immutable and that rather than the people making the law it is the law which made, moulded and remoulded the nation (or nations of Islam) and the people.[36] He says both the outer form and inner spirit bear the impress of the one word – Religion; 'there is but the Law and it is the Religious Law including the civil signified in the word *Shari'ah.* It is the only supreme law' emanating from Allah who decreed its main bases in the Qur'an.[37] For Muslims, the Qur'an is the final, perfected and completed of all revelations reaching mankind through Muhammad the Last of the Messengers who explained and exemplified it as recorded in what developed as the *Sunnah* and second source of the law. Ruxton excludes the Shari'ah from the category of regulations or government orders emanating from temporary authority which should in principle respect the disposition and objectives of the *Shari'ah.*[38]

31 Danny McCain, 'Which road to lead beyond the Shari'a controversy? A Christian perspective on Shari'a in Nigeria', Keynote address in Philip Ostien, Jamila M Nasir and Franz Kogelmann (eds), *Comparative Perspectives on Shari'ah in Nigeria* (Spectrum Books Limited, 2005) 7.

32 Ibid 8.

33 Ibid.

34 Gerrie ter Haar, 'Religion: Source of Conflict or Resource for Peace' in Ostien, Nasir and Kogelmann, above n 31, 303.

35 Geoffrey Parrinder, *Africa's Three Religions* (Sheldon Press, 1969) 200.

36 Fitz Herbert Ruxton, *Maliki Law: Mukhtasar of Sidi Khalil* (NP, 1914) 3.

37 Ibid 1.

38 Ibid.

Joseph Sacht also notes that 'the scared law of Islam is an all embracing body of religious duties. Rather than a legal system per se; it comprises on an equal footing ordinances regarding' group faith and every day worship, 'as well as political and (in a narrow sense) legal rules'.[39]

The dominant Muslim argument is that the *Shari'ah* is not, strictly speaking, a legal system alone. For it reaches much deeper into thought, life, and conduct than as purely legal system can aspire to do. It places the individual in his relationship to society, the universe and his Creator (Allah).

Joseph Stiglitz argues that 'Shari'a has come to constitute a red flag, even without the misrepresentations of so-called Islamophobes'.[40] At the most basic level, Shari'a is the Muslim universe of ideals. It is the result of their collective effort to understand and apply the Qur'an and supplementary teachings of the Prophet Muhammad (called Sunna) in order to earn God's pleasure and secure human welfare in this life and attain human salvation in the life to come. While the Qur'an and Sunna are transcendent and unchangeable, Shari'a itself is the negotiated result of competing interpretations.

Shari'a is not just 'rules.' While the common translation, 'Islamic law', is not entirely wrong, it is under-inclusive, for Shari'a includes scores of moral and ethical principles, from honouring one's parents to helping the poor to being good to one's neighbour. Moreover, most of the 'rules' of Shari'a carry no prescribed earthly sanctions at all. The prescriptions covering ablution or eating pork or how to dress are just as much a part of Shari'a as are those governing sale, divorce or jihad. Yet there are no earthly punishments prescribed for those who violate these dictates. Like the bulk of Shari'a's 'rules', reward and punishment in these areas are the preserve of God in the Afterlife.

Stiglitz observes that many Americans have been led to believe that 'Shari'a equals not only rules but criminal punishments' while 'criminal sanctions constitute a tiny sliver of Shari'a'. God-consciousness spawned by Shari'a, not fear of being punished, sustains these ideals.[41] Stiglitz argues that Shari'a 'matters for Muslims because it represents the ideals that define a properly constituted Islamic existence. Islam without Shari'a would be Islam without Islamic ideals.'[42] Thus it is important to understand Muslims' perspectives of Shari'a and tolerate that for co-existence Shari'a continues to inspire Muslims not only in their personal but also social and national lives. While making a case for Shari'a some scholars, for example Yadudu, says, 'speaking as a Muslim . . . all attempts to evolve a political order for the country will be incomplete and perhaps meaningless if they do not include in their agenda the reinvention of the existing legal system.'[43]

39 Joseph Sacht, *An Introduction to Islamic Law* (Oxford University Press, 1964) 1.

40 Joseph E Stiglitz, 'What Is Shariah and Why Does It Matter?', *Huffpost Religion*, 9 November 2010, accessed 7 April 2016, available at: <www.huffingtonpost.com/sherman-a-jackson/what-is-Shari'a-and-why-d_b_710976.html>.

41 Ibid 2.

42 Ibid.

43 Awwalu H Yadudu, 'We Need a New Legal System' in Ibrahim Sulaiman and Siraj Abdulkarim (eds), *On the Political Future of Nigeria* (Hudahuda Publishing Company Ltd, 1988) 2.

The companions (*sahaba*) should have had a tacit idea of the objectives (*Maqasid*) of Shari'a in the sense of understanding that Shari'a is not merely a set of rules but also a system of values, where the rules were the tangible manifestations of those values.[44] The term appeared in the works of a 10th century Islamic scholar al-Tirmidhi al Hakim and again in the works of a 11th century scholar al-Haramayn al-Juwayni. However, as a written down theory *maqasid al-Shari'a* began its development in the works of the 12th century Islamic scholar Al-Ghazali (d 1111) gaining further articulation in the works of 14th century scholars Ibn Taymiyyah (d 1328) and Abu Ishaq Al-Shatibi (d 1388). In modern times, the more voluminous and more scientific work of the Tunisian scholar Muhammad Al-Tahir Ibn Ashur (d 1973) renewed interest in the *Maqasid* approach. At the turn of the century, notable scholars who contributed to the theory include: Mohammad Hashim Kamali, Ahmad Raysuni, Halim Rane, Jasser Auda.[45]

Scholars of maqasid al-Shari'a have addressed one important aspect, among others albeit that which has attracted the most hatred and condemnation of Shari'a by its antagonist – the criminal (*hudud*) punishments. The third category of *maqasid* – the first two being the essential (*daruriyat*) and the complimentary (*hajiyyat*) – the desirable or embellishment (*tahsiniyyah*) addresses the abhorred criminal law of Islam. The scholars assert that the Shari'a desires that: (i) hardship and severity be removed even in executing punishments; (ii) nonetheless the judiciary and the executive should not to be too eager in the enforcement of penalties; (iii) lesser punishment be sought if any doubt about guilt exists. The primary evidence of the foregoing conclusions is the prophetic tradition (*hadith*) related by Al-Hakim and As-Suyuti: '[r]efrain from enforcing *hudud* on Muslims as much as you can. If you find a way out for a Muslim, let him (or her) go, as it is better for the imam (ruler) to wrongly forgive than to wrongly punish.'[46] For the induction and continuous development of the *maqasid al Shari'a* as the highest normative principles of Islamic jurisprudence, Islamic scholars have opened a tract for scholars who desire co-existence and peace in a world necessarily of different belief traditions.

Robert D Crane developed a strategy to rehabilitate religion in America drawing on the principles of *maqsid al-Shari'a*. His main argument is that the task of Muslims in America or elsewhere is to collaborate with other faith traditions in exploring and applying 'the universal principles of compassionate justice'.[47] The

44 Mohammad Hashim Kamali, *The Principles of Islamic Jurisprudence* (Islamic Texts Society, 2003) 3.

45 See, eg, ibid; Ahmad Al-Raysuni, *Imam al-Shatibi's Theory of the Higher Objectives* (International Institute of Islamic Thought, 2005); Halim Rane, 'The Relevance of a Maqasid Approach' (2013) 28 *Journal of Law and Religion* 489; Jasser Auda, *Maqasid al Shari'ah as Philosophy of Islamic Law* (International Institute of Islamic Thought, 2008).

46 For a detailed analysis of this Hadith/maxim see Intisar A Rabb, 'Islamic Legal Maxims as Substantive Canons of Construction: *Ḥudūd*-Avoidance in Cases of Doubt' (2010) 17 *Islamic Law and Society* 63, 63–125.

47 Robert D Crane, 'Maqasid al Shari'ah: A Strategy to Rehabilitate Religion in America', *i-epistemology.net*, 2009, accessed 7 April 2016, available at: <http://i-epistemology.net/v1/

aim of the task, Crane argues is not merely tolerance or diversity, 'but to work toward pluralism, whereby every faith tradition welcomes the others because each has so much to offer in shaping the agenda of society'.[48]

## Shari'a in pre-colonial Northern Nigeria c 8th century to 1960

Islam is said to have arrived in Kanem (areas in present day Borno state of north-eastern Nigeria) just as Islam was reaching its 1st century in the world (ie 8th century of the Christian Era). The harbingers were Ummayyad refugees flying from the persecutions of the Abbasids who toppled them from the reign of power of the Islamic caliphate in the early 2nd century and were said to have reached and settled in Kanem.[49] Early historical records (for example Ibn Fartu)[50] show that Sayf Ibn Dhi Yazid (Yazan), a 7th century Yamani Arab founded the Sayfawa dynasty believed to be one of the longest in the world (800–1846 CE) which ruled the Kanem-Borno empire. Indeed, many writers as shown below agree that Kanem was born and developed as Kanem and later Bornu with Islam.[51] Palmer quoting very early Arabic sources, including the *Mahram*, says the first Muslim ruler was Mai Humay Jilmi (1085–97)[52] and several modern writers claim Jilmi established the Shari'a in Borno in his reign.[53] The *Mahram* mentioned over a hundred years of reign of subsequent rulers when Islam spread, became established and the Kingdom became the principal focus of Muslim influence in central Sudan. The *Mahram* (letters patent or grant of privilege as Palmer translates) of Ummu Jilmi indicate that by the 11th century the Kingdom began to develop as an Islamic State under its ruler Ibn Abduljalil (1096–1108).[54]

However, Dunama I made Kanem become well known in the Islamic world of the 12th century. Similarly under Dunama II (c 1221–1259) Islam made considerable progress in Kanem with the ruler surrounding himself with experts in Islamic law, and the Maliki school of law (*Shari'ah*) was firmly established. Uthman Ibn

---

islamization-of-kowledge/1220-maqasid-al-shariah-a-strategy-to-rehabilitate-religion-in-america-.html>.

48 Ibid 10.

49 Al-Bakri, 'Kitab masalik wa'l mamalik' in Thomas Hodgkin (ed), *Nigerian Perspectives* (Oxford University Press, 1975) 88.

50 Chieka C Ifemesia, 'States of the Central Sudan' in J F Ade Ajayi and Ian Espie (eds), *A Thousand Years of African History* (Ibadan University Press, 1968) 73–74.

51 W Seidensticker et al (eds), *Borno Muslim Society Newsletter No 38 and 39* (1999); Abubakar Mustapha and Abubakar Garba, *Proceedings of the Conference on the Impact of the 'Ulama in the Central Sudan* (The Centre for Trans-Saharan Studies, University of Maiduguri, 1991).

52 Herbert Richmond Palmer, *Sudanese Memoirs*, 'Kanem-Bornu Wars of Idris Alooma' (Herbert Richmond Palmer, trans, Vol 1, Cass, 1928) 15–72.

53 M N Alkali, 'The question of sovereignty, security and justice in Kanem-Borno History' in Abdalla Uba Adamu (ed), *Chieftaincy and Security in Nigeria* (Government House, 2007) 419.

54 Mai Hume Jilmi, 'Mahram' in Richmond Palmer (ed), *Bornu, Sahara and Sudan* (Negro Universities Press, 1936) 14–15.

Idris (1390–1422), Ali Ghaji (1472–1504) and Mai Aluma were rulers of Borno who showed a good understanding of the values of Islam or Shari'a in leadership and governance. Aluma was particularly noted for being strict in observance of the Shari'a in state affairs.[55] Alkali notes Borno as the land of Islam (*Dar-al-Islam*) from the 15th century onwards and that by the 16th century Borno assumed the role of a super power in the region rivalled in the then Islamic world only by the Ottoman Sultanate and the Sa'adi of Morocco.[56] El Kanemi was a Muslim scholar who established in Borno another dynasty that kept the kingdom together and carried forward claim to Shari'a.

When Islam first reached the Hausa land is still being contested – the 14th, the 13th, and even the 8th century of the Christian Era have all been suggested. The first Muslim ruler (*Sarki*) of Kano, according to the *Kano Chronicle*, was Yaji (1349–1385) who built a mosque, appointed several Muslim immigrants to offices associated with the practice of Islam and ordered all his state to accept Islam. Balogun says by 14th century *Sarki* Umar Dan Kanajeji (1410–1412) must have been such a pious and devoted Muslim as to have abdicated the throne to devote himself to the study and teaching of Islam and to prayer (*salah*), supplication and remembrance of Allah (*zikr*).[57] Leaders in the major Hausa states at Zazzau, Kano and Katsina who are mentioned as Islamic scholars and who pursued the spread of Islam and the application of Shari'a in governance and law with an unmistakable zeal are: Muhammad Labbo in Zazzau, Muhammad Rumfa in Kano and Muhammad Korau (1320–1353) in Katsina. Muhammad Rumfa Dan Yakubu (1463–1499) in particular, the details of whose work are more known, was the first King of the Hausa States who appears to have applied himself seriously to the administration of a multi-religious community in accordance with the Islamic law. To keep to the letters of the Shari'a, Rumfa went abroad (Algeria, North Africa) consulting a jurist of international fame, Muhammad b Abd al-Karim al-Maghili who responded with a well-written treatise on the Islamic (Shari'a-based) principles of government. Rumfa pursued Islamic policies and used Islamic scholars more actively and he established Islam as the state religion which earned him the title of a reformer. From then onwards Kano rulers continued to patronise Muslim scholars and Islamic scholarship so that the Shari'a formed the foundation and framework of governance and administration and the guide of social life.

An important and probably most widespread northern Nigerian Muslim ethnic group is the Fulani who in the 17th century were probably the most devoted to Islamic scholarship in Black Africa (*Bilad al-Sudan*). Even before the Fodio *jihad*, the Fulani founded several polities under *lamidos* (lamidites) with the Shari'ah guiding governance.

55 Alkali, above n 53, 421.

56 Ibid 419.

57 S A Balogun, 'History of Islam up to 1800' in Obaro Ikime (ed), *Groundwork of Nigerian History* (Heinemann for the Historical Society of Nigeria, 1980) 213.

By the early 19th century Uthman dan Fodio, an Islamic scholar led a 30-year intellectual and practical *jihad* that finally led to the establishment of an Islamic state in what is today northern Nigeria. This Islamic state, often referred to with the term 'Sokoto Caliphate', a term rightly described by Murray Last an anachronism,[58] was noted as one of the most significant political and social developments in African history for it was the largest, most territorially extensive, demographically and culturally heterogeneous and literate indigenous state in Africa. Its multi-dimensional impact, as influences or as reactions to it, extended beyond its physical frontiers and beyond 1903 when the British colonialists caused its collapse.[59]

## Shari'a in pre-colonial southern Nigeria (Yoruba land)

While the population of northern Nigeria is unarguably predominantly Muslim the case for the southwestern region remains controversial; however it is generally agreed that the Muslim population in the area is large or a simple majority. However, Noibi claims that the role of the *Shari'ah* in the lives of the Muslims of southwest Nigeria goes back to the 16th century when the people first experienced the coming of Islam to the area.[60] Titilola Euba as well as Murtala Okunola have documented the existence of Shari'a in Lagos as early as the late 18th century.[61]

## Colonial period

It is clear from the foregoing that when the British c 1902–1903 arrived the northern part of what is today Nigeria, they found that most of the areas were under two states both laying claim to being Islamic applying the Shari'a. The vast majority of the inhabitants of the area were Muslims making a conscious effort to apply as much of what they understood of the Shari'a in their political, social and legal systems. Mahmud expresses a sentiment common to elites of these areas that, 'in fact, in all the areas colonised by the British nowhere was Islam being observed as thoroughly as was the case in Northern Nigeria, except perhaps in some parts of the Arab world.'[62] The British found, Mahmud continued, the courts of the local rulers (Emirs) 'filled with learned and pious Jurists whose decisions were always based on authorities from the Qur'an, Hadith or other Islamic law books.'[63] The proceedings of the courts were always recorded in Arabic, which

58 Murray Last, *The Sokoto Caliphate* (Longman, 1967) lix.

59 Bobboyi and Yakubu, above n 17, vii, viii, Vol I, 1, Vol II, 181, 242.

60 Noibi, above n 14, 1.

61 Titilola Euba, 'Muhammad Shitta Bey and the Lagos Muslim Community (1850–1895)' (1979) 2 *Journal of Islam* 7; Muri Okunola, 'The Relevance of Sharīʿa to Nigeria' in Nur Alkali et al (eds), *Islam in Africa: Proceedings of Islam in African conference* (Spectrum Books, 1993) 23–35.

62 Abdulmalik Bappa Mahmud, above n 5, 1.

63 Ibid 1.

Muslims regard as the sacred language of Islam and of Paradise. Indeed colonial reports acknowledge that: the Shari'a judges (*Alkalai*) were of considerable learning and experience; the *Alkalai* courts competed favourably with the English courts and; the natives preferred the former. The reports also extolled the incorruptibility and efficiency of the *Alkali* courts.[64]

The colonialists entered a treaty of indirect rule with the Muslim northern Nigerian leaders. Of what they found existing as Shari'a, the British reduced its operation only in terms of mutilation, torture or any sentence which according to their sense 'is repugnant to natural justice and humanity'.[65] Thus amputation and stoning (which in any case is very rare in the entire history of the Shari'a the world over) stopped, while the sentences that applied to them were commuted to prison sentences. However, lashing continued for offences like alcohol consumption, adultery, and false accusation of adultery.[66]

Of the large volumes of writings on the Shari'a under colonial rule in northern Nigeria Kumo seems to provide an alternative view that is succinct and objective yet bringing out the real cause of tensions that made Shari'a an issue of much discord in Nigeria from independence to date.[67] According to Kumo, all enactments of the colonial government regarding law in northern Nigeria confined British colonial administrative officers to a supervisory role with minimum interference 'as regards its operations and its operators'.[68] Thus the Shari'a ran parallel with the English system, in what Kumo describes as '"good neighbourly" fashion' until 1933 when a new colonial Governor of Nigeria, Cameron, 'decided to bring the Sharia system under the English "executive interference" from emirs and chiefs'.[69] While the colonial 'executive interference' could be resisted in many cases, the advent of party politics added 'political interference' and even thuggery to curb the independence of the judiciary. By the end of the 1950s, Kumo concludes, the interference had intensified which combined with the resultant lowering of the standards and calibre of the judges to destroy the confidence of the people in the system.[70]

As the twilight of the fifties heralded the twilight of British colonial rule, the necessity for a new constitution became apparent, so too did what Kumo calls 'radical measures to the judiciary'. Kumo explains that for one thing the Shari'a criminal law

64 Muhammed Tabiu, 'An Overview of Sharia Law and Practice in Nigeria' in Jibrin Ibrahim (ed), *Shari'ah Penal and Family Laws in Nigeria and in the Muslim World Rights Based Approach* (Global Rights Publications, 2004) 116.

65 Kumo in Bobboyi and Yakubu, above n 17, 287.

66 Alkali, above n 61, 169–78; Mahmud, above n 62; Allan Christelow, 'Islamic Law and Judicial practice in Nigeria: An historical perspective' (2002) 22 *Journal of Muslim minority affairs* 185, 185–204; Ostien, above n 29, 11–27.

67 Kumo, 'The Shari'a Issue: Politics and Legal Technicalities', above n 17, 2; Kumo in Bobboyi and Yakubu, 'The colonial', above n 17, 285, 287–289.

68 Kumo, 'The Shari'a Issue, above n 17, 5; Kumo in Bobboyi and Yakubu, 'The colonial', above n 17, 286.

69 Kumo in Bobboyi and Yakubu, above n 17, 288–9, 292.

70 Ibid 292.

could no longer be applicable since there was a provision in the draft Constitution which made it mandatory for criminal law to be codified; for another, the judiciary had now become substantially integrated, as appeals in all matters other than matters of personal law could go up to the Federal Supreme Court.[71] And furthermore, the laws of criminal procedure and evidence had to be uniform.

Thus by 1958, the northern regional government sought the advice of a panel of jurists[72] to reform the penal law and courts. Paden[73] documents a participant perspective of the reform while Ostein documents list of actors and actions related to the penal reforms of 1958, 1960 and 1962.[74] An interesting aspect of the list of actors is that many non-Muslims were involved in the reforms process. There are arguments as to whether the British lured or forced the northern Muslim politicians into accepting the penal code or it was a 'compromise settlement'. Addressing the House of Chiefs, the Premier of the region, Ahmadu Bello, made it clear that the northern politicians knew what they were doing, believing they were not in any way giving away their rights to be governed by the Shari'a. He said:

> there is nothing in the central recommendation of the Panel that a new Penal Code of criminal law should be introduced into the Region that is in any way contrary to the tenets of our religion. The new code will be almost identical with those which have been in force for years in the Sudan and Pakistan and which have been proved perfectly acceptable to the millions of Moslems among the populations of those countries.[75]

With the eventual 'constitutional' enactment of the *Penal Code* of Northern Nigeria and the *Criminal Procedure Code* of Northern Nigeria operative in all criminal cases in all courts, the only area left entirely under the Shari'a was personal law, for which a new appellate tribunal was established – the Northern Nigeria Shari'a Court of Appeal – as the final court of appeal in matters of Islamic personal law (which were specifically enumerated). Again Shari'a in colonial Nigeria was not restricted to the north. It was practised in the southwest specifically in the following areas: Ede under King (Oba) Habibu (d 1902); Iwo under Oba Memudu Lamuye (d 1906); Ikirun Oba Aliyu Oyewole (d 1912); and in Auchi 1881–1910 and in Iwo 1906.[76] The British abolished the *Shari'ah* Courts in Yoruba land; even the Islamic personal law was outlawed. Between the years 1894 and 1948, Yoruba

71 Ibid 294.

72 The panel was made up of the chief justice of Sudan, a judge of the Supreme Court of Pakistan, one British expert in Islamic Law, and three Nigerians from three provinces of the region.

73 John N Paden, above n 2, 208–211.

74 Phillip Ostien, above n 29, 11–27.

75 Ahmadu Bello, *My Life* (Cambridge University Press, 1962) 217–8.

76 Ishaq Lakin Akintola, 'The Implementation of the Sharīcah in Nigeria: The Impact on the common folks' in Zakariyau I Oseni (ed), *A Digest on Islamic Law and Jurisprudence in Nigeria* (Darun-Nur, 2003) 152.

Muslims sustained chains of agitations under British rule. Lagos Muslims petitioned the colonial governor in 1894 and 1923. In 1938, the Muslims of Ibadan submitted a petition demanding for *Shari'ah*. Muslims in Ijebu-Ode also petitioned for *Shari'ah* in 1948. The *Shari'ah* issue was raised during the reign of General Yakubu Gowon (1966–1975). Muslims also made a spirited attempt during the Constitution drafting Committee meetings (1975–1976).[77]

Okunola, in what he refers to as painstaking research into Nigeria's legal history, gives brief but atomistic history of Shari'a in southwestern Nigeria showing how 'between 1868 and 1894, the *Shari'a* had been firmly established in six principal Yoruba towns. Okunola catalogued 'the demand by the Yoruba people for the application (of Shari'a) before, during and after the colonial administration beginning with the 1881 petition of the Lagos Muslim community.[78] Noibi locates the antiquity of the Shari'a in the 'many Islamic legal terms in the Yoruba language, words which are used by Muslims and non-Muslims alike up to this day.' Noibi argues that:

> although the British contrived and abolished the *Shari'ah* as a recognized legal system in Yorubaland Muslims in places like Lagos, Ijebu-Ode, Ibadan etc, did at different times, demand the revival of the law for the purpose adjudication among Muslims. Therefore, the present call is not new, it only shows that no matter what you do to suppress the desire of a people, that desire will persist and may even grow stronger.[79]

However, there is a dearth of literature on the position of Shari'ah in the western region from then on. The Muslim voices in the Shari'ah heated debates of the late 1970s and the early 2000s are hushed, probably because they have political differences with their counterparts in the northern part of the country which could be affected by a clear support for the northern agitations for Shari'ah.

However, what suddenly became popular is the 'private implementation' of the Shari'ah in three out of six states of the southwestern Nigeria. It started at Oyo in May 2002, followed by Lagos October 2002 and Osun mid-2006. The state branches of the Supreme Council for the Implementation of Shari'ah in Nigeria (SCSN) which draws membership largely from Muslim lawyers, graduates of Shari'ah from local and Arabian universities and activists from other Muslim organisations have been responsible for the initiative and implementation.[80]

77 Makinde and Ostien, above n 14; Abdul-Fatah Kola Makinde and Philip Ostien, *Legal Pluralism in Colonial Lagos: The 1894 Petition of the Lagos Muslims to Their British Colonial Masters* (Leiden, 2012); Ishaq Lakin Akintola, 'The Implementation of the Shari'ah in Nigeria: The Impact on the common folks' in Oseni above n 76, 152.

78 Muri Okunola, 'The Relevance of Sharīʿa to Nigeria' in Alkali, above n 61, 24–9.

79 Noibi, above n 14, 4.

80 Abdur-Raheem Adebayo Shittu, 'Reviewing the prospects and challenges of private initiatives in implementing Shari'ah in South Western Nigeria' (2006–2009), a paper at the 4th *National Conference of Shari'ah Implementing States*, Kano, December 2009.

The instrument for the implementation is what is referred to as Independent Shari'ah Panels. The Judges are usually lawyers and/or graduates of Shari'ah who do not draw salaries or any emoluments for their services. The subject of jurisdiction of these panels are often restricted to Islamic personal law: marriage, divorce, inheritance, succession, will, business contract, endowment, trust, gift, children custody and maintenance etc. The Oyo State Panel is said to have between May 2008–May 2009 resolved a case of fornication/adultery (*zina*) but, whichever way, the punishment of lashing or stoning may have entailed it could not have possibly have resulted in execution).[81] Whether it was a case of fornication (referred to as *zina* in Arabic meaning sexual intercourse of unmarried persons) attracting 100 lashes of adultery (still referred to as *Zina* in Arabic) attracting stoning to death, the state Panel can only pronounce judgement but has no authority/power to enforce its judgment/pronouncement. This is so even where the parties are Muslims ready to submit themselves to the punishment; it cannot be executed without the express approval of the state governor who is most unlikely to grant it because it is a private and not a state jurisdiction process. All parties who appear before the panels are often Muslims who willingly agree to subject themselves to jurisdiction according to the Shari'ah. The panels have no instruments to enforce their judgements which are left to the will of the parties to implement. The Lagos State Independent Shari'ah Panel is said to be the best organised and its publication of ten 'Selected judgements' is said to meet all international standards of law reporting.[82]

## Post-colonial period 1960–1966: Shari'a in post-colonial Nigeria 1960–1966

The Penal Code was for Muslims of northern Nigeria who followed the Shari'a and they never bothered with its shortcomings in terms of non-application of the criminal aspects. Though the real importance of the criminal code in the implementation of Shari'a awaits competent investigation and articulation, it is safe to argue that, as hinted at above, the criminal code of the Shari'a is possibly the least important aspect of the Shari'a. Secondly application of the Shari'a is the responsibility of leaders and the mass of the population to be satisfied that they have Muslim leaders at all levels of a polity that is nonetheless plural.

## The first republic/civilian democracy (1960–1966)

Alhaji Sir Ahmadu Bello, the Sardauna of Sokoto and Premier of the Northern Nigeria, is undoubtedly the most important Muslim figure of the first republic and arguably the most important political figure that has ever existed in post-colonial Nigeria.

81 This is my personal view because as Abdur-Raheem Adebayo Shittu, ibid 5, said 'the Panel does not have any specific office' nor legal status recognised by the state. However, it would have been more scientific if I could interview the judges or some authorities in that area.

82 See Makinde and Ostien, above n 14; Shittu, above n 80, 15–16.

As from the eve of independence, 30 September 1960, according to Paden, the regional government of Northern Nigeria undertook massive efforts to put the reforms of the legal system into effect.[83] The Sardauna was said to have preferred Islamic law in the country to the Penal Code which was developed first in India (Pakistan), then Sudan, and finally brought to Nigeria. Both the Sardauna and Gumi (eventually the first Nigerian Grand Khadi and Chief Adviser to the Sardauna on religious issues) accepted it since it followed the Shari'ah. They felt people could change gradually.

In the early independence period, according to Paden, there was a profound impact of the Penal Code on the judiciary structure and process in Northern Nigeria. A judicial bureaucracy as well as a regional Khadi system emerged with personnel learned in the Shari'a.[84] The situation remained constant for the duration of the northern regional government's administration (1960–1966) and in the period of the military interregnum, without attracting much public discourse.

## The first military Era (1966–1979)

Major Chukwuma Nzeagwu, the southern Christian leader of the 1966 coup at Kaduna (capital of the northern region) clearly had the 'Muslim problem' and so the Shari'a problem as a top priority in his mind for the very first day after the coup he summoned Abubakar Gumi, the Grand Khadi of northern Nigeria. Gumi, said, casually dismissing their crime of the murder of national figures, Nzeagwu first wanted to know where they hid the weapons they supposedly imported from Middle East with which to wage jihad. Nzeagwu presumed that 'they' (meaning Gumi and other Muslim leaders of the then Northern Nigeria) imported weapons from the Middle East with which to wage Jihad against the Christians of the country. Next, Nzeagwu argues that the appointment of Gumi as Grand Khadi (Chief Judge of Islamic law) was of no use since there is already the Chief Justice for the secular law operating in the country. Gumi explained that unlike other religions:

> In Islam, there are very specific laws in respect of all social matters which must be observed correctly. They include those concerning marriage, divorce, rights to offspring and inheritance. In this regard, only an Islamic Court, with a judge versed in the science of the Qur'an and the Prophet's traditions, could properly administer justice on a disputing Muslim couple or their inheritors. As for my position, it is only a natural complement to the Area Courts. The appeals that come to me cannot be handled by the Chief Justice because he has no knowledge of Islamic Law.[85]

83 Paden, above n 2, 210.
84 Ibid 212–3.
85 Sheikh Abubakar Gumi with Ismalia A Tsiga, *Where I Stand* (Spectrum Books, 1994) 116.

Furthermore, that it was a priority of the coup leaders to 'deal' with even the conciliatory 'Shari'a as penal code' is demonstrated by Mahmud as he states that, '[a]t that time the most hated institution (to non Muslims that is) was the Native Courts'.[86] That was why within the four days that Major Nzeagwu was in control of the North, the Attorney General of that region was directed to close all the Native and Emir courts and transfer their cases to the magistrate (common law) courts – a task that turned out to be impossible for one reason among others; for example in Borno, only one out 13 provinces (there were 50 such courts to be closed down), while there was no single magistrate court in that province. Indeed, a magistrate court stationed in Jos was to take care of Plateau, Bauchi, Borno and Adamawa provinces. Some areas of the last two provinces were over 500kms away from Jos. The directive of the coup leaders was withdrawn the following day.[87]

However, the military junta headed by Aguiyi Ironsi, another southern Nigerian Christian who ruled the country for only six months, made a priority of their government the setting up of a study group to look into the administration of justice in the North. Though the group was headed by a Muslim, he and other members were 'English judges' without qualifications in Islamic law. Regarding their terms of reference on the continuous existence of the native courts, the group submitted that it would not be possible to abolish the native courts, because they handled 95 percent of court cases in the North. Furthermore, the majority of such court cases were civil cases determined according to Islamic law while there were 'only three lawyers out of all Nigerian lawyers of that time who knew something about Islamic law.'[88] In spite of the recommendations of the group, the Federal government took over the native courts from native authorities.[89]

Ironically, it was in 1967, under the leadership of a northern Nigerian Muslim and an icon of the royal system, that the northern region abolished the Emirs' courts and in 1968 repealed the Native Courts Law, which merely meant changing the names Native to Area and Provincial to upper Area; but they were still allowed to adjudicate according to Islamic law where litigants were all Muslims.

Northern Nigerian Muslims recognised Shari'a as the core of their religious identity, but anxieties about the operation of the remnants of Shari'a in the public domain remained during the colonial era. Some Muslims complained about elitist manipulations that marred the operation of Shari'ah. To check these manipulations and other unnecessary interference, the British established the first Muslim Court of Appeal (later Shari'a Court of Appeal) in 1956.[90] Non-Muslim religious

86 Mahmud, above n 5, 30.
87 Ibid 30.
88 Ibid.
89 Ibid 31.
90 David D Laitin, 'The Sharia Debate and the Origins of Nigeria's Second Republic' (1982) 20 *Journal of Modern African Studies* 411, 411–430.

minorities, too, resisted, arguing that Shari'a had been a tool for their marginalisation and discrimination.[91]

The remnants of Shari'a in the public domain in the north withered away with the collapse of the First Republic. The military leaders at the centre, who had the task of averting the Nigerian civil war (1967–1970), soon realised that it was politically expedient to expand the federal options by creating more states.

Another military junta headed this time by a Muslim from the north, General Murtala Muhammad, made the 'problem' of the administration of justice in the north a priority of their government necessitating the setting up of an 'Area Court Reform Committee.' That committee, unlike the similar one before it, included an Islamic Jurist, a Grand Khadi. The report of this committee was submitted (23 July 1976) not to General Muhammad (who had by then lost his life ostensibly because of his Islamic identity) but to the then head of the junta, General Obasanjo, a Christian from the South. This committee submitted that they adopt the reasons of the committee set up by the Ironsi junta for maintaining the native courts because they were still valid. The committee further submitted that the area courts being located at the grassroots, employing local languages and local personnel were by far more easily accessible, simpler, speedier, less expensive compared to the magistrate (common law) courts. The committee showed that up to that period 94% of court cases were handled by the area courts. Comparing the two parallel courts, the committee found 769 area court judges while the common law had only 50 magistrates and while there were 19 justices of the High Court, there were 23 justices (Khadis) at the Shari'a Court of Appeal. It thus recommended that all appeal cases pertaining to Islamic law be transferred from High Courts to Shari'a Courts of Appeal. The government accepted the recommendations of the committee.

## The second republic/civilian democracy (1979–1983)

It was from 1977 to 1979 when civilian rule was to resume in Nigeria that the position of the Shari'a in the Nigerian constitution generated heated debates. The conciliatory position was that there would be no Federal Shari'a Court of Appeal, but 'there shall be for any state that requires it, a Shari'a Court of Appeal for that state.'[92] Even then, Shari'a courts were restricted to civil proceedings involving questions of Islamic personal laws.

Shari'a activists were actually proposing an Islamic Penal Code and argued that the reaction against it, which the debate had provoked, was misguided. In the first

91 Mohammed D Sulaiman, 'The Sokoto Jihad, Shari'a and Minorities in Northern Nigeria' in Bobboyi and Yakubu, above n 17, 233–6. Matthew H Kukah, *Democracy and Civil Society in Nigeria* (Spectrum Books, 1999) 125.

92 Section 275 of the *Constitution of the Federal Republic of Nigeria* (1999).

place, the Islamic reformism that had awakened Muslim consciousness must be situated within the context of a multi-religious society, in which the constituent religious groups were stalemating each other's progress. Therefore, the Christian Constituent Assembly members must have thought that if they were to give Muslims an inch, they would take a mile.

## The Shari'a debates

The programme for democratisation necessitated the constitutional debate which, according to Maier,[93] 'unleashed the potentially troublesome genie of Shari'a, Islamic laws.' At issue was Muslims' demand for the application of Islamic laws (*Shari'ah*) on Muslims at all levels of the legal process. The opposition interpreted that as challenging the secular status of the Nigerian state; others go as far as proclaiming it as an attempt at the Islamisation of the state. This has attracted much debate and indeed exacerbated tensions leading to ethno-religious warfare.

At the Constituent Assembly[94] many non-Muslims insisted that establishing the *Shari'ah* courts was tantamount to making Islam a state religion. Muslim members argued their support for Shari'a. Others, for example Unongo, said he was opposed to 'Sharia because the Sharia Court system is basically discriminatory . . .'[95] Nevertheless, Muslims continued to argue for Sharia'a. For example, Shagari, who by October 1979, became the President of Nigeria, said, 'Muslims of the country have made so many sacrifices and compromises in the interest of Nigerian unity.'[96] Yusuf, who eventually became Minister of Commerce and a treasurer of the ruling party, submitted that:

> Unlike in other religions, Islam is a way of life. If you take Sharia away from a Muslim, you are taking his religion away. In fact, this will be the next thing to committing a broad daylight robbery . . . this is why, Mr Chairman we are saying that Sharia is irreducible. This is why Mr Chairman we are saying that we cannot part with an iota of our own fundamental human rights which is the right to worship.[97]

Chiroma emphasised that:

> The Sharia is part and parcel of a Muslim's way of life . . . and I as a Muslim will not feel that I am practising my religion completely without subjecting myself to the provision of the sharia . . . We sit here and mourn about thieves, highway robbers and about materialism. Why should people not be materialistic

93 Karl Maeir, *This House has Fallen* (Penguin Books, 2000) 14.
94 Constituent Assembly (official reports of proceedings), D Adamu (ed), *The Analyst*, Vol 2, No 2 (Dansa Publications Ltd, 1987) 19.
95 Ibid.
96 Ibid.
97 Ibid.

> if you are not telling them that there is some other side to life? If the people are governed by Christian doctrines, they are not going to behave the way they are doing. If they are governed by Islamic doctrines, they are not going to behave the way they are doing.[98]

For non-Muslims in Nigeria, the debate died without success for Shari'a activists' and some uncritical alarmists claim it was the Shari'a issue that 'allowed religion to make a notorious entry into Nigerian politics' – one of the major factors that 'transformed [Nigeria] from a religious peaceable [federation] to a religiously polarized federation'.[99] This is certainly a gross underestimation of the time of entry and the scope of the role of religion in Nigerian politics.

If any loss at all, the Muslims only lost their right to have their criminals tried according to their belief system beyond the 'Area court'. The implication of the foregoing internal restrictions of the Shari'a regime is that Muslims, for the sake of promoting and protecting collective identity under a federal arrangement, could not enjoy their fundamental human rights to have legal pronouncements of their choice and their rights to be protected from having what they abhor – alcohol and prostitutes for example – from being displayed in their public spaces.

## The second military era (1984–1999)

This is the most uneventful period ever for Shari'a in Nigeria; this was partly because of the numerous military coups and counter coups of the period and the anxiety of politicians when several attempts in that period to return to civilian democracy failed.

## The third or fourth republic/civilian democracy (1999–present)

Following the 1999 Nigerian return to democracy, the government of Zamfara state in northwestern Nigeria, acting on an electoral pledge by Sani Ahmed Yerima, in March 2000 expanded the scope of the jurisdiction of Shari'a courts to include criminal cases. Eleven other states in Northern Nigeria immediately followed suit. This 're-introduction' of Shari'a in Northern Nigeria generated much popular and academic literature as well as bloody communal crises.[100] The states claimed legislative competence, under among others, sections 4, 6, and 277, and

98 Ibid 20.

99 Rotimi T Suberu, *Federalism and ethnic conflict in Nigeria* (United States Institute for Peace, 2001) 133.

100 See Rotimi T Suberu, *Federalism and ethnic conflict in Nigeria* (United States Institute for Peace, 2001); Eghosa Osaghe and Rotimi Seberu, *A history of identity and violence in Nigeria*, CRISE Working Paper No 6 (Queen Elizabeth House, 2005); Hakeem Onapajo, 'Politics for God: religion and conflict in democratic Nigeria' (2012) 4 *The Journal of Pan African Studies* 42.

the Second Schedule to the 1999 Nigeria Constitution, to establish Shari'a courts, in addition to existing ones, expand their jurisdiction, and enact laws drawing inspiration from religious and non-religious norms. Thus, the states enacted written laws and punishments prescribed therein for consumption of alcohol, prostitution, and theft, among many other 'sins'. The move to reinstating Shari'a cannot be seen purely as an Islamist drive in the north, but rather a move that also carried much popular support. In June 2000, mass popular demonstrations, forced Kano state government to adopt the reintroduction of Shari'a.

The 'Millennium' Shari'ah issue sparked, in the words of Maier, 'the most serious challenge to Nigeria's survival since the Biafra war.'[101] Reflecting on the Shari'a debates, the Chairman of the Constituent Assembly that designed the 1989 Constitution for Nigeria, Justice Aniagolu said, no issue was, 'Viewed with as much awe, or was as acrimonious, or was as potentially dangerous, or was as emotionally charged or was pursued with as much relentless fervor, or had [that] much capacity of destroying the country'.[102]

Sanusi is one of the few Muslims from Northern Nigeria famous for critical views on the Shari'a implementation 'in an environment filled with poverty and illiteracy, reputed for corruption and parasitism, and integral to an articulate mode of production that has succumbed the de-industrializing predatory form of globalization'.[103] Sanusi concludes that *Shari'ah* in Northern Nigeria has been subjected to criticism from two sources: (i) 'the West, which has carried into northern Nigeria its policy of demanding the capitulation of other cultures to its own values and concepts, without respecting their own right to insist on their own identity'; (ii) the Muslim community in Northern Nigeria, spearheaded by western educated Muslims 'who have ideological leanings of a radical or progressive nature, and who therefore resist what they view as an attempt to legitimate ideological reaction through the appropriation of religious symbols.'[104] He believes that: 'the approach of the West will not lead to fruitful dialogue precisely because of the failure to recognize the authenticity of Islam and respect the sensitivities of Muslim peoples to what is viewed as a grand conspiracy aimed at destroying Islam'.[105]

Na'im, a Sudanese-American well known for his critical views on the Shari'ah, admits that the religious devotion of Muslims for some sort of public role for Shari'ah in their societies makes its total relegation to the so-called private domain, which would be required by 'secularism neither viable nor desirable.'[106] Nonetheless

101 Maeir, above n 94, 15.

102 Anthony N Aniagolu, *The Making of the 1989 Constitution of Nigeria* (Spectrum Books, 1993) 93.

103 Lamido Sanusi, 'The West and the Rest: Reflections on the Intercultural Dialogue about *Shari'ah*' in Kogelmann, above n 31, 293.

104 Ibid 302.

105 Ibid 302.

106 Abdullahi A An-Na'im, 'Sharia and Positive Legislation: Is an Islamic State Possible or Viable?' in Eugene Cotran and Chibli Mallat (eds), *Yearbook of Islamic and Middle Eastern Law* (Kluwer Law International, 2000) 5.

Sanusi says An-Na'im represents not attempt at reform but prescription for abandonment. Sanusi says 'the attempts to seek a "reform" of Shari'ah based on arguments that the law is out dated are counter-productive.'[107]

## Conclusion

In keeping with the appealing theme of this collection of essays, which is to explore the ways in which law means love, the chapter, among others, attempted to show: (i) how Islamic teachings are understood or otherwise misunderstood to cause 'lost love'; (ii) how Islamic (state) laws address 'freedom of religion' and give examples of how, as 'state religion', Islam addresses cohabitation.

Quite very early in Kanem-Borno (11th century) and in Hausa land (about c 13th century) when the Shari'ah was said to have operated there, it did not mean cutting off hands or stoning prostitutes but rather the operation of many apparatuses of government and the facilitation in the public sphere of Islamic teachings and values meant to ensure security, welfare and justice delivery and indeed for socio-economic and political development generally.

Any development paradigm for Nigeria should accord the Shari'ah or, in the Muslim view, Islam in its entirety, as a very serious consideration.

Thus subsequent controversies regarding Shari'a was because Christians, once in leadership in the country, did not desire to follow the 'live and lets live' approach that the Penal Code portends to provide.

## References

Adamu, Abdalla Uba (ed), *Chieftaincy and Security in Nigeria* (Government House, 2007)

Adamu, D (ed), *The Analyst*, Vol 2, No 2, (Dansa Publications Ltd, 1987)

Ajayi, J F Ade and Ian Espie (eds), *A Thousand Years of African History* (Ibadan University Press, 1968)

Alkali, Nur, et al (eds), *Islam in Africa: Proceedings of Islam in African conference* (Spectrum Books, 1993)

Al-Raysuni, Ahmad, *Imam al-Shatibi's Theory of the Higher Objectives* (International Institute of Islamic Thought, 2005)

Aniagolu, Anthony N, *The Making of the 1989 Constitution of Nigeria* (Spectrum Books, 1993)

Auda, Jasser, *Maqasid al Shari'ah as Philosophy of Islamic Law* (International Institute of Islamic Thought, 2008)

Bello, Ahmadu, *My Life* (Cambridge University Press, 1962)

Bobboyi, H and Mahmood Yakubu (eds), *The Sokoto Caliphate: History and Legacies, 1804–2004* (Arewa House, 2006)

107 Lamido Sanusi, 'Democracy, Rights and Islam' in Jibrin Ibrahim (ed), *Shari'a Penal and Family Laws in Nigeria and in the Muslim World Rights Based Approach* (Global Rights Publications, 2004) 2.

Bolaji, Mohammed H A, 'Between Democracy and Federalism: Shari'ah in northern Nigeria and the paradox of Institutional Impetuses' (2013) 59 *Africa Today* 93
Christelow, Allan, 'Islamic Law and Judicial practice in Nigeria: An historical perspective' (2002) 22 *Journal of Muslim minority affairs* 185
*Constitution of the Federal Republic of Nigeria* (1999)
Cotran, Eugene and Chibli Mallat (eds), *Yearbook of Islamic and Middle Eastern Law* (Kluwer Law International, 2000)
Crane, Robert D, 'Maqasid al Shari'ah: A Strategy to Rehabilitate Religion in America', *i-epistemology.net*, 2009, accessed 7 April 2016, available at: <http://i-epistemology.net/v1/islamization-of-kowledge/1220-maqasid-al-shariah-a-strategy-to-rehabilitate-religion-in-america-.html>.
Euba, Titilola, 'Muhammad Shitta Bey and the Lagos Muslim Community' (1850–1895)' (1979) 2 *Journal of Islam* 7
Gumi, Sheikh Abubakar with Ismaila A Tsiga, *Where I Stand* (Spectrum Books, 1994)
Hefner, Robert W (ed), *Shari'a Politics Islamic Law and Society in the Modern World* (Indiana University Press, 2011)
Hodgkin, Thomas (ed), *Nigerian Perspectives* (Oxford University Press, 1975)
Ibrahim, Jibrin (ed), *Shari'a Penal and Family Laws in Nigeria and in the Muslim World Rights Based Approach* (Global Rights Publications, 2004)
Ikime, Obaro (ed), *Groundwork of Nigerian History* (Heinemann for the Historical Society of Nigeria, 1980)
Kamali, Mohammad Hashim, *The Principles of Islamic Jurisprudence* (Islamic Texts Society, 2003)
Kukah, Matthew Hassan, *Religion, Power and Politics in Northern Nigeria* (Spectrum Books, 1993)
Kukah, Matthew Hassan, *Democracy and Civil Society in Nigeria* (Spectrum Books, 1999)
Kumo, Sulaiman, 'The Shari'a Issue: Politics and Legal Technicalities' *Abuja: Workshop on Implementation of the Shari'a in a Democracy The Nigerian Experience*, 7–9 July 2004
Laitin, David D, 'The Sharia Debate and the Origins of Nigeria's Second Republic' (1982) 20 *Journal of Modern African Studies* 411
Last, Murray, *The Sokoto Caliphate* (Longman, 1967)
Maeir, Karl, *This House has Fallen* (Penguin Books, 2000) 14
Mahmud, Abdulmalik Bappa, *A Brief history of Shari'a in the defunct Northern Nigeria* (Jos University Press, 1988).
Makinde, Abdul-Fatah Kola and Philip Ostien, 'The Independent Sharia Panel of Lagos State' (2011) 25 *Emory International Law Review* 921
Makinde, Abdul-Fatah Kola and Philip Ostien, *Legal Pluralism in Colonial Lagos: The 1894 Petition of the Lagos Muslims to Their British Colonial Masters* (Leiden, 2012)
Mustapha, Abubakar and Abubakar Garba, *Proceedings of the Conference on the Impact of the 'Ulama in the Central Sudan* (The Centre for Trans-Saharan Studies, University of Maiduguri, 1991)
National Institute, *Research Reports on Conflict and Integration in Nigeria*, Kuru-Nigeria (National Institute for Policy and Strategic Studies, 2003)
Noibi, Dawud O S, 'Shari'ah in the South West', a paper at the *4th National Conference of Shari'ah Implementing States*, Kano (December 2009)
Onapajo, Hakeem, 'Politics for God: religion and conflict in democratic Nigeria' (2012) 4 *The Journal of Pan African Studies* 42

Osaghe, Eghosa and Rotimi Seberu, *A History of Identity and Violence in Nigeria*, CRISE Working Paper No 6 (Queen Elizabeth House, 2005)

Oseni, Zakariyau I (ed), *A Digest on Islamic Law and Jurisprudence in Nigeria* (Darun-Nur, 2003)

Ostien, Philip (ed), *Sharia Implementation in Northern Nigeria 1999–2006: A Sourcebook* (5 Vols, Spectrum Books, 2007)

Ostien, Philip, Jamila M Nasir and Franz Kogelmann (eds), *Comparative Perspectives on Shari'ah in Nigeria* (Spectrum Books Limited, 2005)

Paden, John N, *Ahmadu Bello Sardauna of Sokoto: Values and Leadership in Nigeria* (Al Hudahuda Publishing Co Ltd, 1986).

Palmer, Herbert Richmond, *Sudanese Memoirs*, 'Kanem-Bornu Wars of Idris Alooma' (Herbert Richmond Palmer, trans, Vol 1, Cass, 1928)

Palmer, Richmond (ed), *Bornu, Sahara and Sudan* (Negro Universities Press, 1936)

Parrinder, Geoffrey, *Africa's Three Religions* (Sheldon Press, 1969)

Political Bureau Report, *Abuja: The Directorate of Social Mobilisation* (Politburo, 1987)

Rabb, Intisar A, 'Islamic Legal Maxims as Substantive Canons of Construction: *Ḥudūd*-Avoidance in Cases of Doubt' (2010) 17 *Islamic Law and Society* 63

Rane, Halim, 'The Relevance of a Maqasid Approach' (2013) 28 *Journal of Law and Religion* 489

Rene Laremont, Ricardo, *Islamic Law and Politics in Northern Nigeria* (Africa World Press, 1st ed, 2011)

Ruxton, Fitz Herbert, *Maliki Law: Mukhtasar of Sidi Khalil* (NP, 1914)

Sacht, Joseph, *An Introduction to Islamic Law* (Oxford University Press, 1964)

Said, Edward, *Orientalism* (Routledge, 1978)

Seidensticker, W, et al (eds), *Borno Muslim Society Newsletter No 38 and 39* (1999)

Shittu, Abdur-Raheem Adebayo, 'Reviewing the prospects and challenges of private initiatives in implementing Shari'ah in South Western Nigeria' (2006–2009), a paper at the 4th *National Conference of Shari'ah Implementing States*, Kano, December 2009

Sodiq, Yushau. 'Can Muslims and Christians Live Together Peacefully in Nigeria?' (2009) 99 *The Muslim World* 646

Stiglitz, Joseph E, 'What Is Shariah and Why Does It Matter?', *Huffpost Religion*, 9 November 2010, accessed 7 April 2016, available at: <www.huffingtonpost.com/sherman-a-jackson/what-is-Shari'a-and-why-d_b_710976.html>

Suberu, Rotimi T, *Federalism and ethnic conflict in Nigeria* (United States Institute for Peace, 2001)

Sulaiman, Ibrahim and Siraj Abdulkarim (eds), *On the Political Future of Nigeria* (Hudahuda Publishing Company Ltd, 1988)

Yadudu, Auwala Hamisu 'Benefits of Shari'a and Challenges of Reclaiming a Heritage', *International Conference on-the Restoration of Shariah in Nigeria*, London, 14 April 2001

Zakariyau I Oseni (ed), *A Digest on Islamic Law and Jurisprudence in Nigeria* (Darun-Nur, 2003)

# Part II

# Legal perspectives

# 6 From law to solidarity

*Slavica Jakelić*

When it comes to religious–secular relations, the realm of law seems to be the last place to look for love. While this point counters some arguments in this volume, it should not be surprising: most stories about law and religion are stories of religious–secular conflict. What is more, such stories are not characteristic only of the United States, France, Turkey, or India, ie, the usual suspects in the studies of the religious–secular relations.[1] The stories of religious–secular antagonism in the legal sphere point to a global and normative crisis, which reflects the need to rethink and renegotiate religious–secular boundaries in order to respond to the challenges of the twenty-first century pluralism.

In this essay, I explore the religious–secular relations in the contexts of law and civil society. I begin the discussion with the focus on two patterns that emerge in the studies of conflict between law and religion. The first is the view that law embodies the powers of the secular, especially the power of the modern states, which are seen as attempting to govern – determine and bound – the domain of religion. The second pattern is the problematisation of the very categories of 'religion' and 'secularism' as they arise in legal debates. Scholars dispute the possibility of a neutral position from which one can define what religion is; they point to the intertwined relationship between, and the evasive character of, the religious and the secular. As a result, some critics argue that we ought to uncover the fluidity and hybridity of religious and secular experiences and identities, as a way to appreciate these identities politically and legally.

There is not much doubt that the genealogies and phenomenology of the religious and the secular are complex. Notwithstanding such complexities, or the importance of hybrid identities for cultural imagination and political creativity,[2] I contend here that the religious and the secular are categories that should also be sustained as indicative of deep and meaningful differences. These categories have

1 For an example of a comparative explorations of secularisms in the US, Turkey, India, and France, see Linell E Cady and Elizabeth Shakman Hurd (eds), *Comparative Secularisms in a Global Age* (Palgrave Macmillan, 2010).

2 See, Kery E Iyall Smith and Patricia Leavy (eds), *Hybrid Identities: Theoretical and Empirical Considerations* (Brill, 2008); especially Iyall Smith's introduction, 5.

been acquired by individuals and communities in powerful and sociologically relevant ways, by giving substance to the individual and communal ontological commitments and by providing platforms for people's political actions. For these reasons, my response to the discussions of religious–secular phenomena in general and in the realm of law in particular is twofold. Firstly, I maintain that the differences between the religious and the secular are constitutive of the ideals of just pluralistic societies but in order to see this we ought to move from the realm of law to the realm of civil society. Secondly, I suggest that one important way to consider religious–secular relations in terms of their role in shaping our political imaginaries is to view those relations through the lens of solidarity, its ethics and its practice.

The concept of solidarity has been a significant subject in the sociological, ethical, and philosophical discussions. For the purposes of this essay, it is the thinking of the American historian David Hollinger that merits special attention. As I elaborate below, Hollinger thinks that the notion of solidarity, while close to the concepts of identity and community, is also very different from them. Identity and community express a fated sense of belonging, he maintains, while solidarity represents first and foremost a willed affiliation. What makes solidarity distinctive, according to Hollinger, is a level of agency – one's choice of commitment to others and expectation of commitment from others in the constitution of the 'we.'

Hollinger's approach to solidarity as a politically robust notion needed for the global age does not fully acknowledge that the willed solidarity – as opposed to the one we develop because we are born into some community – often comes together with ascribed identities. That being said, his understanding of solidarity is pertinent to how we think about religious–secular relations because it gestures toward the ways in which the individuals actively constitute a *pluralistic* 'we.' As I will argue in this essay, solidarity understood as a willed, deliberate affiliation was a foundational ethical component of the 1980s Polish social movement Solidarność. A remarkable event of civil society, the Solidarność was not only a moment when the Polish citizens acted against one common enemy – the power and oppression of the communist secular state. The 1980s were the time when the Poles of all professional backgrounds and worldviews, religious and secular, came together to re-imagine Polish society as a moral, national, and political community. Countering a long history of distrust between the religious and secular Polish citizens, between the Catholic Church and the Polish Left, the Solidarność leaders provided rich philosophical and theological articulations of the ethics of solidarity and translated those ethics into practice. In so doing, they helped create a movement that changed the course of Polish history but also supplies a model for our own thinking about religions and secularisms in public life – a model that can help us understand why it is important to sustain the religious–secular differences in our pluralistic age, as well as to recognise that those upholding the religious and those upholding the secular worldviews also share some important moral orientations.

## Religion, secularism, and the limits of law

According to the British sociologist of multiculturalism Tariq Modood, the US is a society in which secularism is uniquely linked to law: in the US, Modood writes, secularism finds its 'most heightened,' if not 'its only major expression,' in the constitutional arrangements.[3] This US encounter between religion and secularism is shaped by the distinctive religious history, through which the Americans came to be especially protective of the separating line between religion and government,[4] and through which religion acquired the antinomian nature so that 'law is that which is . . . secular' and 'religion is that which is not law.'[5]

While the uniqueness of the US history of separationism is beyond doubt, it is also certain that the American case is just one of many contemporary instances of religious–secular conflict playing out in courtrooms. We have been witnesses to such conflicts all over the globe – in France and Turkey, surrounding the right of Muslim women to wear the hijab in public; in the UK, involving the Sikhs' demand to be exempted from the laws to wear motorcyle helmets; in India, manifested in the demand of Muslim women to have 'civil divorces . . . on the same ground as their Hindu and Christian neighbors';[6] in Russia and Greece, expressed in the quest of minority religions to freely organise and work in the context of religiously homogenous societies; in Australia, mirrored in the debates as to whether the constitution should include provisions dealing with freedom of religion or freedom of conscience.[7]

While the roots of the mentioned disputes should be sought in particular social and religious histories of each society, most of these cases also have important features in common. 'Whenever religion and law today intersect,' writes the American legal and religious studies scholar Winnifred Fallers Sullivan, 'it is usually in one of several familiar ways: in debates concerning certain issues of public policy – such as abortion, homosexuality, cloning, and euthanasia – or in the high-profile stories of the asserted denial of religious freedom.'[8] In other words, what we see in case after case is that religion–law encounters involve tension, antagonism, and sometimes even open clashes between religious traditions and communities on the one hand, and law perceived as representing the state on the other.

The second feature that characterises most religious–secular conflicts in the legal arena arises from the need that law, in order to decide on cases involving

3 Tariq Modood, 'Introduction: Odd Ways of Being Secular' (2009) 75(4) *Social Research* 1169, 1172, 1171.

4 Winnifred Fallers Sullivan, *The Impossibility of Religious Freedom* (Princeton University Press, 2005) 4.

5 Winnifred Fallers Sullivan, 'We Are All Religious Now. Again' (2009) 76 *Social Research* 1181, 1183.

6 For some of these cases, I draw on Fallers Sullivan's discussions, above n 4, 1.

7 Paul Babie and Neville Rochow (eds), *Freedom of Religion under Bills of Rights* (University of Adelaide Press, 2012).

8 Fallers Sullivan, above n 4, 3.

religion, determines what is and what is not religious behaviour, who is and who is not religious. Most countries have an office that regulates whether some community is a religious community and whether it should be free to practise and organise in some society.[9] One exception is the US, where having such an office would be seen as an affront to religious disestablishment and religious freedom. The nobility of these ideals, however, does not absolve the US judges from the fate of their non-American colleagues: in all cases that involve religious communities and individuals, the question '[w]hat *is* religion?' remains at the heart of legal thinking.[10]

And, here begin the problems, since we live in a pluralistic age when there is no shared notion – socially or culturally – of what religion is. Religion, scholars maintain, has been separated from 'place.'[11] What is more, this displacement is directly related to the rise of modern legal thinking, ie, the modern legal disestablishment. In modernity, Fallers Sullivan argues, the law came to be understood as separate, autonomous, transparent, and as being able to transcend specific cultures.[12] Because of this understanding, the law is still often perceived as capable of judging in the matters of religion neutrally and objectively. However, in the context of legal disestablishment – which is a reality or an aspiration characterising many modern societies – the law itself comes to be grounded in 'a narrow and distinctively post-Reformation understanding of religion as appropriately limited to the voluntary association of like-minded individuals.'[13] Contrary to the notion of the law as neutral or objective, then, the legal adjudication of what is religious or non-religious is a normative move: whenever focused on the voluntary aspect of religious life, modern law in effect helps to privatise and individualise religion by reifying its definition 'as faith or conscience rather than as action.'[14]

These Fallers Sullivan's reflections are not equally applicable in all societies[15] but are valuable as they bring together the insights of two quite different areas of inquiry, the legal scholarship and the religious studies scholarship. Her bridging of these two fields uncovers the extent to which much of the modern legal

9 Fallers Sullivan, above n 5, 1185.

10 Ibid 1184–5.

11 One of the most influential religious studies scholars, historian of religions J Z Smith, writes that those who study religion have no firm place to stand on 'apart from the messiness of the given world', see, Jonathan Z Smith, 'Map Is Not Territory' in Jonathan Z Smith (ed), *Map Is Not Territory: Studies in the History of Religions* (Brill, 1978) 289. For the way in which Winnifred Fallers Sullivan uses this notion in relation to the idea of disestablishment, see, 'Religion, Law and the Construction of Identities' (1996) 43 *Numen* 128, 132.

12 Fallers Sullivan, above n 5, 1181–2.

13 Fallers Sullivan, above n 11, 132.

14 Ibid 136.

15 Definitions of religion as voluntary can be contrasted with the cases when religion is viewed as historically embedded in some society, as is the case in societies with collectivistic Christianities. For a comparative look at the European collectivistic Christianities, see Slavica Jakelić, *Collectivistic Religions: Religion, Choice, and Identity in Late Modernity* (Routledge, 2016).

thinking about religion (as disestablished and universally definable) mirrors *and* constitutes the Western approach to religion as a universal human experience.[16] It is important to note that such universalistic definitions of religion have long been refuted by the religious studies scholars, especially those working in the context of feminist, post-modern, and post-colonial studies.[17] Religion, these scholars assert, is always embedded and embodied, can be studied only as such, and only with a sense of reflexivity – about the lived and thus changing nature of religious traditions and about the constant negotiations between religious traditions as lived and scholarly theories about them.[18] Unlike scholars of religion, however, those who make legal determinations about religion still do so in an unreflexive manner, without noting the extent to which the turn toward internalising religion in effect promotes secularisation.

The absence of reflexivity in the legal approaches to religion is only one layer of critique of modern law, the other important aspect pointing to law as an embodiment of modern states. Commenting on the Indian model of secularism, Faisal Devji points to John Locke to note that 'the neutral state does not delimit religion so much as create it as an effect of itself.'[19] Using Devji's lens, the often discussed return of religion to public sphere ceases to be just a matter of religious revival in the face of secularisation;[20] it turns into a question about the public spaces to which religion can – is *permitted to* – return. To use the insights of one of the earliest and most renowned critics of secularism, anthropologist Talal Asad:[21] in the context of modern nation-states the law becomes one of the elements of political strategy and statecraft, next to 'self-discipline,' 'participation,' and 'economy.'[22] The law, in this perspective, comes to embody the powers of the secular – it becomes one modality of that power, which is central to the project of Western modernity and which attempts, as Asad and other scholars working within this normative framework argue, to determine and govern the realm of religion.

16 As Faisal Devji puts it, secularism 'participates in modernization theory as a form increasingly evacuated of historical content', 'Comments on Rajeev Bhargava's "The distinctiveness of Indian secularism"', in T N Srinivasan (ed), *The Future of Secularism* (Oxford University Press, 2008) 54.

17 For an overview of the feminist post-modern, and post-colonial contributions to the study of religion in the context of the history of religious studies as a field, see Slavica Jakelić and Jessica Starling, 'Religious Studies: A Bibliographic Essay' (2006) 74 *Journal of the American Academy of Religion* 194.

18 Ibid 205. For the suggestion that scholars of religion have negotiated between lived religious traditions and scholarly theories about them, Sam Gill, 'Territory', in Mark C Taylor (ed), *Critical Terms for Religious Studies* (The University Press of Chicago, 1998) 298–313, 309.

19 Devji, above n 16, 58.

20 The groundbreaking study of the return of public religions was Jose Casanova's *Public Religions in the Modern World* (The University Press of Chicago, 1994).

21 Talal Asad, *Formations of the Secular: Christianity, Islam, Modernity* (Stanford University Press, 2003).

22 Ibid 3.

Using this line of critique, one way to understand what has been transpiring in the relations between law and religion is to see them as contestations of the realms of sovereignty.[23] At the same time, it is difficult not to see the irony in these contestations: religious communities challenge how law, understood as secular, determines the proper domain of religion while at the same time these communities ask that law adjudicates the described contestations and do so in the very terms established by legal discourse.[24] Scholar of religion Markus Dressler points out this problem when he discusses the ways in which the Alevis group in Turkey worked to differentiate their identity from the Sunni majority. According to Dressler, the Alevis' challenge to the Kemalist, laicist model of Turkish national identity, was articulated in the language of laicism. For Dressler, who is to a great extent representative of the 'Asadian' trajectory in the studies of secularism and religion,[25] this development is not an irony or an unintended consequence; it is an indication of the power of the secular knowledge regimes – the religio-secularist logic, as he calls it – to determine our contemporary discourse and our practice.[26]

Keeping all this in mind, and following some proposals by Winnifred Fallers Sullivan, the right question to ask in the realm of law might not be 'how should religion be defined?' or 'who should define religion?' The question rather seems to be whether the category of 'religion' should be used in law at all.[27] Fallers Sullivan, for one, argues that defining religion with the capital 'R' is not the business of courts and judges: neither can law capture how people at the start of the twenty-first century live their religious lives, she states, nor can it find some neutral space from which to determine what religion is. A number of critics of secularism would concur. For theologian John Milbank and religious studies scholar Elizabeth Linell Cady, the secular can be anything but neutral because it positions itself as a radically different realm from the religious – as reason, knowledge, objectivity, and progress versus faith, revelation, emotion, and tradition.[28]

23 As the political philosopher Wendy Brown argues, the walls erected 'are a feature of the waning, not the waxing, of sovereignty.' For Wendy Brown's point, see Winnifred Fallers Sullivan, 'Separationism and the sex abuse crisis' *The Immanent Frame*, July 20th, 2012, 'Sex abuse in the Catholic Church', accessed 12 December 2015, available at: http://blogs.ssrc.org/tif/2012/07/20/separationism-and-the-sex-abuse-crisis/.

24 Devji, above n 16, 58.

25 For a critique of this Asadian trajectory in the study of religions and secularisms, see Atalia Omer, 'Modernists Despite Themselves: The Phenomenology of the Secular and the Limits of Critique as an Instrument of Change' (2015) 83 *Journal of the American Academy of Religion* 27, 27–71.

26 Markus Dressler, 'Making Religion through Secularist Legal Discourse' in Markus Dressler and Arvind-Pal S Mandair (eds), *Secularism and Religion-Making* (Oxford University Press, 2011) 187–208.

27 Fallers Sullivan, above n 11, 129.

28 John Milbank, *Theology and Social History* (B Blackwell, 1990); Linell E Cady, 'Reading Secularism through a Theological Lens' in Cady and Hurd above n 1, 247–64.

Moreover, Milbank declares, the religious–secular binary did not *gain* normative content; this content was *established* and social scientists were among the most responsible of offenders.

Anthropologist Talal Asad and political scientist Elizabeth Shakman Hurd also critique the religious–secular binary. Asad's genealogies of the secular were a compelling call that we denaturalise the religious–secular distinctions – that we de-normalise the very binary we have come to take for granted. Shakman Hurd follows Asad's proposal in order to unmask what she sees as the politics of secularism in social sciences in general and in the international relations in particular. She also adopts Asad's notion that there is nothing inherent to either the religious or the secular as categories or domains.[29] However, while Asad is careful to say that, even though the two categories have no essence, they are ultimately not the same thing, Shakman Hurd moves one step further. In proposing that we study the categories of the religious and the secular as always 'elusive,' 'shifting,' 'evolving,' interdependent, and fluctuating, she gets very close to the proposition of religious–secular hybridity.[30] Similarly to Janet Jakobsen and Ann Pellegrini, who call for the undoing of the religious–secular binary to 'open new configurations in the political debate structured by these terms,'[31] Shakman Hurd wants us to focus on the mutual transformations in the religious–secular constellations in order to open analytic and epistemological spaces for understanding these constellations.

The intertwined, evolving, fluid nature of the religious and the secular can be traced in the context of the law. Fallers Sullivan points out, for example, that the:

> so-called secular law . . . contains embedded and outdated religious anthropologies and cosmologies, while the religious law is strangely similar to the secular law in its reliance on process and indirection and the primacy of the protection of property.[32]

Put differently, proposals and descriptions that highlight the spaces of intertwined, fluid, or hybrid religious–secular formations are driven by a desire to move beyond the contemporary religious–secular dichotomies. But even if one adopts this trajectory, important questions about the religious and the secular do remain. If we are to describe what is around us and to affirm a framework that can move us beyond the powers of the secular, we are told, we ought to explore the elusiveness, fluidity, and mutual transformation of the religious and the secular. Yet, does this proposal imply that we are to ignore the extent to which the religious and the

29 Asad, above n 21.

30 Elizabeth Shakman Hurd, 'A Suspension of (Dis) Belief: The Secular-Religious Binary and the Study of International Relations' in Craig Calhoun, Mark Juergensmeyer and Jonathan VanAntwerpen (eds), *Rethinking Secularism* (Oxford University Press, 2011) 170, 173.

31 Janet R Jakobsen and Ann Pellegrini (ed), *Secularisms* (Duke University Press, 2008) 10.

32 Fallers Sullivan, above n 23, 2021.

secular have come to shape and claim contemporary individual and social experiences? This is a sensible question because, while the religious–secular binary is a product of the Western Christian history, it has long ceased to be just the property of the West.[33]

Most importantly for our discussion, the emphasis on fluidity and hybridity of the religious and the secular does not only open the novel sites of analysis and critique; it also represents a normative step that leaves behind the notions of 'religion' with the capital 'R' and 'secularism' with the capital 'S'. How should we think of this proposal? Should we take this step as the exclusive trajectory or should we continue to probe *all* meanings of the religious and the secular, especially if we are interested in the value and challenges of twenty-first century pluralism? Let me be concrete and highlight here the case of South African anti-apartheid activists. In this context, we can trace a twofold phenomenology of the religious and the secular as categories. The religious and secular activists in the South African context display their awareness of the ethical affinities and practical sites of encounter between religious and secular worldviews. At the same time, these activists use the notions of the religious and the secular to express the content and depth of their own ontological commitments and to explain how those commitments compelled them to act politically.[34] The cases of the leaders of the labour and civil rights movements in the US, or the Solidarność movement in Poland, are similar in this regard. Consequently, the question arises: should we think of the religious and the secular in their accounts just as elusive, mutually dependent and transformative, or should we *also* identify them as deep ontological motivations without which the political struggles in question would not have had the forcefulness they did?

In her critique of the legal approach to religion, Fallers Sullivan draws on Clifford Greetz to propose that human beings, in a complex and interconnected world, need to keep imagining new principles – new 'fictions', as she puts it – by which

33 For the discussion of the Western Christian origin of the religious–secular binary and the implications of this history, see Slavica Jakelić, 'Rethinking the Religious-Secular Encounters', in Thomas Dienberg, Thomas Eggensperger and Ulrich Engel (eds), *Himmelwärts und weltgewandt/Heavenward and Worldly. Kirche und Orden in (post-)säkularer Gesellschaft/Church and Religious Orders in (Post) Secular Society* (Aschendorff Verlag Muenster, 2014); for the argument about secularism as a global phenomenon, see Slavica Jakelić, 'Secularism: A Bibliographic Essay' (2010) 12 *The Hedghehog Review* 3. As José Casanova explains it, 'the very fact that the same category of religion is being used globally across cultures and civilisations testifies to the global expansion of the modern secular-religious system of classification of reality,' Casanova in Linell E Cady and Elizabeth Shakman Hurd, 'Comparative Secularisms and the Politics of Modernity: An Introduction' in Cady and Hurd, above n 1, 3–24; 20.

34 For interviews with the South African anti-apartheid activists, religious and secular, and the ways in which they speak of their metaphysical and ethical commitments and reasons for taking part in the anti-apartheid struggle, see Charles Villa-Vicencio, *The Spirit of Freedom: South African Leaders on Religion and Politics* (University of California Press, 1996).

to organise their lives.[35] This, she declares, is not something that can be done by judges and in courts. I agree with Fallers Sullivan: law is not the space where the acts of imagining the religious–secular categories happen in a new way. Neither is law the sphere of social life where the individuals and communities have been using their religious and secular imaginaries to probe their moral intuitions and make better societies.[36] But while such acts do not happen in the realm of law, they do take place in the realm of civil society. Here we find rich encounters between the religious and secular individuals and communities, who act in the name of their convictions while also growing open to self-transformation. It is in this kind of encounter of deep religious–secular differences that the idea of solidarity as articulated by historian David Hollinger has a pivotal role to play.

## Solidarity and pluralism: ethical and sociological considerations

Solidarity is not an easy concept to define. Used in various disciplines – from theology, to moral and political philosophy, to sociology – solidarity acquired different meanings dictated by different disciplinary concerns. It can therefore refer to moral obligation or moral motivations that shape our responsibility to others,[37] to the ways in which the sense of solidarity with others emerges and is shaped by the structural differentiation of societies, or to the institutionalisation and the practice of solidarity in social and political life. The history of the concept of solidarity adds more layers to its meanings. Hauke Brunkhorst, for example, points out that in the Greek and Roman contexts the concept of solidarity denoted 'republican civic friendship,' while in the Christian theological contexts it came to stand for the ideal of charity.[38] But whether defined in moral or political philosophy, and notwithstanding the various historical incarnations of solidarity, this notion ultimately has to do with two mutually related phenomena: with the acts we do to support or help others and with the reasons why we do such acts.

Among the most important motivations for being in solidarity with others is a strong sense of interpersonal relations, which often comes with a recognition that we share identity, values, or beliefs with others (in the family, clubs, church, neighborhood).[39] Solidarity is here by definition communal and particular rather

35 Winnifred Fallers Sullivan, 'The Impossibility of Religious Freedom', *The Immanent Frame*, 8 July 2014, *Religious Freedom in the United States*, accessed 12 December 2015, available at: <blogs.ssrc.org/tif/2014/07/08/impossibility-of-religious-freedom>.

36 For social movements as the contexts in which societies probe their moral intuitions, see James M Jaspers, *The Art of Moral Protest: Culture, Biography, and Creativity in Social Movements* (The University of Chicago Press, 1997).

37 Simon Derpmann, 'Solidarity and Cosmopolitanism' (2009) 12 *Ethical Theory and Moral Practice* 3, 303–15; 304–5.

38 See Brukhorst in Derpmann, above n 37, 303–15, 305.

39 Klaus Peter Rippe, 'Diminishing Solidarity' (1998) 1 *Ethical Theory and Moral Practice* 3, 355–74, 356–7.

than universal: 'not everyone, but only the members of a community have these obligations.'[40] For some moral philosophers, such as Alasdair McIntyre, this is in fact the only kind of solidarity that can be truly moral because he does not think it possible for us to have a sense of moral obligation without a sense of loyalty to a particular community.[41]

McIntyre's views are developed within his understanding of particularity and strength of traditions and communities but there are also types of moral obligations and the acts of solidarity with regard to people who are different from each other. These twofold possibilities are reflected in Émile Durkheim's view of social cohesion: the sense of being bound to others because of similarity and fate, and the feeling of being bound to others because of functional necessity. This set of distinctions – ascription and necessity, between what we share with others and what makes us different from each other – shapes Durkheim's renown typology of mechanic and organic solidarity.

Mechanic solidarity, Durkeim proposes, is the solidarity we find in traditional societies. It is grounded in the simple division of labour and is defined through shared values and membership in a particular group. This is the kind of solidarity, American sociologist Michelle Dillon elaborates, we find in communities 'characterized by relative homogeneity' of 'economic and occupational structure' and of 'family and ethnic ancestry, religious affiliation, and political loyalties'.[42] Consequently, what forms one's sense of solidarity with others is automatic and mechanical, and based on shared ideas, values, and institutions. Reinforced by rare occasions for mobility – spatial, occupational, or emotional – the mechanic type of solidarity provides a grounding for a strongly bound collectivity.[43]

Organic solidarity is, in Durkheim's view, very different: it characterises modern societies and it emerges from the developed, more complex division of labour. Rather than through shared values or beliefs, organic solidarity enables social life because of the individuals' dependence on each other – on what they do not have, produce, or create but the others around them do. In the modern, urban societies, then, the word of the day is heterogeneity – heterogeneity of social roles and social relations and heterogeneity of convictions and beliefs.[44]

Durkheim distinguishes between structural and normative aspects of solidarity. Structurally, he establishes links between the sense of dependence on one another and the level of division of labour (division of social roles). Normatively, he proposes that, depending on whether solidarity is based on what is shared or how we differ, societies can have strong or weak 'collective conscience.' His consideration of the strength of collective conscience in some society is crucial: what he wants

40 Derpmann, above n 37, 303–15, 305.

41 Rippe, above n 39, 355–74, 365.

42 Michelle Dillon, 'Multiple Belongings: The Persistence of Community amidst Societal Differentiation' in William A Barbieri Jr (ed), *At the Limits of the Secular: Reflections on Faith and Public Life* (William B Eerdmans, 2014) 276–304, 279.

43 Ibid 276–304, 280

44 Ibid 276–304, 281.

to understand is the change from traditional to modern societies and the uniqueness of the modern condition. Most importantly for our purposes, Durkheim's typology arises from two sets of questions: are we in solidarity with others by virtue of being born into some community (with whose members we share identities and destiny), or are we in solidarity with others because we need them, despite *and* because of the fact they are different?

There are at least two reasons why these questions are pertinent to our discussion of the religious–secular problematic. On the one hand, the structural differentiation – the fact that we depend on others because we play different roles in the division of labour – suggests that modernity presents us with the necessity to regularly encounter those who are different.[45] On the other hand, the situation in which very different people have to live together presents us with challenges: can a sense of moral responsibility toward others emerge solely from the sense of necessity? Dillon argues, correctly in my view, that the 'plurality of identities in contemporary society also means that new group structures are created *intentionally*' and 'seek to knit community out of and across differences.'[46] This intentionality of communal identities, Dillon suggests, is what shapes groups such as support groups for working mothers regardless of their marital status, or the US organisation 'Dignity' that brings together individuals who identify as gay and Catholic. But while Dillon's observations are valuable, she does not probe the question of moral responsibility among modern individuals who do not share immediate needs, or those who differ from each other in terms of ontological positions.

Such questions are urgent today because we live in a global and pluralistic world in which, as David Hollinger puts it, the question of 'the boundaries of responsibility' is strongly contested.[47] And, in such a world we have a problem whenever we think that identity 'implicitly directs solidarity.'[48] For Hollinger, neither family or communal identity nor the functional dependence (which Durkheim posits as a norm of modernity) are robust enough for the kind of solidarity we need. The concept of identity, Hollinger thus writes, is 'quasi-mystical' and as such can promote violence;[49] the notion of community denotes 'a group defined by one or more characteristics shared by its members – whether or not those members are disposed to act together.'[50] Solidarity is different: it transcends the membership in a group into which one is born and it is more than just a matter of fate. It is first and foremost an 'experience of willed affiliation,'[51] entailing 'conscious

45 According to Dillon, what Durkheim shows us is that precisely the 'functional interdependence among institutions, sectors, occupations, and individuals *ensures* that solidarity emerges across difference', ibid 276–304, 281 (italics added).

46 Ibid 276–304, 286 (italics added).

47 David A Hollinger, 'From Identity to Solidarity' (2006) 15 *Daedalus* 4, 23–31, 23.

48 Ibid 23–31, 30.

49 Ibid 23–31, 29

50 Ibid 23–31, 24

51 Ibid 23–31, 24, 26.

commitment,'[52] a level of deliberation and choice, and 'a special claim . . . that individuals have on each other's energies, compassion, and resources.'[53]

Hollinger shares with Durkheim a concern with the nature of solidarity in the world defined by differences, but their inquiries are far from identical. Hollinger insists on a level of choice and agency – of freedom, we might add; Durkheim does not look at those possibilities in the context of cohesion since, in his framework, both mechanic and organic solidarity are dependent on, and even determined by, the structural differentiation of societies. And, while Durkheim's ideas delineate significant structural constraints of modern condition, the boundaries of choice including, Hollinger's argument carries philosophical, ethical, and political significance for our consideration of religious–secular relations. Solidarity is most needed and most difficult to achieve, Hollinger argues, when we have a choice to cross the lines of differences to develop a commitment to the same 'we.'[54] Such 'we,' as a result of the intentionality of affiliation, implies a complicated normative development because it often gives voice, as Dillon writes, 'to intersecting identities that do not fit easily within traditional structures that emphasize a single, overarching, and homogenized identity.'[55] Yet, the possibility of plurality constituting some 'we' is critical for how we envision the religious–secular encounters: the sense of solidarity between those who start with strong and different ontological positions can emerge only in the space of intentionality that Dillon describes and Hollinger posits as a needed norm.

That being said, Hollinger's argument does have two difficulties. First, even though his distinction between solidarity and identity is crucial, he seems to dissociate the two notions altogether. This reflects a view that the break occurs between more traditional, fated forms of belonging and the more modern, agentic ones. However, the relationship between ascribed identity and solidarity as willed needs to be placed on a more complicated – and more interesting – continuum. As the scholars of multiple modernities have been proposing for a while, encounters between tradition and modernity always happen in a more dynamic and dialectic manner.[56] Furthermore, the links between identity and solidarity are not only politically desirable but necessary in the pluralistic democratic societies,[57] in which the national identity is the framework of social cohesion while that very identity is being contested and redefined by cultural pluralisation and globalisation.

In the case of Solidarność, the connection between solidarity and identity was central to the movement's spirit and successes. Solidarność was enacted as the willed affiliation based on a sense of mutual responsibility among Poles of all backgrounds, workers and elites, religious and secular. But while The Solidarność

52 Ibid 23–31, 24.
53 Ibid 23–31, 24.
54 Ibid 23–31, 25.
55 Dillon, above n 42, 276–304, 286.
56 For the multiple cultural programmes involved in the projects of modernisation, see Shmuel N Eisenstadt, 'Multiple Modernities' (2000) 129 *Daedalus* 1, 1–29.
57 For this idea of Herfried Münkler, see Derpmann, above n 37, 303–15, 306.

movement was a result of the deliberate act of unity of the members of this movement, it was also intertwined with their strong sense of Polish national identity – by reflecting it and by informing that identity with the plurality of religious and secular positions. The Solidarność thus proves Jean Harvey's point that solidarity 'applies paradigmatically to moral obligations within communities in the face of oppression'[58] – it becomes critical in those historical moments when there is a need for reimagining and reestablishing the sources of moral obligations to one another.

## Solidarność: 'imperfect solidarity 'as a model of religious–secular pluralism

Solidarność was born in the summer of 1980, as the first labour union in the Soviet bloc over which the communist regime had no control. Within less than a year, this event of democracy in an anti-democratic state grew into 'everything at the same time: a labor union that defends the rights of the working people in their places of employment; an office that prosecutes lawbreakers in the power apparatus; a defender of political prisoners, law and order, and an independent culture.'[59] From a labour union, in other words, Solidarność became a social movement with ten million members of all professions and convictions – workers and intellectuals, Catholics and Jews, priests and the secular Left.[60]

With the advantage of hindsight, we know that the activities of Solidarność announced the beginning of an end of communism, its secular ideology and its model of economics. For these reasons, historians, political scientists, and sociologists have long been studying Solidarność, elaborating on its structure, context, politics, and lasting implications. But the movement's ethical and normative underpinnings that enabled, among others, its non-violent programme, still invite reflection and analysis.[61] The spirit of the Solidarność' ethic was put in motion in October of 1978, with the visit of the first Polish pope John Paul II to his homeland. This was a moment in which, in the words of one secular activist and intellectual Adam Michnik:

> the same people who [we]re so frustrated in everyday life, so angry and aggressive when queuing for goods suddenly transformed themselves into a

58 See Jean Harvey in Derpmann, above n 37, 303–15, 305.

59 Adam Michnik, 'A Year Has Passed' in Adam Michnik *Letters from Prison* (University of California Press, 1985) 124–131, 129–30.

60 As Polish sociologist Jadwiga Staniszkis explains, due to the 'quasi-totalitarian state, where the political sphere is ill-defined and tends to encompass everything', Solidarność had to 'pretend to be a labor union and remain responsive to a huge volume of accumulated grievances and demands of its members that went far beyond the scope of issues that a trade union could hanlde qua trade union'; see Jadwiga Stanizkis *Poland's Self-limiting revolution* (Princeton University Press, 1984) 18.

61 Gerald J Beyer, 'A Theoretical Appreciation of the Ethic of Solidarity in Poland Twenty-Five Years After' (2007) 35 *Journal of Religious Ethics* 207–32, 207–8.

> buoyant collective of dignified citizens. Discovering dignity within themselves, they became aware of their own power and strength.[62]

The papal visit encouraged Poles to stand up to the communist state as a unified nation. This unity did not imply the absence of conflict: there were many tensions among the Solidarność leaders and between the movement's leaders and members, especially about the type of revolution that Solidarność was going to be. There were also anti-intellectual and anti-Semitic Poles in the movement not enthusiastic about the role that the secular Jewish activists and intellectuals came to play. Historian Timothy Garton Ash's words of caution, however, are helpful in this regard: 'it is on its behavior . . . that Solidarity must first be judged', he writes, and what one needs to do is to distinguish between personal agendas of various Solidarność members and the movement's public agenda and activities.[63] Michnik, who was at first sceptical of the Solidarność only to become its adviser,[64] puts it this way: 'there were different people' none of whom 'had achieved that moral elevation,' but what matters, 'after all,' is not only 'how we live but also how we would like to live.'[65]

Aside from being an insider's reflection on the movement's complexities, Michnik's words are crucial for this discussion because they alert us to the centrality of ethics for Solidarność and its members. The latter can greatly influence one's analysis and interpretation. Thus, Polish sociologist and an adviser to the workers in the Gdańsk Shipyards, Jadwiga Stanizkis, remains in the strictly social scientific framework when she writes that Solidarność did not have a clear ideology at first due to its 'tactical silence' and because it was 'a loose coalition' of all opponents to the communist system.[66] But once we become attentive to the ethical considerations of Solidarność members, the openness of Solidarność to all ranks and ideologies ceases to be simply a political strategy; it emerges as an ethical disposition, which came to play the role of ideology. Michnik says something similar, when in the late 1970s he writes about the possibility of religious–secular collaboration. This is not just a political alliance, he argues, this is 'a *community* in humanist values.'[67]

For theological ethicist and scholar of Solidarność, Gerard Beyer, one of 'the most striking features of the Solidarity era' was 'the widespread awareness of the deep bond with others.'[68] The ethical meaning of this unity and trust – despite all the differences – was especially elaborated by one of the Solidarność's most

62 Adam Michnik, 'A Lesson in Dignity', in Adam Michnik (ed), *The Church and the Left* (The University of Chicago Press, 1993) 223–31, 223.

63 Timothy Garton Ash, *The Polish Revolution: Solidarity* (Yale University Press, 2002) 269.

64 David Ost, 'Introduction' to Michnik, above n 62, 1.

65 Michnik in Beyer, above n 61, 207–232, 209.

66 Jadwiga Stanizkis, *Poland's Self-limiting Revolution* (Princeton University Press, 1984) 19.

67 Adam Michnik, 'The Secular Left's Road to Dialogue', in Michnik, above n 62, 188–203, 203 (italics added).

68 Beyer, above n 61, 207–32, 209.

important supporters and its chaplain, Catholic priest Józef Tischner. To be in solidarity, this philosopher states, means 'to carry another's burden' because 'it is right' to do so.[69] Tischner does not posit his ethics of solidarity in a vacuum, as theological abstractions. For him, just like for his close friend John Paul II,[70] solidarity is a social practice and social phenomenon: it 'develops and becomes manifest in a particular social system, in a particular time and place . . . with people and for people', and what is especially important, with these people being who they truly are: believers being believers, the doubtful being doubtful, non-believers being non-believers.[71]

How was it possible for the Poles, so demoralised by the communist regime and exhausted by a long economic crisis, to rise above the most immediate needs and speak and act in the name of highest ethical ideals and common goals?[72] When the first strikes in Poland started, the renowned journalist Ryzszard Kapuściński writes, '[n]o one drank, no one caused trouble . . . Crime fell to zero . . . People became friendly, helpful and open with one another.'[73] How did an impoverished and broken society transcend differences in 'political, economic, and theological views' and, in so doing, counter the historical divisions between the Catholic and secular Poland?[74] For this to be possible, two ethical concepts seemed to have been particularly relevant: dialogue and the recognition of the dignity of each human person.[75]

Dialogue was the key notion and ideal for the Solidarność leaders, religious and secular alike. In the late 1970s, Michnik wrote an influential book entitled *The Church and the Left*. The book was a call for a dialogue and collaboration between the Catholic Church and the Left after decades of disagreements and distrust, and it opened the door for the later active role of secular intellectuals in the Solidarność movement. Michnik's invitation for a dialogue between Polish believers and non-believers draws on the ideas of the Catholic intellectual Tadeusz Mazowiecki, who says that dialogue 'occurs whenever there is readiness to understand the validity of someone else's position . . . whenever there is an openness to the values embodied in other points of view.'[76] As a result of this understanding of dialogue, Michnik attempts to build a bridge between the secular Left he represents and the Polish Catholic Church and Catholics in two ways: he repents for the sins that the Left made toward religion and the Polish Catholicism and its Catholic Church in

69 Józef Tischner, 'The Ethics of Solidarity' (2007) 1 *Thinking in Values* 37, 37–51, 37, 39.

70 As one obituary states, Tischner was such a close friend of John Paul II that he was among a few people who 'could get away with telling the Pope a slightly risqué joke', see *The Times* (London), 4 July 2000.

71 Tischner, above n 69, 37–51, 40, 38.

72 Beyer, above n 61, 207–32, 209.

73 See generally Reyszard Kapuściński in David Ost (ed), *Solidarity and the Politics of Anti-Politics: Opposition and Reform in Poland since 1968* (Temple University Press, 1990).

74 Beyer, above n 61, 207–32, 209.

75 I draw here on Beyer's analysis of the ethics of Solidarity, ibid 207–32.

76 Tadeusz Mazoweicki, 'What is a Dialogue?' in Michnik, above n 62, 172–86, 183.

particular, and, even more importantly, Michnik speaks of the Catholic Church as the main institutional defender of human dignity and rights against the communist totalitarianism.

For Reverend Tischner, dialogue carries an assumption that we can learn the truth only in relation to the other: we need to, he writes:

> look at ourselves as if from the outside, I with your eyes, you with my eyes . . . As long as I look at myself solely with my own eyes, I know only a part of the truth . . . The first condition of dialogue is the ability to sympathize with the other's point of view. It is not only about compassion, but about . . . a *recognition* that the other, from his point of view, is always to some extent right.[77]

Dialogue and solidarity, in Tischner's view, are mutually defined.

Michnik's and Tischner's thinking about dialogue was critical for both the theory and practice of Solidarność in its approach to Polish plurality. It meant that, after decades of divisions, religious and secular Poles could recognise that they did not share just an enemy, the totalitarian communist regime. They also had important moral concepts in common, the principles among which one in particular became speaking the truth. At the start of the Solidarność strike, Stanizkis writes, 'more than 55 percent of workers' could not 'label their political attitudes, and most of the 36 percent who support[ed] opposition groups . . . [could not] give any ideological reason' for what they did 'other than the argument that the "Opposition tells the truth."'[78] In our age, Beyer correctly notes, when people doubt the very possibility of truth and when there is an awareness about the power positions in truth-telling, the emphasis that the Poles put on telling the truth might look as an abstract ideal, or it might be viewed with suspicion and as naive.[79] In the 1980s' Polish context, however, the shared desire to speak the truth, to want to cast 'aside the masks,' and to request to 'be called by [one's] own name,'[80] was an act of courage – it was a stance against the life of fear. Instead of pretending, Tischner explains, '[t]eachers wanted schools to be real schools, universities to be universities, books to be books.'[81] What Poles experienced was something that Michnik – a secular intellectual – called a 'religious renaissance' and 'a collective return to issues of transcendence.'[82] Solidarność, in other words, was not just a movement of hope but a movement that attempted to transcend its historical moment in order to envision and build a better society – by imagining the collective 'we' that is, while particular and Polish, expansive enough to embrace all Poles, Catholic and secular alike.

77 Tischner, above n 69, 37–51, 42 (italics added).
78 Stanizkis, above n 66, 19.
79 Beyer, above n 61, 207–32, 223; Adam Michnik, 'A Year Has Passed' in Michnik, above n 59, 124–131, 129–30.
80 Tischner, above n 69, 37–51, 38.
81 Tischner in Beyer, above n 61, 223.
82 Michnik in Beyer, above n 61, 212.

The religious–secular dialogue enacted in the Solidarność context, to be sure, was not simply a happy celebration of all that the Poles shared. The ethics of dialogue that the Solidarność leaders practised nurtured an open and rigorous disagreement as well. Tischner, for example, sounds intrigued but also very critical in his response to Michnik's book; Michnik, for his part, addresses Tischner's comments critically and with no hesitation. But they can do this because neither one thinks that dialogue is easy or merely about what everyone has in common. For Tischner, 'the building of reciprocity' in a true dialogue means recognising the truth in the other as well as knowing the difference from that other. In a true dialogue, he says, one makes 'the personal truth of the other *a part* of my truth about him, and . . . the truth about myself *a part* of his truth.'[83] Michnik thinks similarly: 'dialogue is not a compromise', he quotes Mazowiecki, but 'an attempt to find a new plane of discourse in which it is possible to meet' with 'the tension of contradiction.'[84] To be in a dialogue in the Polish way, Michnik writes later in his preface to Tischner's book on Marxism and Christianity, is to do it as a polemic, with 'the rigor of brotherhood.'[85]

Michnik's and Tischner's capacity to recognise what the Poles shared and how they were different, their ability to collaborate and to disagree while keeping a sense of respect for one another – all that was enabled by the second ethical component of Solidarność, the idea of dignity of each human being. Emerging from the teachings of the Catholic Church, and especially the personalist ideas of John Paul II, the notion of the dignity of the human person was, according Kapuściński, a major ethical framework and motivation for the Solidarność members. There were instances, to be sure, when the ideals of equal dignity were not put in practice – the place of women in the movement stands as one such case. Yet, as far as the religious–secular encounters were concerned, both the religious and the secular leaders of Solidarność appropriated the language of human dignity and rights. It provided the ethical background for an understanding that a secular intellectual and a Catholic worker could work together and, even more, that they could make sacrifices for each other.[86]

Analysing Solidarność as a sociologist-observer and a participant, Stanizkis speaks of its 'political moralism' and 'moral crusade.' Political scientist David Ost describes the Polish Left, admiring its capacity to be open to various views and its blurring of the ideological boundaries.[87] This was a post-modern kind of politics, Ost maintains, whose goal was a 'permanently open democracy.'[88] Stanizkis and Ost offer careful and thoughtful analyses and interpretations of Solidarność.[89] Yet,

83 Tischner, above n 69, 42 (italics added).

84 Tadeusz Mazowiecki in Michnik, above n 62, 172–86, 183.

85 Adam Michnik, 'Foreword' in Józef Tischner, *Marxism and Christianity: The Quarrel and Dialogue in Poland* (Georgetown University Press, 1987) IX.

86 See Beyer, above n 61, 213–4.

87 Ost, above n 73, 16.

88 Ibid 14.

89 Ibid 14. As Adam Michnik stated in summer of 1980, the public life should be based 'social accord' that emerges from 'the institutionalization of conflict and compromise', see Adam Michnik, 'A Time of Hope' in Michnik, above n 59, 103–10, 105.

their notions of political moralism or post-modern politics do not help us understand why a secular activist such as Michnik could be so moved by the homilies of the Polish pope as to quote his words at length, about human beings as 'free and reasonable . . . conscious, autonomous and responsible subjects, who can and must seek the truth.' I felt, Michnik writes about the papal visit in 1978, that the Pope's words 'never to forsake Him,' were not directed only at Catholics but at 'me, a pagan.'[90]

Neither can the ideas of post-modern politics or moral crusades help us interpret the sight of 'a holy mass in the middle of a strike in the middle of the Lenin Shipyard' and then the moment when these 'same striking workers' refuse to follow the appeals of bishops to end the strikes.[91] What does help explain Michnik's admiration for the Polish Pope and the Catholic workers' commitment to protest (and to disobedience of the church) are the emphases on dialogue and the ethics of solidarity – the ideals that the Poles articulated and practised, and which allowed them see that the Catholic and secular Poles, while remaining different, also shared hopes about a more democratic, free, and pluralistic Poland.

## Conclusion

This chapter started with the focus on the global character and normative roots of the religious–secular conflicts in the legal arena; it also elaborated on some of the more important critiques of modern law in its approach to religions. But the main goal of the essay was constructive: while I affirmed the need to rethink the reified understanding of religious–secular boundaries, I also argued for the importance of religious–secular differences in order to probe their democratic potential. I therefore made a twofold proposition. Firstly, I suggested that it is a look at civil society rather than focus on law that can help us see the complexities of religious–secular pluralism. Secondly, I pointed to the ethics and the practice of solidarity as new trajectories for thinking about religious–secular relations in pluralistic societies: I argued that solidarity is a concept that can affirm both the overlaps and differences between religious and secular orientations.

These ethical and sociological propositions were then explored in the case of Solidarność in 1980s communist Poland. The discussion of Solidarność did not intend to suggest that a labour union such as this one was not about the power struggle against the communist regime – it certainly was. The analysis of Solidarność also did not attempt to show that this religious–secular alliance was not about strategy and politics – it certainly was. But the discussion of Solidarność did want to ask one central question about its historical development: how did something that started as a labour union become a social movement that was simultaneously a political and moral revolution – a turn, to recall Michnik's words, toward the transcendence? That question shaped an inquiry that took us beyond

90 Adam Michnik, 'A Lesson in Human Dignity' in Michnik, above n 62, 223–31, 230–1.
91 Adam Michnik, 'A Response to Critics' in Michnik, above n 62, 233–43, 243.

the concern with strategy and power, into the realm of ethics. And, what this inquiry showed was that, unlike law, the messy life of civil society opens complex and significant paths on which the boundaries between the religious and the secular become porous while they are also being sustained.

The Solidarność ethics and practices did so much for the course of Polish history and its movement toward democracy. By shaking down its own, historically confirmed, belief systems about the division between religious and secular Poland, Solidarność also shook down our own thinking about the interplay between religious and secular worldviews.[92] In so doing, in encouraging us to interrogate 'our own intuitions,'[93] Solidarność emerged as a model of religious–secular encounters that can enrich our approaches to – and maybe even contemporary legal thinking about – the synergies between religions and secularisms and their potential to make our democratic practices closer to the ideal of true, deep pluralism.

## References

Asad, Talal, *Formations of the Secular: Christianity, Islam, Modernity* (Stanford University Press, 2003)

Ash, Timothy Garton, *The Polish Revolution: Solidarity* (Yale University Press, 2002)

Babie, Paul and Neville Rochow (eds), *Freedom of Religion under Bills of Rights*, (University of Adelaide Press, 2012)

Barbieri Jr, William A (ed), *At the Limits of the Secular: Reflections on Faith and Public Life* (William B Eerdmans, 2014)

Beyer, Gerald J, 'A Theoretical Appreciation of the Ethic of Solidarity in Poland Twenty-Five Years After' (2007) 35 *Journal of Religious Ethics* 207

Cady, Linell E and Elizabeth Shakman Hurd (eds), *Comparative Secularisms in a Global Age* (Palgrave Macmillan, 2010)

Calhoun, Craig, Mark Juergensmeyer and Jonathan VanAntwerpen (eds), *Rethinking Secularism* (Oxford University Press, 2011)

Casanova, Jose, *Public Religions in the Modern World* (The University Press of Chicago, 1994)

Derpmann, Simon, 'Solidarity and Cosmopolitanism' (2009) 12 *Ethical Theory and Moral Practice* 3

Dienberg, Thomas, Thomas Eggensperger and Ulrich Engel (eds), *Himmelwärts und weltgewandt/Heavenward and Worldly. Kirche und Orden in (post-)säkularer Gesellschaft/Church and Religious Orders in (Post) Secular Society* (Aschendorff Verlag Muenster, 2014)

Dressler, Markus and Arvind-Pal S Mandair (eds), *Secularism and Religion-Making* (Oxford University Press, 2011)

Eisenstadt, Shmuel N, 'Multiple Modernities' (2000) 129 *Daedalus* 1

Fallers Sullivan, Winnifred, 'Religion, Law and the Construction of Identities' (1996) 43 *Numen* 128

92 For this kind of reading of the role of protests and social movements, see Jaspers, above n 37, 376.

93 Ibid 376.

Fallers Sullivan, Winnifred, *The Impossibility of Religious Freedom* (Princeton University Press, 2005)

Fallers Sullivan, Winnifred, 'We Are All Religious Now. Again' (2009) 76 *Social Research* 1181

Fallers Sullivan, Winnifred, 'Separationism and the sex abuse crisis' *The Immanent Frame*, July 20th, 2012, 'Sex abuse in the Catholic Church', available at: <http://blogs.ssrc.org/tif/2012/07/20/separationism-and-the-sex-abuse-crisis/> (accessed 12 December 2015)

Fallers Sullivan, Winnifred, 'The Impossibility of Religious Freedom', *The Immanent Frame*, 8 July 2014, *Religious Freedom in the United States*, available at: <blogs.ssrc.org/tif/2014/07/08/impossibility-of-religious-freedom>

Hollinger, David A, 'From Identity to Solidarity' (2006) 15 *Daedalus* 4

Jakelić, Slavica, *Collectivistic Religions: Religion, Choice, and Identity in Late Modernity* (Routledge, 2016)

Jakelić, Slavica, 'Secularism: A Bibliographic Essay' (2010) 12 *The Hedghehog Review* 3

Jakelić, Slavica and Jessica Starling, 'Religious Studies: A Bibliographic Essay' (2006) 74 *Journal of the American Academy of Religion* 194

Jakobsen, Janet R and Ann Pellegrini (ed), *Secularisms* (Duke University Press, 2008)

Jaspers, James M, *The Art of Moral Protest: Culture, Biography, and Creativity in Social Movements* (The University of Chicago Press, 1997)

Michnik, Adam, *Letters from Prison* (University of California Press, 1985)

Michnik, Adam (ed), *The Church and the Left* (The University of Chicago Press, 1993)

Milbank, John, *Theology and Social History* (B Blackwell, 1990)

Modood, Tariq, 'Introduction: Odd Ways of Being Secular' (2009) 75(4) *Social Research* 1169

Omer, Atalia, 'Modernists Despite Themselves: The Phenomenology of the Secular and the Limits of Critique as an Instrument of Change' (2015) 83 *Journal of the American Academy of Religion* 27

Ost, David (ed), *Solidarity and the Politics of Anti-Politics: Opposition and Reform in Poland since 1968* (Temple University Press, 1990)

Rippe, Klaus Peter, 'Diminishing Solidarity' (1998) 1 *Ethical Theory and Moral Practice* 3

Smith, Jonathan Z (ed), *Map Is Not Territory: Studies in the History of Religions* (Brill, 1978)

Smith, Kery E Iyall and Patricia Leavy (eds), *Hybrid Identities: Theoretical and Empirical Considerations* (Brill, 2008)

Srinivasan, T N (ed), *The Future of Secularism* (Oxford University Press, 2008)

Stanizkis, Jadwiga, *Poland's Self-limiting Revolution* (Princeton University Press, 1984)

Taylor, Mark C (ed), *Critical Terms for Religious Studies* (The University Press of Chicago, 1998)

*The Times* (London), 4 July 2000

Tischner, Józef, *Marxism and Christianity: The Quarrel and Dialogue in Poland* (Georgetown University Press, 1987)

Tischner, Józef, 'The Ethics of Solidarity' (2007) 1 *Thinking in Values* 37

Villa-Vicencio, Charles, *The Spirit of Freedom: South African Leaders on Religion and Politics* (University of California Press, 1996)

# 7 Love, law and the Judeo-Christian separation–individuation

*Joseph E David*

The study of Law and Religion is a post-enlightenment rapidly growing project that re-examines the consensual disparateness of law and religions, their resemblances and evolutionary history. It traces the ways and trends by which law and religion are articulated conceptually, epistemically, morally, socially, culturally and institutionally in different contexts and manners. The intellectual motives beyond the formation of this field reflect an increasing interest from both angles of legal studies, as well as, religious studies.[1]

Academic orientations of Law and Religion studies are aiming to expend knowledge and understanding of the intrinsic interconnections, interplays and interdependencies between law and religion as realms of normativity and sources of meaning. They reflect an increasing scholarly interest in the legal aspects, and their significance, within religious traditions and religious experiences. On the other edge, scholars of legal studies try to be more sensitive to peculiar features of particular religions and take pain to underscore the limited value of religion as a valid universal category.[2] However, it is important to note that these scholarly trends not only enrich the fields of study. They also lead deep revisions of social and legal theories which were established on the traditional perceptions of both law and religion.

The following analysis is wrestling with the notion of religious legalism and its meaning as a heuristic category in the study of Law and Religion, both academically and regulatory. Our basic inquiry is: how should we understand and treat the ideal of religious legalism within the discourses of religious differences?

Indeed, the conception of religious legalism plays a crucial role through more than two millenniums of history of Judaism and its interfaces with longstanding and established traditions. It seems, however, that regardless the high resolution investigation and serious textual analysis, there is a need to zoom out and develop

1 Besides the development of scholarly literature and research activities related to the study of Law & Religion, the emergence of scholarship about law and legality within religious studies support the observation that the last few years seen a 'legal turn' in religious studies. I elaborate on the characters of this 'turn' elsewhere.

2 Talal Asad, *Genealogies of Religion: Discipline and Reasons of Power in Christianity and Islam* (Johns Hopkins University Press, 1993).

a general outlook on the pragmatics of this conception within the process of separation–individuation of modern Judaism and Christianity as old two sister religions.

The conception of religious legalism encompasses a wide range of attitudes that ascribe religious meaning to legal content or to the compliance to law. Historical and conceptual elucidation of religious legalism challenges both regulatory as well as academic efforts in the study of law and religion. In the following analysis we will not face the regulatory aspects of religious legalism, rather the academic challenges of this conception which dovetails biblical scholarship, religious studies, legal history and theory.

The conception of religious legalism is a central axis of the western metanarrative about the differences between the scriptural religions. Accordingly, an opposition to legalism, or at least its criticism, stands at the essence of Christianity vis-à-vis other religious formats, such as: Judaism, Islam, Roman paganism and more. A tangible depiction of the Christian message as principled antithesis to religious legalism is provided by one of the most critical commentators on Western civilization, Friedrich Nietzsche:

> The law was the Cross on which he (Paul) felt himself crucified. How he hated it! What a grudge he owed it! . . . [f]or from that time forward he would be the apostle of the annihilation of the law [*Lehrer der Vernichtung des Gesetzes*]! To be dead to sin – that meant to be dead to the law also; to be in the flesh – that meant to be under the law! To be one with Christ – that meant to have become, like Him, the destroyer of the law; to be dead with Him – that meant likewise to be dead to the law. Even if it were still possible to sin, it would not at any rate be possible to sin against the law: 'I am above the law,' thinks Paul; adding, 'If I were now to acknowledge the law again and to submit to it, I should make Christ an accomplice in the sin'; for the law was there for the purpose of producing sin and setting it in the foreground, as an emetic produces sickness.[3]

Nietzsche sarcastically describes Christ's death as an illusion of deliberation from the law. He insists on portraying Pauline Christianity not as a new positive message of salvation, but as oppositional religion; a protest against the problematical form-of-life 'under the law', an outcome of the triple-decker nexus of sin, flesh and law. Nietzsche situates the Pauline detection of an intrinsic interconnection of sin–flesh–law at the very essence of Christianity which by justice depicted as antinomian religion. While Nietzsche presents Christian religion as systematic disapproval of morality of legalism (emphasising the law–sin complex), later political-theologians emphasised the political aspect in the Christian rejection

3 Friedrich Nietzsche, *Dawn Thoughts on the Presumptions of Morality* (Brittain Smith, trans, Stanford University Press, 2011) 48–9.

of legalism. Thus, Jacob Taubes (1923–1987) views the birth of Christianity as political transvaluation:

> it isn't *nomos* but rather the one who was nailed to the cross by *nomos* who is the imperator! This is incredible, and compared to this all the little revolutionaries are nothing. This transvaluation turns Jewish-Roman-Hellenistic upper-class theology on its head, the whole mishmash of Hellenism . . . transvaluation of all the values of this world. There is nothing like *nomos* as *summum bonum*. This is why this carries a political change; it's explosive to the highest degree . . . [t]he critique of law is a critique of a dialogue that Paul is conducting not only with the Pharisees – that is with himself – but also with his Mediterranean environment.[4]

The supplementary aspect of the seeing Christianity as anti-legalist religion is the image of the Jews as living 'under the law' and Judaism as law-based religion. Accordingly, religious differences of these two symbiotic–rival religions is summarised and reduced to the question of legalism whereas Christianity embodies rejection and deliberation from legalism, and Judaism extracts adherence to the law. This way, the question of legalism became a matrix for the Jewish–Christian religious differences, and a dichotomy of legalism and its diametric opposition – *anomism* served for self-representations and the marking of religious 'otherness'.[5] In fact, the role that the question of legalism has played within the history of the Jewish–Christian borderlines is an excellent example of the mechanism of which external representation is internalised to become a self-identification.

Thus, the stressing of Christianity as opposition to legalism raised in turn the perception of Judaism as a religion based on legalism, a perception that was well adopted and internalised by Jews themselves. Accordingly, the reduction of Jewish–Christian religious differences to the question of religious legalism became consensual also by those who carried the alleged accusation of living 'under the law'. Apparently, there is correlation between the intensification of the image of Christianity as anti-legalist religion and Jewish apologetics on the religious value of legalism. Jewish reflections on religious legalism not only accept the depiction of Judaism as being 'under the law', but also provided theological and political meanings to the equation of Judaism and legalism.

Moses Mendelssohn (1729–1786), the notable philosopher and scriptural scholar, through his endeavours to promote Jewish civil rights, believed that

4 Jacob Taubes, *The Political Theology of Paul* (Dana Hollander, trans, Stanford University Press, 2003) 24–5.

5 On the important distinction between the concept of 'otherness' and 'approximate otherness' see Jonathan Z Smith, 'What Difference a Difference Makes', in Jacob Neusner et al (eds), *To See Ourselves as Others See Us: Christians, Jews, 'Others' in Late Antiquity* (Scholars Press, 1985) 3–48.

traditional Judaism could integrate in civic life without giving up the religious identity of the Jews and without losing their commitment to their religious laws.[6] He believed to resolve the 'Jewish problem' by disentangling the Jews' tendency to preserve legal insularity and hence to be suspected unfaithful citizens. He thought that full civilian membership and loyalty to Jewish religious laws are reconcilable on the basis of a phenomenology that distinguish between state and religion – between civil laws (*gesetze*) and religious laws (*gebote*).[7] Against Spinoza who ascribed the Laws of the Hebrews as political laws which lost their validity upon the collapse of the Hebrew *politeia*, Mendelssohn insisted on the distinction between political and religious laws and determinedly rejected the voidance of the latter:

> In fact, I cannot see how those born into the House of Jacob[8] can in any conscientious manner disencumber themselves of the law . . . [n]o sophistry of ours can free us from the strict obedience we owe to the law; and reverence for God draws a line between speculation and practice which no conscientious man may cross.[9]

The core of Mendelssohn's integrative vision rests on a phenomenological distinction between the state's political demands and the religion's requirements; in fact, a distinction between different meanings of obedience and being 'under the law'. While political laws are valid and in force also against one's will and approval, the validity and enforceability of religious laws are entirely dependent upon intentional consent, empathy and willingness to obey. Therefore, political laws are essentially coercible and religious laws are intrinsically voluntary and meaningless otherwise. In fact, Mendelssohn argues, political and religious laws are fundamentally incomparable, and using the equivocal term 'law' in both contexts is confusing.[10]

6 Against the endeavours of medieval Jewish thinkers who claimed for harmonisation of the Jewish Law with metaphysics, the notable enlightenment philosopher and scriptural scholar, Moses Mendelssohn attempted to espouse obedience to the Jewish law with the political values of liberty, tolerance and citizenship.

7 'Here we already see an essential difference between state and religion. The state gives orders and coerces, religion teaches and persuades. The state prescribes laws, religion *commandments*. The state has *physical power* and uses it when necessary; the power of religion is love and *beneficence*', Moses Mendelssohn, *Jerusalem, or On Religious Power and Judaism* (University Press of New England, 1983) 45 (emphasis added).

8 A biblical synonym to the Israelites.

9 Mendelssohn, above n 7, 133.

10 This distinction surely parallels to Kant's distinction between political and ethical laws: 'A *juridico-civil* (political) *condition* [*Zustand*] is the relation of men to each other in which they all alike stand socially under *public juridical laws* (which are, as a class, laws of coercion). An *ethico-civil* condition is that in which they are united under non-coercive laws, ie, laws of virtue alone.' Immanuel Kant, Theodore M Greene and Hoyt H Hudson, *Religion within the Limits of Reason Alone* (Immanuel Kant, Theodore M Greene and Hoyt H Hudson, trans, Harper and Brothers, 1960) 87.

In contrast to Mendelssohn, later Jewish thinkers idealised the conception of being 'under the law' dialectically so it was indeed a peculiar trait of Judaism on the one hand, but its significance and meaning were translatable to general ethical, theological and political discourses. Hermann Cohen (1842–1918) is certainly a paradigmatic representative of this pattern. Cohen developed a theory according to which the notion of 'law', and more precisely divine law, should be understood as a communicative device between the deity and humanity in a manner that preserves monotheism and morality. As neo-Kantian,[11] Cohen argued that the notion of law is intrinsic to morality for it postulates its precondition, that is: free individuality.[12] Being 'under the law' therefore means to be responsive, yet fully submissive to one God.[13] Cohen equated the notion of 'law' to revelation and viewed it as a necessary vehicle that makes human beings God's addressees – 'the law of God is a necessary concept in monotheism.'[14] Yet, Cohen maintained the particular identification of Judaism with legalism and embraces the view according to which Judaism is to remain *nomic* insular religion:

> The continuation of the religion of the Jewish monotheism is therefore bound to the continuation of the law in accordance with its general concept – not to the particular laws – because the law makes possible that isolation

11 Kant himself wrestled with the Protestant stigma of Judaism as blind adherence to the law:

> The idea of living 'under the yoke of the Law,' on the other hand, has served since the polemics of the Apostle Paul as the dominant allegation with which to goad, tease, and heckle Judaism; intended as a stigma, it evokes the rebuttal: does not the sacramental rite of the Eucharist in this sense exceed the danger of legal ritualism attributed conventionally to Jewish law? To be sure, our reservation related to the distinction between ethical judgment and ritual laws of religious worship remains. However, the former doubt weighs even more heavily: is ethics at all compatible with an ethical system based on religious service and on the awe and love of God?

Herman Cohen, *The Ethics of Maimonides* (The University of Wisconsin Press, 2004) 26–7.

12 In that regard I am following Batnitzky's articulation of Cohen's position – 'it is the scientific foundation of ethics . . . [because] the norms of right create the possibility of ethics because they create the possibility of the free individual', Leora Batnitzky, Leo Strauss and Emmanuel Levinas, *Philosophy and the Politics of Revelation* (Cambridge University Press, 2006) 192.

13 In fact, Cohen had elevated the existential condition of 'living under the law' to an ethical ideal. Accordingly, man's endeavour was supposed to be directed at the liberation from individuality (his nature), with the goal of becoming a *social* being, ie a member of a state governed by law: 'God commands man, and man of his own free will takes upon himself the "yoke of the Law." The law remains a yoke. Even according to Kant's teaching, man does not voluntarily commit himself to the moral law, but has to subjugate himself to duty', Herman Cohen, *Religion of Reason Out of the Sources of Judaism* (Simon Kaplan, trans, Scholars Press, 1972), 345).

14 'Revelation and law are therefore identical. If the law were not the necessary form of the achievement of the correlation between God and man, revelation would not be so either. Thus, God's law is a necessary concept of monotheism', Ibid 339.

> which seems indispensable to the care for, and continuation of, what is, at once, one's Own as the Eternal [*des Eigenen als des Ewigen*].[15]

The thoughts of Leo Strauss (1899–1973) is another example of a Jewish self-understanding based on the typological religious differences through the anomist–legalist dichotomy. Against Cohen, who celebrated the particularity of Jewish legalism as demonstrative to the basic principle of morality, Strauss took it as a peculiar religious form-of-life that is based on a different perception of the relationship between thought and social life. Strauss' departing point is stating the irreconcilable opposition between philosophy and revelation, theology and law. Strauss blames medieval Christendom for replacing the Jewish understanding of revelation as divine law with a synthesis of revelation and philosophy. Through Christian scholasticism revelation was viewed as a matter of knowledge rather than legislation. In contrast to that, medieval Jewish and Islamic philosophy did not thrive,[16] and both religions succeeded in preserving the identification of the 'word of god' with divine legislation and thus enjoyed further freedom of thought.[17]

The fact that all of the above expressions of Jewish–Christian religious differences are uttered by modern thinkers is certainly not accidental. The reduction of Jewish–Christian differences to the question of legalism pre-dominates modern, rather than pre-modern theological and intellectual discourses. Furthermore, the becoming of legalism as a central axis of Jewish–Christian religious differences, and a conventional 'western metanarrative', is profoundly inspired by Martin Luther's theological construction of the Law–Gospel distinction.[18]

'The Law of God is immaculate, converting the soul'.[19] Thus that immaculate law of the Lord is no other than love (*caritas*):

> law is said to be of the Lord, either because He Himself lives by it or because no one possesses it except by His gift . . . [love] is the eternal law, Creator and Ruler of the Universe. Since all things have been made through it in weight and measure and number, and nothing is left without law, not even He who is the Law of all things.[20]

15 Ibid 366.

16 '[t]his difference explains partly the eventual collapse of philosophic inquiry in the Islamic and in the Jewish world, a collapse which has no parallel in the Western Christian world', Leo Strauss, *Persecution and the Art of Writing* (University of Chicago Press, 1988) 18–19.

17 'The precarious state of philosophy in Judaism as well as in Islam was not in every respect a misfortune for philosophy. The official recognition of philosophy in the Christian world made philosophy subject to ecclesiastical supervision. The precarious position of philosophy in the Islamic-Jewish world guaranteed its private character and therewith its inner-freedom from supervision. The status of philosophy in the Islamic-Jewish world resembled in this respect its status in classical Greece.' Ibid, 21.

18 Indeed, the association of Judaism and legalism does have roots in patristic literature, but the formulation of the two as equivalent is certainly inspired by the Lutheran construction.

19 Psalm 19:7.

20 Saint Bernard Abbot of Clairvaux, *Some Letters of Saint Bernard Abbot of Clairvaux* (Francis Aidan Gasquet, trans, Rallantyne Press, 1904) 197–8.

## Law as problem and as signifier of the other

From a pre-modern perspective, the equation of Christianity and Love and Judaism and Law is certainly not unquestionable. The above formulation of law and love as identical substances deeply associated with the deity is perhaps unique to Bernard of Clairvaux but evidently not foreign to medieval theologians and jurists.[21]

The delineation of Christian–Jewish differences through the anomist–legalist dichotomy is pivotal in Luther's theological reasoning, and Luther himself anchored this dichotomy in the Pauline theology. As it is well known, Luther designated the tension between Law and Gospel as a binary contrast between two incompatible comprehensive alternatives. The Law–Gospel (*Gesetz und Evangelium*) distinction according to Luther is a primer knowledge[22] that enunciates opposing religious realities:

> Therefore the Law and the Gospel are two altogether contrary doctrines . . . [f]or the Law is a taskmaster; it demands that we work and that we give. In short, it wants to have something from us. The Gospel, on the contrary, does not demand; it grants freely; it commands us to hold out our hands and to receive what is being offered. Now demanding and granting, receiving and offering, are exact opposites and cannot exist together.[23]

For Luther, the Law–Gospel distinction folds an all-encompassing dualist division covering a wide range of contrasting dichotomies: Old-New Testaments,[24] Moses–Christ, temporal eternal kingdoms,[25] lawmaking and law-ceasing,[26]

21 Gillian Rosemary Evans, *Law and Theology in the Middle Ages* (Cambridge University Press, 2002).

22 'We believe, teach, and confess that the distinction between the Law and the Gospel is to be maintained in the Church with great diligence', The Book of Concord, *Triglot Concordia*, *Epitome of the Formula of Concord*, Article V, 801; 'Hence, whoever knows well this art of distinguishing between Law and Gospel, him place at the head and call him a doctor of Holy Scripture.' Willard L Buree, 'The Distinction Between the Law and the Gospel: A Sermon by Martin Luther' (1992) 1532 *Concordia Journal* 153, 156.

23 Martin Luther, *Lectures on Galatians*, *Luther's Works*, Vol 26–7 (Concordia Publishing House, Vol 26, 1963) 208.

24 'Know, then, that the Old Testament is a book of laws, which teaches what men are to do and not to do . . . just as the New Testament is gospel or book of grace, and teaches where one is to get the power to fulfil the law'. Martin Luther, *Prefaces to The Old Testament* in Timothy F Lull (ed), *Martin Luther's Basic Theological Writings* (Fortress Press, 1989) 119.

25 'Moses had established the temporal government and appointed rulers and judges. Beyond that there is yet a spiritual kingdom in which Christ rules in the hearts of men; this kingdom we cannot see, because it consists only in faith and will continue until the Last Day. These are two kingdoms: the temporal, which governs with the sword and is visible; and the spiritual, which governs solely with grace and with the forgiveness of sins', Luther, above n 23, 138.

26 Scholastic interpretations that viewed the gospel as s 'new law' and Christ as a legislator comparable to Moses was rejected by Luther: 'For this reason then, when Christ comes the law ceases . . . the office of Moses in them ceases . . . The office of Moses can no longer rebuke the heart and make it to be sin for not having kept the commandments and for being guilty of death, as it did prior to grace, before Christ came,' Ibid 127.

legislation and grace,[27] genuine Christianity and erring and deviating versions of monotheism.[28] To be sure, Luther emphasised that not only Judaism is trapped 'under the law', other religions (Islam) and denominations (Catholicism) also failed to embrace legalism as a comprehensive doctrine.[29] Judaism, however, is portrayed as archetypal legalist religion and the Jewish persistent on legalism as intentional religious, or theo-political, agenda.[30] Over and above previous associations of Judaism and legalism, through Luther's theology legalism has been shifted from the political realm to the religious one, and became by that an indicator of religious identity. Moreover, the Luther's theology had design and shaped the discourse of religious differences upon this semi-gnostic typology; a typology that totalised and essentialised the religious differences as contesting political-theologies. Legalism, or being 'under the law', is thus taken as the most colossal religious mistake against which Christianity appeared to redeem humanity.

Indeed, Luther's antithetical construction of the Law–Gospel distinction is read into Paul's criticism of legalism and for this reason awareness of the Lutheran impact has led critical revisionist scholarship on the Pauline reactions to legalism.[31] The new readings of Paul suggest revised perspectives on the identity of Paul's audience, their religious affiliation and values, and offer better resolution on the targeted subjects of his criticism.[32]

27 '[T]he office of Moses . . . no longer causes us pain and no longer terrifies us with death. For we now have the glory in the face of Christ. This is the office of grace . . . by whose righteousness, life, and strength we fulfil the law and overcome death and hell', Ibid 127–8.

28 'There is no difference at all between a papist, a Jew, a Turk, or a sectarian. Their persons, locations, rituals, religions, works and forms of worship, are, of course, diverse; but they all have the same reason, the same heart, the same opinion and idea . . . [i]f I do this or that, I have a God who is favorably disposed toward me; if I do not, I have a God who is wrathful. There is no middle ground between human working and the knowledge of Christ', Ibid Vol 26, 396.

29 'You hear, therefore, that all the children of men, all who are under the law, Gentiles and Jews alike, come under this judgment in the sight of God, that not even one of them is righteous, understands, or seeks after God, but all have turned aside and become worthless', Martin Luther, 'The Bondage of the Will' in Lull, above n 24, 184.

30 'For you see and hear how they (The Jews) read Moses, extol him, and bring up the way he ruled the people with commandments. They try to be clever, and think they know something more than is presented in the gospel; so they minimize faith, contrive something new, and boastfully claim that it comes from the Old Testament. They desire to govern people according to the letter of the law of Moses, as if no one had ever read it before'. Luther, above n 23, 138.

31 The 'Lutheran Paul' teaches that human beings are fundamentally sinners trapped in the sin-flesh-law complex and they can be justified only by faith in Christ, not by the works done 'under the law'. The 'New perspective of Paul' ('NPP') argues that the tension between law and sin is universal and existential to the humans. Paul, therefore, is critical about it and indicates the possibility to live according to the Spirit, but not a peremptory opponent to 'work-ethic' and living under the law. See Stephen Westerholm, *Perspectives Old and New on Paul: The 'Lutheran' Paul and His Critics* (Eerdmans, 2004).

32 See David F Farnell, 'The New Perspective on Paul: Its Basic Tenets, History, and Presuppositions' (2005) 16 *TMSJ* 189, 189–243.

Evidentially, both revisionists and their opponents would agree that the preconception of Paul's sayings is the equation of *nomos* and *torah*, ie the nominised meaning of the *torah*, and against this backdrop reading Paul's reactions as constitutive to the discourse of religious differences becomes possible. On the face of it, Paul's criticism is not about religious differences and has no direct reference to the biblical *torah*, rather it is directed towards several aspects of the Greek *nomos*. It refers to the theoretical notion of *nomos* rather than a concrete material *nomos*,[33] and discloses an intrinsic tension within *nomoic* form-of-life, rather than rejecting the *nomos* in favour of a religious alternative.

The identification qua reduction of *torah* and *nomos* was indeed not Pauline. It was a product of the confluence of biblical ideas and values with Hellenic political conceptions since the 2nd century BC. Yet it is clear that the equation of *nomos* and *torah* was far more than technical translation; it embraced Hellenic moral and political values,[34] tore out biblical semantic of *torah* and recharged it with legal emphases. Because *torah* is a primer notion of the biblical theological worldview, this process of nominising the *torah* reflects the Jewish–Hellenic amalgamation on a very deep fundamental level. Against this Judeo-Hellenic background, Paul did problematise the *torah–nomos* reduction on theoretical grounds, and his critique opened new horizons of theological, ethical and political aspects of legalism and law obedience. The extract of this critique relates to the fact that the law, or the *nomos*, is essentially heteronomous, external and alien to mental attitudes such as love and faith. The law is not penetrable to the inner world and in fact opposes the inner life.

Nevertheless, the *torah–nomos* reduction is certainly not trivial and as many scholars argue the usage of *nomos* introduced a profound misunderstanding[35] of the very basis of Judaism, which was then perpetuated by the early Christian writers. Thus it is argued that the *torah–nomos* reduction narrowed the meaning and significance of *torah* as 'instruction' and 'teaching' to include only its legalistic elements.[36]

33 He refers to various *nomoi* – 'holy law' (νόμος ἅγιος; 7:12), 'spiritual law' (νόμος πνευματικός; 7:14) 'law of sin' (νόμῳ ἁμαρτίας) and 'God's law' (νόμῳ Θεοῦ; 7:25). More importantly, he outlines the intrinsic tension between the exterior 'flesh' (σαρκί) and the 'inner man' (ἔσω ἄνθρωπον), which corresponds to the distinction between the 'law of mind' (νόμῳ τοῦ νοός) and the 'law of the limbs' (νόμον ἐν τοῖς μέλεσίν; 7:23).

34 It is an embracement of the Greek view according to which living under good order through binging laws (εὐνομία) or lawlessness (άνομος) are excluding alternatives. Accordingly, civilisation emerged from living under *nomos*, while *anomia* or living without law, against the law or outside the law were considered an extreme evil a source of restless and insecure life, that accelerate wars and tyrannical oppressions.

35 Hans J Schoeps, *Paul* (John Knox Press, 1961) 213, for example, places the blame for what he perceives as 'the Pauline misinterpretation of *torah*' on the shoulders of Hellenistic Jewish writers, especially Philo.

36 This censure also oversimplifies the *torah–nomos* reduction, since the Greek idea *nomos* itself was multifaceted so the nominisation of the *torah* was not simply a projection of legalist setting on the biblical lexis of *torah*. In fact, for most Greek thinkers the 'written law' was secondary to 'higher' laws, such as the 'unwritten law' (άγραφος νόμος), the 'living law' (νόμος έμψυχος) and the 'law of nature' (νόμος φύσεως).

Nevertheless, it does not take a lot to acknowledge that the Pauline critique of the *nomos* stands for itself.[37] The application of Paul's critique on Judaism is viable only through asserting that the religion of the Jews is inherently associated with legalism and that the Jews' ultimately adhere to the law in practice. Certainly, these assertions are not free of doubts. Only later commentators viewed the Pauline critique as launching a theology of religious differences around the religious aspects of legalism and the link between religious identity and law.[38]

Marcion's (85–165) gnostic approach elevated the Pauline critique to an ultimate rejection of the *nomic* form of life, hence the Law and Gospel stand as mutually antithetical alternatives that manifest harsh dualism of the true god of the gospel (*deum evangelii*) versus the god of the law (*deum legis*).[39] Nonetheless, most of the patristic and medieval accounts did not follow this antithetical perspective and subscribed to an accommodative perspective according to which the religious differences are narrated through historical progress in which a *nomic* period was merely an intermediate phase in a restorative history.[40] Perhaps it will not be worthless to mention that narrating religious differences through historicising them is an accommodating method that was widespread in late ancient and medieval discourses of religious differences. Beside the Ecclesial traditions that install the Jewish–Christian differences on a historical continuum, it is a central theme of the Quranic theology vis-à-vis earlier forms of monotheism and revelations, and is also embraced by Jewish thinkers who provided meanings to typology of religious differences through historical narratives. Nevertheless, the recognition of legalism as a core and explanatory component of the religious differences was not an overall convention. In fact, for the most predominant medieval Jewish

37 Some commentaries on Paul limited the critique to a precise superfluous parts of the Mosaic Law marking a division between the irrefutable Divine Law and 'Second Legislation' (δευτέρωσις, *tinyan nimosa*, *second nomos*, *secundum legis*) which appeared as circumstantial need. See Charlotte E Fonrobert, 'The Didascalia Apostolorum: A Mishnah for the Disciples of Jesus' (2001) 9 *Journal of Early Christian Studies* 483, 483–509.

38 Paul's autobiography is certainly a crucial backdrop to his critique of the law. Prior to his missionary life, Paul was a student of the rabbis in Jerusalem. He was well acquainted with Hellenic cultural values and political principles, and obviously had complicated affiliation with the Roman legal system; he enjoyed the privileged status of a Roman citizen on the one hand (Acts 22:28), and was persecuted and executed by the same system of laws.

39 Tertullian reports that 'Marcion's special and principal work is the separation of the law and the gospel (*separatio legis et evangelii*), by which he contended the diversity of the gods (*diversitatem deorum*) (*Adversus Marcionem*, I: XIX).

40 Ephrem the Assyrian (4th century), as an example, suggested a tripartite periodisation: The Hebrew epoch, in which people were 'whole in knowledge' living naturally in accord with God's wishes and thus laws were not necessary; The Christian epoch which restored the old religion through God's gift that make laws again unnecessary. In between is the legal epoch in which people were incapable to live in accord to nature and thus laws were necessary. See Christine Shepardson, *Anti-Judaism and Christian Orthodoxy: Ephrem's Hymns in Fourth-Century Syria* (CUA Press, 2008) 75–7.

thinkers, law or legalism were totally not essential component of religious identity and thus irrelevant indicators of religious differences.

The equation of Christianity and Judaism with the Love–Law dichotomy can be countered on various grounds. In fact, the incongruity of this equation can be demonstrated through both religious traditions, Ecclesial and Jewish alike, and it surely deserves a broader exploration. In the following we will outline the incongruity of Jewish legalism from the perspective of medieval Jewish thought.

## Law as vehicle for flourishment and perfection

Reflections on the nature of Judaism as a religion, its legalist components and values by medieval Jewish thinkers, mainly those who lived within Islamic milieus, explicitly counter the identification of Judaism and legalism. By all means, their perceptions of the Jewish religion significantly differ from the ideal of 'being under the law'. Legalism and law, human laws as well as divine laws, in their perspectives are not primer theological elements.

Furthermore, in contrast with the Hellenic propensity to identify *torah* with *nomos*, medieval Jewish accounts on the divine laws and their religious meanings appear to stress the essential gaps between these two conceptions. Their acquaintance with Greek philosophy indicate that they did not only escape this nomenclature and conceptual identification, but consciously rejected the *torah–nomos* reduction even with regard to ostensibly *nomic* elements of the traditional content of *torah*. This anti-*nomic* interpretative trend is manifested in a variety of ways and on different levels; by demoting the legal value of the religious content, dislodging the law from the socio-political realm and by treating the law as means for higher ends. Some aspects of this trend will be illustrated below.

Against the traditional concern with the collective redemption of the Jewish people, intellectual circles in the Judeo-Arabic culture focused their soteriology on the ultimate felicity of the individual. In comparison to Paul's addresses, the target audience of these Andalusian rabbis were those Jews who focused on observing the Law (*Shari'a*) while neglecting the ethical and intellectual demands or goals.

The Saragossian jurist Bachya Ibn Paquda (first half of the 11th century) developed a systematic perspective that displaces the law from the socio-political field to the ethical-spiritual domain. Although lacking acquaintance with the ecclesiastical literature,[41] Ibn Paquda is highly sensitive to a key element of the Pauline critique – the exteriority of the law vis-à-vis the inner life of the self. Yet, while the Pauline critique extensively stressed the incompatibleness of the law, as heteronomous demand, and the inner mental attitudes,[42] Ibn Paquda claims to extend the

41 Though, Ibn Paquda was well acquainted and quoted Islamic sources, Menahem Manssor, 'Arabic Sources on Ibn Pakuda's "Duties of The Heart"', *Proceedings of the World Congress of Jewish Studies* III:C (World Union of Jewish Studies, 1973).

42 On the articulation of Paul's critique in terms of a tension between exteriority of the body and the inner self, see Farnell, above n 32.

applicability of the law to include also mental dispositions. In other words, unlike Paul, Ibn Paquda abolishes the distinction between external conduct and internal mentality, between submission to heteronomous laws and autonomous *affectus*. Instead, he asserts that the law also addresses mental state-of-affairs and that inner self is compliable to demands and duties.

Thus, instead of the antithesis of heteronomous law and autonomous love, Ibn Paquda developed a theory of dual agency encompassing an external-corporal agency and an internal-mental one. Accordingly, religious knowledge and obligatory contexts are also divided into two kinds: external knowledge concerning the obligatory matters of limbs (*jawarih*); and internal knowledge concerning the obligatory matters of hearts (*qulub*). The latter is more important than the former, since it is the heart[43] which decides both inward and outward actions. Consequently, once the internal duties are acknowledged and equated with the external duties the Pauline articulation of legal heteronomy as a problem vanishes, and harmony between religious mentality and behaviour is plausible and marked as a supreme religious goal:

> You should know that the aim and the benefit of the duties of the hearts is the balancing of our outwardness and inwardness [אהר ואלבאטן ’אלט ’מואזנה] in obeying God, so testimonies of the heart, the tongue and the limbs will be equated . . . if our outwardness will contrast our inwardness, and our belief [will contrast] our saying, and the movement of our organs [will contrast] our conscience – our obedience to our creator will not be complete . . . for our adulterated worship and false obedience will not be accepted.[44]

In the same line with his contemporaries, Ibn Paquda also viewed the divine law as historically relative and universal.[45] Thus, also the 'duties of the heart' are depicted as means to universal ends – ten fundamental religious obligations of the heart.[46]

The remarkable poet, scientist, commentator and philosopher, Abraham Ibn Ezra (1089–1167) in the opening session of his book *Yesod Mora*[47] explicitly

43 On Ibn Pauda's Sufi background and in particular role of the heart in the Sufi tradition, see: Saeko Yazaki, *Islamic Mysticism and Abū Ṭālib Al-Makkī: The Role of the Heart* (Routledge, 2013) 145–73.

44 Bahya ibn Paquda, *Hidāyah ilá farā'id al-qulūb* [*Guide to the Duties of the Heart*] (Yosef Kafah, trans, Cambridge University Press, 1973) 30–1.

45 Howard Kreisel, 'Asceticism in the Thought of R Bahya Ibn Paquda and Maimonides' (1988) 21 *Daat* V – XXII.

46 (1) unification (*tawhid*) and sincere devotion to God; (2) contemplation (*i'tibar*) of created beings; (3) obedience (*ta'a*) to God; (4) total reliance upon God (*tawakkul*); (5) the devotion of all acts to God alone; (6) humility (*tawadu'*); (7) repentance (*tawba*); (8) self-examination (*muhasabat al-nafs*); (9) renunciation (*zuhd*) of this world; (10) sincere love (*mahabba*) for God.

47 A monograph on the rationale of the commandments written on 1158 for a London friend, Joseph ben Jacob. On Ibn Ezra works and background see generally the works of Ibn Ezra, which can be accessed at: <http://plato.stanford.edu/entries/ibn-ezra/>.

criticises the conventional trends to attain expertise in the laws of the *torah*, those who aspire to gain juristic prestige (that eventually leads to social friction) and the aim of studying law to improve social order (because any law in a just society would be superfluous).[48] Ibn Ezra seeks an ultimate justification for the commandments that is invariant over any and every social or historical situation, since the divine laws of the *torah* should have an ultimate purpose beyond incidental circumstances. By rejecting a *nomic* view on the laws of the *torah*, Ibn Ezra states that the ultimate purpose of our existence as human beings does not lie in our contribution to communal life, but in the epistemic gains of understanding God's work and knowing Him.[49] Divine laws, therefore, are only one aspect of the divine revelation, not necessarily the most important.

Although Ibn Ezra acknowledged the political gist of medieval Neoplatonism, he evinces no interest in the 'ideal city'. He subscribed to the philosophical view according to which the purpose and goal of human existence is 'knowing God' and as such defined as individual task and responsibility:[50]

> The rationale [שרש][51] of the entire divine commandments is the love of God, with all his soul,[52] and unite with Him. And that would not be completed, only if acknowledging the deity's deeds on heaven and earth and by knowing His patterns . . . and knowing God is possible only through knowing one's mind, soul and body.

Despite the image of the theology of Moses Ibn Maimon (1138–1204) as a paradigmatic synthesis of political philosophy and *halakhah*, it would be wrong to identify the Maimondean thought as advocacy of religious legalism. Moreover, various expressions along his writing give the impression that he also retreats from viewing the divine laws of the *torah* as a case of *nomos*. In the introduction to his theological book, *The Guide of the Perplexed,* he distinguishes between the 'legalist' inquiries into the laws of the *torah* and the philosophical reading into it, by designating experts of the latter as potential addressees and excluding scholars of the former.[53] Moreover, towards the end of the last chapter of his earliest writings *Treatise on Logic* [*Makalah fi-sina'at al-mantik*] he depicts political science and

48 Abraham Ibn Ezra and Joseph Cohen (ed), *Yesod Mora ve-Sod Torah* [*The Foundation of Piety and the Secret of the Torah*] (Bar-Ilan University Press, 2002) 80–7.

49 'The person [*ha-adam*] must set himself aright. He must know the commandments of God, Who created everything. He must try with all of his strength to understand [God's] works – then he will know his Creator . . . and when he knows Him he will find favor in His eyes.' Ezra, above n 48, 84.

50 *Commentary* on Exodus 31:18.

51 Its literal meanings in medieval Hebrew includes: root, principle, reason, purpose and rationale.

52 Referring to Deuteronomy 6:5 – 'Love . . . your God with all . . . your soul'.

53 'It is not the purpose of this Treatise to . . . teach those who have not engaged in any study other than the science of the Law, ie jurisprudence [עלם אלשריעה אעני פקההא]. For the purpose of this Treatise . . . is the science of Law in its true sense [עלם אלשריעה עלי אלחקיקה].'

ends up with an interesting note on the limitation of the *nomoi* vis-à-vis divine standards of conduct:

> The learned men of past religious communities used to formulate, each of them according to his perfection, measures and canons[54] [תדאביר וקואנין], through which their princes governed the subjects; they called them *nomoi*; and the peoples used to be governed by these *nomoi* . . . in these times all the preceding – I mean the policies[55] and *nomoi* [אלנואמיס] – has been dispensed with and men are being coducted by *al-awamir al-ilahiyyah* [באלאואמר אלאלהיה].[56]

How are we to understand this statement? Is the distinction between *nomoi* and *al-awamir al-ilahiyyah* reflecting the distinction between human law and divine law, between *nomos* and *torah*? or something more essential?

The term *amr* (and *amara*)[57] in the Qur'an and in classical Arabic carries a rich variety of meanings. Basically it comprises two distinct groups of meanings, one with the plural *awamir* (اوامر), embraces the notion of 'order', 'command', 'decree' while the second, with the plural *umar* (امور), comprehends 'matter', 'affair', 'concern'. Medieval translations of the Maimonidean texts render the second meaning – 'divine matters' (עניינים אלהיים), 'divine words' (דברים האלהיים) or *res divinae*,[58] while Modern translations tend to emphasise the first meaning – 'divine commands' (צווים האלהיים) or 'divine laws'.[59] Nevertheless, the core meaning of

54 The Arabic term *qawanin* (قوانين; sing. *qanun*) usually translated as 'rules' but can fairly render the literal meaning as 'canons'.

55 The Arabic term *siyasat* (سياسات; sing *siyasa*) indicates both, policies and administrations. Medieval Hebrew translations suggest meanings more approximate with the former (Tibon and Vivas – דתות (Maimonides Efros Israel, *Maimonides' Treatise on Logic (Makalah Fi-Sina'at Al-Mantik): The Original Arabic and Three Hebrew Translations* (American Academy for Jewish Research, 1938) 63, 129)); Ahituv – הנהגות (idem, 99)), while modern English translations tend to the latter (Maimonides Efros Israel, *Maimonides' Treatise on Logic (Makalah Fi-Sina'at Al-Mantik): The Original Arabic and Three Hebrew Translations* (American Academy for Jewish Research, 1938) 64 – 'laws'; Lawrence Berman, 'A Reexamination Of Maimonides' "statement On Political Science"' (1969) 89 *Journal of the American Oriental Society* 106, 110 – 'regimes').

56 Latin *Res divinae.* Medieval Hebrew translations connote divine matters (footnotes added).

57 Joseph Horovitz, 'Jewish Proper Names and Derivatives in the Koran' (1925) 2 *Hebrew Union College Annual* 145, 145–227 argued that the Qur'anic *amr* derived from the Aramaic notion of *memra* which stood in Christian literature for the *logos.*

58 Logica Sapientis Rabbi Simeonis, per Sebastianum Munsterum latine iuxta Hebraismum uersa: quae Hebraeorum Comentaria uolentibus, non tam utilis est quam necessary (Basileae, *The Letter of the Word of God* (1527), accessed 2 March 2017, available at: <https://bildsuche.digitale-sammlungen.de/index.html> 57).

59 Efros, above n 55, 64, Ralph Lerner and Muhsin Mahadi, *Medieval Political Philosophy: A Sourcebook* (Cornell University Press, 1963) 189–90). Berman, above n 55, 110, n 10) righty note that the medieval versions seem to be mistaken as the plural form *awamir* 'can only have the meaning commands.' However, the fact that we have only one Arabic version while all medieval versions embrace the 'non-legal' meaning, allows speculating about the existence

Maimonides' statement is not varying by either meaning.[60] Clearly, Maimonides tells apart two types of guiding standards for human conduct extracted through two notions – *nomos* versus *al-amr al-ilahi*[61] – noting that through history 'divine standards' have replaced human *nomoi*.

Also, vernacular of 'divine standards' should be understood in a 'secularized' way.[62] The adjective 'divine' here basically means 'spiritual' or 'not corporal' as it appears earlier in the same chapter where Maimonides explains that 'divine science' (*al-i'lm al-ilah*) is the science of non-corporal entities that includes theology and metaphysics.[63] 'Divine standards' therefore should be understood as principles that are not human creation and self-imposed norms, but rather principles derived from theological and metaphysical knowledge.[64]

Interestingly, Maimonides narrates the distinction between *nomos* and *al-amr al-ilahi* on a historical sequence. Thus, the two are not only differing conceptually, but also illustrate historical progress. This is certainly not evidencing a factual acquaintance with the ecclesial literature, but it does reflect an anti-Hellenic historisophical view according to which the civilisational progress is a move from epoch in which people were governed by *nomoi* to societies ruled by divine standards.

## Conclusion

Rather than viewing the equation of Judaism and legalism as a consistent and inherent theological content, it is suggested to view it as part of the process of separation-individuation by which Jewish and Christian religious identities designed

of another version, not found yet, in which the Maimonidean text used the term *al-umar al-ilahiyyah*.

60 Berman, above n 55, 110 notes on the originality of this remark and explain it as a neutral account merely describing his contemporary circumstances according to which religious communities claim to be governed through 'divine standards' rather than human-made laws without prejudging the merits of the nomoi and its divine alternative.

61 Elsewhere, Maimonides differentiates between divine law (*sharia*) and nomos in respect to their manufacturing source; the former is a product of the prophets and the later of statesmen: 'Only this law do we call divine law [שריעה אלאהיה], the other political measures, eg the Greek *nomoi* . . . are the works of statesmen, but not of prophets', Moses Maimonides, *The Guide of the Perplexed* (University of Chicago Press, 2010) 39.

62 See Aaron W Hughes, *The Texture of the Divine: Imagination in Medieval Islamic and Jewish Thought* (Indiana University Press, 2004).

63 'The divine science [מלעלא יהלאלא] is divided into two parts. One of them is the study of . . . whatever appertains to God . . . and the transcendent intelligences. The other part of the divine science is the remote causes . . . and divine science is also called metaphysics.'

64 In fact, the devaluation of the *nomoi* certainly corresponds to Maimonides philosophical temper. In that regard she seems to share the views of Ibn Bajjah and Ibn Tufayl that religious laws are merely pointers to philosophical and theological truths. In that respect, medieval philosophers revitalised he ancient optional translation of the *torah* as *logos* rather than *nomos*. In fact, scholars also pointed out the semantic relations between *amr* and *logos*. See Roest A Crollius, *The word in the experience of revelation in Quran and Hindu Scriptures* (Università gregoriana, 1974) 71–9.

and defined themselves as alternatives. The demonstration of this claim has been made emphasising the sharp gap between three cultural settings: the late ancient Judeo-Hellenic backdrop, the medieval Judeo-Arabic and the post-reformation European.

In the wake of that, the predominance of legalism as a central theme in the developing discourse of religious differences seems an indispensable component in inter-religious polemics and dialogs. Nonetheless, a discourse of religious differences is also a constitutive process by which it creates and constitutes the perception of selfness and otherness. The furnishing of Jewish–Christian religious differences through the question of religious legalism is an example of a cyclic mechanism of representation, perception and identification, by which the Jewish 'otherness' is designed by Jews and non-Jews alike.

Whereas the medieval Jewish thinkers contested, or ignored, the ***torah-nomos*** reduction, the nomocentricity of Judaism and the religious values of the divine laws were also challenged and the discourse of religious differences was based on different themes and principles.[65] The Luthern theology at its timing revived and intensified the discourse of religious differences on the bases of religious legalism. Through radicalising Paul's critique of the nomos, Luther essentialised the association of Judaism and legalism, an insight that was internalised as Jewish self-perception and a major theme of the western myth about the Jewish–Christian religious differences.

## References


Asad, Talal, *Genealogies of Religion: Discipline and Reasons of Power in Christianity and Islam* (Johns Hopkins University Press, 1993)

Basileae, *The Letter of the Word of God* (1527), accessed 2 March 2017, available at: <https://bildsuche.digitale-sammlungen.de/index.html>

Batnitzky, Leora, Leo Strauss and Emmanuel Levinas, *Philosophy and the Politics of Revelation* (Cambridge University Press, 2006)

Berman, Lawrence, 'A Reexamination Of Maimonides' "statement On Political Science"' (1969) 89 *Journal of the American Oriental Society* 106

Book of Concord, The, *Triglot Concordia, Epitome of the Formula of Concord*, Article V

Buree, Willard L, 'The Distinction Between the Law and the Gospel: A Sermon by Martin Luther' (1992) 1532 *Concordia Journal* 153

Cohen, Herman, *Religion of Reason Out of the Sources of Judaism* (Simon Kaplan, trans, Scholars Press, 1972)

Cohen, Herman, *The Ethics of Maimonides* (The University of Wisconsin Press, 2004)

Crollius, Roest A, *The word in the experience of revelation in Quran and Hindu Scriptures* (Università gregoriana, 1974)

Evans, Gillian Rosemary, *Law and Theology in the Middle Ages* (Cambridge University Press, 2002)


65 By paraphrasing the brilliant study of Christine Hayes, *What's Divine about Divine Law? Early Perspectives* (Princeton University Press, 2015), we may say that while in ancient times the question of the 'divine law' was 'what's divine about divine law?' medieval thinkers were troubled by a very different question: 'what is legal in the divine law?'

Ezra, Abraham Ibn and Joseph Cohen (ed), *Yesod Mora ve-Sod Torah* (*The Foundation of Piety and the Secret of the Torah*) (Bar-Ilan University Press, 2002)

Farnell, David F, 'The New Perspective on Paul: Its Basic Tenets, History, and Presuppositions' (2005) 16 *TMSJ* 189

Fonrobert, Charlotte E, 'The Didascalia Apostolorum: A Mishnah for the Disciples of Jesus' (2001) 9 *Journal of Early Christian Studies* 483

Hayes, Christine, *What's Divine about Divine Law? Early Perspectives* (Princeton University Press, 2015)

Horovitz, Joseph, 'Jewish Proper Names and Derivatives in the Koran' (1925) 2 *Hebrew Union College Annual* 145

Hughes, Aaron W, *The Texture of the Divine: Imagination in Medieval Islamic and Jewish Thought* (Indiana University Press, 2004)

Israel, Maimonides Efros, *Maimonides' Treatise on Logic (Makalah Fi-Sina'at Al-Mantik): The Original Arabic and Three Hebrew Translations* (American Academy for Jewish Research, 1938)

Kant, Immanuel, Theodore M Greene and Hoyt H Hudson, *Religion within the Limits of Reason Alone* (Immanuel Kant, Theodore M Greene and Hoyt H Hudson, trans, Harper and Brothers, 1960)

Kreisel, Howard, 'Asceticism in the Thought of R Bahya Ibn Paquda and Maimonides' (1988) 21 *Daat* V

Lerner, Ralph and Muhsin Mahadi, *Medieval Political Philosophy: A Sourcebook* (Cornell University Press, 1963)

Lull, Timothy F (ed), *Martin Luther's Basic Theological Writings* (Fortress Press, 1989)

Luther, Martin, *Lectures on Galatians, Luther's Works*, Vol 26–7 (Concordia Publishing House, Vol 26, 1963)

Maimonides, Moses, *The Guide of the Perplexed* (University of Chicago Press, 2010)

Manssor, Menahem, 'Arabic Sources on Ibn Pakuda's "Duties of The Heart"', *Proceedings of the World Congress of Jewish Studies* III:C (World Union of Jewish Studies, 1973)

Mendelssohn, Moses, *Jerusalem, or On Religious Power and Judaism* (University Press of New England, 1983)

Neusner, Jacob, et al (eds), *To See Ourselves as Others See Us: Christians, Jews, 'Others' in Late Antiquity* (Scholars Press, 1985)

Nietzsche, Friedrich, *Dawn Thoughts on the Presumptions if Morality* (Brittain Smith, trans, Stanford University Press, 2011)

Paquda, Bahya ibn, Hidāyah *ilá farā'id al-qulūb* [*Guide to the Duties of the Heart*] (Yosef Kafah, trans, Cambridge University Press, 1973)

Saint Bernard Abbot of Clairvaux, *Some Letters of Saint Bernard Abbot of Clairvaux* (Francis Aidan Gasquet, trans, Rallantyne Press, 1904)

Schoeps, Hans J, *Paul* (John Knox Press, 1961)

Shepardson, Christine, *Anti-Judaism and Christian Orthodoxy: Ephrem's Hymns in Fourth-Century Syria* (CUA Press, 2008)

Strauss, Leo, *Persecution and the Art of Writing* (University of Chicago Press, 1988)

Taubes, Jacob, *The Political Theology of Paul* (Dana Hollander, trans, Stanford University Press, 2003)

Westerholm, Stephen, *Perspectives Old and New on Paul: The 'Lutheran' Paul and His Critics* (Eerdmans, 2004)

Yazaki, Saeko, *Islamic Mysticism and Abū Ṭālib Al-Makkī: The Role of the Heart* (Routledge, 2013)

# 8 From enemy to neighbour?

## The Armenian issue in the Ottoman Turkey and problem of 'de-victimisation' of Armenian society

*Hovhannes Hovhannisyan*

### Introduction

The historical memory of an ethnic group has significant importance for definition of 'national identity', 'nation' and national features.[1] Traditions, customs, religion and historical events play essential roles in forming the national memory, which in its turn defines the relationships amongst the members of a society, and the attitude of the society and its members towards other communities, ethnic groups, countries, etc. The historical memory of Armenians is based on the history of the past and especially on the traumatic history of the Armenian genocide of 1915 which has had an essential influence on the formation of Armenian national identity, especially in the Armenian diaspora. The events which happened in Ottoman Turkey at the beginning of the 20th century should and were somehow overcome by the events that happened after the collapse of the Soviet Union, especially by the independence of the Armenian Republic in 1991 and the Nagorno-Karabakh War between Armenians and Azerbaijan during 1992–94. This article analyses these three major historical events and the process of victimisation caused by the Armenian Genocide and de-victimisation caused by Independence and the Nagorno-Karabakh War. This approach is developed by Harutyun Marutyan as he analyses the iconography of Armenian identity through the memory of genocide and the Karabakh movement.[2]

This chapter is based on the importance of the past and its impact on the formation of national identity which is a multi-layer process constructed and reconstructed according to the needs, interests and perception of an ethnic group.[3] As Anthony Smith indicates, the past of a nation plays a role not only in nation building processes and nationalism but it also creates the present which has a direct

1 Anthony D Smith, *National Identity* (University of Nevada Press, 1991) 14, 40 etc.

2 Harutyun Marutyan, *Iconography of Armenian Identity: The Memory of Genocide and the Karabakh Movement* (Publishing House of NASRA, 2009).

3 Eric J Hobsbawm, 'Social Function of the Past: Some Questions' (1972) 55 *Past and Present* 3; Eric Hobsbawm, 'Ethnicity and Nationalism in Europe today' (1992) 8 *Anthropology Today* 3; Anthony D Smith, *Myths and Memories of the Nation* (Oxford University Press, 1991) 11–17.

influence on political, social processes and forms a new kind of identity.[4] This idea is also developed by Levon Abrahamian while he discusses the four models of national identity based on the relationship of the past and present.[5]

The article also uses the concept of collective memory in the context of reconstruction of the past and its adaptation for the present in the collective conscience of the people. This approach is developed by Maurice Halbwach[6] who asserts that information gained by certain individuals are altered due to adaptation to the reality and widening of the knowledge and views of groups and individuals which change over time. How the group and individuals interact with each other makes their connection stronger as the inter-influence grows and expands. Group knowledge refreshes the memory of the individual whilst the individual tries to enrich the collective memory of the group through analysis, knowledge, new information and adaptation. The adaptation of the past by present was developed in the works of scholars such as Michael Foucault, Eric Hobsbawn, Charles Horton Cooley and others.

George Herbert Mead considers that present includes the past and future and past is reflected in the memory which he calls 'the backward limit of the present'. His theory tries to interpret the present though the historical images and memory of the past; however, he states that the changes in the present irrevocably bring loss of the facts of the past and the memory of the past in turn loses its significance.[7]

Harutyun Marutyan draws attention to various facts about how, after their independence, Armenians revealed many facts about the Soviet past which totally changed their perception about the communist party and its leaders, which had a destabilising effect, as the real facts of the past directly impacted on the present.[8] Using the term of Hobsbawm 'invention of tradition'[9] I explain how the Armenians reinvented their traditional identity after discovering hidden facts of their past, especially concerning the genocide and hidden contract between the communist leaders and Turkey agreeing to the inclusion of Nagorno-Karabakh within the territory of communist Azerbaijan.

The memory on genocide was preserved in the memories of individuals, families, groups and it was transferred through generation to generation by various survival stories, mostly horrible. Armenians usually ask each other the question

4 Smith, above n 1, 14–21.

5 Levon Abrahamian, 'Four Models of Consolidating National Identity' in Albert Stepanyan (ed), *Inknutyan hartser: Taregirk øProblems of Identity, Annualπ* (Yerevan, Zangak, 2002) 43–56 (in Armenian).

6 Maurice Halbwachs, *The Collective Memory*, from the French (F J Ditter Jr and V Yazdi Ditter trans, Harper & Row Publishers, 1980) 24–30.

7 For more details of this theory see David R Maines, Noreen M Sugrue and Michael A Katovich, 'The Sociological Import of G H Mead's Theory of the Past' (1983) 48 *American Sociological Review* 161, 161–173.

8 Marutyan, above n 2, 14–15.

9 Eric Hobsbawm, 'Introduction: Inventing traditions' in Eric Hobsbawm and Terrence Ranger (eds), *The Invention of Tradition* (Cambridge University Press, 1983) 1–14.

'where are you from' meaning not their current address but the region or city of their ancestors. Most of the answers refer to a region or territory in current Turkey which Armenians call 'Western Armenia' in the public discourse. The concept of 'motherland' is also transformed in the collective memory of the generations of Armenians living abroad as they do not consider the contemporary Armenia as their motherland because they have the memory from their ancestors of the 'sacred lands' from which they were coercively expelled. The Armenians who migrated to Eastern Armenia or Russian Armenia named the areas they settled into after the same names of their motherland (Malatia, Sebastia, Zeytun, etc). By such acts, they kept the memory about their past but at the same time found a new reality.[10]

The maintenance of collective memory and especially memory of lost land and the 'unsolved Armenian issue' is seen in the naming of newborns in Armenia. Many of the newborns are named after the towns or historical-geographical places they lived in the lost motherland (Ani, Vaspurakan, Van, etc). Among the Armenian descendants in diaspora it is very popular to name the male newborns Vrezh (revenge) as a manifestation of the restoration of justice in the future.[11] After the declaration of independence the names of newborns are changing due to the time and style and as we see the appearance of more European and American names are having an increasing influence on Armenian and also broader civilisation trends.

The transformation of a nation's collective memory in becoming more nationalistic usually happens when essential facts about the historical background, culture and traditions of the nation are hidden due to different circumstances and causes. The subsequent revelation of those facts may have a shocking effect upon the society; it may bring uprisings and revolts and have the most unexpected consequences. During the Armenian recent history the emergence of such a revolt of revolution happened in 1965 for the rememberance of the 50th year of genocide, which became a movement for independence in 1988 and eventually resulted in the declaration of Armenia as an independent republic in 1991. The chronicling of the events of the past and its commemoration assists the people to keep the link to their history and keep those events rooted in their collective memory.[12] The collapse of the Soviet Union opened the 'Pandora's box' of national identity and the ethnic issue resulted in the Nagorno-Karabakh War where the 'anti-Turkish' element played an essential role in restoring the sense of justice lost about 80 years ago.

10 Peter Burke, 'History as Social Memory' in Thomas Butler (ed), *Memory: History, Culture and the Mind* (Basil Blackwell, 1989) 108.

11 Luisa Passerini, 'Memories Between Silence and Oblivion' in Katherine Hodgkin and Susannah Radstone (eds), *Contested Pasts: The Politics of Memory* (Routledge, 2003) 248–9.

12 Barry Schwartz, 'Social Context of Commemoration: A Study in Collective Memory' (1982) 61 *Social Forces* 377.

## Genocide as a turning point in the formation of Armenian identity

This article does not discuss all the details connected to genocide but explores some essential facts and aspects of it to show why the Armenian genocide became an essential element of Armenian identity and how the victimisation of the nation took place.

Starting from the Russio-Turkish War of 1877–78 the 'Armenian case' became an issue for the diplomatic debates of the European countries of Turkey and Russia. The Armenian case was on the table of negotiations during the San Stefano (Article 16) and Berlin Congresses (Article 61); but no essential reforms took place in Turkey in relation to Armenians. Moreover, during the 1894–95 negotiations the sultan, Abdul Hamid, organised massacres of Armenians in a different part of Turkey.[13] The issue did not get its solution after the Ottoman Constitutional Revolution of 1908 by Young Turks (or Ittihadists).[14]

During the first period of their governance the Young Turks welcomed the equality among the various nationalities living in the territory of Turkey but this policy did not last for very long. Soon Ottomanism, Islam and Turkism formed the integral parts of their ideology which eventually led to the planning and organising of the first genocide at the beginning of the 20th century. Thus, Turkism-centered ideology became the official view in regard to the construction of the new Turkish state.[15]

The first official step was made during the secret conclave of Young Turks in Salonika in 1910, where a decision was made to crush the 'non-Muslim communities' in Turkey and this approach was reinforced in 1911 in a similar forum. The succeeding years showed that the Young Turks Government was taking appropriate steps to turn their ideology into life and to 'clean' the non-Muslim communities in the country. At the same time the Young Turks governments could effectively use the local nationalistic forces, such as the Armenian Revolutionary Party Dashnaktsutyun, and though the Party changed its policy towards the Government in its congress held in Erzurum in July 1914, the Young Turks Government had already made its decision and started to implement the first phase of the genocide.[16]

The first step was to deprive the Armenian population of a resistance force, ie men who could use weapons. About 60,000 men from the population aged between 18–50 were recruited to the Turkish army and sent to the front line and many of them did not return from army service. The Armenians failed to understand the Turkish essence of the Young Turks policy and continued to 'show

13 Richard G Hovhannisyan, 'The Armenian Question in the Ottoman Empire' in Richard G Hohannisyan (ed), *Armenian People from Ancient to Modern Times, vol II* (New York, 1997) 222–6.

14 Ibid 230–3.

15 Christopher J Walker, 'World War I and the Armenian Genocide' in Richard G Hohannisyan, above n 13, 239–42.

16 Hovhannisyan, above n 13, 232.

loyalty to old-fashioned Ottomanism',[17] even holding services in Churches for the Ottoman army. At the same time the Armenians living in the Russian empire had to take part in the war at the ranks of Russian troops as the major military processes were happening mostly in the territories inhabited by Armenians and the Armenians did not have the chance to escape from these processes. Moreover, the major military leader Enver pasha thanked Armenians for taking part in the Sarikamish campaign, (January 1915), where the Turkish forces were defeated. But soon after these failed military actions the Armenians were blamed for supporting the Russian troops and step by step the Armenians were disarmed and subsequently forced to undertake mostly manual labour. The disarming process of Armenians took place in the whole territory of the Ottoman Turkey, which opened the hands of Young Turks to implement the planned and mass killing of Armenians.

During the second stage, starting from April to August 1915, in almost all of the major centres, Armenians were organised for a so-called mass deportation to the desert of Deir ez-Zor and other places. The majority of Armenians were killed on the roads to the final destination, among them the Armenians who had lived far away from the front line and indeed had no known influence over the military processes. The Armenians were deported from Zeitun, Van, Urfa, Erzerum, Mush, Sasun, Bitlis, Kharpert, Sivas and other cities. No mercy was shown to old people, pregnant or nursing women or children. In the houses of those Armenians who had been expelled, the Government settled Muslim refugees (Muhajirs). Brutal mass killings happened in the Van region (where Armenians made up the majority compared to the local Kurdish and Turkish population) headed by Jevdet Bey, where around 55,000 people were killed during several months in 1915. If any Muslims sheltered the Armenians, they were to be sentenced to the death penalty. Notwithstanding these strict measures, many Muslims sheltered the Armenians from these mass killings. In some places the local governors (such as Jelal Bey of Aleppo) refused to implement the orders of the Government and saved thousands of lives.[18]

On 23–24 April, the Turkish Government arrested around 235 community leaders, writers and educators, more than 600 vivid public actors – doctors, members of Parliament (including Hovhannes Serenkiulian and Krikor Zohrab) were arrested and shot nearby the Urfa. Comparatively, no mass killings took place in Constantinople because of the presence there of foreign ambassadors. The famous clergymen and singer Komitas was saved by the intermediation of European ambassadors. Suffering from post-traumatic stress disorder as a result of this ordeal, he later died in Paris.

At the beginning of September 1915, the majority of the Armenian population had been exterminated. The methods used by authorities against the Armenian citizens were numerous, as described by lieutenant Said Ahmed.[19] The massacres

17 Walker, above n 15, 244–5.

18 Johannes Lepsius, *Deutschland und Armenien, 1914–1918* (General Books LLC, 1919) 193, 495.

19 Great Britain, *Public Record Office*, Classes 371 and 424, 7.

of Armenians were implemented by Turkish and Kurdish forces as well as 'Special Organization' and 'butcher battalions' composed of criminals released from gaols for implementing the deportation and massacres of Armenians.[20] Even the requests of Armenian Catholics in Etchmiadzin to the United States and European countries did not change the situation and the extermination of the population continued. The answers received from the leaders of European countries were mostly neutral and even cynical.[21] Instead, humanitarian organisations and individuals started campaigns in different countries to raise money for the survivors of the genocide who had managed to flee to Transcaucasia.

In some places the Armenians took self-defence measures, some of which were successful. The most famous one was the success of Musa Dagh (Mountain), whereupon receiving the order of deportation the local population decided to organise self-protection and moved to higher ground. They fought against the regular Turkish army for seven weeks until they were rescued by a French naval vessel and were able to ship about 4,000 people to Port Said, Egypt.[22]

Professor Bernard Lewis in his book *The Emergence of Modern Turkey* (1968) calculates that approximately 1.5 million Armenians were killed in Turkey and all later studies use this number although there are still debates on this figure.[23] Notwithstanding the official denial by the current Turkish authorities, the voluminous testimonies of the survivors of the genocide, as well as the published testimonies of eyewitnesses, such as US Ambassador Henry Morgentau, Dr Johannes Lepsius, Dr Martin Niepage and many others, on the cruelties, forced conversion to Islam, violence and mass killings prove that the events cannot be described otherwise than as a genocide.

As a result of the genocide thousands of Armenians left their homes and dispersed all around the world, forming the Armenian diaspora, which became the basic maintainer of the collective memory during the Soviet period. Afterwards, the Republic of Armenia took the role to commemorate and chronicle the events of 1915 known as the Armenian genocide.

## Independence of Armenia and first stage of de-victimisation

During the existence of the first Republic of Armenia (1918–20) the Armenian authorities did not possess the political and diplomatic tools to pursue the recognition issue of the Armenian genocide. During the first years after the genocide

20 Arnold J Toynbee, *The Western Question in Greece and Turkey* (Martino Publications, 1922) 280.

21 Great Britain, *The Treatment of Armenians in Ottoman Empire* (Foreign Office, 1916); see generally, Toynbee, above n 20.

22 For more details on the organisation of genocide and its consequences see Vahakn N Dadrian, *The History of the Armenian Genocide: Ethnic Conflict from the Balkans to Anatolia to the Caucasus* (Berghahn Books, 1995).

23 Walker, above n 15, 271–2.

the testimonies of eyewitnesses were also not published and it was not possible to make any kind of campaign against the Turkish State; though the major organisers of the genocide – Taleat, Enver and Jemal pashas were accused by the Turkish court and were murdered by Armenian avengers in different places and circumstances. The murderer of Taleat Pasha, Soghomon Tehlerian, was found innocent by the German Court after he shot the main organiser of the genocide in the centre of Berlin on the grounds of temporary insanity owing to his traumatic experiences suffered during the genocide.

During the Soviet period of Armenia (1920–91) the topic of genocide was prohibited in the context of Soviet policy as a part of the non-circulation of ethnic, religious issues within the empire. However, on 24 April 1965, due to the 50th anniversary of the Armenian genocide, the communist leader of Armenia, Yakov Zarobian, opened the genocide memorial called Tsitsernakaberd on one of the hills of Yerevan and, for the first time in Soviet Union rule, a huge demonstration took place in Yerevan.[24] The demonstrators held posters demanding the recognition of the Armenian genocide by Turkey and the 'solution of the Armenian case'.[25] Large demonstrations took place in a number of cities across the world. Soon after the demonstration, the communist party released Yakov Zarobian as head of the country but the emergence of such a nationalistic movement was quite a remarkable event for Armenian society at the time.[26]

After the declaration of the policies of Glasnost' (Publicity) and 'Perestroyka' (Reconstruction) by the Soviet leader Mikhail Gorbachov, the nationalistic issue was raised in the Soviet republics with a new force. Starting from 1988 the Pan-Armenian Movement started the struggle for a new reality, for breaking the Soviet practices against free choice, freedom of expression and other democratic values. Firstly, the leaders did not have the intention to struggle for independence but the course of the movement changed the initial intentions of the leaders which was supported by the processes happening in the Soviet Union. The leaders of the movement were arrested, but they were later released as a result of the pressure of famous people such as Andrey Sakharov, Elena Staravoytova and others, which even intensified the movement and resulted in the victory of the leaders of nationalistic forces in the elections for the Supreme Council (Parliament) in 1990–91. The communist party was disheartened and could not resist the increasing power of the nationalistic movement. One of the leaders, Levon Ter-Petrosyan, was elected as the head of parliament in 1990. Later, in October 1991, he was elected as the first president of an independent Armenia.

24 Varag Arakelyan, 'April 24, 1965', *Hayk*, 23 April 1996 (in Armenian).

25 Jacob D Lindy and Robert Jay Lifton (eds), *Beyond invisible walls: the psychological legacy of Soviet trauma, East European therapists and their patients* (Brunner-Routledge, 2001) 192; Mark R Beissinger, *Nationalist mobilization and the collapse of the Soviet State* (Cambridge University Press, 2002) 71.

26 Thomas De Waal, *Great Catastrophe: Armenians and Turks in the Shadow of Genocide* (Oxford University Press, 2015) 140–2.

On 23 August 1990, the Declaration for Independence was adopted by the parliament, which eventually led to the referendum for independence on 21 September 1991, when more than 90% of Armenians voted for independence. The march to independence was accompanied by an evaluation of the Soviet past and the revelation of facts hidden during the Soviet period concering Armenia and Nagorno-Karabakh. This in turn fortified the movement to obtain justice for the Armenian case which they identified in the case of Nagorno-Karabakh. As a result of these revelations the discreditation of the Societ past expanded into all aspects of public life, including changes made to museums where the Soviet period was preserved for the archives and Soviet achievements were considered as degradation for the nation.[27]

The Declaration for Independence clearly stated the attitude of the future Armenian State towards the past of Armenia (international recognition of genocide), evaluation of the present and its vision for the future. The Declaration also defines the separation of the legislative, executive and judicial powers and provides some privileges for diaspora Armenians.

The victory of nationalistic forces over the communist party in the democratic elections was conditioned not only by the democratic revolution happening in the country but also the power of the historical-collective memory to re-establish the historical justice. The historical-collective memory may bring mobilisation of the society which may be used by some political forces due to its huge potential.[28] Political elites usually make a great profit out of such mobilisation but in the case of Armenia the newly-developed political elite tried to use the force of mobilised Armenian society for the sake of independence and the solution of the Nagorno-Karabakh issue.

It is also remarkable that the Armenian revolutionary party, which historically played a huge role during the first Republic of Armenia and during the Soviet period in Armenian diaspora – and throughout its main mission to solve the Armenian case and re-establish justice after the genocide – failed to come to power in the newly independent Armenia. This means that the Armenian democratic revolution was not based only on the historical-collective memory but also on the rationale to have a democratic State and it may not be described by merely nationalistic trends but by much wider ideology and approaches. This tends to reject the opinion of the president of Azerbaijan, Ilham Aliev, who stated that 'Armenians live in the past that is why they cannot develop'.[29]

The Independence movement (which is also called the Karabakh movement) gave Armenian society the feeling of victory which they were deprived of during the course of history, as the Armenian history is full of events of torture, capture by other States and invaders, loss of kingdoms and loss of territory. This was the first time when the historical developments proved that Armenians may change the wheel of time and have the first and one of the biggest victories in their history.

27 Marutyan, above n 2, 18.
28 Ibid 26–7.
29 Interview of Ilham Aliev to Turkish paper *Cumhurriet*, July 2006.

## Nagorno-Karabakh War as the second stage of de-victimisation

The collapse of the Soviet Union opened the 'hidden' ethnic conflicts within the territory of the previous empire and one of these such problems was the issue of Nagorno-Karabakh, which is a territory between Armenia and Azerbaijan mostly populated with Armenians. In 1988, the Nagorno-Karabakh Armenians started demonstrations in Stepanakert demanding to re-join the mother Armenia. In December 1989, the parliament of the Autonomous Region of Nagorno-Karabakh adopted a decision to reunite with Armenia. This decision was not accepted by Moscow, which regarded the ethnic problem as one of its major issues and did not want to set a precedent for other ethnic groups who may have been trying to establish their own historical justice.

The Kremlin tried to represent the Karabakh problem as a social-economical, but not a political, problem. To prove this, the Soviet Council of Ministers provided 400 million rubles to solve the social problems in the autonomous region but this money was mostly used by the Azerbaijani leadership for development of Azeri-populated regions.

The local Communist leadership failed to control the protesting people. A newly-formed 'Karabakh' committee became the leader of the movement both in Karabakh and in Armenia. Knowing that there was no chance to suppress the movement the Soviet leadership organised a massacre of Armenians living in a small city, Sumgait near the Baku. On 27–29 February 1988, released criminals killed about 30 peaceful Armenians; many others were wounded and had to leave their homes under the auspices of the Soviet army, which arrived in the city three days late. These events in Sumgait reinforced the feelings of Armenians as the Sumgait was considered as a new genocide[30] implemented by 'turk-azeries' and gave a new impulse to the movement. Thomas De Waal described these events in the following way: 'An orgy of mob violence was unleashed: apartments were burned and ransacked, and ordinary Armenians were attacked, raped, and murdered. The pogroms fuelled themselves, as Soviet officialdom was slow to react.'[31]

In 1989, a year after the Sumgait massacre, thousands of Armenians mourned the victims of Sumgait and marched from the Opera House to the Genocide Memorial of 1915. Harutyun Marutyan made a 'poster-comparison' of the genocide and Sumgait massacre on the Memorial Day of the Genocide, on 24 April, where marchers also carried enlarged photographs of the Sumgait victims in black frames with black ribbons attached, so identifying the victims of the genocide and Sumgait.[32] A cross-stone for Sumgait victims was placed in the territory of the Genocide Memorial making another identification of Armenian 'old and new' victims by means of culture and symbolism. The symbolic identification happened just

30 Thomas De Waal, *The Caucasus: An Introduction* (Oxford University Press, 2010) 111.

31 Ibid.

32 Marutyan, above n 2, 95.

two months after Sumgait (February 1988) on 24 April 1988, where the marchers carried different posters indicating that Sumgait was the continuaton of the great genocide.

The Sumgait massacre and memorial events afterwards enhanced the nationalistic feelings of Armenians and promoted the escalation of conflict. Instead of looking for a peaceful solution for the arising conflict, the Azerbaijani authorities started the blockade of Nagorno-Karabakh and Armenia. The only possible way through was by air transportation. At the same time the authorities tried to implement demographic changes in the region with the assistance of the Republican committee headed by Victor Polyanichko formed by the Soviet Supreme Council. The Armenians made the contrary decision and on 1 December 1989, both of the parliaments of Armenia and Nagorno-Karabakh adopted a decision on unification.

The answer to this decision became the massacres in Baku in January 1990, which was fixed in Armenian collective memory as the continuation of the genocide which had started in Turkey and continued in Sumgait and Baku.

Starting from January 1990 the National Front of Azerbaijan implemented several attacks on Armenian-populated villages along the borderline. The attacks were made not only on the villages in Nagorno-Karabakh but also on the villages situated on the borderline of Armenia and Azerbaijan (Eraskhavan, Vayk, Kapan, Noyemberyan, Tavush, etc). On 5 September 1990, the Armenian Supreme Council suggested the Kremlin undertake appropriate steps towards the aggression of Azerbaijan by implementing termination of the Azerbaijani blockade and isolation of key Armenian villages. However, the central authorities in Moscow did not reply to this announcement. Moreover, the special forces of Azerbaijan with the assistance of Soviet troops implemented the so-called 'ring' operation against the Armenian population of Getashen and Shahumyan. This was the last drop in the glass to ensure the Armenians did not have any other choice other than self-organisation and self-defence.

The war in Nagorno-Karabakh started in mid-1991 and lasted for three years until the ceasefire in December 1994; although war was never officially declared. The Armenians represented themselves not as a party to the conflict – as Armenian authorities stated many times that the conflict was between Nagorno-Karabakh and Azerbaijan – with Armenia rather simply assisting the Armenian population of Karabakh. Notwithstanding this claim, diplomatic announcements stated that Armenia was a part of the conflict and the war in Karabakh was perceived as a conflict between Armenia and Azerbaijan.[33] It is also symbolic that the first victims of the Nagorno-Karabakh conflict were buried in the territory of the Genocide Memorial (Tatul Krpeyan, Movses Georgisyan and others), consolidating beliefs one more time that the Nagorno-Karabakh conflict was the continuation of the genocide and that all Armenians should unite to win the war in Karabakh.

33 Thomas De Waal, *The Black Garden: Armenia and Azerbaijan through Peace and War* (New York University Press, 2003) 159–64.

One of the basic problems of Azerbaijan during these years was the problem of power. Several governments and two presidents (Ayaz Mutalibov and Albulfaz Elchibey) were changed and the situation was stabilised after the former communist leader Heydar Aliev came to power. Compared to Azerbaijan the situation in Armenia was stable. This also was one of the main reasons why Armenians could succeed during the war. The basic events on the battlefield happened during 1992–93 when Armenians successfully took over the city of Stepanakert and also on 9 May 1993, the city of Shusha, which had military importance for the troops for its high location known as a 'citadel of Karabakh'. As Thomas De Waal states, 'the loss of Shusha was the greatest blow to Azerbaijan. It removed its last strategic foothold in Karabakh, but its importance went even beyond that'.[34] During this conflict Azerbaijan lost control not only over Nagorno-Karabakh, but also over several regions surrounding this enclave. The military actions stopped in December 1994 but the conflict remains unsolved up to the present day, though the OSCE Minsk Group (USA, France and Russia) continues its unsuccessful peace mission.

The governing elites of Armenia and Azerbaijan are somehow against the activities of civil society groups and organisations as open debate will promote the conflict resolution process from one side, but also may increase the democratisation process from the other side, which goes against the political interests of governing elites. The relationship of democratisation and conflict resolution was widely discussed by an Armenian and Azerbaijani expert meeting:

> This unhappy relationship between conflict resolution and democratisation processes is a key to the lack of progress in the Nagorno-Karabakh process. No degree of international cooperation will resolve this problem, although a more principled stance on democratic standards from outside powers might help. Yet Armenian and Azerbaijani elites are arguably faced with a choice: risk the fallout of another failed peace process or loosen the reins of power to allow a peace deal to move forward. They need to weigh up where the greater threat to their power comes from – the conflict resolution process or the democratization process. It seems fair to say that the 'colored revolution moment' has passed in the former Soviet Union; is it time to allow effective political participation to enable the peace process to move forward?[35]

The situation in the region proves that the governing authorities in the South Caucasus countries made their choice for none of the above solutions, as they do not try to resolve conflicts, and there is no real and constituent democracy in the region.

34 Ibid 180.

35 Conciliation Resources, *Karabakh 2014: Six analysts on the future of the Nagorno-Karabakh peace process* (Conciliation Resources, 2009).

The establishment of an 'image of the enemy' during the war was seen as one of the main paths to success. Anthropological studies conducted in the years of the Karabakh War and afterwards showed that a majority of the population identify the Azerbaijanis and the Turks as one and the same. This fact has been used with good effect by the political and military leadership by showing films to soldiers about the Armenian Genocide which occurred in Turkey in 1915 and nurturing a patriotic spirit aimed against the enemy – 'the Muslim Turk.'[36] Though Turks and Azeries belong to different branches of Islam this does not play a major role in popular Armenian perceptions which identify the Azeris as Turks. Thus, religion was not the essential part in this identification but common ethnic origin and belonging of Turks and Azeries. The genocide discourse grew stronger as a result of the massacres in Baku and Sumgait, where the instinct of self-defence against the annihilation of Armenians was rekindled.

The Karabakh conflict and the establishment of the non-recognised Armenian state of Nagorno-Karabakh opened the discourse for the first largest success in Armenian history for over many centuries. The success in Nagorno-Karabakh was conditioned by the high spirit of Armenians, although the country faced various challenges in the form of hunger, lack of heat and electricity, economic blockade and new reforms etc. However, the national spirit of the nation and the collective memory to re-establish the justice against 'turks' played the essential role in the conflict.

## Conclusion

After the independence of Armenia the Armenian authorities tried to normalise the relations with Turkey – though emphasising that the genocide may not become a matter for historians to debate (as the Turkish side has always demanded) – as it is an undeniable fact. The position of Armenian authorites was to start the normalisation process and establishment of diplomatic relations without any preconditions. However, this position was changed during the period of president Robert Kocharyan (1998–2008) as his politics had a more nationalistic agenda and he never tried to start any negotiations with Turkey. Just after coming to power in 2008 the Armenian president Serzh Sargsyan invited the Turkish president Abdullah Gul to Armenia for a football match and this step was called the start of a new 'football diplomacy'. After the visit of the Turkish president, Serzh Sargsyan himself visited Turkey for a football match and afterwards Armenian–Turkish protocols were signed in Zurich under the auspices of the US, Russia and Switzerland, although these were later not ratified and relations did not improve when Turkey made a pre-condition for Armenia, conerning the solution of the Nagorno-Karabakh problem, under the pressure of Azerbaijan. The reconciliation process initiated by the

36 The anthropological study was conducted in Nagorno-Karabakh by anthropologist Nona Shahnazaryan. For more information, see 'Child soldiers of the Karabakh War: Life Stories of a Militarised "Youth"' (2008) 8 *The Journal of Power Institutions in Post-Soviet Societies* 1.

Armenian president was badly accepted by the Armenian diaspora who considered him as a national betrayer and organised many demonstrations against such politics as the anti-Turkish rhetoric of diaspora Armenians is the basic component of their identity.

The improvement of relationships between Armenia and Turkey enhanced regional integration and cooperation and enabled the neigbouring countries to get involved in regional and trans-regional projects and substructures. The idea of reconciliation and normalisation of the relationships between two countries was widely promoted by a famous Turkish-Armenian journalist, Hrant Dink, who was assassinated in January 2007 by a young Turkish nationalist. Dink tried to initiate open dialogue between the two States while trying to expose Turkish society to more information and knowledge on the events that happened in Turkey in 1915.[37]

The reconciliation process between Armenia and Turkey became somehow possible because of the de-victimisation of Armenian society as a result of Armenian Independence and victory in the Nagorno-Karabakh conflict. These two stages of de-victimisation supported the Armenian society and, especially its progressive and liberal sections, to overcome the consequences of genocide from the psychological perspective and look for progress and development. Still, the issue of recognition of the genocide both for liberal and conservative parts of Armenian society is no longer an issue for debate. The new positive tendencies in Armenian history made some changes in the identity of Armenians as they became more de-victimised and future-oriented rather than past-oriented as new challanges arose due to independence and the Nagorno-Karabakh conflict. The alteration in identity mostly happened in Armenia rather than in diaspora where victimisation was the basic element for identity maintenance.

Notwithstanding all the above mentioned, the relations between Armenia and Turkey still remain unsolved, but the debates started by civil society organisations in Turkey and in Armenia on normalisation of relations between two neighbouring countries give confidence that in the near future the ice shall break and diplomatic relations may be initiated. The open talk on Armenian genocide in Turkey (which was impossible a decade ago) also supports the process of normalisation. The 'de-victimisation' process in its two stages helped to overcome the traumatic collective memory in order to perceive the 'Turks' not solely as murderers or people responsible for genocide, but as neighbours with whom they can have normal relations.

The 'ice-breaking' process between Armenia and Turkey was witnessed by the recent opening of the Holy Cross on Akhtamar Island in Lake Van, Turkey. The Turkish government had not allowed the Armenian Patriarchate in Constantinople to conduct any religious rituals or to install a cross on the church for many years. However, in March 2007, the Turkish government installed the cross

37 Hrant Dink, 'To Unlock and Transcend History', *Agos*, 27 May 2005. Translation provided by Hrant Dink Foundation.

and allowed a ceremony to be held at the church witnessed by an official delegation from Armenia and the Armenian Patriarchate.[38] Consequently, in October 2011 the Armenian St Kirakos Church was reopened in the city of Diyarbakir, Turkey.[39] The reopening of Armenian churches in Turkey became a solid ground to identify the mutual interest for future cooperation and peace building.

## References


Aliev, Ilham, Interview to Turkish paper *Cumhurriet*, July 2006

Arakelyan, Varag, 'April 24, 1965', *Hayk*, 23 April 1996

Beissinger, Mark R, *Nationalist mobilization and the collapse of the Soviet State* (Cambridge University Press, 2002)

Butler, Thomas (ed), *Memory: History, Culture and the Mind* (Basil Blackwell, 1989)

Conciliation Resources, *Karabakh 2014: Six analysts on the future of the Nagorno-Karabakh peace process* (Conciliation Resources, 2009)

Dadrian, Vahakn N, *The History of the Armenian Genocide: Ethnic Conflict from the Balkans to Anatolia to the Caucasus* (Berghahn Books, 1995)

De Waal, Thomas, *Great Catastrophe: Armenians and Turks in the Shadow of Genocide* (Oxford University Press, 2015)

De Waal, Thomas, *The Black Garden: Armenia and Azerbaijan through Peace and War* (New York University Press, 2003)

De Waal, Thomas, *The Caucasus: An Introduction* (Oxford University Press, 2010)

Dink, Hrant, 'To Unlock and Transcend History', *Agos*, 27 May 2005

Great Britain, *Public Record Office*, Classes 371 and 424

Great Britain, *The Treatment of Armenians in Ottoman Empire* (Foreign Office, 1916)

Halbwachs, Maurice *The Collective Memory* (F J Ditter Jr and V Yazdi Ditter trans, Harper & Row Publishers, 1980)

Hobsbawm, Eric and Terrence Ranger (eds), *The Invention of Tradition* (Cambridge University Press, 1983)

Hobsbawm, Eric, 'Ethnicity and Nationalism in Europe today' (1992) 8 *Anthropology Today* 3

Hobsbawm, Eric J, 'Social Function of the Past: Some Questions' (1972) 55 *Past and Present* 3

Hodgkin, Katherine and Susannah Radstone (eds), *Contested Pasts: The Politics of Memory* (Routledge, 2003)

Hohannisyan, Richard G (ed), *Armenian People from Ancient to Modern Times, vol II* (New York, 1997)

Lepsius, Johannes, *Deutschland und Armenien, 1914–1918* (General Books LLC, 1919)


38 The Turkish government also allowed Armenia to hold liturgy once a year at Holy Cross on Akhtamar Island, which became an important place for tourism and pilgrimage. See generally, PanArmenian.net, 'The Reopening of Holy Cross Church (Surop Khatch on Aghtamar Island)', *PanArmenian.net*, 29 March 2007, accessed 2 March 2017, available at: <www.panarmenian.net/eng/world/news/21593/>.

39 See Rarrta.am, 'St Kirakos church of Diyarberkir to open on Oct 23', *rarrta.am,* 21 October 2011, accessed 2 March 2017, available at: <www.tert.am/en/news/2011/10/21/stkirakos/1279622>.

Lindy, Jacob D and Robert Jay Lifton (eds), *Beyond invisible walls: the psychological legacy of Soviet trauma, East European therapists and their patients* (Brunner-Routledge, 2001)

Maines, David R, Noreen M Sugrue and Michael A Katovich, 'The Sociological Import of G H Mead's Theory of the Past' (1983) 48 *American Sociological Review* 161

Marutyan, Harutyun, *Iconography of Armenian Identity: The Memory of Genocide and the Karabakh Movement* (Publishing House of NASRA, 2009)

PanArmenian.net, 'The Reopening of Holy Cross Church (Surop Khatch on Aghtamar Island)', *PanArmenian.net*, 29 March 2007, accessed 2 March 2017, available at: <www.panarmenian.net/eng/world/news/21593/>.

Rarrta.am, 'St Kirakos church of Diyarberkir to open on Oct 23', *rarrta.am*, 21 October 2011, accessed 2 March 2017, available at: <www.tert.am/en/news/2011/10/21/stkirakos/1279622>.

Schwartz, Barry, 'Social Context of Commemoration: A Study in Collective Memory' (1982) 61 *Social Forces* 377

Shahnazaryan, Nona, 'Child soldiers of the Karabakh War: Life Stories of a Militarised "Youth"' (2008) 8 *The Journal of Power Institutions in Post-Soviet Societies* 1

Smith, Anthony D, *Myths and Memories of the Nation* (Oxford University Press, 1991)

Smith, Anthony D, *National Identity* (University of Nevada Press, 1991)

Stepanyan, Albert (ed), *Inknutyan hartser: Taregirk øProblems of Identity, Annualπ* (Yerevan, Zangak, 2002)

Toynbee, Arnold J, *The Western Question in Greece and Turkey* (Martino Publications, 1922)

# 9 Global Law and Global Ethic

*Leonard Swidler*

## The meaning of the good and ethics

Human beings are *persons*, that is, beings who can know endlessly, choose freely and love. Hence, when we speak of ethics we are talking about the principles of behavior of free beings, of humans. We do not speak of our animal pets having ethics, or complain that trees do not follow their ethics – because only we humans have freedom; only we can choose whether or not to act in a certain way – and as a consequence are responsible. This is what we mean when we talk about ethics: the principles by which free beings, humans, choose to act one way or another.

A clarifying word here about the use of the terms 'ethics' and 'morals': 'ethics' comes from the Greek term *ethos* and means 'custom'; 'morals' comes from the Latin term *moris* and likewise means 'custom.' Some writers project separate meanings for the two terms. However, they are simply synonyms, and can be used interchangeably. Nevertheless, there is a *tendency* to use the term 'morality' when speaking of sexual and private matters and the term 'ethics' when speaking of business and public behavior.

When we speak of *knowing* something we are talking about our *cognitive* faculties. Their purpose is to 'unite' us with reality about us in a variety of ways. For example, through the cognitive faculty of sight, we are united with a myriad of objects via light waves, whereas we are united with certain other realities via sound waves, or through the sense of smell, taste and touch. We humans also have related *appetitive* faculties whereby we also *desire* and *move* to become 'united' with various realities. For example, we want to be *one with* ice cream by eating, *one with* Mozart's music by listening to it, *one with* our friend by being physically near, writing, telephoning . . . these are the *fundamental* ways that we encounter the world and ourselves.

When we speak of ethics/morals, then, we intend to say that certain actions are good or its opposite, bad – or right or wrong. What precisely is meant by the term 'good'? Fundamentally, we have in our minds an idea of the 'purpose' or 'goal' of a thing or action, and if it attains that goal, we say that it is good, or if it does not attain it, it is bad. For example, we will have in mind that the 'goal' of ice cream is to be cool, soft, sweet . . . if this ice cream cone does those things, we say it is 'good', or if it does not quite do so, it is not so good, or if it really misses the goal, we say it is bad. The same is true of music – if it is harmonious to the ears, if it gives pleasure when played well . . . it is said to be good because it does what we think is the goal and purpose of music.

There are many philosophical positions expressed in the field known as 'meta-ethics', that is, the reflection on the meaning of ethical statements, whether they can even make sense, and if so, on what bases? Clearly many of those positions are false, for most of them contradict most of the others. Having surveyed again the myriad articulations, and necessarily disagreeing with most of them – since, as noted, the vast majority contradict each other – let me lay out my basic understanding of the meaning and basis for ethical statements very briefly without giving a name to my position (eg, cognitivist, non-cognitivist, realist, emotivist, prescriptivist etc) – let the reader read and ponder it and decide on its persuasiveness or lack thereof.

When speaking of ethics/morals we normally mean human free *actions*. Hence, we decide that actions do or do not attain the goal that we understand them to have, and hence are judged to be good or bad, right or wrong. For example, the purpose of shooting a person is to cause injury or death. Most would normally judge that goal and action in general to be bad because the purpose of actions physically impacting persons should be life enhancing, or at least life neutral, and surely not life destructive. How does one know that 'actions impacting persons should be life enhancing'? By observing how persons are structured and act in reality: living beings, and most of all self-conscious beings, humans, are observed always striving toward continuing to exist, self-preservation. Hence, to cut short or limit that life is to act contrary to its very structure.

Alleged exceptions to this judgment, such as life-destructive actions including killing in self-defence, do not vitiate this obvious claim. In this case one does not have a choice between 'good' – maintaining life – and 'evil' – destroying a life – but only between two 'evils' – destroying one life or the other. Obviously, if different persons have differing understandings of the purpose of certain actions, their judgments as to those actions being right or wrong will differ. This is true not only of individuals, but also of various groups – religions, cultures, social groups . . . This is considered further when I discuss 'a Global Ethic' below.

## The meaning of the law

When we speak of law in the most general sense, we are talking about the operation of the principle of cause and effect. Thus, we speak of the laws of nature, the law of gravity, and the like. Step out a tenth-storey window and the law of gravity operates to dash us to the ground at a certain rate of acceleration and a certain force – with the consequences being quite predictably smashing. *Cause*: stepping out the tenth-storey window; *effect*: being dashed to the ground – unless, of course, something intervenes, such as a strong awning felicitously placed on the ninth floor.

When the term *law* is used in a human societal context the same fundamental notion applies. Commit murder (*cause*), and we are punished by execution or incarceration (*effect*) – again, unless something intervenes, such as, not being found out. In a way, the same basic principle of cause and effect operates in the field of *ethics* as well. We say in English that we 'ought' to do good and avoid evil; we speak of being 'obliged' to choose the good. Our English word 'obliged' comes from a Latin root, *ob-ligare*, (*ob*, 'to', *ligare*, 'to be bound', as in '*liga*ments binding bones together'). Hence, we are 'bound to', 'obliged to', do the good, which will bring about a good result. If, however, we as free beings choose instead to do evil, we are likewise 'bound to' suffer the evil consequences – again, unless something intervenes, such as, being forgiven by the person offended. (Parenthetically, it is worth noting that the Latin root of the term 'religion' is fundamentally the same as that of 'oblige', ie, '*re-ligare*', 'to be bound back'.)

## The relationship between ethics and law

Fundamentally the relationship between law and ethics in human society is that the law is a public (*external*) expression of an ethical (*internal*) requirement. Thus, all law is a particular, overt specification of some aspect of (*interior*) ethics. Ethics is the broader category. In general, everything required, obliged by law is required, obliged by ethics, but not everything required by ethics is required by law. Many cultures have spoken of all human law as (or should be) a reflection the Divine Law. Such a notion is at the foundation of Confucianism, as in the tenet of *T'ien-ming* (*T'ien* 'Heaven', *ming*, 'mandate'), the 'Mandate of Heaven', that the human person is to follow. It is found also in Roman thinkers such as when 1st century BCE Cicero wrote: '*Lex est ratio summa, insita in natura, quae iubet ea quae facienda sunt, prohibetque contraria*' ('Law is the highest reason, implanted by Nature which commands what ought to be done and forbids the opposite').[1] He went on to say that:

> [l]aw is not a product of human thought, nor is it any enactment of peoples, but something eternal which rules the whole universe by its wisdom in command and prohibition. Thus they have been accustomed to say that Law is the primal and ultimate mind of Jupiter.[2]

Often in human history the laws of a society have largely reflected the ethics of a particular portion of the society, which in a variety of ways dominated the rest of the society, with whose ethics theirs was at variance. In that case, 'might made right.' A prevailing societal ethics, of course, is ultimately determined by the fact that all

1 Cicero, *De legibus*, *Loeb Classical Library* (online), accessed 7 March 2017, available at: <www.loebclassics.com/view/marcus_tullius_cicero-de_legibus/1928/pb_LCL213.317.xml> 316–7.

2 Cicero, *De legibus* in Donald S Guchberg (ed), *Classics of Western Thought, Vol I The Ancient World* (Wadsworth, 4th ed, 1988) 430.

government exists at the sufferance of the governed. Even in those extremely savage dictatorships in which the 'elite', operating according to their 'ethics', killed right and left, the abused population for the time endured the 'ethics' of the elite as the lesser of evils – but they accepted it rather than rebel to the point of their utter self-destruction. For example, Blacks have 'accepted' the (*interior*) ethics of Whites which judged that Whites have superior rights over Blacks – and then passed segregation laws (*exterior*) – rather than rebel and be slaughtered.

In such situations, there obviously exists a kind of schizophrenia, a splintered society wherein the freedom, and hence creativity, of the dominated population is greatly restricted rather than given rein and fostered. Obviously, such a 'split personality' condition is at least as destructive for a society as it is for an individual person. As for the good of the individual person, so also for the good of the whole of society, such a split needs to be overcome. The freedom and creativity of both the individual and society need to be released and encouraged.

Clearly those persons concerned about the welfare of not only individual persons but also of human society in general must/will commit themselves to overcoming that societal split and promoting the freedom and creativity of all. In fact, the long stretch of human history shows clearly that this process is well underway. The move of humankind has been from a primitive tribal condition to the gradual founding of states/civilisations, to the fantastic simultaneous 'great leap forward' of the 'Axial Period' (800–200 BCE) in China, India, Near East and Europe,[3] to the breakthrough of Modernity in the 18th century 'Western Enlightenment', and now to the dawning of the 'Age of Global Dialogue',[4] creating a new global civilisation. Freedom and responsible self-governance, democracy, for all was not even a dream or desideratum until the Enlightenment. Now it is becoming a reality for rapidly increasing numbers around the globe. People can be suppressed today, but they cannot be satisfied. Humankind is 'coming of age', becoming adult – with all the agonies and ecstasies of that process of maturation.

In this new age the continued imposition by law of the ethics of a privileged 'elite' on the non-elite is no longer acceptable. The age-old way of dominance by the few is waning. The possibility of freedom and responsibility of the many is waxing. Law now is increasingly expected to reflect the ethics of freedom and responsibility of all. The rising overt dissatisfaction of the dominated is not a sign of societal deteriorisation, but the first (*interior* – ethics) steps toward further changing of (*exterior* – laws) societal structures.

3 See Karl Jaspers, *Vom Ursprung und Ziel der Geschichte* (Artemis, 1949) 19–43; Michael Bullock (trans), *The Origin and Goal of History* (Yale University Press, 1953).

4 Leonard Swidler, 'The Age of Global Dialogue' (1996) 1 *Marburg Journal of Religion* 1, available at: <www.uni-marburg.de/fb03/ivk/mjr/pdfs/1996/articles/Swidler1996.pdf>.

## The nature of religion and the validation of society's ethics

In those situations, where a law is contrary to the ethical principles of a dominated group, the claim is made that law does not oblige ethically. In the 13th century Thomas Aquinas in his treatise '*De lege*' wrote that laws '*contrarietatem ad bonum humanum*' (laws contrary to human welfare) '*non obligant in foro conscientiae*' (do not oblige in the forum of conscience).[5]

Even far earlier than Aquinas, Cicero wrote:

> Laws were invented for the safety of citizens, the preservation of states, and the tranquility and happiness of human life . . . and when such rules were drawn up and put into force, it is clear that men called them 'laws.' From this point of view it can be understood that those who formulated wicked and unjust statutes for nations, thereby breaking their promises and agreements, put into effect anything but 'laws.'[6]

However, the sanction, the 'effect', of the 'cause' of an ethically invalid law may still be carried out if the law is violated – as in the case of Martin Luther King's being jailed when he non-violently disobeyed US racial segregation laws – or not carried out if successfully avoided by flight, force, etc.

The question then arises: Where does the 'effect', the sanction, resulting from violating an ethical principle come from? It arises from what we in the West have called 'religion', or its functional equivalent, an 'ideology', eg, atheistic Marxism. For example, in the Abrahamic religions – Judaism, Christianity, and Islam – traditionally understood, good behavior merits continued existence in the 'Kingdom of Heaven'. In Indian religions, Hinduism, Buddhism, etc, traditionally understood, the law of 'karma' operates: every human action has its consequences in a future existence – metempsychosis, reincarnation – one's *atman* (Sanskrit 'air', 'breath', – spirit/self; similar to Latin *spiritus*, 'air', 'breath' – spirit/self) is refleshed in a new body according to one's good or bad deeds. Some similar cause and effect procedure exists in every religion and ideology, including very 'critical thinking' modern versions of each older religion.

Whence, then, does the validation of a religion come? The answer lies in the nature of religion. Religion is an 'explanation of the ultimate meaning of life, and how to live accordingly, based on some notion of the Transcendent'.[7] Normally all religions contain the four 'Cs': Creed, Code, Cult, Community-structure:

> *Creed* refers to the cognitive aspect of a religion; it is everything that goes into the 'explanation' of the ultimate meaning of life.

5 Thomas Aquinas, *Summa Theologiae* (1485) I,II, q 96, a 4.

6 Cicero, above n 2, 437f.

7 See generally, Leonard Swidler and Paul Mojzes, *The Study of Religion in the Age of Global Dialogue* (Temple University Press, 2000).

> *Code* of behavior or ethics includes all the rules and customs of action that somehow follow from one aspect or another of the Creed.
>
> *Cult* means all the ritual activities that relate the follower to one aspect or other of the Transcendent, either directly or indirectly, prayer being an example of the former and certain formal behavior toward representatives of the Transcendent, such as priests, of the latter.
>
> *Community-structure* refers to the relationships among the followers; this can vary widely, from a very egalitarian relationship, as among Quakers, through a 'republican' structure like Presbyterians have, to a monarchical one, as with some Hasidic Jews vis-a-vis their 'Rebbe'.
>
> The *Transcendent*, as the roots of the word indicate, means 'that which goes beyond' the everyday, the ordinary, the surface experience of reality. It can refer to spirits, gods, a Personal God, an Impersonal God, Emptiness, etc.[8]

Especially in modern times there have developed 'explanations of the ultimate meaning of life, and how to live accordingly' which are not based on a notion of the Transcendent, eg, secular humanism, Marxism. Although in every respect these 'explanations' function as religions traditionally have in human life, because the idea of the Transcendent, however it is understood, plays such a central role in religion, but not in these 'explanations'. For the sake of accuracy it is best to give these 'explanations' not based on a notion of the Transcendent a separate name; the name often used is: Ideology.

From the very constitutive structure of religion/ideology the validation of its ethics flows: a religion's ethics are the necessary behavioral principles resulting from the religion's 'explanation of the ultimate meaning of life'. If X is determined to be the meaning, the goal of human life, then Y are the actions that one must follow in order to attain X; hence, Y constitutes the ethics one must follow to attain the goal; it is the 'good'.

There will, then, be a basically one-to-one relationship between the law and the ethics of the society – in the sense that all laws will/should be ethically acceptable – if there is but one religion or ideology pervading that society. But what of a society in which there are several influential religions and/or ideologies: what will the relationship be between the law and the ethics flowing from the disparate religions and/or ideologies?

## Varieties of ethics

Before that question can be addressed directly, we need to be aware of the major schools of ethics, at least in the English-speaking world (a full investigation of all the world's ethics systems far exceeds the boundaries of an essay). Recall: when we are dealing with human actions, we need to have in mind what the goal of such an action ought to be in our judgment. Thus, for example, if we judge the 'goal' of speech

8 Leonard Swidler, *The Age of Global Dialogue* (Wipf and Stock Publishers, 2016) 36.

is to express outwardly what we inwardly think, we would say that truth-telling is good. To do the opposite is called a lie, and is usually said to be bad, because it does not move the action of speaking in the direction of its supposed goal.

However, as noted before, and should immediately be clear, deciding that something is good, and therefore ought to be done, very much rides on how we conceive the goal of a particular action. Example: we might argue that in general truth-telling is good. However, what if during the 1940s the Gestapo came to your door in Europe and asked you whether there were any Jews in your house? Knowing that a 'truthful' answer would result in the Jewish mother, father, and child living in your house being sent to torture and death, no 'ethically' concerned person would say that in that case truth-telling was good. Hence, in that situation the householder might think that the 'goal' of the answer to the Gestapo officer was not the customary 'goal' of speaking, namely, expressing out loud what you know in your mind to be the case. Rather, here the goal of speaking was the protection of innocent life.

Over half a century ago when I studied Catholic *Moral* Theology (interesting that that is what it was called, whereas Protestant theologians customarily spoke of the same topic as 'Christian *Ethics*') we learned a number of 'tricks', like 'mental reservation', and similar ones – so-called 'white lies'. (Mental reservation meant that you said out loud, 'No, there are no Jews here', and in your *mind* you would silently add, 'that you need to know about,' or some such.) In the 17th century the Jesuit moral theologians were very creative at devising such 'tricks', and hence, the term 'casuistry' (meaning that the general ethical rules had to be applied with appropriate modifications from case to case) got a bad name, and sometimes was even termed being 'Jesuitical'. In fact, '"The End justifies the Means" is a maxim which originated in an accusation made by Protestants against the Jesuits.'[9]

However, if one thinks about such dilemmas, the basis for ethical decision is clear. In the example just given, as adumbrated above, there clearly are two 'evils'; telling a lie, and handing human beings over to torture and death. Here we do not have a choice between good and bad. There are only two possible choices, both of them bad: tell a lie, send innocent humans to their deaths. One must simply choose the lesser of evils, and in this case which one is lesser is screamingly obvious.

There are of course several conceptualisations of what the proper basis ought to be for deciding on ethical action. One need only put the term 'Ethics' into Wikipedia, Google, or Yahoo to see the almost bewildering wealth of bases for ethics there are in the world.

*Deontological Ethics* is one traditional one, which argues that some things are intrinsically good or bad, and therefore a person must learn and *always* follow the principles and rules of ethics. Before that term was invented in 1930 by C D Broad,[10] the related, though not exactly the same, notion of 'Natural Law' was

9 See the definition of 'Consequentialism', *Wikipedia*, accessed 4 October 2016, available at: <http://en.wikipedia.org/wiki/Consequentialism>.

10 Charlie D Broad, *Five Types of Ethical Theory* (Harcourt Brace, 1930).

articulated by Greek philosophers, preeminently Aristotle and the Stoics. In the West, Gratian in the 12th century and then, most of all, Aquinas in the 13th century, promoted the idea that there is a certain structure or nature (Latin, *natus*, born) with which every human is born, and therefore every human ought to follow this 'natural law' built into us. This thinking has had an immense influence on all Western legal systems, and, indeed, on the global level as well. It is the basis for the now almost universally accepted (but often honoured in the breach!) notion of 'Human rights'.

On the other hand, there is *Situation Ethics*, advocated vigorously by the American Episcopal priest Joseph Fletcher,[11] which emphasised that judging something good or bad depended significantly on the concrete situation. For Fletcher and other situation ethicists the ultimate touchstone is to act lovingly. This puts one in mind of St Augustine's famous saying: *Ama, et fac quod vis!* 'Love, and do what you will!'[12]

Another somewhat similar ethical approach is *Consequentialist Ethics*, which argues that one decides some action is good or bad depending on its consequences. A variation of the latter is *Utilitarianism*, which judges that that is to be done which leads to the greatest amount of good for the greatest number of persons.

A completely different approach to understanding ethics has been put forth in the past half century called *Virtue Ethics*. Here, the argument is that persons should be helped to develop a positively virtuous character – courageous, honest, compassionate . . . such a virtuous person will then know how to act ethically in all different situations. One is reminded of Augustine: *Ama, et fac quod vis!* Viewed in a long-term pedagogical perspective, this approach has much to recommend it. If in growing into maturity a person develops the virtues of prudence and courage, for example, then s/he will not hesitate to send the Gestapo away without betraying the hidden Jews. Prioritising life over lie will be immediately perceived as the prudent and courageous – ethical – move to make.

Each system, of course, has its attractive and unattractive aspects. For example, simply and always to follow the rules eliminates ambiguity and keeps society from sliding down the proverbial 'slippery moral slope'. However, I do not think that the Jews in the above case would be very enthusiastic about such 'ethical' truth-telling action – nor would even the non-Jew 'truth-teller' if s/he had even the slightest twinge of conscience because of the 'consequence' of her/his truth-telling to the Gestapo (even Mary, Joseph, and their child Jesus would all have been sent to the gas chambers!).

Or again, it certainly appears reasonable to choose an action that will bring more happiness to more people rather than to fewer people. However, following

11 See the definition of 'Situational Ethics', *Wikipedia*, accessed 4 October 2016, available at: <http://en.wikipedia.org/wiki/Situational_ethics>.

12 St Augustine of Hippo as quoted in 'St Augustine of Hippo', *Wikiquote*, accessed 4 October 2016, available at: <https://en.wikiquote.org/wiki/Augustine_of_Hippo>.

some version of utilitarianism might, for example, lead some to decide that we have to leave the poor people in a nation go without health insurance because financially that will ensure the highest quality of health care for the largest number in the country (which America claims it has). Even conservative American politicians, however, are beginning to talk as if this were a moral blemish on America (credit on this must be given to Hillary Clinton already back in 1993, and subsequently Barack Obama).

There is something fundamentally attractive about the idea of a Natural Law – despite the valid point of so-called post-moderns who stress the uniqueness of each of the world's cultures, or, indeed, of each individual. Having attained the concept of Human Rights in the 18th century, and still fighting for its universal implementation, I am not willing to abandon it for some kind of hyperbolic notion of post-modern particularity. What the 19th century's sense of history added to the earlier 18th century understanding of Natural Law is that the human being has a historical, evolving nature!

In the end, I am persuaded that some combination of a 'historically' understood version of Natural Law, Situation, and Consequentialist, ethics set in the long-term pedagogical context of fostering Virtue Ethics is the most human. Of course, ethical principles are important. They point us in certain directions that our centuries-long communal experience tells us is vital. For example, if a society did not develop ethical principles insuring that the next generation would be adequately cared for, educated, etc that society would quickly disappear. Further, it is true that a person cannot become a full person except within a community, including giving back to the community in mutuality. However, in the end, the purpose of the *community is for persons*, not the other way around. Similarly, in ethics *principles are for persons*, not persons for principles. (Jesus, for example, seemed to say the same when he stated: 'the Sabbath is for humanity, not humanity for the Sabbath' (Mark 2:27)).

As noted, at the same time, one cannot become a human person alone. One becomes a person in community, so that individual persons ought not to engage in communal destructive actions, because they then are ultimately also destroying themselves. The Golden Rule applies here fully: you love you neighbor exactly *as* you love yourself, and vice versa.

More recently a Monsignor Gianfranco Girotti, Regent of the Vatican Penitentiary, publicly argued that the Catholic Church (and doubtless he would include other Christian bodies as well) needs to come up with a more contemporary 'list of sins'. In the Middle Ages 'Penitentials' were developed, that is, lists of sins to be avoided that one should check in a daily, or at least regular, examination of conscience. Monsignor Girotti argued that contemporary humans are now living in the world of globalisation and hence we need to have our consciences 'informed' about the 'global' sins that we may be so easily tempted to commit – polluting the air and water, unnecessarily buying 'gas-guzzlers', etc – if we are not attentive:

> Norms encoded hundreds of years ago to guide human behavior in a small-scale agrarian society could not account for a globalized postindustrial information

> economy. Polluting the environment, drug trafficking, performing genetic manipulations or causing social inequities, new sinful behaviors mentioned by Msgr Gianfranco Girotti, regent of the Vatican Penitentiary, are arguably more relevant to many contemporary Catholics than contraception.
>
> 'If yesterday's sin had a rather individualistic dimension, today it has a value and resonance that is above all social, because of the great phenomenon of globalization,' Monsignor Girotti told the newspaper *L'Osservatore Romano*.[13]

Let me return now to that previously raised question asking what the relationship will be between the law and the ethics flowing from the now globalised disparate religions and/or ideologies, as Monsignor Girotti also posed it.

## Global civilisation and religions/ideologies in dialogue

In past history the answer to that question was basically that one religion/ideology and its ethics prevailed, with minor concessions reluctantly granted to the other religions/ideologies – for example, Jews were allowed to live in a ghettoised existence within pre-Enlightenment Christendom, and Christians and Jews lived more or less as second-class citizens, *dhimmies*, in the Islamic world. This condition began to change radically with the Enlightenment, as reflected simultaneously in the 1787 American 'Bill of Rights' and the 1789 French 'Declaration of the Rights of Man'. Still, at the beginning of this period of religious liberty the ethics which shaped the laws of America and France were predominantly Christian – Protestant and Catholic, respectively. Only gradually have the ethics, and resultant laws, opened themselves to the influence of other religions and ideologies. That process is one that proceeds by way of dialogue, and is unending.

At the beginning of the second millennium it is evident to all that humankind as a whole is rapidly moving into a Global Civilisation made up of many cultures. In 1993, Harvard University Professor Samuel Huntington wrote of the coming 'clash of civilizations' cultures.[14] He was partially accurate. We did see the violent clash of cultures: Catholicism–Protestantism in Northern Ireland, Islam–Catholicism–Orthodox Christianity in Bosnia, Islam–Orthodox Christianity in Azerbaijan–Armenia, Buddhism–Hinduism in Sri Lanka and Judaism–Islam in the Near East to name a few.

All previous civilisations have had a religion (or in recent modern times occasionally its functional equivalent, an ideology, eg, the Soviet Union and Atheistic Marxism) at its heart, shaping and reflecting its understanding of the ultimate meaning of life and the outflowing values. But what now of the burgeoning Global Civilisation? What religion or ideology will be at its heart? For it too will

13 Eduardo Porter, 'The Vatican and Globalization: Tinkering with Sin', *New York Times* (New York), 7 April 2008, Op Ed Page.

14 See Samuel P Huntington, 'The Clash of Civilizations?' (1993) 72 *Foreign Affairs* 22, 22–49.

need a spiritual life-giving vision and consequent values, otherwise it will die aborning.

The heart of the emerging Global Civilization will be no particular religion or ideology. Rather, it will be 'Religions/Ideologies-In-Dialogue'. This heart began to take shape at the beginning of the 20th century with the launching of the intra-Christian Ecumenical Movement in 1910, gradually drawing the myriad Christian churches into intense dialogue. It was further developed in the 1960s by the initiation of widespread interreligious dialogue, led especially by the Catholic Church in its watershed event of the Second Vatican Council (1962–65).

## A Universal Declaration of a Global Ethic

Both those sets of dialogues, intra-Christian and interreligious/ideological, have increased at a geometric rate, shifting onto another level once more in 1991 when Professor Hans Küng and I issued a call for the drafting and eventual adoption of a *Universal Declaration of a Global Ethic.*[15] That project is proceeding apace.

It is important to clarify what this 'Global Ethic' is and is not. It is *not* an attempt to articulate what *should* be a set of ethical principles across the globe. Rather, it is an articulation after wide investigation and inquiry, of the basic ethical principles of right and wrong that are *de facto* found globally across all major, and not so major, religious and ideological systems. Three such articulations can be identified (see dialogueinstitute.org/global-ethic-documents/).

The year 1993 was the 100th anniversary of the 1893 *World Parliament of Religions* which took place in Chicago. As a consequence, a number of international conferences were held, and at their center was the launching and developing of a *Universal Declaration of a Global Ethic.* The first was held in New Delhi, India in February 1993; the second in August of the same year in Bangalore, India, and the third that year in September in Chicago, United States. For that huge (over 6,000 participants) September 1993 Chicago *Parliament of the World's Religions* conference, Professor Hans Küng drafted a document entitled 'Declaration Toward a Global Ethic', which the Parliament adopted.[16]

Having been commissioned by the January 1992 meeting in Atlanta of the *International Scholars' Annual Trialogue* (*ISAT* – Jewish–Christian–Muslim), I drew up (after wide consultation and research) a draft of a *Universal Declaration of a Global Ethic* and submitted it to the January 1993 meeting of *ISAT* in Graz, Austria. That draft, as modified, was focused on during the spring 1993 semester graduate seminar I held at Temple University entitled: 'Global Ethics–Human Rights–World Religions'. It was also a major focus of the 'First International Conference on Universalism' in August 1993 in Warsaw; a Consultation of the American Academy of Religion in November 1993 in Washington DC was devoted to

15 See Leonard Swidler (ed), *For All Life: Toward a Universal Declaration of a Global Ethic. An Interreligious Dialogue* (White Cloud Press, 1998).

16 Hans Küng and Karl-Josef Kuschel (eds), *A Global Ethic* (Continuum, 1993).

the topic; the sixth '"International Scholars" Annual Trialogue' in January 1994, which concentrated for a second year on the further revised draft of the *Universal Declaration*; in May 1994, it was the subject of a conference sponsored by the *International Association of Asian Philosophy and Religion – IAAPR* in Seoul, Korea; the *World Conference on Religion and Peace – WCRP* in part focused on it in its autumn 1994 World Assembly in Rome/Riva del Garda, Italy; and in June 1995, it was the subject of a conference in San Francisco in honour of the 'Fiftieth Anniversary of the Founding of the United Nations', entitled: 'Celebrating the Spirit: Towards a Global Ethic'.

In March 1997, in Paris, the Philosophy and Ethics Division of UNESCO held the first meeting of its newly established committee to work toward a 'Universal Ethic'. Its second meeting was held December 1997, in Naples, in conjunction with the *Instituto Italiano degli Studii Filosofici.* Both the above drafts (as well as the one described next) were submitted to this UNESCO committee.

Subsequently, a third independent articulartion of the 'Declaration of a Human Ethic' was drafted and published by five graduate students in a graduate seminar of mine. It, along with the prior two and the document referred to immediately below, can be found at: dialogueinstitute.org/global-ethic-documents/.

More recently Professor Küng drafted a fourth text, this time within the context of the *InterAction Council*, entitled 'A Universal Declaration of Human Responsibilities'. The InterAction Council is a committee made up of former heads of states, chaired by retired Chancellor Helmut Schmidt of Germany. All three of these texts have been subjected to numerous consultations and comments by scholars and thinkers from multiple philosophical, religious and other backgrounds.

Now efforts are being made to stimulate as many religious, ethical, ethnic, professional and other groups to join together in dialogue to draw up what they believe to be the basic ethical principles that they and all humans have in common and send them in to the 'Center for Global Ethics' of the *Dialogue Institute* (dialogueinstitute.org/global-ethic/) to be coordinated and eventually synthesised by an appropriate global committee and submitted to a ratification procedure. The three articulations already created and available serve as initial substantive versions of a viable *Universal Declaration of a Global Ethic.* As important, or perhaps even more so, are the efforts that are being mounted to make this Global Ethic increasingly effective on the grassroots level.

## Global Law and Global Ethic

What then ought the relationship be between the developing *Global Ethic* and the Law on the global level? *Global Law* needs to faithfully reflect Global Ethic; Global Law should also contribute to the shaping of Global Ethic, for ethics, as all human realities, is an evolving ethic. To fulfill both parts of its responsibility, the Global Law profession needs to have its experts in Global Law in close and constant dialogue with the other major shapers of Global Ethic. This will include all disciplines, professions, and walks of life, but in an especially intense way it will concentrate on the dialogue with thinkers and scholars of religious and philosophical ethics.

As part of that vital enterprise I propose that the *Union Internationale des Avocats* – as well as other organisations – take a leadership role and join together with the *Dialogue Institute* (www.dialogueinstitute.org/) and the *Weltethos Stiftung* (www.weltethos.org) and *Weltethos Institut* (www.weltethos-institut.org) in forming an ongoing committee of legal experts and experts in ethics, religion and philosophy etc. Surely the funding for such an important undertaking should be forthcoming.

## References


Aquinas, Thomas, *Summa Theologiae* (1485)

Broad, Charlie D, *Five Types of Ethical Theory* (Harcourt Brace, 1930)

Bullock, Michael (trans), *The Origin and Goal of History* (Yale University Press, 1953)

Cicero, *De legibus*, *Loeb Classical Library* (online), accessed 7 March 2017, available at: <www.loebclassics.com/view/marcus_tullius_cicero-de_legibus/1928/pb_LCL213.317.xml>

Guchberg, Donald S (ed), *Classics of Western Thought*, *Vol I The Ancient World* (Wadsworth, 4th ed, 1988)

Huntington, Samuel P, 'The Clash of Civilizations?' (1993) 72 *Foreign Affairs* 22

Jaspers, Karl, *Vom Ursprung und Ziel der Geschichte* (Artemis, 1949)

Küng, Hans and Karl-Josef Kuschel (eds), *A Global Ethic* (Continuum, 1993)

Porter, Eduardo, 'The Vatican and Globalization: Tinkering with Sin', *New York Times* (New York), 7 April 2008

St Augustine of Hippo, 'St Augustine of Hippo', *Wikiquote*, accessed 4 October 2016, available at: <https://en.wikiquote.org/wiki/Augustine_of_Hippo>

Swidler, Leonard, 'The Age of Global Dialogue' (1996) 1 *Marburg Journal of Religion* 1, available at: <www.uni-marburg.de/fb03/ivk/mjr/pdfs/1996/articles/Swidler1996.pdf>

Swidler, Leonard, *The Age of Global Dialogue* (Wipf and Stock Publishers, 2016)

Swidler, Leonard, 'The Relationship Between the Law and a Global Ethic' (International Senate of the *Union Internationale des Avocats*, in the Eschenbach Palace, Vienna, on 21 February 1998)

Swidler, Leonard and Paul Mojzes, *The Study of Religion in the Age of Global Dialogue* (Temple University Press, 2000)

Swidler, Leonard (ed), *For All Life: Toward a Universal Declaration of a Global Ethic. An Interreligious Dialogue* (White Cloud Press, 1998)

# 10 Freedom of expression and legal protection of religious feelings in Europe

## From reconciliation to complementarity

*Davor Derenčinović*

## Introduction

The relationship between freedom of expression and protection of religious feelings has been a matter of scholarly debate for decades. There is no dispute about the well-established fact that some expressions might hurt the religious feelings of believers, but the question arises on whether this amounts to a violation of their rights enshrined in the *European Convention on Human Rights and Fundamental Freedoms* ('Convention'). At the heart of this debate is the dilemma about whether the state has a right to restrict freedom of expression to protect religious feelings; to what extent and under what conditions? Would prior state censorship of certain depictions of objects of religious veneration in cases when no harm is done to the religious feelings of others be considered as a violation of free speech? What about *ex post facto* squashing harsh criticism of religious leaders? Should protection of religious feelings and restriction of free speech be justified through protection of rights of others or public morals? What does it mean in terms of non-discrimination of non-major religions in given societies? Given the fact that criminal law in some European countries still provides for protection of religious convictions, should this system be substituted by the less repressive one? These are just some of the questions that will be addressed in this paper.

The Convention provides for the legal protection of two important fundamental rights and freedoms – freedom of expression (Article 10) and freedom of thought, conscience and religion (Article 9). Exercise of both rights is restricted, inter alia, by the 'protection of the reputation or rights of others'. *Freedom of expression* constitutes one of the essential foundations of a democratic society and one of the basic conditions for its progress and for each individual's self-fulfillment. Intrinsic value theories hold that freedom of expression is cardinal for self-development and self-fulfillment. People develop their personalities and their intellectual capabilities through freely expressing their thoughts whereby they can become more thoughtful and mature. Thus, measures curtailing expression would obstruct those ways of interaction and suppress our personality and its growth.[1] In addition to its intrinsic value, freedom of expression is, above all, the public good protected, inter alia, by the Constitution. This is a democratic standard and as such it goes far beyond the scope of individual self-fulfillment in society with equal opportunities. Due to the fact that democracy cannot be sustained without a broad right to free speech, this right is considered by some commentators as a functional democratic right. In the *Declaration of Principles on Freedom of Expression* it was described as an 'indispensable instrument for the functioning of representative democracy, through which individuals exercise their right to receive, impart and seek information.'[2] The Supreme Court of Canada conceives of freedom of expression as (1) an instrument for the realization of truth; (2) an instrument of democratic self-government; and (3) an aspect of self-realization or human dignity.[3] As one of the commentators correctly observed, 'if the state prevents citizens from participating in public discourse when they would otherwise desire to do so, the state loses democratic legitimacy with respect to those citizens, for it prevents them from attempting to make public opinion responsive to their views.'[4] This multifaceted and multifunctional dimension of freedom of expression in democratic society means that this fundamental human right applies not only to 'information' or 'ideas' that are favourably received or regarded as inoffensive or as a matter of indifference, but also to those that offend, shock or disturb.[5] Such are the demands of that pluralism, tolerance and broadmindedness that without which there is no 'democratic society'.[6] The exercise of these freedoms, since it carries with it duties and responsibilities, may be subject to such formalities, conditions, restrictions or penalties as are prescribed by law and are necessary in a democratic society; in the interests of national security, territorial integrity or public safety; for the prevention of disorder or crime, for the protection of health or morals; for the protection of the reputation or rights of others; for preventing the disclosure of information received in confidence; or for maintaining the authority and impartiality of the judiciary.[7] This means that

1 See generally Nicos Alivizatos, 'Art and Religious Beliefs: The Limits of Liberalism' in *Blasphemy, Insult and Hatred: Finding Answers in a Democratic Society*, Venice Commission (Council of European Publishing, 2010) 508.

2 *Declaration of Principles on Freedom of Expression, Inter-American Commission on Human Rights*, Inter-American Commission on Human Rights, accessed 4 June 2017, available at: <http://www.oas.org/en/iachr/expression/showarticle.asp?artID=26>.

3 Jacob Weinrib, 'What is the Purpose of Freedom of Expression' (2009) 67 *University of Toronto Faculty of Law Review* 1.

4 Robert Post, 'Religion and Freedom of Speech: Portraits of Muhammad' in Susanna Mancini and Michel Rosenfeld (eds), *Constitutional Secularism in an age of Religious Revival* (Oxford University Press, 2014) 331.

5 *Handyside v* UK (1976) 1 EHRR 737 [49].

6 *Ceylan v Turkey* (2000) 30 EHRR 73 [32].

7 *Convention for the Protection of Human Rights and Fundamental Freedoms*, Article 10, par 2, CETS No 005, accessed 23 February 2015, available at: <www.coe.int/en/web/conventions/full-list/-/conventions/treaty/005>.

freedom of expression is not an absolute right and could be restricted if there is legitimate aim. In addition, any restriction should be prescribed by (written) law and imposed only if it is necessary in democratic society.[8] The margin of appreciation is very narrow, for instance, for restrictions on political speech and public interest debates[9] and very broad for limiting freedom of expression that amounts to incitement to violence and hate speech.[10]

*Freedom of thought, conscience and religion*, which is safeguarded under Article 9 of the Convention, is one of the foundations of a 'democratic society' within the meaning of the Convention. It is, in its religious dimension, one of the most vital elements that go to make up the identity of believers and their conception of life.[11] This freedom has two aspects: *internal* and *external*. 'Internal' freedom can only be unconditional, since it concerns deep-seated ideas and convictions formed within an individual's conscience which cannot, in themselves, disturb public order and consequently cannot be limited by state authorities. 'External' freedom, on the other hand, despite its considerable importance, can only be relative. This relativity is logical inasmuch as the freedom in question is the freedom to manifest one's beliefs in which public order may be affected or even threatened. Consequently, although the freedom to hold beliefs and convictions can only be unconditional, the freedom to manifest them can only be relative.[12] Freedom of religion entails many forms such as protection from indoctrination,[13] proselytism[14] etc.

## European Court of Human Rights case law

In a number of cases of alleged violation of Article 10, the European Court of Human Rights ('ECHR') addressed the issue of whether certain forms of public expressions interfered with religious feelings. These cases concern *provocative portrayals of objects of religious veneration* (blasphemy) and *harsh criticism of religious leaders* (religious defamation).[15] The best known and most cited case that belongs to the first group is *Otto Preminger Institute v Austria*.[16] The applicant association announced a series of six showings, which would be accessible to the general public, of the film *Das Liebeskonzil* (*Council in Heaven*). The film

8 See generally Steven Greer, *The Margin of Appreciation: Interpretation and Discretion Under the European Convention on Human Rights* (Council of European Publishing, 2000).

9 *Lingens v Austria* (1986) 8 EHRR 407 [42]; Council of Europe Parliamentary Assembly, 'Blasphemy, religious insults and hate speech against persons on grounds of their religion' (2007) r 1805, par 8.

10 See generally Michael Herz and Peter Molnar, *The Content and Context of Hate Speech: Regulation and Responses* (Cambridge University Press, 2012).

11 *Kokkinakis v Greece* (1994) 17 EHRR 397 [31].

12 Jean-François Renucci, *Article 9 of the European Convention on Human Rights* (Council of European Publishing, 2005) 10.

13 See generally *Kjeldsen, Busk Madsen and Pedersen v Denmark* (1976) 1 EHRR 711.

14 See generally, Renucci, above n 12.

15 Esther Janssen, *Faith in Public Debate: On Freedom of Expression, Hate Speech and Religion in France & the Netherlands* (Cambridge University Press, 2015) 120.

16 *Otto Preminger Institute v Austria* [1994] ECHR 26 (20 September 1994).

ridiculed the Eucharist and the 'portrayal of God the Father, Christ and Mother Mary of God'.[17] This announcement was made in an information bulletin distributed by the application to its 2,700 members and in various display windows in Innsbruck. At the request of the Innsbruck diocese of the Roman Catholic Church, the public prosecutor instituted criminal proceedings against the manager of the applicant. The charge was 'disparaging religious doctrines' (*Herabwürdigung religiöser Lehren*), an act prohibited by section 188 of the Penal Code (*Strafgesetzbuch*). Although the criminal proceedings were discontinued, in the objective proceedings under media law, the Regional Court ordered the forfeiture of the film.[18] In the judgment, the ECHR first focused on difficulties in discerning pan-European uniform conception of the significance of religion in society.[19] Therefore, the ECHR pointed out that it is not possible:

> to arrive at a comprehensive definition of what constitutes a permissible interference with the exercise of the right to freedom of expression where such expression is directed against the religious feelings of others . . . a certain margin of appreciation is therefore to be left to the national authorities in assessing the existence and extent of the necessity of such interference.[20]

The issue before the Court involved weighing up the conflicting interests of the exercise of two fundamental freedoms guaranteed under the Convention, namely the right of the applicant association to impart to the public controversial views and, by implication, the right of interested persons to take cognisance of such views, on the one hand; and the right of other persons to proper respect for their freedom of thought, conscience and religion, on the other hand.[21] The ECHR stressed that the social environment with an owerhelming majority of Roman Catholics would have been affected if the authorities had not seized the film. Restricting the freedom of expression in the concrete case was necessary, as the ECHR pointed out, for ensuring 'religious peace in that region and to prevent that some people should feel the object of attacks on their religious beliefs in an unwarranted and offensive manner.'[22] Therefore no violation of Article 10 was found. This judgment was harshly criticised in the literature for its failure to properly apply the balancing test. The critics questioned whether the measure taken was proportionate to the aim pursued and found that the ECHR was (too) lenient to Austria endorsing the 'state's prerogative to combat intolerance through censorship.'[23] In the joint dissenting judgment, three

17 Paul M Taylor, *Freedom of Religion, UN and European Human Rights Law and Practice* (Cambridge University Press, 2005) 85.
18 Taylor, above n 17, [16].
19 Ibid [50].
20 Ibid.
21 Ibid [55].
22 Ibid [56].
23 Ivan Hare and James Weinstein, *Extreme Speech and Democracy* (Oxford University Press, 2009) 277.

judges (Palm, Pekkanen and Makarczyk) stressed that a less restrictive solution was available and that the:

> need for repressive action amounting to complete prevention of the exercise of freedom of expression can only be accepted if the behaviour concerned reaches so high a level of abuse, and comes so close to a denial of the freedom of religion of others, as to forfeit for itself the right to be tolerated by society.[24]

They shared the view that:

> it should not be open to the authorities of the State to decide whether a particular statement is capable of contributing to any form of public debate capable of furthering progress in human affairs because such a decision cannot but be tainted by the authorities' idea of progress.[25]

The ECHR reiterated its position in *Wingrove v UK*.[26] The applicant was a film director who made a video entitled *Visions of Ecstasy*. According to the applicant, the idea for the film was derived from the life and writings of St Teresa of Avila, the 16th century Carmelite nun and founder of many convents, who experienced powerful ecstatic visions of Jesus Christ. The video contained scenes of her erotic ecstasies with Jesus Christ and another woman. After the competent authorities refused to issue a certificate of distribution (the appeals in administrative proceedings was not granted), the applicant turned to ECHR claming that the state violated his right under Article 10. As regards the content of the law itself, the Court observed that the English law of blasphemy does not prohibit the expression, in any form, of views hostile to the Christian religion. Nor can it be said that opinions which are offensive to Christians necessarily fall within its ambit.[27] The ECHR stressed that the aim of the interference was to protect against the treatment of a religious subject in such a manner:

> as to be calculated (that is, bound, not intended) to outrage those who have an understanding of, sympathy towards and support for the Christian story and ethic, because of the contemptuous, reviling, insulting, scurrilous or ludicrous tone, style and spirit in which the subject is presented.[28]

This is an aim which 'undoubtedly corresponds to that of the protection of "the rights of others" within the meaning of paragraph 2 of Article 10 . . . it is also fully consonant with the aim of the protections afforded by Article 9 to religious

24 See Taylor, above n 17, Joint Dissenting Opinion of Judges Palm, Pekkanen and Makarczyk.
25 Ibid [3].
26 *Wingrove v UK* [1996] ECHR 60 (25 November 1996).
27 Ibid [60].
28 Ibid [48].

freedom.'[29] The ECHR confirmed that the 'extent of insult to religious feelings must be significant, as is clear from the use by the courts of the adjectives "contemptuous", "reviling", "scurrilous", "ludicrous" to depict material of a sufficient degree of offensiveness.'[30] As a result, the ECHR found that the high degree of profanation that was attained constitutes, in itself, a safeguard against arbitrariness. Therefore, it was decided that the state did not overstep its margin of appreciation under Article 10. The argument for criticism by commentators and dissenters were very similar to those in the *Otto Preminger* case (lack of balancing, arbitrariness etc). One of the arguments raised by Judge Lohmus was that:

> the law of blasphemy only protects the Christian religion and, more specifically, the established Church of England . . . the aim of the interference was therefore to protect . . . the Christian faith alone and not other beliefs . . . this in itself raises the question whether the interference was 'necessary in a democratic society'.[31]

The ECHR in obiter also expressed disagreement with such 'anomaly of this state of affairs in a multidenominational society'[32] but correctly concluded that the Court does not have jurisdiction to 'rule in abstracto as to the compatibility of domestic law with the Convention.'[33] The extent to which 'English law protects other beliefs is not in issue before the Court which must confine its attention to the case before it.'[34] The uncontested fact that the 'law of blasphemy does not treat on an equal footing the different religions practised in the United Kingdom does not detract from the legitimacy of the aim pursued in the present context.'[35]

A similar line of reasoning was adopted in *I A v Turkey*.[36] The applicant was a book publisher who was convicted for publishing insults against 'God, the Religion, the Prophet and the Holy Book.' In its 2005 judgment, the ECHR came to the conclusion that the Turkish authorities did not violate the applicant's freedom of expression as guaranteed by Article 10. According to the Court, one part of the book indeed contained an abusive attack on the Prophet of Islam, whereas it is asserted that some of the statements and words of the Prophet were 'inspired in a surge of exultation, in Aisha's arms . . . God's messenger broke his fast through sexual intercourse, after dinner and before prayer'. In the book, it is stated that 'Mohammed did not forbid sexual intercourse with a dead person or a living animal'. The Court accepted that believers could legitimately feel that these passages of the book constituted an unwarranted and offensive attack on

29 Ibid.
30 Ibid [60].
31 *Wingrove v UK* [1996] ECHR 60 (25 November 1996), see the dissenting opinion of Judge Lohmus [4].
32 Ibid [50].
33 Ibid.
34 Ibid.
35 Ibid.
36 *I A v Turkey* [2005] ECHR 590 (13 September 2005).

them.[37] Therefore, according to the Court, the present case 'concerns not only comments that offend or shock, or a "provocative" opinion, but also an abusive attack on the Prophet of Islam.'[38]

Unlike the insult of religious feelings through provocative portrayals of objects of religious veneration, *harsh criticism of religious leaders* has not been considered by ECHR as a violation of religious feelings. The applicant in *Giniewski v France*,[39] as a response to the papal encyclical *Veritatis Splendor*, published an article in a French newspaper critising the Catholic Church and the position of the Pope. He wrote, inter alia, that 'many Christians have acknowledged that anti-Judaism and the doctrine of the "fulfilment" of the Old Covenant in the New lead to anti-Semitism and prepared the ground on which the idea and implementation of Auschwitz took seed.'[40] The Court observed that:

> although the applicant's article criticises a papal encyclical and hence the Pope's position, the analysis it contains cannot be extended to Christianity as a whole, which, as pointed out by the applicant, is made up of various strands, several of which reject papal authority. Although the issue raised in the present case concerns a doctrine upheld by the Catholic Church, and hence a religious matter, an analysis of the article in question shows that it does not contain attacks on religious beliefs as such, but a view which the applicant wishes to express as a journalist and historian.[41]

By reasoning that in democratic society 'debate on the causes of acts of particular gravity amounting to crimes against humanity should be able to take place freely'[42] the Court concluded that the state overstepped the margin of appreciation and consequently violated Article 10 to the detriment of the applicant. Similarly, in *Klein v Slovakia*,[43] the ECHR unanimously found violation of Article 10. The case concerned an applicant who sharply criticised the Archbishop J Sokol following the latter's call, in a TV broadcast, for the withdrawal of both the film *The People vs Larry Flynt* and the poster accompanying that film.[44] The ECHR was not persuaded that by his statements the applicant discredited and disparaged a sector of the population on account of their Catholic faith, finding that:

> The fact that some members of the Catholic Church could have been offended by the applicant's criticism of the Archbishop and by his statement that he did

37 Drik Voorhoof, 'European Court of Human Rights, Case of I A v Turkey' (2005), accessed 23 February 2016, available at <http://merlin.obs.coe.int/iris/2005/10/article3.en.html>.
38 Özgür Heval Çınar and Mine Yıldırım (eds), *Freedom of Religion and Belief in Turkey* (Cambridge Scholars Publishing, 2014) 78.
39 *Giniewski v France* (2007) 45 EHRR 23.
40 Ibid [14].
41 Ibid [51].
42 Ibid.
43 *Klein v Slovakia* [2006] ECHR 909 (31 October 2006).
44 Ibid [51].

not understand why decent Catholics did not leave that Church since it was headed by Archbishop J Sokol cannot affect the position.[45]

## Discussion

### *Protection of religious feelings from expressions not functional in democratic society*

The central issue here is whether authorities have a right to restrict certain expressions that hurt religious feelings of believers. Supporters of unlimited free speech opine that the state should not have even minimum scrutiny over the 'marketplace of ideas'.[46] They suggest that government must remain neutral with regard to different contents. Otherwise, restricting certain viewpoints would amount to 'viewpoint discrimination'.[47] Yet, the realities of a legal regulation in Europe in this matter are quite the opposite. While strong distrust against governmental control over the content of expression is typical for the United States of America where speech may only be prohibited if it poses a 'clear and present danger'[48] (imminent lawlessnes doctrine),[49] different categories of content-based bans on free speech have been firmly established in Europe (for instance hate speech, speech discriminatory to minorities, apology of terrorism etc). Numerous grounds for restriction of freedom of expression under the free speech provision itself (Article 10, para 2) serve the purpose to protect some other values indispensable for functioning of democratic societies. As these values also serve some important functions in a society, those who willingly abandon their duties and responsibilities in exercising their right to freely express themselves should reasonably expect certain reaction(s) either through formalities, conditions, restrictions or penalties. In other words, as long as the particular expression has a function in democratic society there will be no legitimate ground for its restriction. On the contrary, when it has been established that some other value of functional importance is affected by certain expression, the functional dimension of free speech comes into question. And that would be a legitimate ground for its restriction justified by pressing social need. In the light of the foregoing, who should have a right and duty, if not the state who on behalf of the citizens holds the keys of the Constitution, to assess whether certain form of expression, by departing from its function in democratic society, breach some other rights and values protected under the Convention? Again, arguments of those who claim that the state does not have a right to judge on functional aspects of free speech would be valid only where freedom of expression is an absolute right; which is obviously not the case. Therefore,

45 Ibid [52].
46 *Otto Preminger Institute v Austria* [1994] ECHR 26 (20 September 1994) [28].
47 Ibid.
48 *Schenck v United States* 249 US 47 (1919).
49 *Otto Preminger Institute v Austria* [1994] ECHR 26 (20 September 1994) [26].

the state has a right, under the legitimate margin of appreciation doctrine, to restrict certain expressions that violate, inter alia, the rights of others. It is true that expressions that 'offend, shock or disturb' must be tolerated in democratic society but, as already pointed out, this is not without limits whatsoever. If such expressions are 'gratuitously offensive' to the rights of others and serve no other purpose than simply to 'offend, shock or disturb', the state has a right to restrict them. There are some expressions that are so lacking in social or democratic virtue that they do not deserve to shelter behind the shield of free speech.[50] In terms of protection of religious feelings, the standard of 'gratuitously offensive' speech that emerged in ECHR case law is very similar to the narrow interpretation of 'blasphemous' speech established in the House of Lords jurisprudence:

> Every publication is said to be blasphemous which contains any contemptuous, reviling, scurrilous or ludicrous matter relating to God, Jesus Christ, or the Bible, or the formularies of the Church of England as by law established. It is not blasphemous to speak or publish opinions hostile to the Christian religion, or to deny the existence of God, if the publication is couched in decent and temperate language. The test to be applied is as to the manner in which the doctrines are advocated and not as to the substance of the doctrines themselves.[51]

Back to the circumstances of the case in *Otto Preminger*, it is implausible that portraying the Virgin Mary as a promiscuous woman and Jesus as a mentally insufficient and impotent man would have any social function whatsoever. At the same time, it is very probable that such portrayals, if available to the public, would offend those who believe in their sanctity. Therefore, the conclusion that such an expression amounts to 'gratuitously offensive' speech in abstracto is correct.

### *Prior restraint*

However, the dissenting judges and other critics are right in questioning whether prior restraint by the authorities interferes with freedom of expression because the members of the society whose feelings they seek to protect have not called for such interference. In other words, they claim that prior interference, by not corresponding to a 'pressing social need', was not justified under the margin of appreciation doctrine.[52] This brings us to the question whether there is a positive obligation of a state to prevent religious criticism and expressions that *could be* offensive to the feelings of the believers. Most of the commentators suggest that freedom of religion statutes do not impose positive obligations on the state, but rather affirm freedoms of the individual which the state is not to breach. The very

50 Rex Tauati Ahdar, 'The Right to Protection of Religious Feelings' (2005–2008) 11 *Otago Law Review* 629, 654.

51 *Whitehouse v Gay News Ltd* [1979] AC 617 (21 February 1979) 665.

52 *Wingrove v UK* [1996] ECHR 60 (25 November 1996) [3].

nature of these rights and freedoms means that they are freedoms from state interference.[53] Notwithstanding the ECHR case law that might suggest otherwise (*Otto Preminger* and *Wingrove*), it seems that *opinio juris* in this matter denies *prior facti* protection of religious feelings in the sense that a state has been held to be under a duty and thus required to positively protect a believer's feelings. States have the power to protect religious feelings and they may, in suitable instances, do so and capitulate to complaints by outraged citizens by intervening to curtail the offensive material.[54] However, this does not mean that the state is relieved from positive obligations regarding some other aspects of freedom of religion. For instance, when a state does not afford individuals any protection against religiously inspired violence and does not take any steps to investigate the discriminatory motives of such violence, that state violates a positive obligation on the ground of Article 3 para 9, para 14 of the Convention.[55] In *Dubowska and Skup v Poland*, ECHR went even further confirming that:

> there may be certain positive obligations on the part of a state inherent in an effective respect for rights guaranteed under Article 9 of the Convention, which may involve the adoption of measures designed to secure respect for freedom of religion even in the sphere of the relations of individuals between themselves . . . such measures may, in certain circumstances, constitute a legal means of ensuring that an individual will not be disturbed in his worship by the activities of others.[56]

## *Protection of religious feelings and satirical form of expression*

Rights of the citizen not to be insulted in their religious feelings by 'gratuitously offensive' expressions *does not necessarily mean full protection against ridiculing these feelings* by the others. Dworkin describes the ridicule as a distinct kind of expression; its substance cannot be repackaged in a less offensive rhetorical form without expressing something very different from what was intended.[57] That is why cartoons and other forms of ridicule have for centuries, even when illegal, been among the most important weapons of both noble and wicked political movements.[58] So in a democracy no one, however powerful or impotent, can have a right not to be insulted or offended.[59] This brings us to the question of satire as a form of expression that enjoys broad protection under the Convention.

53 *Whitehouse v Gay News Ltd* [1979] AC 617 (21 February 1979) 634.
54 Ibid 639.
55 *Otto Preminger Institute v Austria* [1994] ECHR 26 (20 September 1994) [136].
56 *Dubowska and Skup v Poland* (1997) 24 EHRR CD 75 [5].
57 Ronald Dworkin, 'Even Bigots and Holocaust Deniers Must Have Their Say', *The Guardian*, accessed 3 January 2017, available at: <www.theguardian.com/world/2006/feb/14/muhammadcartoons.comment>.
58 Ibid.
59 *Whitehouse v Gay News Ltd* [1979] AC 617 (21 February 1979) 631.

In ECHR case law, satire has been recognised as a form of artistic expression and social commentary, by exaggeration and distortion of reality which naturally aims to provoke and agitate. Accordingly, any interference with an artist's right to such expression must be examined with particular care.[60] The ECHR found that there was no pressing social need to criminalise symbolic retorsion (made by a farmer who publicly displayed the sentence to the President '*Casse toi pov'con*'/'Get lost, you sad prick'/, a phrase uttered by the President himself several months previously when a farmer had refused to shake his hand at the International Agricultural Show).[61] The Court opined that prosecuting and convicting the perpetrator in such a case would deter satirical intervention which could have a severe effect on free debate questions of general interest, without which there is no democracy. The imposition of a criminal penalty by the authorities in this case was therefore disproportionate to the aim pursued and was not necessary in a democratic society.[62] In *Leroy v France*,[63] the ECHR went in the opposite direction. The case concerned French cartoonist Denis Leroy who, in the close aftermath of the 11 September 2001 attacks on the World Trade Center in New York, depicted the attacks with the text '[w]e have all dreamt about it . . . Hamas did it'. The Court, unanimously, disagreed. It held that the interference in this case served the legitimate aims of public safety and the prevention of disorder or crime in the sensitive context of the fight against terrorism.[64] In deciding the case, the Court took into account 'global chaos' caused by the attacks, the fact that large-scale violence was used against civilians and that such a message could produce negative impact in a politically sensitive region (Basque country).

In the case *Ben El Mahi and others v Denmark*[65] (also known as *Jyllands-Posten*), the Court was dealing with a privately owned Danish newspaper that published 12 cartoons, most of which were caricatures of the Prophet Muhammad. The most controversial of the cartoons showed the Prophet Muhammad with a bomb in his turban. After the case was discontinued by the Danish public prosecutor, the ECHR found that there was no jurisdictional link between any of the applicants (Moroccan nationals) and the relevant member state, namely Denmark, and therefore declared the case inadmissibile.[66] Soon after this case was dismissed by the Court, the Parliamentary Assembly of the Council of Europe adopted the

60 *Vereinigung Bildender Künstler v Austria* [2007] ECHR 79 (25 January 2007) [33].

61 Rosalind English, 'Satirical Insult of Head of State Should not be a Criminal Offence', *Rules Strasbourg*, UK Human Rights Blog, accessed 23 February 2016, available at: <http://ukhumanrightsblog.com/2013/03/14/satirical-insult-of-head-of-state-should-not-be-a-criminal-offence-rules-strasbourg/>.

62 Ibid.

63 *Leroy v France*, Application no 36109/03 of 2 October 2008.

64 ECHR Blog, 'Judgment on Apology of Terrorism', *ECHR Blog*, 2 October 2008, accessed 23 February 2016, available at: <http://echrblog.blogspot.hr/2008/10/judgment-on-apology-of-terrorism.html>.

65 *Ben El Mahi and others v Denmark*, Application no 5853/06 of 11 December 2006.

66 Ibid.

*Resolution on Freedom of Expression and Respect for Religious Beliefs* which stated that:

> attacks on individuals on grounds of their religion or race cannot be permitted but blasphemy laws should not be used to curtail freedom of expression and thought . . . modern democratic societies tend to be secular and more concerned with individual freedoms . . . the recent debate about the Danish cartoons raised the question of these two perceptions . . . critical dispute, satire, humour and artistic expression should, therefore, enjoy a wider degree of freedom of expression and recourse to exaggeration should not be seen as provocation.[67]

This position was confirmed in *Recommendation on Blasphemy, Religious Insults and Hate Speech Against Persons on Grounds of Their Religion*:

> in a democratic society, religious groups must tolerate, as must other groups, critical public statements and debate about their activities, teachings and beliefs, provided that such criticism does not amount to intentional and gratuitous insults or hate speech and does not constitute incitement to disturb the peace or to violence and discrimination against adherents of a particular religion.[68]

Similar conclusions can be found in the *Venice Commission 2006 Report*.[69] These statements should be understood as a reaction of a regional organisation (Council of Europe) to the affair of the Danish Cartoons (regrettably not decided on the merits) and the United Nations 'defamation of religions' resolutions.[70] Although it might seem that the tone and the content of these documents depart from the ECHR position taken in *Otto Preminger* and *Wingrove*, two major standards remain the same to those established in ECHR jurisprudence: blasphemy laws should not be used to curtail freedom of expression and thought in general, but they can be used to restrict intentional and gratuitous insults and discrimination against adherents of a particular religion. The statement that 'critical dispute, satire, humour and artistic expression should enjoy a wider degree of freedom of

67 Council of Europe Parliamentary Assembly, *on Freedom of Expression and Respect for Religious Beliefs*, (28 June 2006) Resolution 1510.

68 Council of Europe Parliamentary Assembly, 'on Blasphemy, Religious Insults and Hate Speech Against Persons on Grounds of Their Religion' (29 June 2007), Recommendation 1805.

69 The Venice Commission, *The Relationship Between Freedom of Expression and Freedom of Religion: The Issue of Regulation and Prosecution of Blasphemy, Religious Insult and Incitement to Religious Hatred*, Report of the Venice Commission, Study no 406 (Council of European Publishing, 2006).

70 *Otto Preminger Institute v Austria* [1994] ECHR 26 (20 September 1994) [125].

expression' is also just a confirmation of a stance firmly established by the ECHR.[71] In *Müller and others v Switzerland* the ECHR concluded that 'through his creative work, the artist expresses not only a personal vision of the world but also his view of the society in which he lives . . . to that extent art not only helps shape public opinion but is also an expression of it and can confront the public with the major issues of the day.'[72] It is also true that critical dispute (even sharp criticism) of certain religious beliefs, notwithstanding the form it has been conveyed to the public (ie artistic or non-artistic), offers at least some kind of argument that contribute to the public debate. Although the religion is not necessarily about the reason but about belief, for the sake of fostering debate in plural societies believers must tolerate not only those who, even publicly, declare that they do not share their convictions, but also those who expose some views that might seem hostile to their beliefs. Such criticism must have been protected because of its function in democratic societies. However, extreme satirical (as well as other artistic and non-artistic) expressions made with a sole purpose of provoking and insulting religious feelings of others lacks that function and states must have a possibility for their restriction relying on the margin of appreciation doctrine. Ostensible artistic or quasi-artistic nature of expression must not be used as *carte blanche* for violation of the rights of others. Otherwise, the expressions that call for a person or group to be subjected to hatred, discrimination or violence and that are disguised in some form of artistic or quasi-artistic expression (sometimes satirical), might quite easily spill over the margin of tolerance in contemporary European societies.

### *Religious feelings, morality and non-discrimination*

Religious feelings and religious freedoms in general are closely linked to the notion of the *morality*. They both share common understanding of 'right and wrong', as is also the case with some secular value frameworks like humanism. Yet, protection of religious feelings in the ECHR case law is not justified under the 'public morals', but under the 'rights of others' as a ground for exclusion of the free speech envisaged in Article 10. It might seem perplexing why these two inseparable systems (religion and morality) do not rely on each other under the protective human rights mechanism of the Convention. The answer lies in the non-discriminatory dimension of religious freedoms provision. In other words, if religious feelings would have been protected by invoking public morals, religions other than major ones and other denominations would not be adequately protected under the Convention. This is the best argument to those critics who suggest that inherent interconnection between notions of 'public health', 'national security' and 'public

71 Council of Europe Parliamentary Assembly, 'on Blasphemy, Religious Insults and Hate Speech Against Persons on Grounds of Their Religion' (29 June 2007), Recommendation 1805.

72 See Michel Verpeaux, *Freedom of Expression in Constitutional and International Case Law* (Council of European Publishing, 2010), 149.

morals' provide for protection only for major monotheistic religion(s) while other religions and denominations have not been entitled to the same level of protection.[73] However the criticism is well founded when it comes to certain domestic legislation that provide for protection of the major religion while neglecting the others. That kind of legislative discrimination was criticised by both majority and dissenting judges in *Wingrove v UK*. In *Choudhury v United Kingdom*[74] it was argued that the United Kingdom had failed to protect the religious sensibilities of Muslims insofar as the English courts ruled that the blasphemy law did not extend beyond Christianity to the protection of Islam. The victim, Mr Abdul Choudhury, along with certain other British Muslims, had been outraged at the publication of Salman Rushdie's *The Satanic Verses*, and unsuccessfully sought to bring a criminal prosecution against Rushdie and Viking Penguin, the book's publishers, on the ground that the book blasphemed against Allah and the religion of Islam. The ECHR found that Choudhury had not claimed 'and it [was] clearly not the case' that the state authorities had directly interfered with his freedom to manifest his religion. That being so, it could see no link between Article 9 and the applicant's complaint at all, and it declared the complaint to be inadmissible.[75]

### *Moral limits of criminal law and protection of religious feelings through reactive prevention*

According to Jeremy Bentham, legislation and morality have the same object. Morality in general is the art of directing the actions of men in such a way as to produce the greatest possible sum of good.[76] For Feinberg 'the basic question' is 'one about the moral limits within which states may encroach upon individual liberty.'[77] The alternate formulation has the advantage of making explicit the 'presumption in favor of liberty,' a Feinbergian first principle that assigns the 'burden of argument to . . . the advocate' of governmental intervention.[78] The need to prevent harm (private or public) to parties other than the actor is always an appropriate reason for state interference with a citizen's behaviour.[79] This concept of 'harm to others' is in a way rooted in the protective dimension of the Convention. By suggesting that state has a right to interfere with a citizen behaviour when such behaviour caused or is likely to cause harm to the others, means nothing else than invoking the protection

73 Talal Asad et al, *Is Critique Secular?: Blasphemy, Injury, and Free Speech* (Fordham University Press, 2009) 79.

74 *Choudhury v United Kingdom*, Application no 00017439/90 (1991).

75 *Whitehouse v Gay News Ltd* [1979] AC 617 (21 February 1979) 639.

76 In general, see Jeremy Bentham, *Theory of Legislation* (Prometheus Books, 1864).

77 See Joel Feinberg quoted in Harlon L Dalton, *Offense to Others: The Moral Limits of the Criminal* (1987), Faculty Scholarship Series Paper 2047, accessed 3 January 2017, available at <http://digitalcommons.law.yale.edu/fss_papers/2047>.

78 Ibid.

79 Ibid.

principle when this is necessary in democratic society. This stems from the *ultima ratio* nature of a criminal law norm and, in theory, this principle is known as the subsidiarity principle. In essence it means that criminal law intervention either from a legislator or from law enforcement is justified only if the protection of certain public good cannot be achieved by using some less repressive and less intrusive instruments of social control. Fuller requests that the arbiter must not lose sight of the fact that in the course of arriving at his decision he was compelled to engage in a process of compromise and accommodation of conflicting objectives.[80] His final judgment should not be viewed as the only possible solution. Properly, it should be regarded as nothing more than the most desirable when tested by the standards used by the decision maker.[81] Hart distinguishes between primary and secondary rules.[82] Primary rules are 'duty-imposing' rules.[83] They impose certain specific duties upon the citizens of a state to act in a certain manner, or they may be subject to certain legal sanctions.[84] Hart characterises primary rules as 'basic' rules. Secondary rules are not duty-imposing rules. They are what Hart calls power-conferring rules. They state the manner in which primary rules may be recognised, changed and adjudicated.[85] They state the procedure one must follow in order to make a legal will. Secondary rules are, as Hart puts it, 'rules about primary rules'.[86] Applying these principles to the issue at stake ends up with the conclusion that there is no doubt that criminal legislation is designed to prevent harm. Given the fact that criminal law is *ex post facto* mechanism that takes place only after the harm is done, its preventive dimension must be understood as a positive impact upon the perpetrator not to reoffend (special prevention) as well as on the general public to abstain from violating duty-imposing rules (general prevention). Having said that, criminal law should not be used as a mechanism of prior restraint externally but only internally. Furthermore, within its moral limits, criminal law in general does not protect feelings but rights. It is true that in some legislation insult and defamation are still criminalised but the *ratio legis* for these offences is not protection of other people's feelings but their rights to be respected by the others as equal members of the society. It has rather to do with their right to dignity, ie social construct or the way they are seen by the others, than the right to be protected by any verbal or symbolic questioning by others of their self-perception. The criminalisation of the insult is primarily aimed at protecting the honour of a single individual. This legal protection

80 Edwin W Tucker, 'The Morality of Law by Lon L Fuller' (1965) 40 *Indiana Law Journal* 270, 271.

81 Ibid.

82 William C Starr, 'Law and Morality in H L A Hart's Legal Philosophy' (1984) 67 *Marquette Law Review* 673.

83 Ibid.

84 Ibid.

85 Ibid.

86 Ibid.

entitles every person to a 'moral integrity' not as internal personal honour but as a social value of a person's honour in the eyes of others. The same goes for the rationale of protecting religious feelings. They should not be understood as a psychological concept but rather as a legal one. Religion is far from being the private matter of an individual. It is the social construct with very specific social meaning that is entitled to certain form(s) of social protection. However, this protection has not been focused on internalised values of a certain individual that relate to his religious beliefs (convictions) but to his right to be respected by others in free exercise of his religious customs. By analogy, the legal threshold for protection of religious feelings through criminal law is the determination of circumstances that degrade the respectability of a believer in the eyes of the others. It is always up to the authorities to decide whether criminal law should be used as a tool for reactive (not proactive) prevention of religious feelings as a right enshrined in Article 9 of the Convention. ECHR jurisprudence confirmed the right of the state to protect religious feelings through criminal law mechanisms. In *Dubowska and Skup v Poland* the Commission found that:

> the applicants had at their disposal a legal remedy in case of an insult to their religious feelings . . . in their decisions discontinuing the investigations they carefully assessed all circumstances of the case and the importance of the issue at stake . . . thus, the present case is not one in which the applicants were inhibited from exercising their freedom to hold and express their belief . . . moreover, the fact that the authorities eventually found that no offence had been committed does not in itself amount to a failure to protect the applicants' rights guaranteed under Article 9 of the Convention.[87]

## Conclusion

To sum up, in the case law of the ECHR it has been established that religious feelings enjoy protection under the Convention. This mirrors the expectation that others show respect for religious feelings of believers as an important aspect of their religious freedoms.[88] In this regard, states may legitimately consider it necessary to take measures aimed at repressing certain forms of conduct, including the imparting of information and ideas, judged incompatible with the respect for the freedom of thought, conscience and religion of others.[89] The *Right of the citizens not to be insulted in their religious feelings*[90] by excessive freedom of expression is guaranteed under protection of rights of others envisaged in Article 10, para 2. Whereas there is little scope under Article 10, para 2 of the Convention

87 *Whitehouse v Gay News Ltd* [1979] AC 617 (21 February 1979) [5].
88 Taylor, above n 17, [47].
89 Renucci, above n 12, [48].
90 *Wingrove v UK* [1996] ECHR 60 (25 November 1996) [47].

for restrictions on political speech or on debate of questions of public interest, a wider margin of appreciation is generally available to the Contracting States when regulating freedom of expression in relation to matters liable to offend intimate personal convictions within the sphere of morals or, especially, religion.[91] However, this protection would be limited only to such expressions that either inhibit those who hold such beliefs from exercising their freedom to hold and express them or that are 'gratuitously offensive'. In general, believers in democratic societies are expected to cultivate tolerance and broadmindedness and thus they have no right to expect that their religion will be immune from criticism.[92]

Freedom of expression and freedom of religion are not juxtapositioned. Indeed, the rights enshrined in Articles 9 and 10 of the Convention have very similar purposes – promoting the spirit of tolerance and pluralism in democratic society. They are not exclusive but inclusive and both have a function in democratic societies. These two rights are on the same side of the human rights spectrum. They are not confronted as it may seem from the outset and their function is closely connected with promoting tolerance among those who share different values. There are no conflicting objectives of these two fundamental rights (in the United States' Constitution, for instance, both rights are guaranteed under the First Amendment). What might be conflicting, as already pointed out, is the excess of free speech that violates the rights of others. When there is a pressing social need, states have a right to restrict, even through repressive mechanisms of substantive criminal law, speech that lacks any social function in order to protect other functional social values. The grounds for these restrictions must be narrowly interpreted. This is supported by the fact that freedom of religion can be seen as a special form of freedom of expression. This means that unreasonable and unlimited restriction of free speech could be just one step on the way to restricting religious freedoms. There have been numerous examples of simultaneous repression of both rights throughout history, particulary in totalitarian regimes. Having said that, the dominant paradigm that presupposes these two rights as conflicting ones should be reconsidered taking into account their substantive complementarity.

## References

Ahdar, Rex Tauati, 'The Right to Protection of Religious Feelings' (2005–2008) 11 *Otago Law Review* 629

Asad, Talal, et al, *Is Critique Secular?: Blasphemy, Injury, and Free Speech* (Fordham University Press, 2009)

Bentham, Jeremy, *Theory of Legislation* (Prometheus Books, 1864)

*Ceylan v Turkey* (2000) 30 EHRR 73

*Choudhury v United Kingdom*, Application no 00017439/90 (1991)

Çınar, Özgür Heval and Mine Yıldırım (eds), *Freedom of Religion and Belief in Turkey* (Cambridge Scholars Publishing, 2014)

91 Ibid [58].

92 Ahdar, above n 50, 638.

*Convention for the Protection of Human Rights and Fundamental Freedoms*, Article 10, par 2, CETS No 005, accessed 23 February 2015, available at: <www.coe.int/en/web/conventions/full-list/-/conventions/treaty/005>

Council of Europe Parliamentary Assembly, 'on Blasphemy, Religious Insults and Hate Speech Against Persons on Grounds of Their Religion' (29 June 2007)

Dalton, Harlon L, *Offense to Others: The Moral Limits of the Criminal* (1987), Faculty Scholarship Series Paper 2047, accessed 3 January 2017, available at <http://digitalcommons.law.yale.edu/fss_papers/2047>

*Declaration of Principles on Freedom of Expression, Inter-American Commission on Human Rights*, Inter-American Commission on Human Rights, accessed 4 June 2017, available at: <http://www.oas.org/en/iachr/expression/showarticle.asp?artID=26>

*Dubowska and Skup v Poland* (1997) 24 EHRR CD 75

Dworkin, Ronald, 'Even Bigots and Holocaust Deniers Must Have Their Say', *The Guardian*, accessed 3 January 2017, available at: www.theguardian.com/world/2006/feb/14/muhammadcartoons.comment

ECHR Blog, 'Judgment on Apology of Terrorism', *ECHR Blog*, 2 October 2008, accessed 23 February 2016, available at: <http://echrblog.blogspot.hr/2008/10/judgment-on-apology-of-terrorism.html>

*El Mahi, Ben and others v Denmark*, Application no 5853/06 of 11 December 2006

English, Rosalind, 'Satirical Insult of Head of State Should not be a Criminal Offence', *Rules Strasbourg*, UK Human Rights Blog, accessed 23 February 2016, available at: http://ukhumanrightsblog.com/2013/03/14/satirical-insult-of-head-of-state-should-not-be-a-criminal-offence-rules-strasbourg/

*Giniewski v France* (2007) 45 EHRR 23

Greer, Steven, *The Margin of Appreciation: Interpretation and Discretion Under the European Convention on Human Rights* (Council of European Publishing, 2000)

*Handyside v* UK (1976) 1 EHRR 737

Hare, Ivan and James Weinstein, *Extreme Speech and Democracy* (Oxford University Press, 2009)

Herz, Michael and Peter Molnar, *The Content and Context of Hate Speech: Regulation and Responses* (Cambridge University Press, 2012)

*I A v Turkey* [2005] ECHR 590 (13 September 2005)

Janssen, Esther, *Faith in Public Debate: On Freedom of Expression, Hate Speech and Religion in France & the Netherlands* (Cambridge University Press, 2015)

*Kjeldsen, Busk Madsen and Pedersen v Denmark* (1976) 1 EHRR 711

*Klein v Slovakia* [2006] ECHR 909 (31 October 2006)

*Kokkinakis v Greece* (1994) 17 EHRR 397

*Leroy v France*, Application no 36109/03 of 2 October 2008

*Lingens v Austria* (1986) 8 EHRR 407

Mancini, Susanna and Michel Rosenfeld (eds), *Constitutional Secularism in an age of Religious Revival* (Oxford University Press, 2014)

*Otto Preminger Institute v Austria* [1994] ECHR 26 (20 September 1994)

Renucci, Jean-François, *Article 9 of the European Convention on Human Rights* (Council of European Publishing, 2005)

*Schenck v United States* 249 US 47 (1919)

Starr, William C, 'Law and Morality in H L A Hart's Legal Philosophy' (1984) 67 *Marquette Law Review* 673

Taylor, Paul M, *Freedom of Religion, UN and European Human Rights Law and Practice* (Cambridge University Press, 2005)

Tucker, Edwin W, 'The Morality of Law by Lon L Fuller' (1965) 40 *Indiana Law Journal* 270

Venice Commission, *Blasphemy, Insult and Hatred: Finding Answers in a Democratic Society* (Council of European Publishing, 2010)

Venice Commission, *The Relationship Between Freedom of Expression and Freedom of Religion: The Issue of Regulation and Prosecution of Blasphemy, Religious Insult and Incitement to Religious Hatred*, Report of the Venice Commission, Study no 406 (Council of European Publishing, 2006)

*Vereinigung Bildender Künstler v Austria* [2007] ECHR 79 (25 January 2007)

Verpeaux, Michel, *Freedom of Expression in Constitutional and International Case Law* (Council of European Publishing, 2010)

Voorhoof, Drik, 'European Court of Human Rights, Case of I A v Turkey' (2005), accessed 23 February 2016, available at <http://merlin.obs.coe.int/iris/2005/10/article3.en.html>

Weinrib, Jacob, 'What is the Purpose of Freedom of Expression' (2009) 67 *University of Toronto Faculty of Law Review* 1

*Whitehouse v Gay News Ltd* [1979] AC 617 (21 February 1979)

*Wingrove v UK* [1996] ECHR 60 (25 November 1996)

# Part III

# Synthesis

# 11 The International Forum on Religions and Democracy – a path of civic mediation for Islam in Italy

## The pros and cons of integrative university education

*Alessandra Gaetani*

## When: before and after the fall of the Twin Towers

Like many other countries in Europe, Italy, albeit belatedly and with certain peculiarities, has become involved in a process of change caused by the transition from a culturally homogeneous society to a plural society in need of renewed synthesis on a social level. Compared to the multicultural and multi-religious society, the state of the art of legislation in Italy shows, on one hand, obsolescence and gaps[1] and, on the other, a series of constraints that at times make it difficult to access rights for religious minorities, especially Islam.

From a socio-cultural standpoint, Law 40/1998[2] outlined a good model of integration which promoted both the universalism of rights and recognition of the

1 Under the Italian Constitution the laws safeguarding religious freedom are among the most complex in the world, with seven articles dedicated to the subject (2, 3, 7, 8, 18, 19 and 20), and religion is given a prominent role as a recognised social factor of great importance, emblematic for its authoritative doctrine of '*favor religionis*'. Cf Giuseppe Dalla Torre, *Il fattore religioso nella Costituzione: Analisi e interpretazioni* (Giappichelli, 1995) 28–9. On this subject, meanwhile, the Italian law is outdated, incoherent and not consistent with constitutional principles. It dates back to 1929, the Fascist period, and is entitled 'Provisions regarding the conducting of religious worship permitted in the country'. The use of the word 'permitted' in reference to worship (ie religious confession) suggests that the State has the power to condition or tolerate the existence or non-existence of a religion rather than a duty to grant the social expression of a human right to be protected.

2 Italy: Law No 40 of 1998, *Provisions Governing Immigration and Regulations Concerning the Status of Foreigners*, 6 March 1998. The legal definition of integration is: 'the process of non-discrimination and inclusion of differences and, therefore, of fusion and the experimentation of new relational and behavioural forms, in a constant and daily attempt to keep together universal principles and particularisms. It should, therefore, prevent situations of marginalisation, fragmentation and ghettoisation, which threaten social balance and cohesion, and affirm universal principles such as the value of human life, personal dignity; recognition of women's freedom and the valorisation and safeguarding of childhood, regarding which no exceptions may be made, even in the name of the value of difference.'

value of the diversity of cultures of origin, as long as there is no conflict with the fundamental values of Italian society that we are all indiscriminately required to uphold and respect. In terms of the right to religious freedom there have been a number of legislative proposals which have run aground and have never come to light.

Three years after the enactment of Law 40/1998, the event of September 11 produced such a general upheaval that even Muslims living in European countries were faced with critical issues caused by the relentless struggle against international terrorism.

In the name of national security many countries of the world have adopted security policies which, by contrast, have often led to an overall sense of insecurity among Islamic immigrants, who are regarded with suspicion and often considered as having more to do with terrorism than with citizenship – with the risk of receiving the Muslim immigrant communities as if they were the enemy. These were the years when the term Islamophobia was re-introduced into the current lexicon.[3]

In 2002 there was a tightening of legislation with Law No 189 which, repealing the previous law, established that only those with an employment contract, that enabled them to support themselves financially, may enter the country. Under this law a person found in extra-territorial waters may be sent back to their country of origin, based on bilateral agreements between Italy and neighbouring countries, and introduced the offence of aiding and abetting illegal immigrants, including, where appropriate, immediate expulsion if identified or after identification, escorting the offending immigrants without residence permit to the border. Living in the country as an illegal immigrant was now also an offence. In the eye of this migratory cyclone, European countries enforced restrictive laws which led, at least in part, to the problem of new *clandestini*.[4] Immigration, especially that of an illegal nature, became a

3 Cf Monica Massari, *Islamofobia: la paura e l'islam* (Laterza, 2006) and also Gordon Conway, *Islamophobia: A Challenge for Us all*, (Runnymede Trust, 1997); accessed on 2 January 2016, available at: <www.runnymedetrust.org/publications/17/32.html>.

4 For example in France: Law 2001–1062 '*loisur la sécurité quotidienne* (or LSQ)', 15 November 2001, Law 2002–1094 '*orientation et programmation sur la sécurité intérieure*', 29 August 2002, Law 2006–64 '*relative à la lutte contre le terrorisme et portant dispositions diverses relatives à la sécurité et aux contrôles frontaliers*', 23 January 2006, Law 2008–1245 amending Law 2011–267 for the acquisition of computer data; Law 2012–1432, '*sur la securité et la lutte contre le terrorisme*', 21 December 2012; Law 2014–1353, JORF no 0263 '*renforçant les dispositions relatives à la lutte contre le terrorisme*', 13 November 2014; Law 2015–912 JORF no 0171, 24 July 2015 (see also, IIE Publique, 'trente-ans-legislation-antiterroriste', *IIE Publique,* 3 August 2016, accessed 29 December 2016, available at: <www.vie-publique.fr/chronologie/chronos-thematiques/trente-ans-legislation-antiterroriste.html>; see also, in the UK the *Anti-Terrorism, Crime and Security Act* 2001 (ATCSA), *Prevention of Terrorism Act* 2005 was approved.

scapegoat for counterbalancing the modest results achieved in the struggle against terrorism.[5]

In Italy, the massive eruption of migration took place in a period when the centre-right government was in power.[6] Apart from an interval of two years, when legislation was introduced in 1998–1999 in compliance with EU recommendations, the government did not take any suitable initiatives for preparing forward-looking policies, intervening only in cases of emergency[7] (a trend that was later also maintained by the centre-left government).

The strong political biases created in that period produced extremely conflicting alignments, allowing certain demagogue-oriented parties to increase greatly their electoral support by carrying out propaganda against Muslim immigrants who 'must go home'. Political factionalism and the media contributed to fueling distorted sentiments regarding Muslim migrants who, it was said, were spending too long in temporary transit.

The university, of course, did not remain insensitive to the overall situation, conscious of the fact that for the transition to be as little confrontational as possible the specific new cultural and religious characteristics would have to find room for peaceful coexistence in respect of the legal and social coordinates of the Italian context. And in the encouragement of mutual exchange processes, two essential stages are the promoting of interventions geared to studying the regulatory framework in depth and the raising of awareness regarding intercultural perspectives.

Before having a closer look at the work of the International Forum on Religions and Democracy ('FIDR') it might be useful to outline the national situation and its peculiarities starting from a retrospective look at Islam.

5 By way of example, in the USA: on 25 October 2001, the *Uniting and Strengthening America by Providing Appropriate Tools Required to Intercept and Obstruct Terrorism Act* of 2001, ie the *USA Patriot Act*, geared to reinforcing national security after the attack on the Twin Towers. In a UN context: the *International Convention for the Suppression of Terrorist Bombings* was signed on 10 October 2002. In Europe: EC Regulation 2580/2001 and EC Regulation 881/2002 on the subject of terrorism, adopted in national law, amending article 270 of the *Penal Code*, renamed '*Associazioni con finalità di terrorismo anche internazionale o di eversione dell'ordine democratico*', and introducing a sector-specific provision with Law No 144/2005, geared to '*Misure urgenti per il contrasto del terrorismo internazionale*'.

See also Christina Boswell, 'Migration control in Europe after 9/11: Explaining the absence of securitization' (2007) 45 *Journal of Common Market Studies* 589–610; Pierre Berthelet, 'L'impact des événements du 11 septembre sur la création de l'espace de liberté, de sécurité, et de justice' (2002) 42 *Cultures et Conflits* 1.

6 From June 2001 to November 2011.

7 In 1998, with Law No 40/98, the so-called 'Turco Napolitano law', and with the consolidated law issued with Legislative Decree of July 1999, No 286 on the immigration of 1999, national legislation conformed to that of Europe, granting immigrants similar rights and duties to those applied to citizens, with the exception of the right to vote and with other preclusions for those coming from certain countries of origin not conforming to regulations regarding the conditions of reciprocity.

## Islam in Italy

### *Origins*

Italy has just under 61 million inhabitants,[8] of which around 1.36 million are migrants from geographical areas where Islam is the dominant religion.[9] Considering the very varied nature of the countries of origin we talk about a plurality of Islams,[10] the Islamic worlds,[11] 'Islam and Islam',[12] and so on. Most Muslims are Moroccans, numbering around 500,000, a figure similar to that of Albanians (highly secularised); there are around 123,000 Tunisians, 100,000 Egyptians and Bangladeshis, and 90,000 Pakistanis and Senegalese. These populations are randomly scattered throughout the country.[13] Most are Sunni, but there are also Shiites.[14]

### *Migratory flows in Italy*

Although Islam is not a new phenomenon in Italy[15] there was no Islamic presence in the country until the last century. Italian Islam does not have its roots in a colonial

8 These figures are taken according to the data published on Istat, 'Popolazione e famiglie', *Istat – Istituto nazionale di statistica*, available at: <www.istat.it/it/popolazione> there were approximately 60,795,612 inhabitants in December 2015. See also, Tuttitalia, 'Popolazione per età, sesso e stato civile 2015', *Tuttitalia,* December 2015, available at: <www.tuttitalia.it/statistiche/popolazione-eta-sesso-stato-civile-2015/>; Caritas, 'Rapporto Immigrazione Caritas e Migrantes 2013', *Caritas Italiana*, available at: <www.caritasitaliana.it/home_page/area_stampa/00003960_Rapporto_Immigrazione_Caritas_e_Migrantes_2013.html>.

9 The Italian census does not take into account information on religious affiliation. The data is from Caritas Italiana Migrantes (a Catholic association with social welfare aims) which furnishes an annual report on immigration. The most recently published report is available at: <www.caritasitaliana.it/home_page/area_stampa/00003960_ Rapporto_Immigrazione_Caritas_e_Migrantes_2013.html>. Ibid.

10 Cf Renzo Guolo, 'Un Islam plurale', in Augosto Tino Negri and Silvia Scaranari Introvigne (eds), *Musulmani in Piemonte: in moschea, al lavoro, nel contesto sociale* (Guerini e Associati, 2005); Chantal Saint-Blancat, 'Tra identità e fede: una religiosità plurale' in Chantal Saint-Blancat (ed), *L'Islam in Italia. Una presenza plurale* (Edizioni Lavoro, 1999) 119–40.

11 Cf Felice Dassetto, *L'incontro complesso. Mondi occidentali e mondi islamici* (Città Aperta Edizioni, 2004).

12 Stefano Allievi, *Il multiculturalismo alla prova. L'Islam come attore sociale interno* (Scidà, 2000) 50.

13 It is estimated that in Italy there are approximately 1,360,000 Muslims. Cf 'Le religioni in Italia', a project by Massimo Introvigne and Pierluigi Zoccatelli, which takes the figure and extrapolates it from religious affiliation in the countries of origin of the immigrants, updated 4 March 2017, accessed 22 November 2015, available at: <www.cesnur.com/lislam-e-i-movimenti-di-matrice-islamica in italia/lislam-sunnita-unintroduzione/>. See also Stella Coglievina, 'l'Italia', in Jörg Nielsen (ed), *Yearbook of Muslims in Europe* (Brill, Vol 5, 2013) 351–67.

14 ISTAT data from 2010, available at: <www.demo.istat.it>; cf also Maria Bombardieri, 'l'Islam in Italia: Numeri, protagonisti e dinamiche sociali' (2013) 1 *Ad Gentes* 1, 7–24.

15 Its presence dates back to the Middle Ages, in the period of military expansion in the Mediterranean during the first half of the 8th century AD. Traces are found in Sicily and Sardinia, as well as in various other places in Southern Italy, such as Taranto, Bari, Brindisi, Naples and

legacy, as it does in France and the UK; it is, rather, a consequence of economic migration based on the personal initiative of a younger generation willing to take on hard labour, who considered themselves as just 'passing through', to the extent that they learned just enough Italian to get by at work.

During the economic boom resulting from post-war reconstruction, the first unskilled workers arrived from Maghreb. These were the years of the first major migratory flow from Islamic areas that hit more or less the whole of Europe. Other Northern European countries benefited from immigration organised on the basis of bilateral agreements between countries[16] for the supply of manpower. Italy, which was not as economically attractive as the northern countries for employment, acted as a sort of a transit or fallback corridor.

The migrant regarded himself and was regarded as temporary. He was not interested in gaining public visibility. Foreigners were simply workers with distinctive characteristics of an ethnic (but not religious) nature. Being perceived as temporary, therefore, immigrants were quite happily received by the Italian people.

With the coming of the oil crisis, 1974 marked the watershed between the first and second waves of European migration. The economic crisis and rising unemployment, in fact, brought about a radical turnabout. Jobs had to be reserved for natives – foreigners were no longer needed.

With Britain, Germany and France closing their borders, the migrants in Europe were faced with the choice of returning home definitively or remaining and renouncing the opportunity to go home. Italy, therefore, which was already considered a second-best option, became the destination of those who no longer had access to the more industrialised countries because of restrictive laws resulting from migration policies that rigorously controlled entry permits.

At this time, however, the phase of individuals coming to join their families began. The policy of migratory flow containment, in fact, produced the opposite effect from that intended, ie the reunion of families and their settlement. The migratory phenomenon, meanwhile, was no longer perceived only from the point of view of the people's ethnic and cultural difference. The religious connotation became more evident with the appearance of veiled women walking in the streets with their children. It became clear that most immigrants wanted to settle. And at a time of rising unemployment all this was beginning to arouse concern among part of the native population.

Migration has continued to this day. Part of this is illegal immigration, which is difficult to quantify and, up until the 1990s, was encouraged by periodic amnesties. Over the years attempts have been made to introduce scheduled immigration

the Pontine Islands. The siege of the coastlines began in 652 AD with the first naval attacks on Sicily, which was under the protection of the Byzantine Empire; the beginning of the conquest is dated as 827 AD but the period of actual stabilisation covers roughly 100 years, ie from 956 to 1061 AD. Raids by the Barbary pirates and Turkish incursions did not cease until the 16th century. Cf Stefano Allievi and Felice Dassetto, *Il ritorno dell'Islam – I musulmani in Italia* (Edizioni lavoro, 1993).

16 For example, agreements between Germany and Turkey and between France and Algeria.

flows into the country,[17] but due to social conditions (often unpredictable) these have all come to naught.[18]

In the space of 30 years the foreign population coming from Islamic areas has increased seven-fold. The 1981 census, in fact, showed that in Italy there were 210,937 immigrants,[19] that of 2001 revealed 1,334,889 and the last one, in 2011, set the figure at 1,317,928.[20] In 2015 in the *Oxford Handbook* report the rough estimate was 1,505,000.[21]

Today's Islam may be defined as an anagraphically young community, allocated within a demographic context that has for years been witnessing a drastic decline in birth rates and the consequential ageing of the native population.[22]

17 *Martelli Law*, Law No 39/90.

18 In 1991 there was a mass immigration from Albania following the collapse of the Communist bloc, which Italy tried, with limited success, to manage in respect of bilateral agreements. The agreement-based approach was also adopted with some of the Mediterranean countries in an attempt to regulate admissions. In the same years, however, there was an increase in the general influx from Tunisia, Senegal and Egypt, as well as Pakistan and Bangladesh. Containment strategies also included forms of repression and control both within the country (a sad example of which as were the detention centres geared to providing 'internal support' on the national boundary line) and beyond the borders, by attempting to enlist the active cooperation of the countries of origin in the transit of migratory movements. Control measures at sea borders and in international waters were reinforced. In addition, in order to delocalise border controls on the southern shore of the Mediterranean bilateral agreements were signed with North African countries, implementing international cooperation between police forces for repatriation. The countries involved in these agreements were Libya, Morocco, Tunisia, Egypt and Algeria. Cf Paolo Cuttitta, 'Borderizing the Island. Setting and Narratives of the Lampedusa Border Play' (2014) 13 *ACME: An International E-Journal for Critical Geographies* 196–219; Paolo Cuttitta, 'Migration Control in the Mediterranean Grenzsaum. Reading Ratzel in the Strait of Sicily' (2014) 29 *Journal of Borderlands Studies* 117–31.

19 Giovanna Zincone, Rinus Penninx and Maren Borkert (eds), *Migration Policymaking in Europe: The Dynamics of Actors and Contexts in Past and Present* (Amsterdam University Press, 2011) 247. It is important to bear in mind, however, that the national census does not take into account information on religious affiliation and, therefore, data on foreigners are mostly taken from surveys published in the annual reports on immigration policy of the Italian Caritas (cf, Caritas Italiana, above n 8).

20 See, Censimento della Popolazione, 'Gli stranieri al 15° Censimento della popolazione', *Censimento della Popolazione*, accessed 13 December 2015, available at: <www.istat.it/it/files/2013/12/Notadiffusione_stranieri20122013.pdf>.

21 Chantal Saint Blancat in Jocelyne Cesari (ed), *The Oxford Handbook of European Islam* (Oxford University Press, 2014) 270. The estimate is based on the average of the data published by ISTAT, Caritas and ISMU.

22 Around 2.5–3% of the Italian population (against a European average of 4%, with 6.5% in France and 6.1% in the Netherlands) is from Islamic areas. Statistics regard Muslims as foreign immigrants from countries dominated by Muslim culture. Obviously, within this group not all are practising Muslims. Often Albanian, Tunisian and Algerian immigrants have a cultural more than a religious bond with their countries of origin, which have undergone processes of marked secularisation. Cf Stefano Allievi, 'La presenza dell'islam nello spazio pubblico italiano: a che punto siamo?' in Paolo Naso and Brunetto Salvarani (eds), *I ponti di Babele. Cantieri, progetti e criticità nell'Italia delle religioni* (EDB, 2015) 209.

In a certain segment of the common people there is a pronounced fear of an increase in the immigrant population, considered as a threat to jobs and a cost to welfare, especially in this time of economic crisis that has held Italy in its grip since 2008. The censuses of 2001 and 2011, however, produced figures that are very close to the current estimate, and in any case in that period the curve at times decreased. Since 2014 the massive exodus from the war zones and the poverty of Africa is putting Europe more and more under stress due to the irrepressible influx of forced migrants (refugees, asylum seekers and displaced persons). Arrivals by sea have increased in Italy also, amounting to 65,000 new admissions (out of a total of 628,000 in the EU).[23] These figures are approximate. In Italy around 100,000 immigrants from Muslim areas have been regularised.[24] The reason for such a small number after 40 years from the beginning of immigration is the long bureaucratic process required for the granting of Italian citizenship, which is symptomatic of the underlying political reticence.[25]

## *Peculiar aspects of Islam in Italy: a mosaic*

In Italy, Muslims are a large minority that are having to deal with a context that is pluralist, secularised and heavily Catholic, as it seeks a way to adapt to change without distorting its own culture of origin. As the ethnic origins are so varied, the traditions of reference offer different interpretations of the religion, manifesting faith through expressions and rituals specific to the cultural background and quite distinct from each other. This pronounced differentiation also reflects inconsistency in organised Islam. There are religious, socio-cultural or ethnic associations, some of which support transnational political movements, while

23 See, IDOS Research Centre, 'Dossier Statistico Immigrazione 2015: 15 punti chiave', *Centro Studi e Ricerche IDOS – Rivista Confronti*, accessed 24 December 2015, available at: <www.dossierimmigrazione.it/docnews/file/Dossier%20Statistico%20Immigrazione%202015%20 15%20punti%20chiave(1).pdf>. According to 2014 data from the IDOS research centre there were around 4,922,085 foreign citizens in Italy out of a population of 60,782,668, with a percentage of 8.1%. IDOS gives the total number of legal immigrants as 5,364,000, of which around one-third are Muslims.

24 Cf Stefano Allievi, *I nuovi musulmani* (Edizioni Lavoro, 1999).

25 Law No 91/1992: article 1. 'Citizen by birth: a child of a father or mother with citizenship'; article 4 par 2: 'A foreigner born in Italy, who has legally resided in the country on a continual basis . . . up to . . . adulthood, may become a citizen if he/she declares the desire to obtain Italian citizenship within one year of said data'. For second generation applicants, being born and studying in Italy is not enough to grant automatic Italian citizenship. In the case of interrupted residence, moreover (which involves 37%), applicants are granted the intermediate status of 'Italian with foreign citizenship': cf Milena Santerini, 'Le seconde generazioni e il nodo della cittadinanza' curatorship Antonio Angelucci, Maria Bombardieri, Davide Tacchini (eds), *Islam e integrazione in Italia* (Marsilio, 2014) 140.

Citizenship is also granted in the case of marriage to an Italian citizen or after ten years of legal residence.

others are not concerned with political ideologies. Islam is commonly spoken of as *one* religion, but:

> in actual fact the problem we are facing is not religious pluralism but cultural pluralism . . . and poses a new set of issues as the spectrum of diversity is greater and no longer covers only religious, theological or dogmatic aspects but also concerns attitudes towards relations between men and women and between citizen and State, as well as relations in an employment context, and so on . . . [t]he problems that Muslim presence poses . . . involve not only religious but also cultural aspects.[26]

In the magmatic Islamic world, besides the congregations there are also a considerable number of secular, non-gregarious Muslims who are not members of any established group but place 'the Islamic religious reference in the subjective and private sphere of personal religious experience'.[27]

In outlining the characteristics of the Islamic communities in the following paragraph I shall be covering the main features of national relief organisations.

## *Associative Islam of national importance*

In Italy organised Islam tends to prefer legal forms of a private-law type, emphasising the socio-cultural rather than the religious purpose, apart from a few exceptions.[28] Many of those taking part in the FIDR process are leaders or delegates of the leading associations.[29]

The pioneers of Islamic associationism were students of the Union of Muslim Students in Italy ('USMI'). In the late 1960s, in addition to diplomats and businessmen, students began to arrive from Syria, Jordan, Somalia, Egypt and Palestine to study medicine and engineering at the University of Perugia. They formed an association (now extinct) of a religious and politicised character.[30] The goal was to set up places of worship for the purpose of maintaining and strengthening the

26 Silvio Ferrari, 'Aspetti giuridici e istituzionali dell'Islam' in Costanza Bargellini and Elisabetta Cicciarelli (ed), *Islam a scuola esperienze e risorse* (Quaderni ISMU, 2007) 67, accessed on 12 January 2016, available at: <www.ismu.org/wp-content/uploads/2014/04/vol-intero_islam-a-scuola.pdf>; cf Antonio Angelucci, 'Associazionismo religioso musulmano tra diritto speciale e diritto comune: la centralità dello statuto' in curatorship Angelucci, Bombardieri and Tacchini, above n 25, 71–91.

27 Andrea Pacini, 'I musulmani in Italia una presenza plurale' in Andrea Pacini (ed), *Chiesa e islam in Italia: esperienze e prospettive di dialogo* (Paoline, 2008) 22.

28 Alessandro Ferrari, *Islam in Italy: The 'Ghost' Religion – A 'non-religion' in a 'religious country'*, 2015, accessed on 8 March 2016, available at: <www.academia.edu/15027163/Islam_in_Italy>.

29 Maria Bombardieri, 'Mappatura dell'associazionismo islamico in Italia' in curatorship Angelucci, Bombardieri and Tacchini, above n 25, 11–34.

30 Association affiliated with the International Islamic Federation of Student Organisations, based in Kuwait.

Islamic identity among Muslim students. It was the first example of structured relations with the local government and the religious institutions.[31] USMI was the forerunner of the first Islamic centres, which today are affiliated with the Union of Italian Islamic communities that are active in many Italian cities.[32]

In the same period the Islamic Cultural Center of Italy ('CCII') was founded in Rome. This is the most prominent organisation and represents the 'Islam of the embassies', since its board members,[33] sitting in rotation, include[34] 15 ambassadors from 28 Muslim-majority countries with diplomatic offices in the capital. In the multi-coloured panorama of Islamic associations the CCII is the only one to have achieved the status of a non-profit[35] (religious) entity since 1974.[36] It took 20 years to perfect the process, but finally in 1995 the CCII succeeded in opening a mosque in Rome with a dome and minaret. The centre, which is well integrated from the point of view of relations with national (and international) institutions, is perceived as distant and 'foreign' by the religious community, which prefers to affiliate with other associations, especially the Union of Islamic Communities and Organisations in Italy (UCOII),[37] which has branches throughout the country.

Established by the founders of USMI in 1990, this association still supervises some of the 18 branches scattered throughout 20 Italian regions. It is a different example of organised Islam, which from the very beginning brought together the first Italian converts who, with the advantage of language and an in-depth knowledge of the context, have played a leading role of intermediation with the institutions. UCOII represents an intricate network with the largest number of prayer halls in Italy (200 places of worship[38] according to some sources, 300 according to others[39]), and has received permission to build two of the five Italian mosques[40]

31 Stefano Allievi, *Islam italiano: viaggio nella seconda religione del paese* (Einaudi, 2003) 99–101.

32 Bari, Bologna, Camerino, Ferrara, Genoa, Aquila, Milan, Naples, Padua, Parma, Pavia, Perugia and Siena.

33 The main sponsors are Saudi Arabia and Morocco. Saudi Arabia appoints the chairman of the board and Morocco appoints the Secretary General, who is responsible for the management of the mosque and CCII. Egypt is in charge of appointing the Imam.

34 Group of general members including the Italian Muslims and the vice president of the Islamic Religious Community in Italy (COREIS).

35 D P R decree No 712 of 21 December 1974. This recognition as a juridical entity was the result of a political calculation by the Italian state and the Vatican, geared to improving relations with the countries of the Gulf, given the very critical historical period sparked by the oil crisis.

36 Cf Giuseppe Casuscelli, 'Le proposte d'intesa e l'ordinamento giuridico' in Silvio Ferrari (ed), *Musulmani in Italia: la condizione giuridica delle comunità islamiche* (Il Mulino, 2000) 83.

37 See generally, the Union of Islamic Communities and Organisations in Italy (UCOII) website, available at: <www.ucoii.org>.

38 Maria Bombardieri, 'Mappatura dell'associazionismo islamico in Italia' in Antonio Angelucci, Bombardieri and Tacchini, above n 25, 15.

39 See Massimo Introvigne and Pierluigi Zoccatelli, 'L'Unione delle Comunità Islamiche d'Italia (UCOII)', *Le Religioni in Italia*, 2016, available at: <www.cesnur.com/lislam-e-i-movimenti-di-matrice-islamica-in-italia/lunione-delle-comunita-islamiche-ditalia-ucoii/>.

40 The mosque of Segrate is run by the Islamic Centre of Milan and Lombardy and that of Colle Val d'Elsa, directed by the president of UCOII, Izzedin Elzir.

with dome and minaret in Colle Val Elsa and Ravenna. Also, affiliated with UCOII, though independent, are the Association of Muslim Women in Italy ('ADMI'), the Islamic Alliance of Italy ('IIA')[41] and the Italian Islamic Association of Imams and Religious Leaders;[42] the Association of Young Muslims in Italy ('GMI') also supports UCOII, while preserving its own status of emancipation from the adults of the first generation. The union advocates a conception of religious practice that is predominantly community-oriented, 'placing religion at the centre of the public sphere as the main factor of political and social regulation'[43] by restoring from the bottom up the values that the Muslim members are called to respect. The association does not have a recognised legal status but a private-law profile oriented to 'social advancement.'[44]

This entity is active in terms of interreligious dialogue and invests in publishing and culture.[45] It issues scholarships in State universities for courses relating to Islam and interculturalism.[46] It holds cultural and social activities open to the general public. A number of scholars recognise a strategy committed to the deculturation and communitisation of practising Muslims[47] as a ploy to escape the secular world by means of centripetal retreat.[48] In fact, from the point of view of legal pluralism the Union strives for recognition by the State of a differentiated legal community status that is regulated by Islamic law[49] but still compatible with common law.

41 The Islamic Alliance of Italy has been active for over ten years but only took on an associative character in 2010. Formally also a member of the Federation of Islamic Organizations in Europe.

42 Founded in 2012 for the purpose of improving the training of imams.

43 Renzo Guolo, *Le organizzazioni islamiche in Italia e le reti transnazionali di riferimento, Relazione presentata al Convegno L'islam in Italia. Appartenenze religiose plurali e strategie diversificate*, Turin, 2–3 December 2004, accessed 27 December 2015, available at: <www.fga.it/fileadmin/storico/UPLOAD/ALL/CEA/65.pdf>.

44 The association of social advancement is one of the types of private association whose main aim is to operate in a social context. Cf § 2.2

45 The translation of the Qur'an and religious works.

46 Recently it funded, together with Morocco, scholarships for a Master's degree in Studies on Islam in Europe at the FIDR Inter-University Centre of the University of Padua.

47 See Renzo Guolo, 'La Sinistra, I'Islam e il complesso di Kurtz', 2002, *Italianieuropei*, available at: <www.italianieuropei.it/italianieuropei-4-2010/item/456-la-sinistra-lislam-e-il-complesso-di-kurtz.html>.

48 Sociologist Renzo Guolo defines the UCOII model as 'neotraditionalist and fundamentalist' and of 'externalised integration', ie based on the pursuit of economic and social integration while preserving cultural integration. In my opinion, however, these terms, especially 'fundamentalist', risk being too easily associated with forms of extremism or politicisation in which religion is exploited for power purposes. This does not seem to be the case with UCOII, which practises religion in respect for tradition while seeking its place in contemporary society. It lives the authenticity of its practice by creating in its centres (which are open to all) areas of prayer reserved exclusively for Muslims. Ibid.

49 Renzo Guolo poses the question of whether a demand for recognition that includes 'the legal safeguarding of subjects which regard as exclusive role models founded on cultural and religious identities favours not so much pluralism as the fragmentation of society in non-communicating communities' (Renzo Guolo, 'La rappresentanza dell'Islam italiano la questione dell'intesa' in Ferrari, above n 36, 89).

Demands for the introduction of Shari'a are also typical of the Muslim Brotherhood ideology. Affinity with this movement has often been the reason behind the shadow of fundamentalist adherence that has hovered over UCOII, fueling distrust and suspicion not only among certain outside observers but also in an intra-religious context. At the same time, however, it has close ties with the movement of Tunisian rebirth, Ennahda, which represents a moderate political Islam.[50] It was precisely the public controversy over ultra-national political sympathies, in fact, that led to the exclusion of UCOII from certain of the Interior Ministry advisory meetings.[51]

Like CCII, another religious association that has focused its main activity on 'top-down' relationships is the Italian Islamic Religious Community ('COREIS'[52]), which was founded in 1993 as the Italian Association for Information on Islam and in 2000 changed its charter and took its current name in the hope of obtaining recognition by the President of the Republic as a non-profit organisation of Islamic worship in 2001.[53] It was, in fact, approved by the Interior Ministry and the State Council, but today still lacks the decree of recognition by the President of the Republic. The community comprises around 100 Italian intellectuals converted to Sufism and inspired by the Gnostic esotericism of Rene Guénon.[54] Its aim is to represent the exclusively religious interests of those faithful to Islam in Italy and is very active in the public sphere in terms of interreligious dialogue with Catholics and Jews. To this end, it founded the Centre of Documentation on Islam and the Interreligious Studies Academy ('ISA'), which has signed an agreement with the Ministry of Education, Universities and Research for introducing intercultural and religious training projects into education programmes. The prestigious main branch is in the centre of Milan, while secondary branches are located in seven Italian regions. The COREIS has been involved with all the advisory committees set up in the Interior Ministry on the subject of integration. It has legal status, and has also presented to the government an agreement proposal.[55] As regards relations with the rest of the traditional Sunni context, the

50 See generally, Grazia Lissi, 'La transizione ecologica di Gaël Giraud', *Atlante*, updated January 2017, accessed 5 January 2016, available at: <www.treccani.it/geopolitico/saggi/2014/tunisia-ennahda-alla-prova-del-governo.html>.

51 See § 2, No 84.

52 See Una comunità islamica nel cuore dell'Occidente, available at their website: <www.coreis.it>.

53 Cf §2.1, 23.

54 Independent branch of the brotherhood Ahmadiyya Idrîsiyya Shâdhilyya.

55 For the agreement see §1.5, 2.2. Being composed of converted Italians the COREIS has an advantage in terms of relationship and communication strategies with the institutions, since it is familiar with their crucial points and is more easily able to gain access to the public arena than other associations. Its competence in the national context makes it easier to understand the political and organisational dynamics of the decision-making systems, media, cultural networks and all that furthers the construction of authoritative national and international public relations, eg those with important European Islamic entities such as the Great Mosque of Paris or the mosque of Lyon, whose vice president is a member of COREIS. In a non-European context, the community has forged relations with the Gulf countries and

community maintains a certain distance (except with the CCII) since the Sufism professed by the brotherhoods is not regarded as orthodox by all.[56]

Concerning the second generation there are the Young Muslims of Italy ('GMI'),[57] whose members include one[58] of the only two Muslim MPs ever elected in Italy. Founded in 2001 as a constructive reaction to the 9/11 attacks, this association counts 1,000 members[59] and has 16 offices in 15 regions of Italy. Many of its members are children of immigrants, who were born and/or have been educated in Italy and who feel Italian in all respects.[60] Unlike their parents they are fluent in Italian as their mother tongue. This enables them to relate to their environment as natural mediators, being part of many different contexts (family, social, religious, cultural, ethnic, professional, etc). Accustomed to coping with differences, speaking more than one language and moving among different cultures while recognising the relative codes and rules, these young people act as a bridge to bring across, with an 'Italian' approach, innovative aspects into Islam.[61] The GMI has its own line of action, with leadership aspirations. Its large number of members may soon begin to exercise a significant electoral weight in national politics.[62]

Of a more pronounced ethnic character, meanwhile, is the Union of Muslims in Italy ('UMI'). Founded in 2008 following the split resulting from political dissent with the UCOII, of which it is now a direct competitor, the Union associates some

---

Indonesia, whose cooperation has allowed it to gain the necessary know-how for setting up a halal certification body, registering the trademark Halal Italia.

56 The brotherhoods in Italy are inconspicuous but numerous, spiritually and organisationally united and dedicated to religious life and the practice of solidarity among their own brethren. The emphasis is on the personal affective dimension with Allah and mediated by the spiritual message of the various founders. Of Turkish origin in Italy there are the Suleymanci, deriving from the Indian brotherhood Naqshabandiyya which settled in Anatolia; from sub-Saharan Africa, outside the Arab cultural hegemony, there is the Murid brotherhood, which includes most of the Senegalese immigrants in Italy, who participate in *dahire muridi* (fixed meetings of the members of the brotherhood) for collective prayer. Economic solidarity is strongly practiced among members, favouring cohesion and social control and minimising marginalisation and deviance.

57 Giovani Musulmani d'Italia, Protagonisti noi, con l'aiuto di Dio, website available at: <http://giovanimusulmani.it/>.

58 Khalid Chaouki, founding member of the GMI. The other was Khaled Fouam Allam.

59 The association GMI was born from the ashes of other Islamic youth associations of the UCOII.

60 This is the youth group of the UCOII and, in fact, its founders include the sons of two of the original leaders of the UCOII. GMI is a member of the FEMYSO ('Forum of European Muslim Youth and Student Organisations'), a European umbrella organisation founded in 1996 under the aegis of the FIOE (Federation of Islamic Organisations in Europe). Both represent the Muslim brothers on a European level.

61 See Annalisa Frisina, Università di Padova, Italia, 'Giovani Musulmanid' Italia, *Transformazioni Socio-Culturalie Domande Di Cittadinanza,* Relazione presentata al Convegno internazionale Giovani musulmani in Europa, 11 June 2000, available at: <www.cestim.it/argomenti/02islam/02islam-frisina-giovani%20musulmani.pdf>.

62 Cf Annalisa Frisina, *Giovani Musulmani d'Italia* (Carocci, 2007).

150 Islamic centres of Moroccan origin throughout Italy. It collaborates with COREIS and has strong ties with the Ministry of Islamic Affairs in Morocco. The Union has federated 45 prayer halls frequented exclusively by Moroccans.[63]

Even from this brief excursus we can see the dissimilarities between the different ways of practising the organised Italian Sunni Islam and the internal conflicts involved.

On one hand there is the 'Islam of the mosques' which, within the social context, tends to create identified spaces around the mosques, based on the collective religious experience of the faithful, ie 'from below'; on the other hand there is the 'Islam of the States',[64] which is subjected to the scrutiny of the Islamic countries through the diplomatic missions and related entities which influence it with their respective politico-religious orientations. This model uses its considerable political influence to weave institutional relations from above but is not ramified throughout the country and therefore is unable to set itself up as the representative body of Muslims in Italy.[65]

Another level of differentiation is determined by the attribution of moderation. The UMI and the COREIS would like to be regarded as 'moderate' towards the public authorities, as an alternative to the UCOII, which they consider as having non-moderate characteristics. The Shiites, meanwhile, have six associations, plus a small group of Ismailis. The groups of non-Arab Muslims have the Senegalese Murid, with associations scattered throughout Italy, and in the north, there are various Turkish associations (Süleymanci, Fetullah Gülen or Milli Görüsh).

This brief description of the widespread diffusion of Islamic centres gives us an idea of the internal complexity of Islam in Italy. The various interpretations, the many currents represented, the national influences and the peculiarities reflected in the different associations all correspond to the vast assortment of approaches that influence integration into Italian society and make it hard to achieve a workable intra-Islamic agreement for a possible unified representation before the Italian State, because although Islam is polyhedrically one, the cultures that profess it are countless.

## *Italian law and Islam: the reasons for a failed agreement*

The Italian Constitution dedicates ample space to the right to religious freedom in order to regulate relations between confessions and the Italian State. The main instruments are the agreement reserved for the Catholic Church and that established for permitted religions, ie those granted the legal status of religious moral institution

63 UMI was about to build a mosque in Turin, which would have benefited from Moroccan government funding; the 2011 elections, however, were won by the Party of Justice and Development, upholder of the Muslim Brotherhood which, as mentioned earlier, in Italy has affinities with several of the UCOII leaders. The new Moroccan premier, therefore, supported the establishment of a Regional Islamic Federation for Piedmont, affiliated with the Italian Islamic Confederation, which includes a dozen Islamic centres in Piedmont, excluding the UMI.

64 The expressions in inverted commas are by sociologist Renzo Guolo.

65 Pacini, above n 27, 21.

(or religious confession).[66] The latter form represents a negotiating tool reserved for non-Catholic confessions seeking an agreement with the State. The combination of an outdated and inadequate ecclesiastical policy, intra-religious conflicts and the lack of initiative on the part of many Islamic communities (which tolerate the fact that the existing law remains unenforced) does not encourage the government to adopt sustainable, organic and decisive measures for guaranteeing the right to religious freedom. The request for the granting of this status must be promoted by unified representation acting on behalf of the holistic interests of the religious confession.[67]

And this is where the first problem arises. Unified representation is typical of a hierarchical structure, as in the case of the Catholic Church. In Islam, however, especially the Sunni branch, since priesthood does not exist the structure is not top-down and individualised but horizontal and communitarian. It is, in fact, defined as a religious denomination 'with no centre',[68] pulverised into a multitude of communities each with its own representative.

The second problem lies in the fact that the regulation of relations between the Italian State and non-Catholic religious denominations is dominated by a high level of discretionality. There is no general law that regulates the situation of religious pluralism by formalising criteria for identifying the subjects qualified to undertake negotiations with the Executive Council in accordance with the agreement.

Consequently, there are acknowledged elements of resistance among non-institutionalised minorities that sabotage the applicability of the right to religious freedom. Such sabotage results from the difficulty in negotiating, which is inherent to the aspects of structural weakness typical of the Nation State Identity and accentuated by the lack of basic cultural and religious homogeneity and the dissimilarity of interests among different social players, which need to be balanced.

This difficulty is made even greater by the interference on the national stage of a number of unofficial but weighty *comprimari* (the Catholic Church, for example), whose influence is exercised to varying degrees of conspicuousness.

Despite the rulings of the Constitutional Court[69] there is still hesitation to apply the principle of secularism according to a procedural model 'for the regulation of

66 Cf § 2.2, 23.

67 To date this has only been practically implemented with the Waldesians, Adventists, Pentecostals, Jews, Lutherans, Baptists, Jehovah's Witnesses and Buddhists.

68 Illaria Biano, 'Questioni di libertà religiosa: il caso dell'Islam italiano – CESPEC Summer school', accessed 2 November 2015, *Academia,* N/A, available at: <,www.academia.edu/6115875/Questioni_di_libert%C3%A0_religiosa_il_caso_dell_Islam_italiano_-_CESPEC_Summer_school>.

69 The organisation of secularism oriented in a pluralistic sense should integrate the protection of the fundamental rights granted to the individual with the protection of the same rights to be granted in relation to the group, and as the Constitutional Court has established, the State, on the basis of secularism, must guarantee 'the safeguard[ing] of religious freedom within a regime of religious and cultural pluralism', see Giancarlo Anello, '2016 Freedom of Religion vs Islamophobia: Lombardy's "Anti-Mosque Law" is Unconstitutional', *Academia,* 2 April 2016, accessed 6 March 2017, available at: <www.academia.edu/24053495/2016_Freedom_of_Religion_vs_Islamophobia_Lombardys_Anti-_Mosque_Law_is_Unconstitutional>.

a pluralism good enough to contribute to the success of a democratic system',[70] which may be used as a regulating principle of social pluralism in general applied to all denominations.

The issuing of a law on religious freedom would guarantee a basic standard for rendering effective the freedom of worship of religious denominations that have been excluded from contractual relations with the State, by subjecting the stipulation of agreements to criteria designed to define, regardless of the 'moods' of institutional discretionality, the range of pertinence of the collective subjects, consistently with the spirit of Article 8 of the Constitution, which refers to reasonable equality that allows for differences rather than formal equality.[71]

In drawing up agreements, in fact, the characteristics of the individual denominations should be valorised (even in the case of the stipulation of several agreements with the State by various communities of the same denomination).[72] However, according to a current and increasingly consolidated practice, the text of the agreements is copied almost word for word from the initial agreement stipulated with the Waldensian church, to the extent that they are referred to as photocopy agreements.[73]

While the State, when it grants this stipulation, standardises and aligns the agreements with the churches, the local institutions vested with the powers to act in religious matters apply them in vastly different ways. The reform of Title V of the Constitution establishes a regional decentralisation in order to implement the fundamental right of religious freedom and the free expression of the religious practice, producing different results in different regions. These results depend on how each region conceives the relationship between the individual local administrations and the Islamic communities. It is the responsibility of the regional

70 Sara Domianello, *Diritto e religione in Italia – Rapporto nazionale sulla salvaguardia della libertà religiosa in regime di pluralismo confessionale e culturale* (il Mulino, 2012) 8. The author considers 'procedural secularism as starting-point or projectual secularism and substantial secularism as juridical arrival-point or balanced secularism'.

71 Felix E Oppenheim, 'Under Justice', in Noberto Bobbio, Nicola Matteucci and Gianfranco Pasquino (eds), *Dizionario di politica* (Turin, 2004) 1006.

72 In favour of the possibility of stipulating multiple agreements cf Barbara Randazzo, Article 8, in curatorship of Raffaele Bifulco, Alfonso Celotto and Marco Olivetti (eds), *Commentario alla Costituzione, Vol I* (UTET Giuridica, 2006) 206–7. Against cf Nicola Colaianni, 'Intese (diritto ecclesiastico)' in Giuffrè, *Enciclopedia del diritto Aggiornamento, Vol V* (Giuffrè, 2001) 716–7. In addition, in the guidelines of the department for civil freedom and immigration and the central management for religious affairs (Internal Ministry of Italy), entitled *Religioni, Dialogo, Integrazione* we read that 'Islam, with its historical structure and in its current form, has organisational models that are different from those for which the religious policies in Italy were conceived, and it is therefore necessary to reconsider how we approach it, with a view to integrating it in the variegated world of relations between the State and the various religious communities in our country.' Available at: <www1.interno.gov.it/mininterno/export/sites/default/it/assets/files/26/2013_06_18_vademecum_esecutivo_low.pdf> (Unione Europa, 2013) 65.

73 Francesco Alicino in LUM J Monnet (ed), *La legislazione sulla base di intese: I test delle religioni 'altre' e gli ateismi* (Cacucci, 2013) 18, 42.

council, therefore, to regulate the construction and opening of places of worship, spiritual assistance in hospital environments and compliance with food safety laws and burial laws, regardless of the agreement.

From this brief outline, we can deduce that the problem regarding the policies on religious freedom in Italy has to do with the relationship between the centre and the peripheral areas, and that there is a dispersal of regulations on religious matters due to a somewhat motley and unpredictable management of responses to demands from religious minorities.

In the Islamic context, the high litigation rate makes it difficult to work together on identifying common ground for submitting collective requests. Competition between communities, based on their different religious, legal and political views, inevitably leads to divergent approaches, which at times cause relations to be instable. Even bonds within the same community routinely become strained by competitive exuberance in the conquest of leadership roles. The situation is also aggravated by the stagnancy of the generational change in leadership, which frequently leads to further fragmentation as the younger generation asserts itself, creating new associations and centres of worship.

For decades, the leaders of the Islamic community have each been striving for recognition as the most suitable spokesman before the State for profiting from the agreement.[74] Consequently, the dispute is likely to stall even more the process of discussion needed for identifying a viable way towards the agreement with the Interior Ministry. These disputes are between the Islam of the grassroots communities (UCOII), that of the embassies (CCII) and that of the Sufis and the brotherhoods (COREIS). Each of these, in 1992, 1993 and 1996 respectively, attempted to form an agreement, and all were unsuccessful due to the difficulty in identifying who represents whom.

The lack of political and legislative enterprise in Italy, which still struggles to deal with social change:

> favours the emergence of the contradictions of a system that is wary of actual pluralism and incapable of finding, between such a highly discretionary and very special[75] law and a common law of great potential but basically blind to religious diversity, a happy medium that can guarantee the reasonable safeguarding of religious freedom.[76]

The absence of a pyramid structure and polycentricism make it difficult for the Italian government to choose who to deal with in the magmatic and intricate system

74 Ibid 120–1.

75 Privileged pactional bilaterality reserved for the Catholic Church.

76 Alessandro Ferrari, *La libertà religiosa in Italia- un percorso incompiuto* (Carocci, 2012) 103. See also Alessandro Ferrari, 'Libertà religiosa e nuove presenze confessionali (ortodossi e islamici): tra cieca deregulation e super-specialità, owerodel difficile spazio per la differenza religiosa', *Stato e Chiese*, July 2011, accessed 10 February 2016, available at: <www.statoechiese.it/index.php?option=com_content&task=view&id=467&Itemid=40>.

of Islam. Locating a unitary representation is complicated, but so is identifying a partial representation of significant and stable portions of Muslims. Furthermore, the manifestation of the various nationalist sentiments and the unwavering ethnic solidarity of the associations are additional external resistances against the State, which regards with suspicion the strong institutional bonds maintained by the organised Islamic communities with their countries of origin. At the same time, there are also internal resistances among Muslim communities due to transversal antagonism between ethnic groups, which does not help to lower the level of intra-community conflict. It is partly because of such close ties with its roots that the Islamic religion in Italy continues to be regarded as alien.[77] Moreover, to date, only around 100,000 Italians have become Muslims, ie less than 10% of the total Islamic population.[78]

## *Factors of integration: the Italian spectrum*

The inertia of the government and its policies has led to the integration process being activated on a grassroots level due to social factors.[79]

Politics should presuppose the top-down management of public interventions referring to identified system and regulatory models for immigration and related issues, including the religious factor. Social integration, in fact, runs parallel to interaction with the various religious affiliations.

With regard to the social profile the Italian State is not referring to a specific model of integration.[80] When the model exists, it enables (thanks to the vote) forms of participatory democracy to be exercised, making it easy even for non-natives to make

77 Ferrari, above n 28, 1.

78 See Stefano Allievi, 'La presenza dell'islam nello spazio pubblico italiano: a che punto siamo?', *De Stefano*, 29 May 2015, accessed 18 December 2015, available at: <www.stefanoallievi.it/2015/05/la-presenza-dellislam-nello-spazio-pubblico-italiano-a-che-punto-siamo/>.

79 Ferrari, above n 28, 1.

80 In other countries that have had to deal with the same problems before Italy, legislation has been oriented on the basis of an ideal type as a defining criterion. The ideal type provides the framework that facilitates understanding (including among citizens) of the arrangement by the government of the plural society and the reconciliation of the interests involved. The adopting of a model (eg multiculturalism in Britain or assimilationism in France) allows all those involved to see (more) clearly how the State conceives and organises the implementation of integration, for example through clear criteria regarding the formal attribution of citizenship status and clear regulations that govern the legal relationship between the host society and the migrant, between the State and the religious confession. For a more in-depth study on models of citizenship cf Christian Joppke and Ewa T Morawska (eds), *Toward Assimilation and Citizenship* (Palgrave, 2003). See also Sergio Carrera, *In search of the perfect citizen? The intersection between integration, immigration and nationality in the EU* (Martinus Nijhoff Publishers, 2009); Cf Tariq Modood, Anna Triandafyllidou and Ricard Zapata-Barrero, *Multiculturalism, Muslims and Citizenship: A European Approach* (Routledge, 2006) 17; see also Alessandro Ferrari, 'Laïcité et multiculturalisme à l'italienne, Archives de sciences sociales des religions' (2008) 78 *Archives of Social Sciences of Religion* 1, 135.

proposals and contribute more or less actively to the decisions that affect the quality of their lives and the contexts in which their daily experience of citizenship takes shape. For the time being, however, in Italy it is the principle of *ius sanguinis*[81] that rules.

In view of its state-nation character[82] (which implies a special emphasis on the sharing of a common history, language, religion and culture,[83] as opposed to the nation-state, which is dominated by the centrality of the institutional principles that support the national culture), Italy does not impose a policy geared to the application of a principle of equality oriented to the levelling and uniforming of citizens that is typical of state-centricity. In the non-centralised Italian system, more than the dirigism of State law it is the social and family mechanisms of the natural composition of interests that contribute to integration through spontaneous processes of the accommodation of cultural and religious diversity. And it is this accommodation that acts as a compensatory process in which immigrants become members with equal rights and opportunities, based on the willingness of the majority of individuals making up the community to correctly and effectively coordinate their actions with those of other individuals at different levels of the social structure, resulting in a relatively low degree of conflict.[84]

Consequently, the local authorities[85] have assumed legal responsibility for the issues related to the settlement of migrants, and likewise, spontaneously, also the

81 Citizens, therefore, are those who are born of other citizens, who share the same culture, made up of principles, laws, moral codes, values, customs, symbols and beliefs, including of a religious nature. We should note, nevertheless, that since October 2015 the Italian Parliament has been debating a reform aimed at enabling children born in Italy of foreign parents with long-term EU residence permits to obtain citizenship, a right that would be extended also to children under 12 coming to Italy, providing they have concluded an educational cycle of at least five years.

82 Ferrari, above n 76, 133; see also Loredanna Sciolla, 'Italia una e plurale' in Annick Magnier and Giovanna Vicarelli (eds), *Mosaico Italia. Lo stato del Paese agli inizi del XXI secolo* (FrancoAngeli, 2010) 57.

83 Luciano Orabona, Antonio Magliulo, Ulderico Parente, *Cattolicesimo e identità nazionale* (Editrice Apes, 2011) 44; Cf also Simonetta Soldani and Gabriele Turi (ed), *Fare gli italiani. Scuola e cultura nell' Italia contemporanea. 1, La nascita dello stato nazionale* (Il Mulino, 1993).

84 Luciano Gallino, *Dizionario di sociologia*, under 'integrazione' (UTET, 2004) 694–5.

85 The town councils collect the social requests and evaluate whether and how to manage them, either to apply policies geared to integration in the pluralistically intended civic fabric or to de-legitimise them. A good example of the compensation of the inadequacies of the central policy is the resolution of the board of the Milan town council meeting of 6 July, 2012, No 1444, which represents the first prototype of ecclesiastical policy on the part of the council. The resolution is dedicated to the 'approval of the guidelines for the promotion of inter-religious dialogue and support of the freedom to vote of the religious communities in the city area' and established the creation of a register for the associations of the religious organisations accessed by groups with specific requisites. On the municipal management of issues related to religious freedom, see Elisa Rebessi, 'Diffusione dei luoghi di culto islamici e gestione delle conflittualità. La moschea di via Urbino a Torino come studio di caso', *Dipartimento POLIS*, December 2011, accessed 6 March 2017, available at: <www.fidr.it/cgi-bin/materiale/123/Rebessi.pdf>.

welfare and charity organisations, led by Caritas, along with the trade unions, non-profit organisations and individuals who have offered jobs. In short, the local social factor has shown an enterprising spirit and resilience *sui generis* in trying out factual methods of inclusion[86] in which a key role was played by local, relational and cultural elements and the free operation of the market.

The fact that the spatial allocation of the ethnic groups in Italy has always manifested itself in forms of dispersion rather than concentrating in specific areas has helped to limit certain risks of social peripheralisation, as has occurred in other European countries; in other words, this dissemination has avoided the formation of ethnic ghettos. The inclusion mechanisms have been inseparably linked to regularised labour and the possibility of entering the employment system. This has occurred mainly in the north, where, however, Muslims have long been generators of resources.[87]

It can be said that up until now the Italian situation has been that of 'a country that has acted on an experimental basis. We have a very vibrant, very lively civil society which has succeeded in carrying out a series of experiments on a local level',[88] where cultural integration and the preservation of traditional or ethnic aspects, mixed with local customs and habits, have developed into a culture of accommodation[89] in the form of what has been called 'reasonable integration', applied both in the private and the public sphere.[90] The latter, when it is accomplished, is in fact made possible by forms of inclusive voluntarism through the actual encounter between locals and immigrants in everyday life contexts, ie schools, neighbourhood, at work, in recreational activities and in the offering of

86 Cf Fabio Berti and Andrea Valzania (eds), *Le dinamiche locali dell'integrazione: Esperienze di ricerca in Toscana* (FrancoAngeli, 2011).

87 The enterprises of immigrants count for 6.5% of the national added value (over 94 billion euro). The record is held by individual companies, but companies with local shareholders are also increasing. Joint-stock companies represent more than one-tenth of the 525,000 immigrant businesses registered with the Chambers of Commerce (57,000, 10.8%). The six most numerous national groups among entrepreneurs are Moroccans (15.2%), Chinese and Romanians – the only immigrants from non-Islamic areas (11.2% each), Albanians (7.3%), Bangladeshis (6.2%) and lastly Senegalese (4.3%) – data from IDOS Study and Research Centre, see, 'Rapporto-Immigrazione e Imprenditoria 2015', *Aggiornamento Statistico*, 2015, accessed on 12 January 2016, available at: <www.dossierimmigrazione.it/docnews/file/2015_Rapporto%20Imprenditoria_Scheda.pdf>.

88 Ferrari, above n 26, 70. On the subject of the experimentation Ferrari continues, 'I refer to companies with Muslim workers which strive to find work schedules allowing for prayer or holiday periods that enable Muslims to return to their country of origin, to hospital facilities that in the case of patients of Muslim or other religions contact the Muslim community in the city to guarantee spiritual assistance for patients of Muslim or other religions, etc. This is experimentation'.

89 Eve Hepburn and Ricard Zapata Barrero (eds), *The Politics of Immigration in Multilevel States, Palgrave Politics of Identity and Citizenship Series* (Macmillan Distribution Ltd, 2014) 5–17.

90 Cf Giovanna Zincone, *Introduzione e sintesi. Un modello di integrazione ragionevole*, in Giovanna Zincone (ed), *Primo rapporto sull'integrazione degli immigrati in Italia*, (Il Mulino, 2000).

jobs within the Italian entrepreneurial network consisting mainly of small family businesses. And the interactions have been based on rules deriving from the free interpretation of the political institutions, local entities and civil society in consideration of the mutual resources that can be activated, moving as far as possible towards adapting the newcomers' customs to the values, principles and practices of the host country.

Only after local resources were activated did politics make a move, and then only to assess the possibility of granting citizens' rights and prerogatives to foreign workers. The State, in addition to intervening *ex post*, often does so to prepare temporary and emergency solutions through amnesties. Problems have been, and still are, managed on a knife-edge without carrying out the necessary prior theoretical analysis for preempting crisis situations. What is needed is not uncertain and sometimes impulsive solutions but, rather, well thought-out actions that tend to be not only socially appreciable but also, and above all, sustainable in the medium and long term.

In the long run, institutional weakness is turning into social conflict. Italian society, which has been experiencing a state of economic crisis for eight years now, is no longer able to be as accommodating and welcoming as in the past. The excessive burden that has fallen on the shoulders of individual towns has produced anger and polarisation, spurred on by populist movements.

Consequently, society loses even the perception of the economic added value brought by Muslim immigrants, who are still too often considered, if not a foreign body, a 'disconnected' and temporary entity that takes advantage of welfare while giving nothing in return, when in fact the entrepreneurial initiative of Muslims has a positive impact on the GDP.[91]

These convictions are also a result of the delay in initiating a public debate[92] (which is still, in fact, confined to the academic world) in favour of an updated and non-stereotyped reformulation of the concept of citizenship that also considers the inclusion of Muslims as a positive factor.

In addition to the above, the parliamentary deadlock is also leaving incomplete the necessary initiatives designed to more effectively and homogeneously safeguard the right of religious minorities to religious freedom, despite the fact that in Italy the civil right profession of one's religious faith is given particular importance.

As is fairly obvious, the fact that the Catholic religion stands out from the others as having an acquired right (being inevitably part of a historical, economic and social context) emphasises even more clearly how much the religious factor represents

91 See again the comments of Ferrari, above n 88.

92 The 'religious question' is not the subject of political debate in its global and general aspects. At most, it deals with the religious theme in relation to individual issues regarding cultural factors, and religious freedom is mainly considered in relation to the exercising of the right on an individual level, while it is difficult to take a consistent stand with respect to an approach that takes into account the community aspect.

a critical mass, extending its power beyond the realm of spiritual life, and in dealing with Islam it is precisely this consequence that is opposed.

## The 'standing-in' of the Academy

The inaction of legislators has had an inevitable impact on the systemic implementation of religious freedom, especially with regard to the exercising of the right on a community level.

In the absence of a confederation representing the interests of Islam, the Interior Ministry has, since 2000, attempted to stand in by organising regular advisory meetings for formulating proposals and opinions with experts and representatives of Islam on issues concerning the religious practice of Islamic groups and their relative rights. After four unfruitful attempts, in late January 2016 a fifth meeting was held, which focused also on the training and accreditation of the role of the imam.

It should be emphasised that the (political) tool of meetings has ambivalent aspects. While the constructive aim is to find a way to progress from 'Islam in Italy' to 'Italian Islam',[93] at the same time there is a risk of creating ambiguity through contradiction with the constitutional principles of non-interference on the part of the State in religious matters, when Islam is 'exceptionalised'.[94]

Not least of the problems is the fact that the stratagem of the meetings ends up by favouring only the politically accredited Islamic elites, since these are included in the special circuit of meetings of the Interior Ministry, placing them in a position that allows them a privileged dialogue with top government officials, thereby increasing intra-community conflict.

The FIDR project, therefore, began by acknowledging the institutional impasse created by the set of factors that have contributed to exacerbating the exclusion of Islam from access to religious and citizenship rights (the obsolescence of the law of 1929,[95] although it was made compatible with the Constitution; the objective difficulty of Parliament to implement a general law; the decentralised devolution of responsibility for the fact that it is interpreted on the basis of regional and local discretionality, and the provision of special measures reserved by the government for Islam without, however, establishing anything concrete) in order to facilitate, through technical and legal support, constructive interaction with the Directorate-General of Religious Affairs of the Interior Ministry and the most important Islamic associations in Italy.[96]

To meet the challenge of the complexity of the religious phenomenon in terms of contemporary pluralistic democracy FIDR has worked towards strengthening

93 Elena Dusi, 'Il fantasma della Consulta', *Limes*, Issue 4, 2007, 150.

94 The aim of the executive council was to adopt and adapt a European model like that of Belgium and, more recently, that of France.

95 Treaty of Conciliation (one of the Lateran Pacts of 1929) concluded by the Holy See (Vatican City State) and Italy during the facist period.

96 The project underway has also obtained the patronage of the Ministry for International Cooperation and Integration.

the awareness of Muslims in relation to the Italian context, focusing primarily on the historical and political framework that has helped define the Italian constitutional approach to the religious phenomenon, and subsequently analysing the contemporary world and the social dynamics relating to the new religious pluralism and its social consequences, the forms of dialogue between Islam and society, Islam and other religions and intra-religious dialogue, the encounter with secularisation and secularism, and the relationship between religion and State democracy, offering cognitive tools of an interdisciplinary type – all necessary theoretical steps for getting to the heart of the problems to be solved regarding the practical issues of rights and duties.

The Academy has therefore created a laboratory on neutral ground, providing a space for developing studies and strategies geared to identifying the legally effective way to influence the actual exercising of Italian Islam's right to religious freedom.

The participants are mainly Muslims, but include also members of groups that do not attend the national advisory meetings, for the purpose of training them as cultural mediators acting as an interface with the prefectures and municipal bodies based on the areas of competence of local authorities such as municipalities and regional councils. Importance is given to the training of an interlocutor qualified to combine:

> democratic syntax and cultural differences in an intercultural perspective . . . geared to identifying democratic solutions of a negotiational, transactional type and therefore inclusive of the different identities . . . and discursive strategies for rendering that which is different mutually comprehensible.[97]

To facilitate an effective action locally with the peripheral and central institutions it was deemed necessary for Muslims to be suitably equipped for transparently moving within the public space. A key step was to provide the legal means to highlight the religious and cultural connotation of the communities, which are often disguised behind a cultural connotation.

This is because the requisite of religious identity is, in fact, essential in accessing the special framework.

The main stages of the training process concerned the issues related to the practising of religion in places suitable for the purpose and the role of the imam as a spiritual guide and community spokesperson.

## *The International Forum on Religions and Democracy*

The founding of the International Forum on Religions and Democracy ('FIDR') was based on the realisation of the urgency to combine academic research with socially significant actions. The Centre is backed by five universities in northern Italy which have taken the decision to embark on a venture of research/action with

97 Mario Ricca, 'Sul diritto interculturale. Costruire l'esperienza giuridica oltre le identità' (2008) 8 *Daimon, Annuario di diritto comparato delle religioni* 10–11.

the intention of transferring the necessary skills to Muslims or reinforcing these skills, in the awareness that a more knowledgeable use of existing legal instruments based on a deeper understanding of the social framework favours the activation of processes of mediation and dialogue with institutions and within the society.

The interdepartmental centre was established in 2009 and became operational in 2010. It consists of a consortium of five universities: the University of Eastern Piedmont, the University of Insubria in Como, the State University and Catholic University of the Sacred Heart in Milan, and the University of Padua, all of which are situated in northern Italy, the area with the densest Muslim population. The centre involved national and international experts in law, economics, literature and philosophy, sociology and communications. It was created with the aim of formulating sustainable solutions for enabling Muslims to access the right to religious freedom. The proposed route, of an interdisciplinary and experiential nature, was entitled 'New religious presence in Italy' and focused on the training of the incoming leadership of the Islamic associations.

The aim of FIDR was to develop, together with the Muslims, a set of best practices.

The establishing of a series of milestones, both beforehand and during the process, has been the subject of periodic meetings with the Directorate-General of Religious Affairs of the Interior Ministry, which, in fact, offered itself as sponsor (free of charge)[98] and interlocutor in dialogues aimed at reaching certain concrete goals, such as the public recognition of the value of a three-year training period in civic education.

Taking part in this three-year programme were individuals from different backgrounds, including some 40 representatives and leaders of first and second-generation Islamic associations, especially religious leaders and linguistic–cultural mediators of Islamic origin, Italians converted to Islam (who act as a point of reference for at least 60,000 Muslims),[99] delegates from Islamic organisations of national importance and independent men and women.

The forward-looking idea was to target not only the most prominent and well-established leaders in the Italian public space, but also the second line of organised Islam, since this is probably the level that is most willing to consider something new, to experiment with new attitudes in order to find the most suitable way of helping to promote citizenship in the interests of social cohesion.

FIDR offers to act as a facilitative figure for deciphering and matching the codes of the society of origin with those of the host society, helping immigrants, in terms of both technico-legal and socio-cultural aspects, to better understand the dynamics of Italian society and therefore effectively access rights.

98 In the end it was not the State which came through with funds, but the Compagnia di San Paolo, one of the leading foundations in Europe, which pursues goals of public interest and social utility and is backed by one of the major Italian banks, Banca Intesa San Paolo.

99 The figure suggests a potentially positive impact. There were imams of mosques who every Friday alternated three prayer shifts, itinerant imams and leaders of associations with tens of thousands of members.

The work of FIDR began by mapping all the problems and resources relating to the Islamic situation in Italy, with the aim of working towards the validation of inclusive rights.

The crucial issue addressed by FIDR is based on two closely related questions: why is the right to religious freedom still ineffective for Muslims, and what can be done? The underlying sub questions were oriented to analysing how the State manages relations with Islamic pluralism in Italy and what difficulties of self-organisation do Muslims face in obtaining an agreement with the State.[100]

FIDR sought, therefore, to trigger mediatory processes aimed at identifying possible common objectives both on a Muslim intra-community level and between Muslims and the public authorities. Identifying points of convergence would make it possible to set the lowest common denominator, based on which Muslims could first of all establish a common front among themselves and then leverage the public authorities to secure the effective recognition of the right to religious freedom.

The road map that ensued made it possible to tackle complex practical aspects through a series of small but systematic rather than episodic steps, in order to outline (and where possible resolve) some of the major problem areas that contribute to relegating Islam to the sidelines in the Italian context. Thematic meetings concentrated on all the aspects of the integration.

## *Places of worship*

There is a shortage of mosques in Italy today. In all the country, there are only six mosques that are identifiable for the fact that their architectural features include dome and minaret[101] and, in accordance with the law, are open to all. This encourages Muslims to pray or gather in unsuitable places, eg basements, depots, private apartments, etc. Yet the right to religious freedom demands that everyone has the right to a place of worship where they can pray and perform religious ceremonies. The mosque is not only a place where people pray. Besides having its own cultural centre it may include a halāl butcher, a bookshop and recreational spaces. Identifying the applicable laws and the procedure required in the construction or opening of mosques is complicated, and in different regions different practices are followed. Consequently, the number of prayer rooms recorded amounts to 769.[102] These are places that belong mainly to associations which reserve admission for their members. This is because there is no general law regulating places of worship, and because decentralisation with the devolution of the relative responsibilities to the

100 Felice Dassetto, Silvio Ferrari, Brigitte Maréchal, *Islam in the European Union: What's at Stake in the Future?*, Directorate General Internal Policies of the Union, Policy Department Structural and Cohesion Policies – Culture and Education, European Parliament, May 2007; see also Ferrari, above n 76, 103–8.

101 Rome, Catania, Segrate (Milan), Brescia; Ravenna; Colle di Val d'Elsa (Siena).

102 Maria Bombardieri, *Moschee d'Italia. Il diritto al culto. Il dibattito sociale e politico* (Zoom Italia, 2011) 59.

local institutions[103] allows a wide margin of discretion in granting or refusing permission. Regional authorities, in exercising their powers in the field of urban planning, often impose conditions and requisites for the opening of such places that are difficult to maintain, presenting legal quibbles to oppose requests to change the use of the buildings from 'civil' to 'religious'. Administrative refusal is often disguised behind pretexts such as the unsuitability of the premises or incompatibility with urban planning.[104]

As outlined in the 'associational Islam' part of this chapter, the religious groups that claim the right to a place of worship form associations. This is because in Italy the system of the regulation of religions (as briefly mentioned earlier) is of a tripartite pyramidal type, with the associations on the most simplified and basic level. It is here that common law applied to associations is put into effect. Religious communities may organise themselves as associations and govern themselves on the basis of the laws on freedom of association established by the Civil Code. This arrangement guarantees, in this case, a degree of freedom from the forms of control applied by the State, which is basically disinterested.[105]

The intermediate level of the pyramid is accessed by religious groups demanding recognition under the law of 1929.[106] The State may discretionally decide to recognise the religious group and grant it the status of religion confession (or, technically, non-profit organisation). In such case, it is allowed various prerogatives[107] and advantages,[108] in exchange, however, for a level of State control that the first layer is not subject to.

103 Regional councils.

104 For an analysis of an emblematic case see Alessandro Ferrari, 'La nuova legge lombarda sui luoghi di culto: una risposta sbagliata al pluralismo culturale e religioso', *Oasis*, 2 February 2015, accessed 20 January 2016, available at: <www.oasiscenter.eu/it/articoli/libert%C3%A0-religiosa/2015/02/02/la-nuova-legge-lombarda-sui-luoghi-di-culto-una-risposta-sbagliata-al-pluralismo-culturale-e-religioso>.

105 First the charter must be drawn up and registered with the Tax Office and then an office and a current bank account can be opened. The social purpose to be indicated in the charter, however, does not include religious aims of a cultural type, since common law provisions are oriented to cultural and social purposes. Associations do not have access to State funding and religious communities adopting this configuration are not permitted to teach their own religion in public schools.

106 At this level the State, as represented by the Interior Ministry, steps in and interacts, requesting proof of organisational requisites, stability, equity consistency and non-conflict with public order and morality.

107 Religious ministers approved by the government can perform wedding ceremonies with civil effects, pursuant to R D 289/1930 on the opening of places of worship, subject to verification by the administrative authority of the necessity for such 'in order to meet actual religious needs of substantial groups of followers' and the existence of 'sufficient means to meet maintenance costs'; the followers of a permitted religion may hold public meetings, without prior authorisation, only in buildings open to worship and provided that the meeting is 'presided or authorised by a religious minister' appointed by the required authorisation; the power to provide religious assistance in places of treatment and withdrawal, in the armed forces, prisons, etc.; exemptions from military service.

108 Buy and hold property in their own name and take advantage of tax benefits.

At the top, there is the third level; this includes both the Catholic Church, which enjoys a privileged position and has its agreement with the State in place, and the other denominations with which the State has formed an agreement. Here the level of political and administrative discretionality is at its highest.

It is the Italian government that decides independently whether or not to enter into an agreement with a given religious confession. Signing this agreement means establishing with the State a very high-level relationship of cooperation, which presupposes the obtaining of grants on taxes, the possibility to teach religion in public schools and a special level of organisational autonomy.[109] Since Muslims in Italy, despite repeated applications, have never succeeded in entering into an agreement with the Italian State, the first-level forms of association have proliferated. Even without the necessary permission these associations still open places of worship and hold religious services for their members. This leads to the illegalisation of worship and forms of juridical camouflage,[110] causing the religious communities to separate their religious identity from their civil identity by specifying cultural purposes as the aim of the association.

The result is the creation of pseudo cultural associations whose purpose is to mask secret places of worship that end up with marginalisation and the corroboration of a suspicious image of Islam.

Operating without a recognised religious status produces various spin-off effects. It prevents dialogue with the public authorities, which is often unable to either identify which groups there are in the area or deal with issues relating to the exercising of religious freedom; it encourages a misinformed use of tax concessions available for certain forms of association that are adopted by Muslim communities for purposes not of (unofficial) religious worship but of cultural or social promotion, common good, solidarity, etc (for-profit endeavours instrumental to denominational activities are, in fact, permitted by law exclusively for legitimate religious associations).

The democratic-based internal organisation is a *conditio sine qua non* of the deed of incorporation of all associations except those of a religio-cultural nature, given that they operate in the field of spirituality, which is not subject to State interference (Catholic religious associations do not necessarily consider the democratic character of their structure).[111]

109 Exemption from work for religious reasons (Fridays and Islamic holidays).

110 Ferrari, above n 28, 11; G Anello, 'Categorie ermeneutiche dei diritti religiosi e libertà di culto' in Gianfranco Marci, Marco Parisi and Valerio Tozzi (eds), *Diritto e religione, L'evoluzione di un settore della scienza giuridica attraverso il confronto fra quattro libri* (Pletica, 2012), accessed 9 March 2016, available at: <www.olir.it/areetematiche/libri/documents/diritto%20e%20religione.pdf>; see Ferrari, 'Libertà religiosa e nuove presenze confessionali (ortodossi e islamici): tra cieca deregulation e super-specialità, ovvero del difficile spazio per la differenza religiosa', above n 76; see also Erminia Camassa in Carlo Cardia and Giuseppe Dalla Torre (eds), *Caratteristiche dei modelli organizzativi dell'Islam italiano a livello locale: tra frammentarietà e mimetismo giuridico* (Giappichelli Publisher, 2015).

111 Pierangela Floris, *Autonomia confessionale – Principi-limite fondamentali e ordine pubblico*, (series of the Faculty of Law at the University of Cagliari (Cagliari, 1992) 175.

In order to meet the need of Islamic associations to conform to the law, FIDR has reviewed with the participants how to use the instruments of common law in order to benefit from the same in accordance with the *ratio legis* based on which the legislation was drafted, with the aim of establishing an association charter sample for religious purposes.[112] This instrument, which has been discussed and reviewed with the participants, sets out the purposes in a clear and undisguised manner and is geared to facilitating interaction with the public authorities on the basis of criteria of transparency. The intention is to consolidate the appropriate civic integration conditions necessary for maintaining the constitutional promise of the right to religious freedom.

### *Imams and leaders of the communities*

Another subject of study and debate in the course of the training was, of course, that of the imam, since the FIDR programme represented the first ever initiative for training religious leaders to be held in Italy in an academic context.

The imam is the figure who leads the faithful in collective prayer in the mosque. In Islamic countries, the imam is a purely religious figure. A solid religious education involves the consideration of at least three main aspects: religious training (ie doctrinal and language skills), knowledge of the national context, and the procedures for selection and responsibility for the apprenticeship process.

The training of a spiritual guide requires a diploma in theology. And, as in a Catholic context, where religious studies are taught by confessional institutions and in Catholic universities,[113] likewise the training of Muslim religious experts is the exclusive prerogative of the Islamic academies, which are lacking in Italy.[114] For this reason, where requested the Islamic countries send imams who have been trained in their universities and pay their salary. The inevitable price for this, however, is the external conditioning of the local Islamic community that benefits from it. The Islamic countries offer cultural support, but by paying the religious personnel as State officials they create a subordination which could lead to the 'training of compatriots' for the purpose of maintaining control. Indeed, one of the concerns of the Islamic leaders and religious authorities established in Italy is that of being able to rely on the regularisation of the figure of the imam in order that the training process in Italy might be institutionalised. This is also because the imam who comes from abroad inevitably brings with him another tradition and mentality, does not know the Italian language, history, or culture, finds it difficult to understand the context and needs time to integrate.

Building on the experience of other countries where the training models are clearly quite dependent on and conditioned by the Islamic countries, which tend

112 Angelucci, above n 26, 81.

113 Since based on the principle of secularity religion is not a responsibility of the State.

114 Silvio Ferrari, 'La formazione degli imam', in *XV° rapporto sulle migrazioni 2009* (Angeli, 2009) 238.

to export their own model (France, for example, which adopts the models of Turkey, or Algeria and Morocco, which require the subjection of the imam to the respective States), FIDR incorporates civic education[115] in the training of imams, considering it an essential part of the Islamic integration process.

In Italy, the imam, besides acting as officiant and contributing to preserving the cultural identity of his flock so it might be passed down to the younger generations, also plays a key role in helping the Muslim community in the integration process.

In a sense, unlike in Islamic countries where the imam traditionally carries out his duty without being assigned any particular office, the 'Italian imam' is increasingly called to perform the tasks typical of the Catholic parish priest. It is as if there were underway a sort of 'auto-reformatting' of the traditional function, which, in fact, within the host context is becoming institutionalised, almost clericalised. Essentially, the 'Italian imam' proceeds by adjusting to accommodate the needs that arise. In order to gain access to the public space, the process of adaptation appears increasingly to be based on the ex-novo reinvention of the role in a local key, creating a sort of innovative form of 'Italian imam', shaped more to accommodate the situation at hand than on a theological basis. A striking example of this reinvention are the imamates set up to provide spiritual assistance to Muslim hospital patients[116] and prison detainees,[117] which are today found throughout Europe[118] though are not part of the tradition of Islamic countries.

FIDR believes that the imams and leaders of associations and communities may act as a sort of bridge for transmitting the principles and values of Italian society, seeking solutions geared to reconciling respect for the religious identity of Muslims with the legal paradigm of constitutional rights, primarily that of religious freedom.[119] The acquisition of knowledge in the history, culture, traditions and especially the law of the country in which the guide (whether religious or community-oriented) fulfils his role qualifies him, in fact, to act as an inter-cultural and intra-community bridge, which is an essential step in creating an Italian Islam.

115 The ideal requisites are generally: age, knowledge of Arabic and the Qur'an for leading prayer, an overall knowledge of the Shari'a and the ability to interpret it, knowledge of the Sunna, the ability to correct a prayer in case of error, preparation on the four schools, moral qualities and communication skills. The imam also performs duties of social assistance and mediation of a confessional nature, geared to settling intra-community disputes, and takes an active part in helping the Muslim community become integrated.

116 Khalid Rhazzali, 'The end of Life from an Intercultural Perspective: Mediators and Religious Assistants in the Health Service' (2014) 6 *Italian Journal of Sociology of Education* 2, 224–55.

117 Khalid Rhazzali in Irene Becci and Oliver Roy (eds), *Religious care in the reinvented European Imamate. Muslims and their guides in Italian prisons, in Contemporary religious diversity and rehabilitation issues in European correction facilities* (Springer, 2015).

118 M K Rhazzali, 'In and around the mosque: profile and territory of the Italian Imam' in M Hashas, N V Vinding, K Hajji and J de Ruiter (eds), *The Imamate in Western Europe: Developments, Transformations, and Institutional Challenges* (Amsterdam University Press, 2016) in press.

119 Chantal Saint-Blancat and Fabio Perocco, 'New modes of social interaction in Italy: Muslim leaders and local society in Tuscany and Venetia', in Jocelyne Cesari and Sean McLoughlin (eds), *European Muslims and the secular state* (Ashgate, 2005) 99–112.

The approach adopted by FIDR, and offered in a spirit of critical openness, is of a secularised type and conveys a variety of content, including sociological, legal and historico-cultural; it is also an approach geared to intercultural education and to the running of the associations. The lessons have been designed to focus on thematic studies on the subjects of a) rights and duties of citizenship; b) religious freedom and non-discrimination; c) the concept of secularism in Italy; d) dialogue between public authorities and religious communities in a local government context; e) the charter model of religious communities and the legal aspects of associationism; f) religious pluralism; g) places of worship, cemeteries, the celebration of religious acts in public places and respect for law and order; h) religious assistance in hospitals and prisons; i) problems involving halal ritual slaughter.

An in-depth study of the context anchored in social life and placed within the coordinates set by legal sources allowed the Muslims, during the workshops, to formulate hypotheses on how to concretely rationalise the role of the imam (or its current revisitation) in order to make it a lever for integration.

Even the role of women[120] in preaching was given space for discussion with a view to finding workable methods of valorisation.[121]

For women in Morocco, for example, there are the *murshidates*, who are assigned to guide and instruct the faithful in places of worship.[122] During FIDR workshops, on the basis of the theological background, Moroccan women specifically outlined the possible interpretations of this role, favouring especially the integration of women immigrants into Italian society. As we know, female immigration is due largely to family reunification, and this tends to cause the migrant woman to be defined not, like the migrant Muslim man, as an individual, but as an element of a family, often confining her to the same and assigning her to the internal social dynamics of the communities, profoundly redefined as 'Islamic'.

The figure of the *murshidat* may prove to be a useful support and a way to become emancipated from the critical community restrictions that tend to condition the lives of immigrant women. In Syria, Lebanon and Jordan, moreover, a similar figure, known as *qubaysiyat*,[123] has been recognised for decades – an indication that part of Africa may be predisposed (albeit with some difficulty)[124] towards an inclusive attitude to women.

120 According to three out of four Sunni schools and many Shiites, a woman may lead other women in the *Ṣalāt* (obligatory Islamic prayer). The idea of a guide of either gender is controversial. Almost all the Muslim women on the course agreed that women are entitled to lead both men and women in public prayer, while almost all the men disagreed.

121 In Morocco, the figure of the *murshidate* already exists, and a degree course in Islamic sciences is held at the University of Rabat.

122 Morocco funds training programmes for women, to be held in mosques, prisons, schools and disadvantaged urban areas.

123 A nickname deriving from the name of Munira al-Qubaysi, founder of a movement that demands a role for women in public religious activities.

124 Authoritative teachers of the Islamic faith are increasingly considering women as an important resource for the Islam of the future. These include Sudanese leader Hassan al-Turabi, PhD in law from the Sorbona and PhD from Oxford, the power behind the Muslim

Also in relation to the function of the imam, a subject that was particularly close to the heart of the young participants of the three-year course, regards the establishing of an apprenticeship that takes into account, on one hand, the problems of young people who live astride two worlds, acting as sort of generational bridge, and on the other hand the need for a suitable language (not only for the older generation) for putting into practice the message of the great values espoused by the faith. Young people, more than adults, disapprove of the importation of imams from Muslim countries – which, in fact, would not respond adequately to the needs of the second generation since the imam would first have to be trained, informed and integrated.

## Conclusion

The safeguarding of religious freedom in a pluralistic (and also cultural, seeing that Islam is not only a religion) regime has prompted FIDR to develop training, in a secular key, geared to making the best possible use of the legal toolbox already available with a view to providing Muslims with a more in-depth citizenship education. The representatives of the Islamic community in Italy invited to participate in the course covered a potential group of over 80,000 practising Muslims. The 40 or so participants, including leaders, imams and especially second-generation youths (who are more open to the idea of combining different cultures), met together every weekend for three years, for a total of 34 days, completing over 400 hours of workshops. The fact of being a residential course, moreover, provided an additionally singular experience. Discussing the issues of integration and comparing with the current laws, culture and customs in Italy on a continual basis and in a casual setting also gave them an opportunity to get to know each other. Sitting together and enjoying social interaction between cultures while sharing a meal was not accidental. Providing occasions for exchange outside the classroom encouraged discussion and communication in a world in which heated debate is far more common than constructive dialogue. Different groups of Muslims are, in fact, accustomed to respecting each other, but from a distance. The use of mediation methods to support dialogue with a view to identifying common goals perhaps helped to shorten these distances between the individual aggregations, which traditionally tend to group together and compete against each other. Each group of Muslims was then given the freedom to choose, based on their common goals, whether to join forces in dialoguing with the State.

As mentioned earlier, this three-year integration course was patronised by the Interior Ministry, with all costs borne exclusively by private entities.[125]

---

Brotherhood in Sudan, who declared that Muslim women may freely perform the function of the imam, including in collective prayer in the mosque. This statement sparked disapproval and the issuing of a *fatwa* for apostasy.

125 The main sponsor was the bank foundation Compagnia di SanPaolo of Turin.

The lack of participation from Parliament, which is as yet reluctant to enter into an in-depth debate on the Islamic question, resulted in some resistance on the part of the Executive Council which, lacking political support, did not have the courage to take a decisive step forward in substantially opening up to change – eg, by validating with an imprimatur the identification of practices conforming to the State framework within which to exercise constitutional rights and duties.[126]

While still in the developing stages, the situation today 'highlights the current difficulty [not only in Italy but also] in European countries of translating into living law constitutional directives aimed both at the management and the promotion of cultural and religious pluralism.'[127] Slowly but surely, however, we are making progress.

In this sense, therefore, rather than talking about conclusions it would be more accurate to say that a process is underway. New steps towards the configuration of an Islam that can be said to be Italian are being taken, hopefully with increasing sensitivity on the part of all the institutions responsible for the building of social cohesion.[128]

## References

Allievi, Stefano, *I nuovi musulmani* (Edizioni Lavoro, 1999)

Allievi, Stefano, *Islam italiano: viaggio nella seconda religione del paese* (Einaudi, 2003)

Allievi, Stefano, 'La presenza dell'islam nello spazio pubblico italiano: a che punto siamo?', *De Stefano*, May 29 2015, accessed 18 December 2015, available at: <www.stefanoallievi.it/2015/05/la-presenza-dellislam-nello-spazio-pubblico-italiano-a-che-punto-siamo/>

Allievi, Stefano and Felice Dassetto, *Il ritorno dell'Islam – I musulmani in Italia* (Edizioni lavoro, 1993)

Anello, Giancarlo, '2016 Freedom of Religion vs Islamophobia: Lombardy's "Anti-Mosque Law" is Unconstitutional', *Academia*, 2 April 2016, accessed 6 March 2017, available at: <www.academia.edu/24053495/2016_Freedom_of_Religion_vs_Islamophobia_Lombardys_Anti-_Mosque_Law_is_Unconstitutional>.

126 A particularly unfavorable circumstance, coinciding with the last day of the first year of the course, was the publication of an article in *Corriere della Sera* (5 December 2010, 285) bearing the inept title 'With the introduction of the first local imams Islam becomes a little less problematic'. This, in fact, prompted the Interior Ministry to take a position of neutrality rather than committal with respect to the Academy's proposal, despite the fact that the aim of the course was clearly only to provide legal and sociological training for the leaders of the communities and associations and not to 'certify' future Italian imams. The website 'Fidr.it' includes publications and press releases rebutting the allegations presented. The controversy was further fueled by a misunderstanding regarding the alleged issuing of accreditation to imams by the prefectures (which can only occur as a result of the political work of the councils); Cf Federica Paci, 'Gli imam moderati attaccano il Viminale "Scelti gli estremisti"', *La Stampa*, 12 June 2016.

127 Alessandro Ferrari, 'introduzione. Una libertà per due? Oltre l'incommensurabilità, per un diritto di libertà religiosa mediterraneo' in Alessandro Ferrari (ed), *Diritto e religione nell'Islam mediterraneo -rapporti nazionali sulla salvaguardia della libertà religiosa: un paradigma alternativo* (Mulino, 2012) 8.

128 Cf § 2 on advisory meetings and the accreditation of the imam.

Angelucci, Antonio, Maria Bombardieri, Davide Tacchini (eds), *Islam e integrazione in Italia* (Marsilio, 2014)

*Anti-Terrorism, Crime and Security Act* 2001 (UK)

Bargellini, Costanza and Elisabetta Cicciarelli (ed), *Islam a scuola esperienze e risorse* (Quaderni ISMU, 2007)

Berthelet, Pierre, 'L'impact des événements du 11 septembre sur la création de l'espace de liberté, de sécurité, et de justice' (2002) 42 *Cultures et Conflits* 1

Berti, Fabio and Andrea Valzania (eds), *Le dinamiche locali dell'integrazione: Esperienze di ricerca in Toscana* (FrancoAngeli, 2011)

Biano, Illaria, 'Questioni di libertà religiosa: il caso dell'Islam italiano – CESPEC Summer school', accessed 2 November 2015, *Academia*, N/A, available at: <www.academia.edu/6115875/Questioni_di_libert%C3%A0_religiosa_il_caso_dell_Islam_italiano_-_CESPEC_Summer_school>

Bifulco, Raffaele, Alfonso Celotto and Marco Olivetti (eds), *Commentario alla Costituzione, Vol I* (2006, UTET Giuridica)

Bombardieri, Maria, 'l'Islam in Italia: Numeri, protagonisti e dinamiche sociali' (2013) 1 *Ad Gentes* 1

Bombardieri, Maria, *Moschee d'Italia. Il diritto al culto. Il dibattito sociale e politico* (Zoom Italia, 2011)

Boswell, Christina, 'Migration control in Europe after 9/11: Explaining the absence of securitization' (2007) 45 *Journal of Common Market Studies* 589

Cardia, Carlo and Giuseppe Dalla Torre (eds), *Caratteristiche dei modelli organizzativi dell'Islam italiano a livello locale: tra frammentarietà e mimetismo giuridico* (Giappichelli Publisher, 2015)

Caritas Italiana, 'Rapporto Immigrazione Caritas e Migrantes 2013', *Caritas Italiana*, available at: <www.caritasitaliana.it/home_page/area_stampa/00003960_Rapporto_Immigrazione_Caritas_e_Migrantes_2013.html>

Carrera, Sergio, *In search of the perfect citizen? The intersection between integration, immigration and nationality in the EU* (Martinus Nijhoff Publishers, 2009)

Censimento della Popolazione, 'Gli stranieri al 15° Censimento della popolazione', *Censimento della Popolazione*, accessed 13 December 2015, available at: <www.istat.it/it/files/2013/12/Notadiffusione_stranieri20122013.pdf>

Cesari, Jocelyne (ed), *The Oxford Handbook of European Islam* (Oxford University Press, 2014)

Cesari, Jocelyne and Sean McLoughlin (eds), *European Muslims and the secular state* (Ashgate, 2005)

Conway, Gordon, *Islamophobia: A Challenge for Us all* (Runnymede Trust, 1997)

Cuttitta, Paolo, 'Borderizing the Island. Setting and Narratives of the Lampedusa Border Play' (2014) 13 *ACME: An International E-Journal for Critical Geographies* 196

Cuttitta, Paolo, 'Migration Control in the Mediterranean Grenzsaum. Reading Ratzel in the Strait of Sicily' (2014) 29 *Journal of Borderlands Studies* 117

Dalla Torre, Giuseppe, *Il fattore religioso nella Costituzione: Analisi e interpretazioni* (Giappichelli, 1995)

Dassetto, Felice, *L'incontro complesso. Mondi occidentali e mondi islamici* (Città Aperta Edizioni, 2004)

Dassetto, Felice, Silvio Ferrari, Brigitte Maréchal, *Islam in the European Union: What's at Stake in the Future?*, Directorate General Internal Policies of the Union, Policy Department Structural and Cohesion Policies – Culture and Education, European Parliament, May 2007

Domianello, Sara, *Diritto e religione in Italia – Rapporto nazionale sulla salvaguardia della libertà religiosa in regime di pluralismo confessionale e culturale* (il Mulino, 2012)

Dusi, Elena, 'Il fantasma della Consulta', *Limes*, Issue 4, 2007

*Enciclopedia del diritto Aggiornamento, Vol V* (Giuffrè, 2001)

Ferrari, Alessandro (ed), *Diritto e religione nell'Islam mediterraneo -rapporti nazionali sulla salvaguardia della libertà religiosa: un paradigma alternativo* (Mulino, 2012)

Ferrari, Alessandro, *Islam in Italy: The 'Ghost' Religion – A 'non-religion' in a 'religious country'*, 2015, accessed on 8 March 2016, available at: <www.academia.edu/15027163/Islam_in_Italy>. (Paoline, 2008)

Ferrari, Alessandro, 'La nuova legge lombarda sui luoghi di culto: una risposta sbagliata al pluralismo culturale e religioso', *Oasis*, 2 February 2015, accessed 20 January 2016, available at: <www.oasiscenter.eu/it/articoli/libert%C3%A0-religiosa/2015/02/02/la-nuova-legge-lombarda-sui-luoghi-di-culto-una-risposta-sbagliata-al-pluralismo-culturale-e-religioso>

Ferrari, Alessandro, '*Laïcité et multiculturalisme à l'italienne, Archives de sciences sociales des religions*' (2008) 78 *Archives of Social Sciences of Religion* 1

Ferrari, Alessandro, 'Libertà religiosa e nuove presenze confessionali (ortodossi e islamici): tra cieca deregulation e super-specialità, ovverodel difficile spazio per la differenza religiosa', *Stato e Chiese*, July 2011, accessed 10 February 2016, available at: <www.statoechiese.it/index.php?option=com_content&task=view&id=467&Itemid=40>

Ferrari, Alessandro, *La libertà religiosa in Italia- un percorso incompiuto* (Carocci, 2012)

Ferrari, Silvio, 'La formazione degli imam', in *XV° rapporto sulle migrazioni 2009* (Angeli, 2009)

Ferrari, Silvio (ed), *Musulmani in Italia: la condizione giuridica delle comunità islamiche*, (Il Mulino, 2000)

Floris, Pierangela, *Autonomia confessionale – Principi-limite fondamentali e ordine pubblico*, (series of the Faculty of Law at the University of Cagliari (Cagliari, 1992)

Frisina, Annalisa, Università di Padova, Italia, 'Giovani Musulmanid' Italia, *Trasformazioni Socio-Culturalie Domande Di Cittadinanza*, Relazione presentata al Convegno internazionale Giovani musulmani in Europa, 11 June 2000, available at: <www.cestim.it/argomenti/02islam/02islam-frisina-giovani%20musulmani.pdf>.

Frisina, Annalisa, *Giovani Musulmani d'Italia* (Carocci, 2007)

Gallino, Luciano, *Dizionario di sociologia*, under 'integrazione' (UTET, 2004)

Giovani Musulmani d'Italia, Protagonisti noi, con l'aiuto di Dio, available at: <http://giovanimusulmani.it/>

Guolo, Renzo, 'La Sinistra, I'Islam e il complesso di Kurtz', 2002, *Italianieuropei*, available at: <www.italianieuropei.it/italianieuropei-4-2010/item/456-la-sinistra-lislam-e-il-complesso-di-kurtz.html>.

Guolo, Renzo, *Le organizzazioni islamiche in Italia e le reti transnazionali di riferimento, Relazione presentata al Convegno L'islam in Italia. Appartenenze religiose plurali e strategie diversificate*, Turin, 2–3 December 2004, accessed 27 December 2015, available at: <www.fga.it/fileadmin/storico/UPLOAD/ALL/CEA/65.pdf>.

Hashas, M, N V Vinding, K Hajji and J de Ruiter (eds), *The Imamate in Western Europe: Developments, Transformations, and Institutional Challenges* (Amsterdam University Press, 2016)

Hepburn, Eve and Ricard Zapata Barrero (eds), *The Politics of Immigration in Multilevel States, Palgrave Politics of Identity and Citizenship Series* (Macmillan Distribution Ltd, 2014)

IDOS Research Centre, 'Dossier Statistico Immigrazione 2015: 15 punti chiave', *Centro Studi e Ricerche IDOS – Rivista Confronti*, accessed 24 December 2015, available at: <www.dossierimmigrazione.it/docnews/file/Dossier%20Statistico%20 Immigrazione%202015%2015%20punti%20chiave(1).pdf>

IDOS Study and Research Centre, 'Rapporto-Immigrazione e Imprenditoria 2015', *Aggiornamento Statistico*, 2015, accessed on 12 January 2016, available at: <www.dossierimmigrazione.it/docnews/file/2015_Rapporto%20Imprenditoria_Scheda.pdf>

IIE Publique, 'trente-ans-legislation-antiterroriste', *IIE Publique*, 3 August 2016, available at: <www.vie-publique.fr/chronologie/chronos-thematiques/trente-ans-legislation-antiterroriste.html>

Internal Ministry of Italy, *Religioni, Dialogo, Intergrazione* (Unione Europa, 2013) available at: <www1.interno.gov.it/mininterno/export/sites/default/it/assets/files/26/2013_06_18_vademecum_esecutivo_low.pdf>

Introvigne, Massimo and Pierluigi Zoccatelli, 'Le religioni in Italia', 4 March 2017, available at: <www.cesnur.com/lislam-e-i-movimenti-di-matrice-islamica in italia/lislam-sunnita-unintroduzione/>

Irene Becci and Oliver Roy (eds), *Religious care in the reinvented European Imamate. Muslims and their guides in Italian prisons, in Contemporary religious diversity and rehabilitation issues in European correction facilities* (Springer, 2015)

ISTAT, 'Demographical Data', updated January 2017, available at: <www.demo.istat.it>

Istat, 'Popolazione e famiglie', *Istat – Istituto nazionale di statistica*, available at: <www.istat.it/it/popolazione>

Joppke, Christian and Ewa T Morawska (eds), *Toward Assimilation and Citizenship* (Palgrave, 2003)

Lateran Pacts of 1929, Treaty of Conciliation 1929 (Italy)

Law 2001–1062 'loisur la sécurité quotidienne (or LSQ)', 15 November 2001

Law 2002–1094 'orientation et programmation sur la sécurité intérieure', 29 August 2002

Law 2006–64 'relative à la lutte contre le terrorisme et portant dispositions diverses relatives à la sécurité et aux contrôles frontaliers', 23 January 2006

Law 2012–1432, 'sur la securité et la lutte contre le terrorisme', 21 December 2012

Law 2014–1353, JORF no 0263 'renforçant les dispositions relatives à la lutte contre le terrorisme', 13 November 2014

Law 2015–912 JORF no 0171, 24 July 2015

Law No 40 of 1998, *Provisions Governing Immigration and Regulations Concerning the Status of Foreigners*, 6 March 1998

Magnier, Annick and Giovanna Vicarelli (eds), *Mosaico Italia. Lo stato del Paese agli inizi del XXI secolo* (FrancoAngeli, 2010)

Marci, Gianfranco, Marco Parisi and Valerio Tozzi (eds), *Diritto e religione, L'evoluzione di un settore della scienza giuridica attraverso il confronto fra quattro libri* (Pletica, 2012)

Massari, Monica, *Islamofobia: la paura e l'islam* (Laterza, 2006)

Modood, Tariq, Anna Triandafyllidou and Ricard Zapata-Barrero, *Multiculturalism, Muslims and Citizenship: A European Approach* (Routledge, 2006)

Monnet, LUM J (ed), *La legislazione sulla base di intese: I test delle religioni 'altre' e gli ateismi* (Cacucci, 2013)

Naso, Paolo and Brunetto Salvarani (eds), *I ponti di Babele. Cantieri, progetti e criticità nell'Italia delle religioni* (EDB, 2015)

Negri, Augosto Tino and Silvia Scaranari Introvigne (eds), *Musulmani in Piemonte: in moschea, al lavoro, nel contesto sociale* (Guerini e Associati, 2005)

Nielsen, Jörg (ed), *Yearbook of Muslims in Europe* (Brill, Vol 5, 2013)

Noberto Bobbio, Nicola Matteucci and Gianfranco Pasquino (eds), *Dizionario di politica* (Turin, 2004)

Orabona, Luciano, Antonio Magliulo, Ulderico Parente, *Cattolicesimo e identità nazionale* (Editrice Apes, 2011)

Paci, Federica, 'Gli imam moderati attaccano il Viminale "Scelti gli estremisti"', *La Stampa*, 12 June 2016

Pacini, Andrea (ed), *Chiesa e islam in Italia: esperienze e prospettive di dialogo Prevention of Terrorism Act* 2005 (UK)

Rebessi, Elisa, 'Diffusione dei luoghi di culto islamici e gestione delle conflittualità. La moschea di via Urbino a Torino come studio di caso', *Dipartimento POLIS*, December 2011, accessed 6 March 2017, available at: <www.fidr.it/cgi-bin/materiale/123/Rebessi.pdf>

Rhazzali, Khalid, 'The end of Life from an Intercultural Perspective: Mediators and Religious Assistants in the Health Service' (2014) 6 *Italian Journal of Sociology of Education* 2, 224

Ricca, Mario, 'Sul diritto interculturale. Costruire l'esperienza giuridica oltre le identità' (2008) 8 *Daimon, Annuario di diritto comparato delle religioni* 10

Saint-Blancat, Chantal (ed), *L'Islam in Italia. Una presenza plurale* (Edizioni Lavoro, 1999)

Soldani, Simonetta and Gabriele Turi (ed), *Fare gli italiani. Scuola e cultura nell' Italia contemporanea. 1, La nascita dello stato nazionale* (Il Mulino, 1993)

Tuttitalia, 'Popolazione per età, sesso e stato civile 2015', *Tuttitalia*, December 2015, available at: <www.tuttitalia.it/statistiche/popolazione-eta-sesso-stato-civile-2015/>

Una comunità islamica nel cuore dell'Occidente, available at: <www.coreis.it>

Union of Islamic Communities and Organisations in Italy (UCOII), <www.ucoii.org>

*Uniting and Strengthening America by Providing Appropriate Tools Required to Intercept and Obstruct Terrorism Act* of 2001 ('*USA Patriot Act*') (US)

Zincone, Giovanna (ed), *Primo rapporto sull'integrazione degli immigrati in Italia* (Il Mulino, 2000)

Zincone, Giovanna, Rinus Penninx and Maren Borkert (eds), *Migration Policymaking in Europe: The Dynamics of Actors and Contexts in Past and Present* (Amsterdam University Press, 2011)

# 12 The boundaries of religious ethics, secular ethics and law

*Robert Crotty*

## Introduction

The sharing of common space by conventional religionists of more than one religious tradition and non-conventional religionists has always caused difficulty. At times the religious persons have been discriminated against; at other times the others have been discriminated against.

That problem has never been more obvious than at the present moment. Too often, those who follow Islam are either in the ascendency in a community or they are a despised minority. Although other world religions have exclusivist triggers – such as the Christian '*extra ecclesiam nulla salus*', n'o salvation outside the church' or the 'chosen people' of the covenant of Israel – Islam is in a particular bind.

Islam's formula to describe this division of the world has long been: *dar ul-islam* (the sphere of Islam) and *dar ul-harb* (the sphere of war). The *dar ul-islam* would have a Muslim ruler, a Caliph, and the way of life within this sphere would be controlled by the Shari'a, the way of life of Islam. The *dar ul-islam* had the obligation to expand into the *dar ul-harb*. When early Islamic conquest took place, the inhabitants either converted to Islam or were accepted as 'Peoples of the Book' (if they were Christians or Jews). Thus, the *dar ul-harb* was transformed into an extension of the *dar ul-islam* by means of *jihad*. The very fact of the division imposing the obligation of *jihad* or 'striving' could be interpreted as a belligerent expansion of Islam. This religious exclusivism became a cornerstone of Islamic religious culture, utilised in periods of political and social tension to galvanise general Islamic support.

Many Western modern societies are thus faced with a confrontation of religious ethics, secular ethics and the law of the land. Four research points are raised relative to this question:

- Where are the boundaries between religion, ethics and the law of the land?
- How can competing systems of secular ethics be reconciled?
- How can competing systems of religious ethics be reconciled?
- How can competing systems of religious ethics and secular ethics be reconciled?

This chapter is intended to consider these four research questions.

## Ethics

We can begin a discussion with a clarification on the meaning of 'ethics'.

Whether religious or secular, ethics is that system of principles by which human actions and intentions can be adjudged good or bad, right or wrong. It defines a judgemental system that informs humans as to what is right or wrong in a particular situation. Ethical theory and ethical reasoning have subsequently developed because it is not always clear how a human should rightly respond in a particular situation and substantiation is often required.

Generally speaking, there are three standard elaborations of ethical reasoning in Western thought. First, there is consequentialism. This approach takes regard of the consequences that will follow from making a certain response to a human situation. Its basis is that the consequences of a particular human response determine the morality of that response.

An important subcategory of consequentialism is called utilitarianism. This theory goes one step further and holds that consequences that promote welfare are ethically preferable to those that do not do so, and those consequences that promote welfare more are ethically preferable to those that do not maximise welfare. Following from this, Jeremy Bentham's utilitarian principle (as refined by John Stuart Mill) was that so long as people do not interfere with the freedom and happiness of others they should be allowed to think and do as they like.

Another approach is to focus on the duties and obligations of those who perform human actions. These are called deontological theories. Immanuel Kant held to the principle of unconditional respect for others, treating people not as means to an end but as ends in themselves. Kantians struggle to do what duty demands as against what the human spirit wants to do.

Yet another approach is called virtue ethics which concentrates on the particular qualities of the person involved in making a human decision. A response is deemed good and right if it is what a good person would normally do. The virtue ethicist therefore must identify those virtues which good people should possess if they are to live fulfilling lives.

Each of these broad approaches has its problems. How does the ethicist who follows consequentialism or utilitarianism decide on the relative value of more than one consequence of an action? The decision maker's duties and obligations, given precedence by the deontologist, can themselves sometimes seem to be in conflict. And who decides the necessary virtues of the morally upright person for the virtue ethicist?

I would like to take another approach and begin with the claim that human life is dominated by the interaction of genes and human culture. Human culture is similar to a software program within a computer, while the genes are like the computer itself. Culture directs the output of the computer. If a glitch develops within the software, then usually the output will be skewed. If the computer is faulty, culture cannot rectify it.

To tease out this point, we need to look in the first place at genetics and the human condition.

## The genetic basis of humanity

At the moment, our human species, *homo sapiens*, has been the only hominid for the last 10,000 years.[1] Hominids evolved within Africa some 2.5 million years ago, and then migrated to North Africa, Europe and Asia. From these points, they branched off into different species. The hominids were at that point in time weak and marginal on the scale of living carnivores, somewhere in the middle of the food chain. Only with *homo sapiens*, dating from some 200,000 years ago, has the hominid reached the top of the food chain. And *homo sapiens* have survived as the sole hominid today.

What explains the superiority of *homo sapiens* that allowed it to dominate other species (including other hominids)? Most probably the development of language. It reflected and brought about a revolution in *homo sapiens'* cognitive abilities. Perhaps quite accidental genetic mutations enabled the species to think in new ways and to form a much more efficient form of communication in the human ability to speak. In any case, this manipulation of human sound was superior to any of the communication methods known in other species, human or otherwise.

It is at this point, with the refinement of linguistic communication, that human myths began to play their part. Since then, religious myths, national myths, the myth of justice and human rights have enabled people to live together with some degree of co-operation. Strangers could co-operate because of a shared imagined reality of a created, fictional 'world'. This fiction allowed *homo sapiens* to co-operate effectively, to share innovation and to adapt social behaviour in the face of new challenges. When we speak of myth and fiction, we are moving into the area of culture. The way was open to quick cultural evolution.

In all species, genetic control, the particularised DNA, controls that species. But there can be significant changes to the influence of DNA because of the environment and individual circumstances. The behaviour patterns of *homo sapiens* remained generally fixed (allowing for some changes due to climate and habitat). However, it can be argued that it was the development of language and the use of fiction that brought about rapid change that outstripped genetics.

In short, it is the diversity of imagined realities, based on the invented myths and the diversity of possible behavioural patterns that make up what we call 'culture'.

## Culture

I understand culture to mean the total shared way of life of any given *homo sapiens* group; substantially, culture is composed of that group's modes of thinking, acting, feeling, valuing. Culture is both apprehended internally and expressed externally by a system of symbols.[2]

1 Yuval Noah Harari, *Sapiens: A Brief History of Humankind* (Harvill Secker, 2014) Ch 1–2.
2 Clifford Geertz, *The Interpretation of Cultures* (Basic Books, 1973) 89.

Culture is a human fiction. It is not something static; it develops and adapts, just as the human group, within which it has its being, develops and adapts to a changing physical environment. The development and adaptation of a culture and the development and adaptation of its attendant human group are not separate issues. Without human beings, there could be no culture; development and adaptation of culture and humans must happen synchronically.

The very notion of being human requires being programmed by culture.[3] While other animal species, to a large extent, have their behavioural patterns predetermined by their genetic code, the behaviour of human beings is regulated genetically to a far lesser extent.

Why is there a need for culture? Humans must put a construction on those events in which they are involved and they do so by means of this very system of fictional symbols, a culture. They need to construct order; culture enables them to achieve order. What other animals achieve through genetically developed instinct, humans largely achieve – more extensively, with more variety and more efficiently – through culture.

Does this vital human culture exist in reality or only in the human mind? It would seem that there is a tendency for humans to situate culture 'out there', in what they would define as reality. It is natural, accordingly, for people to consider that their own particular culture is the 'true' culture, that their way of living is really real; it comes as a shock to realise that there are other humans of the same species who regard their own, different cultures equally as valid. There are many cultures, many cultural choices for humans. Cultures exist primarily in the mind.

## Cultural relativism

Hence, looking across the contemporary world we can review such different cultures as Chinese, Japanese, European, Aboriginal Australian – even granted that there are many variants within each of them. Looking back in time, we can reconstruct from texts and artefacts ancient Greek culture, ancient Mesopotamian culture, ancient Celtic culture. Are they comparable?

In the past, common, universal characteristics have been confidently identified as existing in all cultural systems.[4] For instance, in the 1970s the well-known anthropologist Melville Spiro was able to identify 'invariant dispositions and orientations' which stemmed, he claimed, from 'pan-human biological and cultural constants'.[5] He cited abhorrence of incest, rejection of murder and gregariousness as examples of these universal cultural traits. On the basis of 'invariant dispositions

3 Ibid Ch 2.
4 Clyde Kluckholm, 'Universal categories of Culture' in Alfred Kroeber (ed), *Anthropology Today* (University of Chicago Press, 1953) 507–23.
5 Melville Spiro, 'Culture and human nature' in George Spindler (ed), *The Making of Psychological Anthropology* (University of California Press, 1978) 330–60.

and orientations' he was able to postulate 'a universal human nature' as a base underlying all human cultures.[6]

There are other scholars who hold that any such perception of a universal human nature is illusory. While most anthropologists would agree that the basic parameters for the behavioural scope of *homo sapiens* is set by the genetic makeup, the DNA, they temper this with the claim that *homo sapiens* has developed the ability to create fiction, to tell myths. More and more possibilities for living, for creating a future, can be fictionalised by each human generation.

Every culture, the anthropologists maintain, is unique, formed within the parameters of the life experience and ecological habitat of a particular group and variously shaped by non-recurrent historical events. Each element of a culture can only be judged by what it contributes to the totality of that culture. A particular form of government (which is a cultural artefact), such as ancient Greek democracy, cannot meaningfully be compared to a similar form of democracy in another culture, such as Western democracy; each cultural element only has meaning within the total culture of its own group. Such complete cultural relativism has, of course, its own philosophical difficulties.[7]

A variant, more moderate relativism has been proposed and deserves attention. The case could be put that while the behaviour patterns of animals are for the most part genetically determined and the genetic code orders their activity within a narrow range of variation, human beings are genetically endowed with very general response capacities. These are not the cultural universals proposed above by Spiro and others; they are response capacities that allow humans to learn and to adapt within broad ranges of activity.

These would be similar to the list of 'innate modules of the human mind' identified by Pinker, which he also calls 'families of instincts'. Pinker writes specifically about language:

> Language is a complex, specialized skill, which develops in the child spontaneously, without conscious effort or formal instruction, is deployed without awareness of its underlying logic, is qualitatively the same in every individual, and is distinct from more general abilities to process information or behave intelligently. For these reasons some cognitive scientists have described language as a psychological faculty, a mental organ, a neural system, and a computational module. But I prefer the admittedly quaint term 'instinct.' It conveys the idea that people know how to talk in more or less the sense that spiders know how to spin webs.[8]

In this sense, we have an innate response capacity or 'instinct' to speak, but our capacity to speak English, for example, is culturally determined. Perhaps this principle

6 Ibid 349–50.

7 Clifford Geertz, 'Distinguished lecture: anti-relativism' (1984) 86 *American Anthropologist* 263, 263–78.

8 Steven Pinker, *The Language Instinct* (Penguin, 1994) 18.

can be applied to the whole of human development: response capacity is determined and controlled by biology; how this capacity will be activated and manifest itself will normally depend upon the culture into which the individual has been socialised.[9]

However, a human being with capacities *simpliciter* would be an incomplete animal, uncontrollable; it is culture that completes the human being by activating these capacities in a number of quite specific ways.

Following this line of thought, culture would be 'learned' in a way analogous to language:

> 'Culture' refers to the process whereby particular kinds of learning contagiously spread from person to person in a group and minds become coordinated into shared patterns, just as 'a language' or 'a dialect' refers to the process whereby the different speakers in a group acquire highly similar mental grammars.[10]

There is a fear that any form of relativism, including the moderate form I have described above, will constrain the observer to accept blindly everything proposed in an alien culture. 'Everything', opponents claim, might entail cannibalism, infanticide or female genital mutilation. Yet, what has been described is not determinism. Just as an individual is free to depart from the 'rules' of language and invent neologisms or even speak nonsense, so too the individual retains freedom and can depart from the 'rules' of culture, learned by 'contagion', more generally and so behave, think and value in a variant or even a nonsensical way.

In other words, moderate relativism does not require its followers to be uncritical of their own culture or even of alien cultures. However, in the case of alien cultures, care must be taken. For a critique of an alien culture to be valid, a cultural proposition must be evaluated within its own cultural framework and context, just as it would be critiqued spontaneously by its adherents within their own cultural parameters. When critiquing an alien culture, the canons of evidence and epistemology, proper to that particular cultural discourse, need to be respected.[11]

For example, the practice of female genital mutilation cannot be accepted or rejected on any absolutist grounds. It cannot be critiqued from the vantage point of a European culture. It can only be validly critiqued from within the total cultural context of the society in which it is practised. Multiculturalism would raise the question: can female genital mutilation, admittedly acceptable in a North African culture, be allowed in a Western space?

9 Stated as such, there seems to be a determinism and lack of difference in both human biology and human culture. However, it must be remembered that the biology, principally the structure and composition of the brain, differs from human to human, access to cultural learning also differs. There will always be serious problems in human society where the biological brain development of individual members is skewed or where cultural immersion is inadequate for the particular person's needs.

10 Pinker, above n 8, 411.

11 F Allan Hanson, 'Does God have a body? Truth, reality and cultural relativism' (1979) 14 *Man New Series* 515–29.

## The need for order

What does culture, understood in the way proposed, offer to the human being? The human individual has a need for order. To make sense of the universe, self and others, the individual within the group requires a direction, a purpose, a sense of meaning. All cultural activity takes place in the context of the construction of a cultural 'world' of meanings. These constructed worlds, shaped according to perhaps significantly different configurations of values, power relationships and knowledge, achieve viability because they are supported by a group which, by its general acceptance, gives plausibility to such constructed worlds. The supportive group commits itself to its 'world' and defines its own roles and identities vis-à-vis it.

Culture, every culture, offers this advantage to its adherents. In order to find meaning and direction, individuals and groups must accept and then adapt themselves to this cultural heritage of a constructed world. When the group has achieved meaning and direction, it acts to retain its cultural heritage (so often seen as 'real' and 'out there') with the same tenacity as an individual displays in maintaining personal, physical life. Hence there is always an element of adherence and continuity in culture, together with a capacity to adapt and change.

It is the universal need for order (the most tenacious of all general response capacities) together with other human capacities that give rise to the impression of so-called cultural traits or universals. The general response capacities of the human group are activated and directed in different ways by a particular culture. Because of these two factors, general response capacities and diverse activation, there will be both similarity and diversity when any two human cultures are compared.

## Sexuality as an example

In order to illustrate the basic point of this paper, I will take the instance of sexuality. Sexuality is primarily determined by genetics.[12] This is the general response capacity to the need for sexual satisfaction. Human genetics has produced this sexual need to ensure reproduction. But this need is blind in its satisfaction; genetically it could be fulfilled in many and indiscriminate ways. We can think of monogamy, polygamy, polyandry, casual copulations. How should the genetic need to reach sexual satisfaction be ordered in societies of people? We need to look more in detail at the genetic basis of sexual satisfaction, although this will be superficial.

Human sexuality is largely determined in the womb. It is linked to the development of the foetal brain. The normal foetus has 23 pairs of chromosomes. One pair of these are sex chromosomes. They can be XX or XY – XX is a genetic female and XY is a genetic male. Early in the pregnancy the sex organs remain neutral; then in the second month genes on the Y chromosome produce a protein that effect the male testes. With no Y activity, as in a female, the sex organs become

12 Patricia Churchland, *Touching a Nerve: Our Brains, Our Selves* (W W Norton, 2013) 131–49.

ovaries. As term approaches, testosterone is produced by the male testes and eventually reaches the foetal brain. It affects the brain's anatomy and the person is masculinised. The female brain is what develops if there is no testosterone.

Thence begins a veritable cacophony of hormonal interactions in the human brain. Mood, personality, aggression, trustfulness are engendered. With regard to all of these traits, one human male or female differs from another; the same individual can differ from one time to another. Variability is the order of the day in this sexual development: unusual chromosome patterns are known and they usually result in genetic abnormalities; the process of masculinisation of the brain can be disrupted; gender identity can be confused; sexual orientation can take a number of significantly different forms.

Scientists, for example, have isolated a small hypothalamic region of the brain that is anatomically different in homosexuals. It is the result of specific hormonal interaction. Homosexuals are formed in the womb, not by later lifestyle choices. In general, sexual orientation is largely genetic; it is largely determined from conception.

But it needs to be recognised that the human brain is a very large organism, the most complex machine known in the universe. It is capable of massive variations in individuals and it controls later extra-womb development. This means that while genetic process does to a large extent control sexual orientation, culture is also very important.

Sexual orientation, determined by genetics, is ordered in the life-situation by culture. Human social institutions have long seen the need to stabilise and mature the basic sexual expressions. Sexual satisfaction cannot be allowed free play in an ordered society. The possibilities for sexual satisfaction listed above have been scrutinised by culture for possible ways forward. Societies construct myths which fictionally depict the supposedly universal way by which sexual humans should attain sexual satisfaction. Hence, different groups have constructed systems of sexual ethics to control their human population; sometimes these systems are secular (eg this is how humankind is expected to act sexually or there will be grave consequences for society), sometimes religious (eg God or the gods or an Ancestor commanded humans to have only one sexual partner and to practise sex only within the limits of monogamous relationship) and there is the complication of law (some sexual practices, such as homosexuality, may be forbidden; certain sexual liaisons, such as polygamy, may be forbidden).

We need to see how this cultural direction links up with ethics.

## Culture and ethics

I have proposed that human culture primarily exists to provide order in human affairs. I now identify ethics with a system of principles that determine how a particular person can achieve what is ordered in human affairs and avoid what is disordered in human affairs. For the purposes of this exercise, I am going to pretend at first that humans live their lives in separate groups, each group having its own everyday culture. That is never or rarely the case in reality.

To achieve order in everyday life, human beings must marshal thinking, acting, feeling and valuing towards that end, ensuring that they think, act, feel and value in such a way as to bring their ordered life in line with an ordered community. A human culture, contemporary or in the past, has been refined over time to do just that. Cultures that endure over a length of time have endured precisely because of their capacity to achieve such a purpose.

In this light, the three broad theoretical approaches to ethics, as listed above, begin to make sense. Consequentialism is based on the output: an ordered individual should live harmoniously within an ordered community. If the consequence of some human activity is to bring about disorder for the individual or the community, then it is wrong and bad. But how can that disorder be identified and how can one determination of order be compared, for better or worse, with another?

The answer lies within the cultural thinking, the valuing patterns, of the individual culture. There are general response capacities, but their expression is culturally determined in this particular culture. The ethicist can only decide about consequences for this particular culture, arguing back from particular human actions to those general response capacities. Carrying out this work, the ethicist may, in the end, uncover certain constant ethical principles across all or most cultures ('thou shalt not kill without due reason'; 'thou shall protect the weak and helpless'). This is only to be expected in the one species of *homo sapiens.*

Hence, in one community, the killing of a convicted murderer will be judged as part of the ordering of the community and fulfilling the ethical dictum 'thou shalt not kill without due reason'; in another the same action of killing a convicted murderer will be judged as part of the disorder of the community and contrary to the dictum 'thou shalt not kill without due reason'. Some groups hold to the justice and deterrent value of capital punishment; others see the need for the unconditional protection of human life, with 'eye for an eye' as inapplicable. For both communities, the constant ethical principle remains the same; its expression differs drastically in the two constituencies. The ethicist cannot migrate from one cultural group to another, without changing the focus of decision making on ethical behaviour.

The second group of theories, the deontological, looks to the duties and obligations of the decision makers. From where do those duties and obligations arise? They come from the cultural direction amongst humans towards order. They are based on the general response capacities and their particular expressions. We should remember that there are those who would want to say that these general response capacities are genetically determined or they are religiously ordained and no further argument for or against needs to be advanced. There is no evidence for this. The cultural direction is relativistic.

Virtue ethics, as one proponent has put it, declares as immoral what every right-minded person considers to be immoral. But who is the 'right-minded person'? This is an appeal to a society as a community of ideas that has a certain cultural foundation. In other words, it is an appeal to an accepted culture: common ways of thinking, acting, feeling and valuing. But this appeal is dependent on the particular expression adopted over time by the community. That is also a relative matter.

In short, the three main approaches to ethical reasoning, whose proponents would each claim some degree of objectivity for their theory, end up in a form of relativism once the inevitable cultural ambience is taken into consideration.

But this discussion has presumed that we are dealing with simple, homogeneous cultural groups. There are two other very relevant considerations to be taken into account when considering the ethical scenario.

One is religion and the other is multiculturalism linked with religious pluralism.

## Culture and religion

How can what has been said earlier about culture be applied to religion? Like secular culture generally, religion is a meaning-seeking activity and presents itself as an organised system of symbols. While we can catalogue the religious phenomenon by means of typology, religion is no different from other cultural systems.

Typologically, the symbols of religion can be catalogued mainly under the subsets of myth and ritual, but they also include beliefs, objects, natural phenomena, clothing and so forth.[13]

Religion, seen as religious culture, must be appreciated in its vital role of attaining a unique form of order, what Geertz called 'the general order of existence'[14] and Berger and Luckman called more simply 'reality'.[15] I prefer to use the terms 'ultimate order' and 'ultimacy', but intend to say much as they did.

What we have been discussing to this point could be called 'secular culture', which provides its adherents with everyday order; human beings depend on their secular symbol systems for everyday viability. Secular culture allows human beings to find order amid a chaos of common human experience, to explain historical events, to solve problems of identity.

However, there are certain points along the plane of human experience where chaos could reassert itself. Insuperable ignorance, the experience of suffering and the problem of evil (with the concomitant problem of cosmic injustice as demonstrated, for example, by the random devastation wrought by *tsunamis* in recent times) can threaten both an ordered, cultural world and the interpretability of human experience. Should there be the remotest indication that a secular culture is unable to cope with a significant human experience, for example a specific instance of death or dying, then severe anxiety results. In such a situation human beings face the dire inability to interpret their experience. There is no order.

At this point of the potential disintegration of a secular cultural world, there is an urgent need for religious culture. A 'religious culture' could include the living world religions, indigenous religions, syncretistic religion, nature religions as well

13 Robert Crotty, 'Towards Classifying Religious Phenomena' (1995) 8 *Australian Religion Studies Review* 34–41.

14 See generally Geertz, above n 2.

15 See Peter Berger and Thomas Luckman, *The Social Construction of Reality: A Treatise in the Sociology of Knowledge* (Penguin, 1971).

as philosophical systems such as Marxism, Humanism, Existentialism and so on. It could also include individually constructed personal religious systems. By means of these religious cultures, the religious person construes the world, others and self in terms of ultimacy, of ultimate order.

In keeping with what was said with regard to secular culture, I would now claim that all humans have the innate and genetically endowed capacity to construe in terms of ultimacy; cultural circumstances, whereby they gain access to one or other religious culture, activate the capacity in mature humans. All human persons who have reached a level of discretion and are not mentally handicapped to a significant degree should therefore be designated as 'religious persons', although the 'religion' of some of them might not be recognised as a conventional religion.

Although the two might be separable in theory, secular culture and religious culture are not distinct in real terms. Each affects the other and each is interconnected with the other. The division between the two is in the mind of the modern beholder. It would not be evident in indigenous societies or in ancient societies. In fact, the symbols of ultimate order and direction are shaped in a specific way within a particular secular culture. Alternatively, once it has been constructed, a religious culture then deeply affects the secular culture by its particular cultural logic.

Further, I understand ultimacy, the state of ultimate order and meaning that goes beyond everyday order, to be formulated in a religious culture by means of symbols; ultimacy is not postulated as an object *in se*, an autonomous reality. While the existence of a symbol of ultimacy could be and commonly is taken to infer a noumenal reality, such inference does not by any means prove its real and separate mode of existence;[16] ultimacy is noumenal. Any symbolisation of ultimacy is produced, as must be expected, within the historical and social context of a particular individual's cultural worldview. The symbol, once historically established, operates as a focus on ultimate order and takes on a seeming substantiality of its own.

If the cultural worldview employed by an individual postulates that this symbolic focus and the human group are widely separated, with a distinct gulf lying between them, then the focal symbol will have a separate, personal form, such as a particular and identifiable god or a pantheon of gods. By definition, these deities, such as Zeus or Allah, would be distinct from, and distant from, the group. If, on the other hand, the worldview postulates an intimate closeness between the focus and the human group, with easy access between them, then the symbolisation will take an impersonal form. An example is Brahman, the Hindu symbol of infinite being that encroaches on an individual's personal space and yet extends into infinity.

Religious cultural activity is about bridging the gulf or activating the intimate closeness between the individual and ultimate order and meaning by means of that focus.

The attainment of ultimate order is, of course, an ideal; there is no absolute guarantee that this ideal will be or has ever been achieved in reality. The human

16 Gerard Loughlin, 'Noumenon and Phenomenon' (1987) 23 *Religious Studies* 495–508.

person has a general response capacity for ultimate ordering and seeks instinctively to achieve it; every mature person seeks a form of liberating order and meaning not offered by secular culture.

Similarly, in secular culture, the human person has a biological need for sexual satisfaction. Culture determines how this need may be fulfilled in an ordered society. There is no guarantee that this determination will actually bring about perpetual satisfaction.

What has been proposed so far is that humans have a universal capacity to seek ultimate order, and that specific religions, in the broad sense of the word, offer them the ability to activate that capacity in culturally diverse ways by adopting a particular culturally constructed religious focus.

## Religious ethics

From this discussion on religion, religious ethics (as notionally distinct from secular ethics) must be viewed in the light of the human individual marshalling thinking, acting, feeling and valuing towards the accomplishment of this ultimate order. This ethical character of the devotee is one of the identifying features of a religious community.

The three approaches to ethical reasoning then need to be adapted. How are values apportioned to the consequences of human actions, when seen from a religious viewpoint? That may be an entirely different scenario when compared to secular culture since the consequences would be evaluated from the vantage point of religious myth, religious ritual, religious text or other phenomena of religion. Likewise, deontological theories would be primarily informed by religious duties and observances, derived from religious myth, beliefs, texts or other. Virtue ethics would rely on the identification of virtues necessary for human advancement, virtues which may be derived from religious sources, since 'human advancement' would now have an ultimate endpoint. Religious virtue ethics would often be imagined in a Founder or an elite believer.

In short, religious ethics are as relativistic as secular ethics. For example, Islamic ethics will be specifically different from Christian ethics because the two religions derive from an entirely different religious system.

The second and related issue relates to multiculturalism and religious pluralism.

## Multiculturalism and religious pluralism

The confrontation of secular ethics and a variety of religious ethics is not the only complication. As stated in the introduction, each geographical area in the modern world is more usually the site for more than one cultural cohabiting group. Each would presumably have its own secular culture; accordingly, each would have its own secular ethical system.

There are two attitudes, at diverse ends of a continuum, which become evident once such culturally diverse groups cohabit. One is ethnocentrism: the attitude that only one culture is valid for all human beings. Ethnocentrism is a natural reaction to enculturation; other cultures are considered to be misplaced, deviant, perhaps corrupt ('they wear confronting clothes; eat disgusting food; speak inarticulate languages'). At the opposite end of the continuum is some form of multiculturalism: a programme directed towards harmonious and unified cohabitation.

Multiculturalism maintains that there are many humanly constructed cultures, all of which presumably give adequate order and meaning to their constituencies and activate the general response capacities of these constituencies in variant ways; it maintains and encourages the preservation of a variety of cultures. It esteems and promotes the variant configurations of culturally different groups, including their different patterns of family structure, their languages and their ethical systems.

In a multicultural society, a variety of relationships between the dominant (frequently the majority) group and the minorities can exist. Minorities can be suppressed by the dominant group. But, if such a culturally diverse society is governed by a degree of voluntary consensus, rather than coercion, a set of shared values could be evolved that overarch the differences between various ethnic groups. Under such a cultural 'umbrella', ethnic groups may retain certain core values, such as a distinct language or family tradition, while adhering to other values included under the umbrella.

Hence, a Vietnamese living in Australia, where knowledge and facility in the use of English is a core value of the cultural umbrella, would learn English but also would be encouraged to retain Vietnamese; the Vietnamese would accept Australian democracy and avoid eating delicacies that disgust other groups. This would seem a laudable form of multiculturalism. Ethical diversity is not so straightforward. An Australian male aborigine whose culture allows him to be betrothed to and have sexual relations with a female child under 12 would be expected to defer to the core value of the cultural umbrella that defines a higher age for sexual access because of the value of sexual consent.

Such a multicultural society would share in a dynamic equilibrium between the overarching or shared values of a broad-based community, on the one hand, and its ethnic core values on the other. The dominant group in that community would exhibit its own set of values, many of which would percolate into the overarching framework. Such shared values within the umbrella should not be regarded, however, as the dominant group's own private domain, but as common to all in the society; if the dominant group did totally control the umbrella, the result would be assimilation not multiculturalism.

The opposite of assimilation is separatism, where the overarching framework is only vestigial and each ethnic group is encapsulated within its own value system. This is cultural apartheid. There would be little interaction between the different cultural groups. Much of the earlier official government policy dealing with Aboriginal Australians was based on this separatism.

Assimilation and separatism are both the result of, and the breeding ground for, ethnocentrism: the conviction that only one cultural system is valid. The eventual forestalling or destruction of a cultural umbrella, which remained open to the insertion of values other than those of the dominant group, is the blatant aim of ethnocentrism.

Beyond these assimilationist and separatist positions lies the vast area that is covered by the label of multiculturalism. This position involves some form of on-going interpenetration between the overarching or shared values of the broad community within the umbrella on the one hand, and the separate ethnic values of the constituent groups on the other.

Just as there are a variety of possible attitudes to secular culture, stretching along a continuum from ethnocentrism to multiculturalism, so there is an analogous continuum of attitudes towards religious culture. Three major points along the continuum can be isolated.

The first is exclusivism, similar to ethnocentrism, the attitude that one religious cultural system is valid and all others are invalid, even if they might be right-minded and sincere. Midway is inclusivism, the view that one religious system is certainly valid while certain other, but not all, systems share partially and imperfectly in that valid system. This is the position, formulated since Vatican II, of the Roman Catholic Church.

Thirdly, there is religious pluralism. It holds that all existing religious cultures are valid. They differ simply because they employ variant symbolisations of ultimate order, providing alternative foci, and so relate the individual to ultimate order by a different route. If then the one transcendent reality of ultimate order is differentially conceived, experienced and consequently achieved from within the many religious systems by a number of foci, then choice between one of these systems and another is simply a matter of prior enculturation, of later choice, even of serendipity.[17] *Convivienca* (the term used to describe the unique Spanish experience of religious harmony in the later Middle Ages) could always be maintained by a religious cultural umbrella and at various historical moments this has been achieved.

What has been said of secular and religious ethics now needs to be modified by the role of law in society.

## Ethics and the law

Ethics and the law are not necessarily coextensive in a society. Long ago, John Stuart Mill maintained that the State cannot enact laws forbidding behaviour simply because that behaviour was considered to be immoral or religiously immoral. This is clear enough. So, ethics and law cannot be coextensive. In 1954, the Wolfenden Report, following this liberal line of thought, considered how British law should regard prostitution and homosexuality. It stated that the law exists:

> to preserve public order and decency, to protect the citizen from what is offensive or injurious, and to provide sufficient safeguards against exploitation or corruption of others, particularly those who are specially vulnerable

17 See, eg, John Hick, *An Interpretation of Religion* (Macmillan, 1989).

> because they are young, weak in body or mind, inexperienced, or in a state of special physical, official or economic dependence.[18]

If behaviour does not involve public disorder or offence to others, does not exploit vulnerable people, then the law has no call to legislate against such behaviour. To emphasise further the difference between ethics and the law, it can be pointed out that in order to preserve order in society, not only are certain actions forbidden because they are immoral (*prohibitum quia malum*) but the law can forbid actions which are wrong only because they are forbidden (*malum quia prohibitum*). The law forbids and punishes both murder and driving down the wrong side of the road. Hence, there can be a distance between the law and ethics.[19]

In the terminology proposed above, I would recognise the role of law as protecting the public order of a cultural group or of a multicultural society; its purpose, in other words, is to maintain the cultural umbrella.

## Conclusion on ethical reasoning

Here we are at the hub of the central ethical question. We rarely have, in the modern world, a homogeneously cultural society. First, we have secular cultures and religious cultures and they do not always overlap. Also, we usually have some form of multiculturalism and of religious pluralism in the broad sense of competing systems, the blunt recognition that there are a number of secular ethical systems and religious ethical systems.

There are various stances thereafter along the continuum from ethnocentrism/exclusivism to multiculturalism/religious pluralism that can be adopted. That means that, as far as ethics are concerned, there will be variety and relativity. That variety will be controlled or not by the cultural umbrella. Just as values are taken up into the umbrella, so too ethical reasoning must take account of the umbrella. That is where secular ethics, as a system of principles, is lodged – not in the individual culture but in the umbrella.

We return to the four research questions enunciated at the onset:

- Where are the boundaries between religion, ethics and the law of the land? Religion provides a supplementary cultural system, including ethics, to the adherent. A variety of secular ethics and religious ethics requires the intervention of the law to protect the common umbrella required by this particular delineation of human society.

18 Wolfenden Committee, *The Wolfenden Report: Report of the Committee on Homosexual Offences and Prostitution* (Stein and Day, 1963) 23f.

19 While this liberal position is opposed to legal moralism, there is still obviously room for debate. Certainly, most Muslim states would debate against it. '*Sharia* law' is seen by most Muslims as rightly embodying all the ethical stances of the *sharia*.

- How can competing systems of secular ethics be reconciled? By recourse to an overarching system of cultural values, an umbrella.
- How can competing systems of religious ethics be reconciled? In the same way, even if it is more difficult to achieve.
- How can competing systems of religious ethics and secular ethics be reconciled? Once more, by the umbrella.

It was Aristotle who told us that in the ethical field we must be content if we attain as high a degree of certainty as the matter of it admits.[20] This paper is endeavouring to show just that. It puts forward a case for moderate relativism as the best way to understand ethical reasoning, but it also makes the case that achieving ethical reasoning can never be homogenous for all.

## References

Aristotle, *The Ethics of Aristotle: the Nichomachean Ethics Translated* (J Thomson, trans, Penguin, 1953)

Berger, Peter and Thomas Luckman, *The Social Construction of Reality: A Treatise in the Sociology of Knowledge* (Penguin, 1971)

Churchland, Patricia, Touching *a Nerve: Our Brains, Our Selves* (W W Norton, 2013)

Crotty, Robert, 'Towards Classifying Religious Phenomena' (1995) 8 *Australian Religion Studies Review* 34

Geertz, Clifford, 'Distinguished lecture: anti-relativism' (1984) 86 *American Anthropologist* 263

Geertz, Clifford, *The Interpretation of Cultures* (Basic Books, 1973)

Hanson, F Allan, 'Does God have a body? Truth, reality and cultural relativism' (1979) 14 *Man New Series* 515

Harari, Yuval Noah, *Sapiens: A Brief History of Humankind* (Harvill Secker, 2014)

Hick, John, *An Interpretation of Religion* (Macmillan, 1989)

Kroeber, Alfred (ed), *Anthropology Today* (University of Chicago Press, 1953)

Loughlin, Gerard, 'Noumenon and Phenomenon' (1987) 23 *Religious Studies* 495

Pinker, Steven, *The Language Instinct* (Penguin, 1994)

Spindler, George (ed), *The Making of Psychological Anthropology* (University of California Press, 1978)

Wolfenden Committee, *The Wolfenden Report: Report of the Committee on Homosexual Offences and Prostitution* (Stein and Day, 1963)

20 Aristotle, *The Ethics of Aristotle: the Nichomachean Ethics Translated* (J Thomson, trans, Penguin, 1953) 15.

# 13 *Imago* and *imitatio*

## Perfection of the individual and society in Maimonides' theory of religious law

*Raphael Dascalu*

'Thus do you learn that the laws of the Torah are not vengeance upon the world, but rather compassion, mercy, and peace upon the world'.[1]

## Introduction

In the opening lines of Moses Cordovero's (1522–1570) popular kabbalistic ethical manual, *Tomer Deborah* (*The Date Palm of Deborah*), the author writes as follows:

> A person should imitate the Creator, in order to enter into the secret of the supernal form (*ha-tzurah ha-ʿelyonah*): Image and Likeness (*tzelem u-demut*; cf Gen. 1:26). For if one is similar in body, but not in actions, one renders the form untruthful (*harei hu makhzib ha-tzurah*), and they will say: 'Nice form, ugly deeds.' For actions are the fundamental quality of the supernal Image and Likeness. So what does it achieve if one is like the supernal form in terms of the likeness of the structure of one's limbs, when one is unlike the Creator in one's actions?[2]

Here, Cordovero draws upon the concept of *imitatio dei* in order to illuminate what he understands to be the deeper sense of the biblical concept of *imago dei*. That is to say that not only are human beings created in the image of God in terms of their physical form and configuration in some sense, but the imperative to live godly lives in imitation of the Creator actually constitutes a more profound stratum of human embodiment of the Divine. The fullest expression of the Divine Image is a human being whose external, physical visage is in harmony with her

1 Maimonides, *Mishneh Torah*, Laws of the Sabbath, 2:3.

2 See Nisan Vaksman (ed), *Tomer Deborah* (Shoshanim, 1960) 3. Translations are mine unless otherwise indicated, with the exception of citations from Maimonides' *Guide*, for which I have followed the convention in Maimonidean studies and utilised Shlomo Pines (trans), *The Guide of the Perplexed* (University of Chicago Press, 1963). In citations from that work, italics indicate verses and terminology in Hebrew or Aramaic.

disposition and deeds. Thus, for Cordovero, *imitatio dei* is simply the deepest realisation of *imago dei.*

This understanding of *imago dei*, *imitatio dei*, and the relationship between those concepts is profoundly different from that of Moses Maimonides' (1138–1204). Both ideas feature prominently in his works. The opening chapters of his philosophical *magnum opus The Guide of the Perplexed*[3] are a lexicon of philosophical exegesis. Here, the problem of *imago dei* as formulated in Genesis 1:26–27 is accorded a distinguished place: it is the subject of the first chapter of the first part of the book. The idea that one must live a life that mirrors the activity of the Divine as described in Scripture is also formulated in various places in Maimonides' works. However, while many other writers before and after Maimonides' lifetime have employed the concept of *imitatio dei* to interpret the biblical account of the creation of human beings in the Divine Image, Maimonides made a sharp distinction between them. This is not to say that the concepts are not related: they converge when we consider Maimonides' teleology of the commandments (*mitzvot*) as a means of attaining all modes of human perfection. As a whole, *imago dei* and *imitatio dei* represent aspects of the full perfection of the human being as a rational, moral, and political being.

## *Imago dei* in Maimonides

Maimonides' conception of human perfection has been the subject of much scholarly discussion.[4] From numerous passages in Maimonides' writings it is clear that the cultivation of ethical virtue is a prerequisite for the acquisition of intellectual virtues,[5] that the ultimate stage of the individual's intellectual development entails

3 See Moses Maimonides, *The Guide of the Perplexed* (University of Chicago Press, Vol I – Vol II, 1963). Hereinafter, referred to as '*Guide*'.

4 For an overview of the major approaches, see Menachem Kellner, *Maimonides on Human Perfection* (Scholars Press, 1990) 1–11. See also Howard Kreisel, *Maimonides' Political Thought: Studies in Ethics, Law, and the Human Ideal* (State University of New York Press, 1999). The underlying Greek term upon which this technical use of the Arabic *kamāl* (perfection) is based is *entelecheia*, which carries a similar connotation of 'wholeness, completion.' The term should not be understood in an absolute sense, as there are many degrees to which such perfection may be attained; Cf see Pines, above n 2, 8. According to Maimonides, Moses, who achieved the highest degree of perfection available to humans, remained morally flawed – see 'Eight Chapters', in Raymond Weiss and Charles Butterworth (eds), *Ethical Writings of Maimonides* (Dover Publications, 1975) 73–4. In fact, in order to achieve this highest level of intellectual perfection, *complete* moral perfection is not necessary; indeed, the latter appears to be unattainable (ibid 73, 81).

5 In *Guide* I.34, Maimonides writes as follows: 'it has been explained, or rather demonstrated, that the moral virtues are a preparation for the rational virtues, it being impossible to achieve true, rational acts – I mean perfect rationality – unless it be by a man thoroughly trained with respect to his morals and endowed with the qualities of tranquility and quiet. . . . [i]t is accordingly indubitable that preparatory moral training should be carried out before beginning with this science [ie metaphysics], so that a man should be in a state of extreme uprightness and perfection' in Pines, above n 2, 76–7.

some kind of communion with the Active Intellect,[6] and that one may attain such a degree of perfection that one may then become instrumental in perfecting others.[7] Like many Islamicate Peripatetics,[8] Maimonides believed that the attainment of some degree of intellectual perfection is necessary in order to enable the intellectual soul to survive the death of the body.[9] More importantly for the present discussion, the individual's attainment of intellectual perfection represents the highest realisation of human nature, and the full expression of *imago dei*.[10]

This conception of *imago dei* as expressive of some property of the human intellect has its background in several streams of thought that merged in Maimonides' own exegetical project.[11] First, and most obviously, there is the biblical account of the human being as an image of the Divine,[12] and its reception in rabbinic thought – often in explicitly imagistic terms.[13] Then there is the Platonic

6 Maimonides, *Guide* II:36 in Pines, above n 2, 369. According to medieval Peripatetic cosmology, the Active Intellect is the lowest of ten intellects that emanate from the Divine, and it governs the sublunary realm. For the Active Intellect as that which leads the human intellect from potentiality to actuality, see Herbert Davidson, *Alfarabi, Avicenna, and Averroes, on Intellect* (Oxford University Press, 1992) 4. Maimonides identified the emanated intellects, including the Active Intellect (along with the other emanated intellects), as angels; see Maimonides, *Mishneh Torah*, Laws of the Foundations of the Torah, 2:3–8. In this he followed Ibn Sina; see Seyyed Hossein Nasr, *An Introduction to Islamic Cosmological Doctrines* (State University of New York Press, 1993) 238.

7 See discussion below.

8 I prefer the term 'Peripatetic' to 'Aristotelian' for two major reasons: (1) It is less foreign to the Arabic philosophical tradition, where the equivalent term (*al-mashshā'ūn*) is used to describe the intellectual tradition that includes Alfarabi, Ibn Sina (Avicenna), Ibn Bajja (Avempace), and Ibn Rushd (Averroës); and (2) the term 'Aristotelian' sets up a misleading dichotomy between Aristotelianism on the one hand and Platonism/Neoplatonism on the other. In fact, Platonic and Neoplatonic elements were quite central to this tradition. As it was put by Herbert Davidson: 'The universe envisioned by Alfarabi is fashioned of Aristotelian bricks and of mortar borrowed from Neoplatonic philosophy', see Davidson, above n 6, 44.

9 See Menachem Kellner, *Maimonides on Human Perfection* (Scholars Press, 1990) 1–5. Cf also Davidson, above n 6, 203; Sarah Stroumsa, *Maimonides in His World: Portrait of a Mediterranean Thinker* (Princeton University Press, 2009) 162, 181.

10 Maimonides, *Guide*, I:1 in Pines, above n 2, 21–3. On intellectual perfection as the *telos* of human existence, see *Guide*, III:27 in Pines, above n 2, 511, and *Guide* III.54, 635.

11 Although Maimonides never wrote biblical commentaries per se, he has been increasingly studied as a serious exegete. For important studies in this vein, see Sara Klein-Braslavy, *Maimonides as a Biblical Interpreter* (Academic Studies Press, 2011); Mordechai Z Cohen, *Three Approaches to Biblical Metaphor: From Abraham Ibn Ezra and Maimonides to David Kimhi* (Brill, 2003); Mordechai Z Cohen, *Opening the Gates of Interpretation: Maimonides' Biblical Hermeneutics in Light of His Geonic-Andalusian Heritage and Muslim Milieu* (Brill, 2011).

12 For which, see Genesis 1:26–27, 5:1–2, 9:6. For imagistic understandings of these passages, see Benjamin D Sommer, *The Bodies of God and the World of Ancient Israel* (Cambridge University Press, 2009), 69–70. See also Esther J Hamori, *'When Gods Were Men': The Embodied God in Biblical and Near Eastern Literature* (De Gruyter, 2008).

13 For a comprehensive study of the concept in classical rabbinic Judaism, see Yair Lorberbaum, *In God's Image: Myth, Theology, and Law in Classical Judaism* (Cambridge University Press,

conception of the human soul as sharing a kinship (*sungeneia*) with the gods, a notion that was enthusiastically embraced by the Stoics.[14] A similar understanding is echoed in rabbinic literature,[15] and brought into full and explicit conversation with the biblical narrative by medieval exegetes such as Abraham Ibn Ezra (d 1164), who asserted that human beings may only be considered to be 'in the Divine Image' insofar as 'the supernal soul of the human being [*nishmat ha-adam ha-'elyonah*]' shares something of the divine nature.[16]

Like Ibn Ezra, Maimonides adopts a non-imagistic interpretation of Genesis 1:26–27. However, he formulated his understanding in distinctly Aristotelian terms: since the human intellect is an entelechy of the organism, rather than an emanated entity, the divine image and likeness (*tzelem* and *demut*) consist of the human ability to attain true intellectual insight.[17] Thus, according to Maimonides, one attains the fullest expression of *imago dei* upon achieving intellectual perfection.

## *Imitatio dei* as ethical, social, and political activity

If Maimonides' understanding of *imago dei* is focused on individual intellectual realisation, his understanding of *imitatio dei* is deeply enmeshed in the ethical and political aspects of human life. To some degree, Maimonides' owes his understanding of this conception to earlier non-imagistic understandings of Genesis that emphasise human social and political activity as the full realisation of *imago dei*. Thus, some classical rabbinic sources locate the full expression of *imago dei* in the embodiment of divine compassion,[18] while for Saadia Gaon (d 942) *imago dei* signifies the establishment of human rulership over the natural world.[19] However,

---

2015). For a distinctly imagistic understanding of *imago dei* in rabbinic thought see Menahem Kister (ed), *Avoth de-Rabbi Nathan: Solomon Schechter Edition*, version B (Macmillan, 2007) Ch 30, 66.

14 See John R Lenz, 'Deification of the Philosopher in Classical Greece,' in Michael J Christensen and Jeffrey A Wittung (eds), *Partakers of the Divine Nature: The History and Development of Deification in the Christian Traditions* (Fairleigh Dickinson University Press/ Associated University Presses, 2007) 59; Guy G Stroumsa, *The End of Sacrifice: Religious Transformations in Late Antiquity* (The University of Chicago Press, 2009) 12.

15 Cf Babylonian Talmud, Tractate Berakhot, 10a.

16 Namely, immortality and incorporeality; see Ibn Ezra's commentary to Genesis 1:26.

17 Maimonides, *Guide* I.1 in Pines, above n 2, 21–23.

18 Mekhilta de-Rabbi Yishma'el – Tractate *Shirta*, Parashah 3: 'Abba Shaul says: Be like Him {Heb. *edmeh lo*; etymologically related to the *demut* [likeness] of Genesis 1:26 – RD}. Just as He is gracious, you be gracious; just as He is compassionate, you be compassionate.' For text and translation, see Jacob Z Lauterbach (ed), *Mekhilta de-Rabbi Ishmael* (The Jewish Publication Society, 2nd ed, 2004), vol 1, 185, lines 43–4 and variants. Cf parallel in Babylonian Talmud, Tractate Shabbat 133b, where the text reads *heve domeh lo* ('be like him').

19 Saadia Gaon (d 942), *Tafsīr* (Arabic translation) to Gen. 1:26: 'Let us make a human being in our image [and] in our likeness [insofar as that human is] appointed as an overlord [*musallaṭan*]'. For the Judeo-Arabic text, see J Derenbourg (ed), *Oeuvres Complétes de R Saadia ben Iosef al-Fayyoûmî* (E Leroux, 1893), vol 1, 6. Cf the Qur'ān's account of the

Maimonides' discomfort with anthropomorphism,[20] combined with a desire for a greater degree of conceptual clarity,[21] may have been the primary motivators behind his narrower definition of *imago dei* and his sharper distinction between that concept on the one hand, and *imitatio* on the other hand.

There are two broad contexts in which Maimonides articulates his conception of *imitatio dei*. The first is in an ethical context. Maimonides grounds his Aristotelian ethics of following the 'golden mean' in Deuteronomy 28:9 (*and walk in His ways*).[22] In the *Mishneh torah*, he writes as follows:

> One who is particularly careful in this matter and distances himself from the mean disposition in one direction is called 'pious' [*ḥasid*]. How so? One who distances himself from arrogance to the opposite extreme, so that he is very lowly in spirit, is called 'pious', and this is the attribute of 'piety' [*ḥasidut*]. If one moves only to the mean, becoming [moderately] humble, he is called 'wise' [*ḥakham*], and this is the attribute of 'wisdom' [*ḥokhmah*]. And this is true of all of the other dispositions. The pious ones of old [*ḥasidim ha-rishonim*] would guide their dispositions towards the extremes – they would guide one disposition towards one extreme and another towards the other extreme. But this is more than the law requires of us.[23] We are commanded to follow the middle ways [*ba-derakhim ha-ellu ha-benonim*], these being the good and upright ways, as it is said, *and walk in His ways.*
>
> (Deut 28:9).

creation of Adam as the appointment of a ruler representative of God (*khalīfa*; in *Sūrat al-baqara* [2], 30).

20 For which see Maimonides, *Guide* I:1. See also Kenneth Seeskin, 'Metaphysics and Its Transcendence', in Kenneth Seeskin (ed), *The Cambridge Companion to Maimonides* (Cambridge University Press, 2005) 82–104.

21 It is notable that the Bible's articulation of *imago dei* is descriptive, while the biblical exhortation to 'walk in [the Lord's] ways' (Deut 28:9 and elsewhere – discussed below) is clearly prescriptive. Still, the creation of humans in the Divine Image certainly carries normative implications, for the most obvious of which, see Genesis 9:6; see also Yair Lorberbaum, *In God's Image: Myth, Theology and Law in Classical Judaism* (Cambridge University Press, 2015). There is also a prescriptive element in Maimonides' understanding of *imago dei* insofar as its fullest realisation *in actu* remains to be achieved by the individual.

22 Cf Maimonides' enumeration of the commandments in his introduction to the *Mishneh Torah*, positive commandment 8. Maimonides' interpretation of the verse appears to be based on a passage in *Tanna de-be eliyahu*: '*and walk in His ways* (Deut 28:9) – in the ways of Heaven [ie in the ways of God]. Just as [it is in] the ways of Heaven [to be] compassionate and merciful to the wicked and receive them through repentance, so shall you be merciful to one another.' See Meir Ish-Shalom (ed), *Seder eliyahu rabbah ve-seder eliyahu zuṭa ha-muba'im be-shem tanna de-be eliyahu* (Achiasaf, 1902) 135.

23 Hebrew: *lifnim mi-shurat ha-din* (lit. 'within the boundary of the law'). For a discussion of this concept, see Shubert Spero, *Morality, Halakha, and the Jewish Tradition* (Ktav Publishing House/Yeshiva University Press, 1983) 51, 167. For Maimonides on this concept, see also 173.

> And so they learned concerning the explanation of this commandment:[24] Just as He is called Gracious, you be gracious; just as He is called Compassionate, you be compassionate; just as He is called Holy, you be holy. And in this fashion did the prophets apply the various epithets to God: Slow to Anger, Abundant in Kindness, Righteous and Upright, Perfect, Mighty and Strong, and so on – in order to instruct [us] that these are good and upright ways and that one must conduct oneself in them, and imitate these [paths] to the greatest of one's ability.
>
> (Laws of Dispositions 1:5–6).

Here, Maimonides is careful to avoid interpreting biblical epithets for the Divine in anthropomorphic or anthropopathic terms. The purpose of descriptive prophetic discourse is not to *describe God* – a project that Maimonides utterly rejects[25] – but to inform human behaviour. In this sense, biblical accounts concerning divine attributes might best be understood in consequentialist terms: they lead human beings to cultivate positive dispositions and to live in moderation. Rather than being mere description, the biblical accounts of divine attributes generally carry normative value for Maimonides, expressed in this context in the ethical cultivation of the individual.[26]

The second, related context in which Maimonides develops his conception of *imitatio dei* is in his discussions of wise governance. In *Guide* III:54, he rejects the position that divine providence does not extend to the sublunar world, before writing as follows:

> Rather is it as has been made clear to us by the Master of those who know:[27] *That the earth is the Lord's.* (Ex 9:29) He means to say that His providence also extends over the earth in the way that corresponds to what the latter is, just as His providence extends over the heavens in the way that corresponds to what they are. This is what he says: *That I am the Lord who exercise long-kindness, judgment, and righteousness, in the earth.* (Jer 9:23) Then he completes the notion by saying: *For in these things I delight, saith the Lord.* (Jer 9:23). He means that it is My purpose that there should come from you *loving-kindness, righteousness, and judgment in the earth* in the way that we have explained with regard to the *thirteen attributes*:[28] namely, that the purpose

24 Ie the commandment mentioned in the previous clause (*halakhah*).

25 For example, see *Mishneh Torah*, Laws of the Foundations of the Torah, 1:5–12; *Guide* I.54–60 (Pines, above n 2, 123–43).

26 See *Guide* I.54 (Pines, above n 2, 123–8). This is one of two functions that such descriptions perform. The other is the elimination of even more problematic understandings of the Divine – cf *Guide* I.47 (104–6).

27 Arabic: *sayyid al-ʿālimīn*; ie Moses. Cf Maimonides, *Guide* I.54 in Pines, above n 2, 123 (citation added).

28 This is the traditional rabbinic name for the divine epithets listed in Exodus 34:6–7. On them, see Maimonides, *Guide* I.54 in Pines, above n 2, 124–8 (citation added).

> should be assimilation to them [*al-tashabbuh bi-hā*] and that this should be our way of life. Thus the end that he sets forth in this *verse* may be stated as follows: It is clear that the perfection of man that may truly be gloried in is the one acquired by him who has achieved, in a measure corresponding to his capacity, apprehension of Him, may He be exalted, and who knows His providence extending over His creatures as manifested in the act of bringing them into being and in their governance as it is [*fī ījādihā wa-tadbīrihā kayfa huwa*]. The way of life of such an individual, after he has achieved this apprehension, will always have in view *loving-kindness, righteousness, and judgment*, through assimilation to His actions [*tashabbuhan bi-afʿālihi*], may He be exalted, just as we have explained several times in this Treatise.[29]

This passage provides a bridge between the ethical and political aspects of *imitatio dei*. Twice in this passage, Maimonides mentions 'assimilation' (*tashabbuh*) to the divine attributes. This very term is used in Maimonides discussion of the eighth commandment in his *Sefer ha-mitzvot* (*Book of Commandments*): 'That which we were commanded, concerning assimilation [or likening ourselves] to him according to our ability [*alladhī umirnā bi-ʾl-tashabbuh bihi bi-ḥasab ṭāqatinā*].'[30] The terminology of *tashabbuh* – imitating, making oneself alike something or someone – is as explicit a formulation of the concept of *imitatio* as can be, and Maimonides once again grounds this commandment in Deuteronomy 28:9 (as well as a similar formulation from Exodus 11:22): *And walk in his ways*. As we have seen, in the *Mishneh torah* Maimonides applies this verse to the cultivation of desirable dispositions (ie ethics). However, in the passage cited above, there is a distinctly political element: the Arabic term *tadbīr*, used in this passage, has unmistakable political implications.[31] Human beings thus become a conduit for divine providence, and should engage in *governance* through their assimilation to the divine attributes: Compassionately and justly. Full 'assimilation' or 'likening of oneself' to the Divine entails an outward engagement, the guidance of one's society towards its greatest perfection.

The background to Maimonides' conception of wise governance – or, indeed, any activity directed at guiding others or securing their welfare – lies once again in his Peripatetic view of human perfection. According to this view, although there are modes of perfection that pertain only to the individual, there are others that allow one individual to affect another, depending on the degree of intellectual

29 Pines, above n 2, 637. Arabic in Munk, *Dalālat al-ḥāʾirīn*, 470 line 24–471 line 7 (citations added) (italics in original).

30 Joseph Qafih (ed), *Sefer ha-mitzvot le-rabbenu mosheh ben maymon* (Mossad Harav Kook, 1971) 62.

31 Cf The discussions of 'governance of the city (*tadbīr al-madīna*), and governance of the great nation or the nations (*tadbīr al-umma al-kabīra aw al-umam*)'. English in Israel Efros (ed), *Maimonides' Treatise on Logic (Maḳāla fi-ṣināʿat al-manṭiḳ): The Original Arabic and Three Hebrew Translations* (American Academy for Jewish Research, 1938) 62–4.

inspiration from above.[32] One who attains this higher degree of perfection may guide others towards their own perfection through instruction:

> It is fitting that your attention be aroused to the nature of that which exists in the divine overflow coming toward us, through which we have intellectual cognition and through which there is a difference of rank between our intellects. For sometimes something comes from it to a certain individual, the measure of that something being such that it renders him perfect, but has no other effect. Sometimes, on the other hand, the measure of what comes to the individual overflows from rendering him perfect toward rendering others perfect. This is what happens to all things: some of them achieve perfection to an extent that enables them to govern others, while others achieve perfection only in a measure that allows them to be governed by others, as we have explained [*minhā mā ḥaṣala lahu al-kamāl mā yudabbiru bihi ghayrahu wa-minhā mā lam yaḥṣal lahu min al-kamāl illā qadr yakūnu mudabbaran bi-ghayrihi kamā bayyannā*] . . .
>
> [i]t has already become clear to you that, were it not for this additional perfection, sciences would not be set forth in books and prophets would not call upon the people to obtain knowledge of the truth.[33]

According to this passage, all true guidance of others towards human perfection is the product of an individual's surplus in a particular kind of perfection.[34] True prophetic and philosophical instruction is necessarily the product of such a degree of perfection. Indeed, Maimonides is not unique in portraying the pursuit of the welfare of others (including wise instruction and governance) in one's society in terms of *imitatio dei* – in this, he echoes earlier medieval Peripatetic traditions.[35]

32 *Guide*, II:37 in Pines, above n 2, 373–4; Avraham Melamed, 'Ha-Rambam 'al ha-ofi ha-medini shel ha-adam – tzerakhim u-meḥuyyabut,' in Moshe Idel, Devora Dimant and Shalom Rosenberg (eds), *Tribute to Sara: Studies in Jewish Philosophy and Kabbala presented to Professor Sara O Heller Wilensky* (The Magnes Press, 1994) 327–8.

33 Pines, above n 2, 373–4, 375; Munk, *Dalālat al-ḥā'irīn*, 264 line 3–265 line 8.

34 Melamed in Idel, Dimant and Rosenberg, above n 32, 327–8.

35 Haim (Howard) Kreisel, 'Maimonides' Political Philosophy', in Seeskin, above n 20, 195, 197, 208; Haim (Howard) Kreisel, *Maimonides' Political Thought* (State University of New York Press, 1999) 125–58; Abraham Melamed, *The Philosopher-King in Medieval and Renaissance Jewish Political Thought* (State University of New York Press, 2003) 35–40, 48–49; and cf Menachem Kellner, above n 4, 8. Cf also the *Chapters on Felicity*, spuriously attributed to Maimonides, in which the author states: 'Therefore, the individual who has attained perfection must perfect others, and emanate upon humans that which God has emanated upon him'. For the Judeo-Arabic and Hebrew of the passage, see H S Davidowitz and D H Baneth (eds), *Peraqim ba-hatzlaḥah* (Mekize Nirdamim, 1939) 10. For the work's spurious attribution to Maimonides, see Herbert A Davidson, *Moses Maimonides: The Man and his Works* (Oxford University Press, 2005) 309; Itzhak Shailat, *Letters and Essays of Moses Maimonides* (Shailat Publishing – Ma'aleh Adumim, 1995 AM) Vol 2, Appendix B, 696–7.

Thus, according to Maimonides, we can speak of the embodiment of desirable dispositions and the pursuit of the welfare of others as *imitatio dei*. Such activity entails the imitation of divine behaviour as described in the Hebrew Bible and rabbinic tradition. Furthermore, human political activity in these modes mirrors – and is an extension of – the deity's governance of the world.[36]

## Maimonides' conception of divine law: prophetic legislation versus imitative jurisprudence

Maimonides held the Torah to be the product of Moses' unique prophecy. He understood the Torah of Moses to be the most extensive work of divinely inspired legislation ever produced, and to be immutable; yet no law is truly comprehensive – legislators and jurists must interpret and apply the law in ever-changing circumstances.[37] Maimonides' conception of prophetic legislation versus its interpretation and application appears to be rooted in Alfarabi's typology of the sciences. According to Alfarabi, jurisprudence (*fiqh*) is fundamentally an imitative art: Jurists (*fuqahā'*, sing *faqīh*) employ formal legal parameters in order to apply the existing law to new situations, and in order to create laws as unforeseen situations arise:

> The art of jurisprudence [*ṣināʿat al-fiqh*] is that by which a human being is able to infer, from the things the lawgiver [*wāḍiʿ al-sharīʿa*] declared specifically and determinately, the determination of each of the things he did not specifically declare.[38]

According to Alfarabi, the discipline of jurisprudence does not constitute philosophical knowledge at all; rather, it is the application of norms produced through somebody else's insight, or a formal method of deduction based in that person's insight.[39] Alfarabi considers this art to contain two distinct parts: one dealing with

36 Cf Haim (Howard) Kreisel, 'Maimonides' Political Philosophy' in Seeskin, above n 20, 195, 208; Haim (Howard) Kreisel, *Maimonides' Political Thought* (State University of New York Press, 1999) 125–58; Melamed, *The Philosopher-King in Medieval and Renaissance Jewish Political Thought*, above n 35, 35–40, 48–9; and cf Kellner, above n 4, 8. For the homology between the human organism and the cosmos, and for the human mind occupying the role of the deity in this scheme, see Maimonides, *Guide* I.72 in Pines, above n 2, 184, 190–1.

37 Cf Kreisel, above n 4, 16–23, 80–2.

38 Charles Butterworth, 'Enumeration of the Sciences' in Charles Butterworth (ed), *Alfarabi: The Political Writings ('Selected Aphorisms' and Other Texts)* (Charles Butterworth, trans, Cornell University Press, 2001), 80, section 4; Arabic text in Osman Amine, *Enumeration of the Sciences* (Alfarabi, 1968) 130.

39 However, Alfarabi's understanding of jurisprudence is not purely mechanistic. Indeed, the jurist must have a comprehensive knowledge of the law, combined with an understanding of human society and its customs, and the original languages of the legal sources. See Butterworth, above n 38, 99–101.

actions and one dealing with opinions.[40] It must be stressed, however, that the *originator* of the law ('the lawgiver' – *wāḍiʿ al-nawāmis* or *wāḍiʿ al-sharīʿa*)[41] is a truly wise figure, as are the lesser prophets who continually exhort the population to adhere to the law.[42] It is true knowledge (or even prophecy, the highest knowledge possible for human beings) that *produces* the law, and indeed enables the foundation of the *polis*,[43] but deriving legal conclusions on the basis of that original law remains an imitative art.[44]

For Alfarabi, there exists a boundary between 'religion' and philosophy. Religion (*milla*, *dīn* and *sharī'a*)[45] is essentially an imitative representation of philosophical truth that may be taught to those who have not pursued or cannot pursue knowledge via demonstration.[46] Jurisprudence based on revealed law is a derivative art,

40 Cf Butterworth, above n 38, 80, section 4.

41 For the exclusive use of the latter term in the *Book of Religion*, see Butterworth, above n 38, 96, fn 9.

42 See Howard Kreisel, 'Maimonides on Divine Religion', in Jay M Harris (ed), *Maimonides after 800 Years: Essays on Maimonides and His Influence* (Harvard University Press, 2007) 157. In 'The Political Regime', Alfarabi makes a distinction between a first ruler (*ra'īs awwal*) and a secondary ruler (*ra'īs thāni*) – see Arabic in Fauzi M Najjar, *Al-Fārābī's The Political Regime (Al-Siyāsa Al-Madaniyya also Known as the Treatise on the Principles of Beings)* (Imprimerie Catholique, Beyrouth, 1964) 79. This distinction, particularly when compared with Alfarabi's use of this terminology in the *Book of Religion* corresponds closely with the Ismaili distinction between the *rasūl* (messenger, apostle; also known as the *nāṭiq*, or speaker) and the *nabi* (prophet; also known as the *waṣī*, or deputy): The former is the bearer of a founding revelation, while the latter are identified with all lesser prophets and the Imams who rule based on the system revealed by the *rasūl/nāṭiq* – for the first ruler (*ra'īs awwal*) as the founder of a polity and its norms, see Alfarabi, 'Book of Religion' in Charles Butterworth (ed), *Alfarabi: The Political Writings ('Selected Aphorisms' and Other Texts)* (Cornell University Press, 2001) 93, section 1, 98–9, section 7; for the Ismaili distinction, see Paul Walker, *Early Philosophical Shiism: The Ismaili Neoplatonism of Abu Yaʿqub al-Sijistani* (Cambridge University Press, 1993) 28–9. In 'The Attainment of Happiness', Alfarabi equates the founder-legislator, philosopher, statesman and Imam, claiming that they represent a single idea – see 'Attainment of Happiness' in Muhsin Madhi (ed), *Philosophy of Plato and Aristotle, Alfarabi: Philosophy of Plato and Aristotle* (Cornell University Press, 2001) 47, section 58; although different ranks may apply within these categories.

43 Muhsin Mahdi, *Alfarabi and the Foundations of Islamic Political Philosophy* (University of Chicago Press, 2001) 131–9.

44 In light of this discussion, we might offer an alternative translation for Maimonides' description of the jurists as *wa-yatafaqqahūn fī aʿmāl al-ʿibādāt* (Maimonides, *Guide* III.51; Munk, *Dalālat al-ḥā'irīn*, 22). Pines translates: 'and study the law concerning the practices of divine service', Pines, above n 2, 619. Based on the Alfarabian background to Maimonides' conception of the art of *fiqh*, and his discussion of Talmud in the *Mishneh Torah* (Laws of Torah Study, 1:12), I would suggest the following translation: 'and extrapolate concerning acts of [divine] service by means of the juristic art.' This is admittedly less elegant, but I believe that it is more accurate.

45 See Alfarabi, 'Book of Religion' in Butterworth, above n 42, 96, section 4. Here it is also suggested that *sunna* refers only to the practical component of *fiqh* and is thus a more limited term.

46 Ibid 94–7, sections 2–5, particularly section 4. In 'The Opinions of the Virtuous City', Alfarabi discusses the place of religion in the virtuous city as follows: 'The philosophers

based on the inspired legislation of the original lawgiver (of which there may be many throughout history as changing circumstance requires) – it is not knowledge proper (*ʿilm*). According to Alfarabi, the scope of 'religion' ends where true philosophical insight begins. It is at the point that one advances beyond accepting opinions and prescribed practices on the authority of tradition that knowledge properly begins, and one enters into the realm of both practical and theoretical philosophy.[47]

In *Guide* III.51, Maimonides appears to adopt Alfarabi's typology of the sciences, according to which the art of jurisprudence does not demand true philosophical insight.[48] However, as is well known, the esoteric sciences of *maʿaseh bereshit* ('The Account of the Creation') and *maʿaseh merkavah* ('The Account of the Chariot') were understood by Maimonides to correspond with physics and metaphysics respectively.[49] That is to say that the most profound esoteric disciplines of the Torah are in fact identical with two of the major theoretical sciences.[50] Indeed, these are also included in Maimonides' definition of *talmud*, extending it beyond mere imitative jurisprudence (*fiqh*).[51]

---

[*ḥukamā'*] in the city are those who know these things {including physics, metaphysics, cosmology, prophetology, the qualities of the virtuous city which facilitates the attainment of intellectual and spiritual felicity, and the wicked city that renders felicity impossible – RD} through strict demonstration and their own insight; those who are close to the philosophers know them as they really are through the insight of the philosophers, following them, assenting to their views and trusting them. But others know them through symbols which reproduce them by imitation, because neither nature nor habit has provided their minds with the gift to understand them as they are. Both are kinds of knowledge [*maʿrifatān*], but the knowledge of the philosophers is undoubtedly more excellent . . . But what is best known often varies among nations, either most of it or part of it. Hence these things are expressed for each nation in symbols other than those used for another nation. Therefore it is possible that excellent nations and excellent cities exist whose religions differ, although they all have as their goal one and the same felicity,' in Richard Walzer (ed and trans), *Al-Farabi on the Perfect State: Abū Naṣr al-Fārābī's Mabādi' ārā' ahl al-madīna al-fāḍila* (Clarendon Press, 1985) 278–81.) For Alfarabi then, philosophy is privileged over religion not only in its epistemological grounding, but also in its universality.

47 See discussion in Alfarabi's 'Book of Religion', in Butterworth, above n 38, 97, section 5; See discussion in Alfarabi's, 'The Attainment of Happiness' in Mahdi, above n 42, 44.

48 See Maimonides' parable of the king's palace, in *Guide* III.51 in Pines, above n 2, 618–9. Cf also the dichotomy that he proposes between jurisprudence and philosophical or 'true' religion: 'It is not the purpose of this Treatise to . . . teach those who have not engaged in any study other than the science of the Law – I mean the legalistic study of the Law [*ʿilm al-sharīʿa aʿnī fiqhihā*]. For the purpose of this Treatise and all those like it is the science of the Law in its true sense [*ʿilm al-sharīʿa ʿalā al-haqīqa*]' in Pines, above n 2, 5; Arabic in Munk, *Dalālat al-ḥā'irīn*, 2, lines 12–3.

49 See *Mishneh Torah*, Foundations of the Torah, 2:11–12, 4:10–13; Maimonides' commentary to Mishnah Ḥagigah 2:1; Isadore Twersky, *Introduction to the Code of Maimonides* (Yale University Press, 1980) 493.

50 For the tripartite division of the theoretical sciences into mathematics, physics, and metaphysics, see Efros, above n 31, 62–3.

51 *Mishneh Torah*, Laws of Torah Study, 1:12.

According to Maimonides, Alfarabi's definitions of religion and jurisprudence represent only the most superficial stratum of the disciplines contained within the Torah. Beliefs accepted on the basis of authority and laws derived from inspired legislation – as necessary as these may be – are not the product of true insight. After mastering the law and the introductory philosophical arts, the more advanced pupil proceeds to the study of the philosophical underpinnings of the religion and its doctrines, and enters the 'orchard' (*ha-pardes*), a deeper level of the Torah.[52] It seems that Maimonides' use of the terms *torah* in Hebrew and *dīn/sharī'a* in Arabic is significantly broader than the equivalent categories were for Alfarabi.[53] In fact, strongly implied in the opening passage of The Laws of the Foundations of the Torah in the *Mishneh torah* is the belief that there exists a profound unity between Torah and the philosophical sciences.[54] The purpose of the Torah is thus to lead the individual through the process of ethical and intellectual perfection, and to create a society that will maximally facilitate the individual's pursuit of such ends.

In sum, Maimonides argues for a profound unity between the philosophical sciences and Torah. The norms and teachings of Torah are intended to lead human beings through a process of ethical and intellectual development, to psychological stability, and ultimately to true philosophical insight. In the following sections, we shall broadly discuss the ways in which Maimonides understood revealed law to achieve such ends. In the absence of direct prophetic governance, humans must turn to the revealed law in order to enable society to attain the greatest possible degree of stability, and to enable individuals to attain the highest degree of ethical and intellectual perfection that they can.

## Revealed law and the attainment of human perfection

As is implied in Maimonides' classification of the commandments (*mitzvot*), and stated in various forms throughout his oeuvre, legislated norms play a central role in facilitating the acquisition of individual perfection.[55] Proscriptions teach one a

52 'The Torah' as a book thus transcends genres for Maimonides: It teaches physics, metaphysics, ethics and proper political theory. For a broad treatment of Maimonides' philosophical understanding of the Torah, see Sara Klein-Braslavy, 'Bible Commentary,' in Seeskin, above n 20, 245–72. In general, classical Jewish genres break down for Maimonides: The term *mishnah* ceases to refer to a particular compilation and refers instead to the study of law in an apodictic fashion; *talmud* appears to refer to any analytical study, and spans the gamut of *midreshei halakhah*, *talmudim*, physics and metaphysics.

53 Cf also Maimonides' use of the term *sharī'a* to denote imitative jurisprudence as well as (and as opposed to) philosophical or 'true' religion: *'ilm al-sharī'a a'nī fiqhihā . . . 'ilm al-sharī'a 'alā al-haqīqa* (Munk, *Dalālat al-ḥā'irīn*, 2 lines 12–3).

54 Understanding *ḥokhmot* to refer to all true sciences, as a calque of the Arabic *'ulūm*. Cf Menachem Kellner, *Science in the Bet Midrash* (Academic Studies Press, 2009) 177. Kellner also quotes Rabbi Joseph Qafih as having denied the possibility of secular knowledge according to Maimonides: 'if a discipline yields truth, it is not secular', ibid.

55 Cf Maimonides, *Guide* III.27 in Pines, above n 2, 510–1. The term that Pines translates as Law is *sharī'a*, with its specifically legal sense.

mild mode of asceticism, subduing the passions and helping one to free oneself from vices[56] and from attachment to the physical world;[57] Torah study imbues one with the correct opinions that facilitate further intellectual development and apprehension of truths.[58]

Cultivation of the individual self certainly occupies a central place in Maimonides' religious programme. In some passages, he interprets even the most social elements of Jewish law to be directed towards this end. This is particularly pronounced in his commentary to the Mishnah.[59] For example, Hillel's advice against separating from the community (Tractate Avot 2:5) is interpreted by Maimonides in terms of the individual's training in the face of society's challenges. According to this interpretation, one is to remain involved in society as a guard

56 Weiss and Butterworth, above n 4, 72.

57 Maimonides, *Guide*, III:51 in Pines, above n 2, 622.

58 In *Guide* III.35, Maimonides divides the commandments into 14 categories, in each case identifying the sections in the *Mishneh Torah* that deal with the laws of that particular category. (A number of points regarding this classification remain unclear, and he develops his treatment of the rationales behind the commandments in chapters III.36–49 of the *Guide*, which are devoted to the further explication of the fourteen classes of commandments.) The fourteen categories are as follows: (1) Laws that communicate or affirm true doctrines, such as divine incorporeality and unity; (2) laws that negate idolatrous beliefs and practices, – this being the negative corollary of the previous category; (3) laws that improve one's moral qualities; (4) laws that prescribe charitable gifts – '[f]or one who is rich today will be poor tomorrow, or his descendants will be poor; whereas one who is poor today will be rich tomorrow, or his son will be rich'; (5) laws that prevent wrongdoing and aggression; (6) laws concerning punishment for transgressions, which provide deterrence against wrongdoing; (7) laws that dictate or constrain one's ownership of property, participation in trade, and entry into contracts – '[f]or these property associations are necessary for people in every city, and it is indispensable that rules of justice should be given with a view to these transactions and that these transactions be regulated in a useful manner'; (8) laws concerning days on which work is forbidden (Sabbaths and festivals), serving either to teach a correct doctrine, or to facilitate bodily rest, or both; (9) laws concerning worship (prayer, *Shema*, etc), inculcating correct theology (to a degree) and love of God; (10) laws concerned with the sacrificial cult of the Sanctuary and Temple, and the details of how and by whom its service is to be conducted; (11) laws concerned with the sacrifices themselves, the logic of which is bound up in Israelite cultural history [for which see *Guide* III.32] (12) laws concerning purity, creating an atmosphere of veneration around the Sanctuary; (13) laws concerning food taboos, the purpose being to cultivate a mild asceticism; (14) laws concerning sexual taboos (linking *kil'e ha-behemah* and circumcision to this, it becomes clear that this is also about cultivating a mild asceticism) in Pines, above n 2, 535–8.

59 I would like to note that it is possible to interpret the different accounts of charitable norms as a product of diachronic development in Maimonides' thought. But two elements lead me to prefer a synchronic approach: (1) I do not believe that there is a very substantial shift in Maimonides' attitude, but rather a difference in emphasis – in his commentary to Avot (including the introduction, 'Eight Chapters'), he is more interested in the moral cultivation of the individual, while in *Guide* III.35 the scope of his discussion is broader; (2) Maimonides continuously updated his commentary to the Mishnah, but did not significantly revise these passages. For Maimonides' continuous editing and updating of his commentary to the Mishnah, see Moshe Halbertal, *Maimonides: Life and Thought* (Princeton University Press, 2014) 93; Herbert Davidson, above n 35, 166.

against complacency, and in order to maintain a degree of vigilance in one's moral training.[60] He even goes so far as to interpret overtly communal religious activities through the prism of individual perfection. The most striking examples are marriage and obligatory donations to the poor, which he understands to be practices that instruct the individual in moderate behaviour (that is, behaviour according to the golden mean).[61]

Although it is necessary for people to receive guidance in the initial stages of moral and scientific education,[62] both of which are necessary for the attainment of intellectual perfection, it seems that the highest stages of self-cultivation ought to take place in a state of solitude. Thus, Maimonides writes as follows:

> It is clear that after apprehension, total devotion to Him and then employment of intellectual thought in constant passionate love for Him should be aimed at. Mostly this is achieved in solitude and isolation. Hence every excellent man stays frequently in isolation and does not meet anyone unless it is necessary.[63]

For Maimonides, then, the most advanced stages of the perfection of the self must take place internally and individually, in some degree of isolation from others. Such efforts cannot be effectively prescribed by legislation, but they can be encouraged, eg through the prescription of prayer and contemplation of Torah, with a minimal degree of focus and intent.[64]

It would be a mistake to think that Maimonides regards the individual as an island, whose internal life has no impact upon society as a whole. A striking illustration of his sensitivity to the societal import of individual cultivation may be found in the distinction that he makes between personal and interpersonal transgressions, with which Maimonides concludes his broad categorisation of the commandments in *Guide* III.35. It is significant that Maimonides retains the original mishnaic formulation, defining the commandments by the scope of direct harm when transgressed. That is to say that Maimonides does not refer to interpersonal and private *commandments*, but *transgressions*: 'It is known that all the

60 In his commentary to this Mishnah, Maimonides writes: 'We have already stated that it is not appropriate to separate from the community unless they are corrupt . . . [Hillel] stated that even though a person has attained a lofty virtue in himself and it has become firmly embedded, let him not desist from repeating good actions in order to embed it further, and let him not be too certain and say, "This lofty characteristic has already been attained"'.

61 Weiss and Butterworth, above n 4, 73–4.

62 *Misneh Torah,* Laws of Character Traits, 6:1–2.

63 Maimonides, *Guide* III:51 in Pines, above n 2, 621.

64 Cf his introduction to the *Mishneh Torah*, in which he states that the 'Book of Love' treats those commandments 'in which we are commanded, in order to love the Omnipresent and remember Him always, such as the recitation of the *Shema* and prayer and *tefillin* and benedictions' (translation mine). In Maimonides, *Guide* III:51 in Pines, above n 2, 622, the *Shema* and prayer are mentioned as a means by which the first stages of contemplative consciousness may be developed.

*commandments* are divided into two groups: *transgressions between man and his fellow man* and *transgressions between man and God*.'[65] According to the Mishnah, one who sins against God alone may repent and attain atonement without the involvement of another human being. But one who sins against another human being must make amends with the victim before repenting before God in order to attain atonement. Thus, this is not so much a classification of commandments as it is a measure of the scope of the direct harm that results from their transgression. As useful as this distinction may be in the context of repentance,[66] Maimonides notes that the norms that constrain the individual ultimately do have an impact on others.[67] Thus, for example, norms that train the individual in personal restraint and compassion will hopefully reduce violence in society; the absence of such norms is likely to increase violence in society.

Still, it must be emphasised that for Maimonides, the ultimate purpose of social stability is to enable individual human beings to acquire the full range of ethical and intellectual virtues that will lead them to the greatest possible degree of intellectual perfection – the full realisation of *imago dei* as described in *Guide* I.1. A particularly clear expression of this ideal may be found in Maimonides' *Maqāla fī ṣināʿat al-manṭiq* (*Treatise on the Art of Logic*), in the classification of the philosophical sciences included in its 14th chapter.[68] Describing political science, the author writes as follows:

65 Pines, above n 2, 538. The citation is from the *Mishnah Torah*, Tractate Yoma 8:9 (italics in original).

66 It is maintained by Maimonides in the *Mishneh Torah*, see Laws of Repentance 2:5.

67 'For every *commandment*, whether it be a prescription or a prohibition, whose purpose it is to bring about the achievement of a certain moral quality or of an opinion or the rightness of actions, which only concerns the individual himself and his becoming more perfect, is called by them [ie by the talmudic Sages] *between man and God*, even though in reality it sometimes may affect relations *between man and his fellow man*. But this happens only after many intermediate steps' in Pines, above n 2, 538 (italics in original).

68 For this work, see Israel Efros' critical edition, with partial Arabic text, English translation, and three Hebrew translations: Efros, above n 31. A complete edition of the Arabic (in Arabic script) was published in Türker, '*Al-maqāla fī ṣināʿat al-manṭiq*.' Subsequently, Efros published a study of the MSS, accompanied by a complete and improved critical edition (in Hebrew script) – see Israel Efros, 'Maimonides' Arabic Treatise on Logic: Introduction,' (1966) 34 *Proceedings of the American Academy for Jewish Research* 155, 155–60; and 'Maqāla fī ṣināʿat al-manṭiq,' Ibid. (Hebrew section) מ-מא.Maimonides' authorship of this work was called into question by Herbert Davidson; see 'The Authenticity of Works Attributed to Maimonides' in Ezra Fleischer et al (eds), *Me'ah she'arim: Studies in Medieval Jewish Spiritual Life in Memory of Isadore Twersky* (The Magnes Press, 2001) 118–25; Davidson, above n 35, 313–22. Cf also Charles H Manekin, 'Logic in Medieval Jewish Culture' in Gad Freudenthal (ed), *Science in Medieval Jewish Cultures* (Cambridge University Press, 2011) 116–7. For cogent critiques of Davidson's position, see Joel Kraemer, 'Is There a Text in This Class?' (2008) 8 *Aleph: Historical Studies in Science and Judaism* 268, 268–72, and in particular 273–5 n 62–3; Sarah Stroumsa, 'On Maimonides and on Logic' (2014) 14 *Aleph: Historical Studies in Science and Judaism* 259, 259–63. Additional considerations in favour of Maimonides' authorship of the treatise have been offered by a number of scholars; see Steven Harvey, 'Maimonides and the Art of Writing Introductions', in Arthur Hyman (ed),

> The government of a city is a science imparting to those who possess it a knowledge of true happiness [*al-sa'āda al-ḥaqīqiyya*], showing them the way to obtain it, and a knowledge of true evil, showing the way to avoid it. It shows them how to use their habits in abandoning presumed happiness so that they will not desire or delight in it, and it explains to them what is presumed evil so that it will cause them no pain or grief.[69]

Maimonides' reference to 'true happiness' in this context carries unmistakably soteriological implications. That is to say that Maimonides believes political philosophy to be ultimately oriented towards guiding its individual subjects towards their greatest perfection,[70] so that they might attain felicity (*sa'āda*) in the afterlife.[71] Indeed, precisely this point is made in the *Guide*: The Torah aims to establish societal and bodily welfare, not for their own sake, but so that individuals might ultimately be able to attain intellectual perfection.[72]

## Insiders and outsiders in Maimonides' world: Jews and non-Jews

We have established that, according to Maimonides, intellectual perfection represents the fullest realisation of *imago dei*; that the true meaning of *imitatio dei* lies in ethical cultivation, and social and political activity; and that the purpose of the Torah is to create a stable society, and lead individual human beings towards these modes of perfection (understanding that ethical virtue and the profession of correct doctrines are a prerequisite for intellectual perfection). But what are the boundaries for the Torah's concern with human beings? According to Maimonides, does the Torah care for the welfare of all human beings, or only for that of Jews?

Before answering this question, it is worth noting that rabbinic tradition is divided on the subject of the relationship between Gentiles and the Torah. According to one school of thought, the Torah is specifically intended for Jews, to the point that Gentiles are actively discouraged from studying it.[73] Another

---

*Maimonidean Studies* (Yeshiva University Press, 2008) Vol 5, 86–8; Cohen, above n 11, 101 fn 12; Stroumsa, above n 9, 127–8. Cf also the parallels noted by Efros, above n 31, 63 fn 43.

69 Translation with changes from Israel Efros, above n 31, 64. For the Arabic text of this passage, see Türker, above n 31, 109; and in Efros, above n 31, 'Maqāla,' מא.

70 Kreisel, above n 4, 3–5.

71 This conception is reflected in a number of medieval classifications of the sciences. Cf al-Ghazali's statement in *Maqāṣid al-falāsifa* that the utility of practical philosophy (the highest part of which is political philosophy) lies in determining the actions that will result in the welfare of human beings in this world and the hereafter; see Sulayman Dunya (ed), *Muqaddimat tahāfut al-falāsifa al-musammāh maqāṣid al-falāsifa lil-imām al-ghazālī* (Dār al-ma'ārif bi-'l-miṣr, 1961) 134.

72 Maimonides, *Guide* III.27 in Pines, above n 2, 510–1.

73 See Babylonian Talmud, Tractate Sanhedrin 59a. In theory, this law is codified by Maimonides (see *Mishneh Torah*, Laws of Kings and Wars, 10:9); however, in practice he permits

school of rabbinic thought holds that the very location of the human encounter with the Divine in the desert is indicative of the universal relevance of the Torah: 'The Torah was given in a public, ownerless place. For if it had been given in the Land of Israel, they would have said that the nations of the world have no portion in it. Therefore, it was given in the desert – a public, ownerless place. Let whomever wishes to do so receive it.'[74] Despite the wide appeal of universalism in our own time, it has been powerfully argued that universalism can lead to intolerance, and that particularism may paradoxically facilitate a greater accommodation of difference in beliefs and cultural and religious practices.[75] On the other hand, particularism may encourage apathy towards the needs and concerns of those outside of one's group (or worse, active antipathy).[76] Both attitudes entail a certain danger, and both contain the seeds of violence. By focusing on universalistic aspects of Maimonides' thought, I do not intend to judge whether or not they are superior to more particularistic attitudes.[77]

For Maimonides, the capacity for intellectual insight and perfection is something that characterises – and defines – the human race as a whole. In this sense, all human beings are created in *imago dei*.[78] This is particularly clear in connection with Maimonides' statement that non-Jews may attain prophecy – the highest realisation of intellectual perfection.[79] Indeed, according to Maimonides, an ethically cultivated and philosophically sophisticated non-Jew must meet a better fate in the hereafter than an uncultivated Jew who lacks a philosophical education.[80] His theoretical attitude also translated into the practical sphere: in his commentary to the Mishnah, Maimonides famously defends his integration of philosophical

---

the study of Torah by Christians (who recognise the sanctity of the Hebrew Bible), but not by Muslims (who believe the text of the Hebrew Bible to have been corrupted) – see discussion below.

74 Tractate Ba-Ḥodesh. *Mekhilta de-Rabbi Yishma'el, parashah* 1; see text and alternative translation in Lauterbach, above n 18, 293–4.

75 Jonathan Sacks, *The Dignity of Difference: How to Avoid the Clash of Civilizations* (Continuum, 2002) 45–66; Daniel Boyarin, *A Radical Jew: Paul and the Politics of Identity* (University of California Press, 1994) 228.

76 Ibid.

77 In this context, it is worth noting that it may be no coincidence that, among countless other statements, the Babylonian Talmud ascribes two statements to Rabbi Johannan that have a bearing on the relationship between particularism and tolerance: He strongly discourages non-Jews from studying Torah (Sanhedrin 59a); and he states that practitioners of (presumably polytheistic) religions outside of the Land of Israel are not to be regarded as idolatrous, as they are simply following their ancestral practices (Ḥullin 13b). I am not implying that these traditions were espoused by the same historical figure – I am merely pointing out that the tradents and students of the Talmud saw no contradiction between these positions when ascribed to a single authority who is expected to hold coherent views.

78 See Maimonides, *Guide* I.1; Kellner, above n 54, 296–7, 306.

79 For which see Maimonides', 'Epistle to Yemen' in Abraham Halkin and David Hartman (ed), *Crisis and Leadership* (Jewish Publication Society, 1985) 111; Menachem Kellner, *Maimonides on Judaism and the Jewish People* (State University of New York Press, 1991) 26–9.

80 Kellner, above n 54, 297.

material from non-Jewish philosophers (both pagan and Muslim) by stating that one should 'accept the truth from whomever states it.'[81]

Just as Maimonides' psychology, soteriology, and prophetology reflect a fundamentally universalistic (if thoroughly elitist) understanding of individual human nature, his eschatology reveals a universalistic vision of the ideal society. The following passage is particularly illuminating in this respect:

> Let it not occur to one that during the days of the Messiah some element of the natural order will change, or that some new thing will occur in the laws of nature.[82] Rather, the world follows its law[s].[83] And that which is stated in Isaiah (11:6) – *The wolf shall dwell with the lamb, the leopard lie down with the kid* – is a parable and a metaphor. Its meaning is that the Israelites shall dwell securely with the wicked [nations] of the world, who are likened to a wolf and eagle . . . [a]nd they shall all adopt[84] the religion of truth, neither stealing nor destroying, but peacefully consuming permitted food like[85] Israelites . . .[86]

Whether or not Maimonides is referring to the conversion of non-Jews to Judaism, their adoption of Noahide or Abrahamic practice, or some other sense,[87] one matter is clear: according to Maimonides, in the messianic period, non-Jews will adopt a greater set of divinely revealed norms.[88] When we recall that the purpose of the Torah and its laws is to lead society and individuals towards their fullest perfection, the universalism of this vision becomes apparent.

We might then conclude that on a theoretical level, Maimonides is a true universalist.[89] Humans are all created in *imago dei* (ie human beings are distinguished by their capacity to attain intellectual insight); divinely inspired laws lead us to our

81 Weiss and Butterworth, above n 4, 60.

82 Hebrew: *o she-yihyeh sham ḥiddush be-ma'aseh bereshit.* This phrase is an excellent example of impact of Arabic language and discourse on Maimonides' writing. To illustrate: *sham* = *thamma* (there, there is), a locution that makes little sense in Hebrew; *ḥiddush* = *iḥdāth* (production, creation of something anew); *ma'aseh bereshit* = [the laws of] physics.

83 Hebrew: *'olam ke-minhago noheg*. For this phrase in its talmudic context, see Babylonian Talmud, Abodah Zarah 54b. See also Isadore Twersky, above n 49, 145–6. For another case of Maimonides' use of the phrase 'the world proceeds according to its law[s]' (*'olam ke-minhago holekh*) in an eschatological context, see *Mishneh Torah*, Laws of Repentance, 9:2.

84 Hebrew: *ve-yaḥzeru*, lit. 'they shall return.' On the meaning of this expression, see Kellner, above n 54, 300; cf Kreisel, above n 42, 152.

85 Or: as Israelites. Some versions read 'with the Israelites'; cf Kellner, above n 54, 291 and fn 3.

86 *Mishneh Torah*, Laws of Kings and War, 12:1.

87 For the interpretive possibilities for this passage, see Kellner, above n 54, 291–319.

88 See Kreisel, above n 42.

89 For the limits and contours of Maimonides' universalism (including the problematic aspects of the very term 'universalism'), see Kellner, above n 54, 273–90.

fullest perfection; and just as the religious community[90] founded by the Patriarchs was to expand into a fully developed *polis* with its divinely-inspired *nomoi*, the law of the Israelites will ultimately become the source of guidance for all of humanity.

However, the imperfect world in which Maimonides lived was far from his messianic ideal: Jews existed in a state of exile, without political self-determination; they were ruled by Muslims and Christians, and lived side by side with followers of these faiths. If the teachings of the Patriarchs and the Law of Moses are to be effectively and sustainably transmitted from generation to generation in exile, boundaries between Jews and Gentiles must remain intact.[91] Indeed, the concern to maintain such social boundaries as a means of guaranteeing the transmission of Judaism goes back to the oldest rabbinic sources.[92]

The real, breathing Gentiles that Maimonides and most other Jews encountered in the world were Muslims and Christians.[93] How were members of these faiths to be treated? Maimonides believed Christianity and Islam to be fundamentally imitative of Mosaic revelation and its accompanying interpretive tradition (ie rabbinic Judaism), rather than the product of true insight.[94] In his view, each of these traditions serve to guide their believers towards ultimate recognition of the true religion in the messianic era.[95] Each of these religions also presents unique challenges. On the one hand, Muslims accuse Jews of corrupting Scripture, and deny the sanctity of the Hebrew Bible in the form that Jews and Christians have transmitted it.[96] On the other hand, Maimonides understood Muslims to be true monotheists in a way that he did not consider Christians to be.[97] As a consequence, Jews may teach

90 The Arabic term used by Maimonides to describe this religious community is *milla* – see Maimonides, *Guide* III.51 in Pines, above n 2, 624; Munk, *Dalālat al-ḥā'irīn*, 459, line 8.

91 Cf his discussion of the contents of *Sefer ha-qedushah* (*The Book of Sanctity*) in his introduction to the *Mishneh Torah*, where he describes the laws of forbidden foods and sexual relations as creating/maintaining boundaries between Jews and Gentiles.

92 A *locus classicus* for dietary laws as a social boundary intended to prevent the adoption of non-Jewish religious practices may be found in the Babylonian Talmud, Tractate Abodah Zarah 36b.

93 A related but distinct facet of Maimonides' thought is his treatment of Jewish outsiders, heretics, and in particular Karaites. In general, Maimonides is harsher in this context than the talmudic precedents would warrant. For a study of this topic, see Gerald J Blidstein, 'The "other" in Maimonidean law' (2004) 18 *Jewish History* 173, 173–95.

94 See Maimonides' comments in *Iggeret teman* (*Epistle to Yemen*) in Halkin and Hartman, above n 79, 99.

95 See *Mishneh Torah*, Laws of Kings and War, 11:4, in uncensored editions. On this passage, see Kellner, above n 54, 208–9, 303.

96 The term for this act of corruption or misrepresentation in Arabic is *taḥrīf*. For *taḥrīf* in the context of Muslim anti-Jewish polemics, particularly as applied to the problematic portrayal of biblical prophets, see Jacques Waardenburg, 'The Medieval Period: 650–1500' in Jacques Waardenburg (ed), *Muslim Perceptions of Other Religions: A Historical Survey* (Oxford University Press, 1999) 52–3.

97 For Maimonides' view of Christianity as an idolatrous, see his commentary to the Mishnah, Tractate Abodah Zarah 1:3, 4; *Mishneh Torah*, Laws of Idolatry and Gentile Practices, 9:4; Laws of Forbidden Foods, 11:7. For Islam as truly monotheistic, see Maimonides' letter to Obadiah the Proselyte, in Itzhak Shailat, *The Letters and Essays of Moses Maimonides* (Shailat

Torah to Christians, as they consider it to be an authoritative revelation – but they may not teach Torah to Muslims.[98] Conversely, Jews may convert to Islam on pain of death, but not to Christianity.[99] Indeed, Maimonides' overall attitude towards Islam seems to have been considerably more positive than his attitude towards Christianity.[100]

Beyond certain social boundaries that must exist in a pre-Messianic world, and certain limitations that emerge from the challenges posed by specific communities that live alongside Jews, Maimonides' fundamental understanding of both human nature and the function of Torah reflects a deep universalism.[101] It is important to note that in the aforementioned cases of Christians and Muslims, his positions are based on his understanding of the specific content of an individual's faith rather than their status as a non-Jew per se. According to Maimonides, the Torah is ultimately destined to guide all of humanity towards their ethical, social, and intellectual perfection – that is, towards *imitatio dei*, and the fullest expression of *imago dei*.

## Conclusion

As is well known, Maimonides understood the identification of human beings with *imago dei* in entirely non-imagistic terms. Indeed, such a position reflects his strongly anti-anthropomorphic and anti-anthropopathic theology, with its ultimate emphasis on apophasis. Many other interpreters sought to illuminate this concept with recourse so some notion of *imitatio dei*, whether their interpretation of the biblical verses tended to be imagistic or not. That is to say, they sought to illuminate the concept of *imago dei* by appealing to the notion that human beings must live in some kind of divine mode – whether by governing the world, or embodying divine attributes such as compassion and justice.

---

Publishing, 1995) Vol 1, 238–9; *Mishneh Torah*, Laws of Forbidden Foods, 11:7. Cf Davidson, above n 35, 293–4.

98 Responsum No 149, in Joshua Blau (ed), *Teshubot ha-Rambam* (Mekize Nirdamim, 1960) Vol 1, 284–5 (Arabic with Hebrew translation); discussed in Davidson, above n 35, 294. Apart from the danger of providing Muslim students with fodder in anti-Jewish polemics discussed in the responsum, cf also the rabbinic dictum that 'just as one is commanded to say something that will be accepted, one is commanded *not* to say something that will not be accepted.' (Babylonian Talmud, Tractate Yebamot 65a.) That is to say, instruction may only be offered if the student is likely to accept the content of that instruction.

99 See Maimonides' 'Epistle on Martyrdom', in Halkin and Hartman, above n 79, 15–45; for Hebrew translation (the Arabic being no longer extant), see Itzhak Shailat (ed), *The Letters and Essays of Moses Maimonides* (Shailat Publishing – Ma'aleh Adumim, 1995), Vol 1, 25–59. See also Maimonides' 'Epistle to Yemen' in Halkin and Hartman, above n 79, 93–149; Arabic original and Samuel Ibn Tibbon's Hebrew translation in Itzhak Shailat (ed), *The Letters and Essays of Moses Maimonides* (Shailat Publishing – Ma'aleh Adumim, 1995) vol 1, 77–168.

100 Cf Maimonides' epistle to Obadiah the Proselyte; Hebrew original in Shailat, above n 99, 238–9.

101 Kreisel, above n 42; Kellner, above n 54, 273–319, 339–46.

In contrast with these thinkers, Maimonides makes a sharp distinction between these concepts. According to him, they are grounded in different biblical verses: *imago dei* (Genesis 1:26–27, 5:1–2, 9:6) represents the human capacity to attain true intellectual insight; *imitatio dei* (Deuteronomy 28:8 and elsewhere – 'walking in God's ways') constitutes a formal commandment, according to which human beings must cultivate within themselves the positive attributes of the Divine as they are described in Scripture. Intellectual perfection is the fullest expression of the former; moral perfection and wise governance of others are the fullest expression of the latter.

Although he believes that only Jews currently live (to a large degree) in accord with divine law, Maimonides envisions a world in which that law becomes universal. The Torah ultimately aims to guide all human beings towards attaining their true welfare. That is to say that the Torah aims to establish a peaceful and prosperous society, in which individuals may pursue moral and intellectual perfection. The purpose of the Torah, its true *telos*, is thus the maximal realisation of *imago dei* and *imitatio dei* in the world.

## References

Amine, Osman, *Enumeration of the Sciences* (Alfarabi, 1968)

Blau, Joshua (ed), *Teshubot ha-Rambam* (Mekize Nirdamim, 1960)

Blidstein, Gerald J, 'The "other" in Maimonidean law' (2004) 18 *Jewish History* 173

Boyarin, Daniel, *A Radical Jew: Paul and the Politics of Identity* (University of California Press, 1994)

Butterworth, Charles (ed), *Alfarabi: The Political Writings ('Selected Aphorisms' and Other Texts)* (Charles Butterworth, trans, Cornell University Press, 2001)

Butterworth, Charles (ed), *Book of Religion, Alfarabi: The Political Writings ('Selected Aphorisms' and Other Texts)* (Cornell University Press, 2001)

Christensen, Michael J and Jeffrey A Wittung (eds), *Partakers of the Divine Nature: The History and Development of Deification in the Christian Traditions* (Fairleigh Dickinson University Press/Associated University Presses, 2007)

Cohen, Mordechai Z, *Opening the Gates of Interpretation: Maimonides' Biblical Hermeneutics in Light of His Geonic-Andalusian Heritage and Muslim Milieu* (Brill, 2011)

Cohen, Mordechai Z, *Three Approaches to Biblical Metaphor: From Abraham Ibn Ezra and Maimonides to David Kimhi* (Brill, 2003)

Davidowitz, H S and D H Baneth (eds), *Peraqim ba-hatzlaḥah* (Mekize Nirdamim, 1939)

Davidson, Herbert, *Alfarabi, Avicenna, and Averroes, on Intellect* (Oxford University Press, 1992)

Davidson, Herbert A, *Moses Maimonides: The Man and his Works* (Oxford University Press, 2005)

Derenbourg, Joseph (ed), *Oeuvres Complétes de R Saadia ben Iosef al-Fayyoûmî* (E Leroux, 1893)

Dunya, Sulayman (ed), *Muqaddimat tahāfut al-falāsifa al-musammāh maqāṣid al-falāsifa lil-imām al-ghazālī* (Dār al-ma'ārif bi-'l-miṣr, 1961)

Efros, Israel, 'Maimonides' Arabic Treatise on Logic: Introduction,' (1966) 34 *Proceedings of the American Academy for Jewish Research* 155

Efros, Israel (ed), *Maimonides' Treatise on Logic (Makāla fi-ṣinā'at al-manṭiķ): The Original Arabic and Three Hebrew Translations* (American Academy for Jewish Research, 1938)

Fleischer, Ezra et al (eds), *Me'ah she'arim: Studies in Medieval Jewish Spiritual Life in Memory of Isadore Twersky* (The Magnes Press, 2001)

Freudenthal, Gad (ed), *Science in Medieval Jewish Cultures* (Cambridge University Press, 2011)

Halbertal, Moshe, *Maimonides: Life and Thought* (Princeton University Press, 2014)

Halkin, Abraham and David Hartman (ed), *Crisis and Leadership* (Jewish Publication Society, 1985)

Hamori, Esther J, *'When Gods Were Men': The Embodied God in Biblical and Near Eastern Literature* (De Gruyter, 2008)

Harris, Jay M (ed), *Maimonides after 800 Years: Essays on Maimonides and His Influence* (Harvard University Press, 2007)

Hyman, Arthur (ed), *Maimonidean Studies* (Yeshiva University Press, 2008)

Idel, Moshe, Devora Dimant and Shalom Rosenberg (eds), *Tribute to Sara: Studies in Jewish Philosophy and Kabbala presented to Professor Sara O Heller Wilensky* (The Magnes Press, 1994)

Ish-Shalom, Meir (ed), *Seder eliyahu rabbah ve-seder eliyahu zuṭa ha-muba'im be-shem tanna de-be eliyahu* (Achiasaf, 1902)

Kellner, Menachem, *Maimonides on Human Perfection* (Scholars Press, 1990)

Kellner, Menachem, *Maimonides on Judaism and the Jewish People* (State University of New York Press, 1991)

Kellner, Menachem, *Science in the Bet Midrash* (Academic Studies Press, 2009)

Kister, Menahem (ed), *Avoth de-Rabbi Nathan: Solomon Schechter Edition*, version B (Macmillan, 2007)

Klein-Braslavy, Sara, *Maimonides as a Biblical Interpreter* (Academic Studies Press, 2011)

Kraemer, Joel, 'Is There a Text in This Class?' (2008) 8 *Aleph: Historical Studies in Science and Judaism* 268

Kreisel, Haim (Howard), *Maimonides' Political Thought: Studies in Ethics, Law, and the Human Ideal* (State University of New York Press, 1999)

Lauterbach, Jacob Z (ed), *Mekhilta de-Rabbi Ishmael* (The Jewish Publication Society, 2nd ed, 2004)

Lorberbaum, Yair, *In God's Image: Myth, Theology, and Law in Classical Judaism* (Cambridge University Press, 2015)

Mahdi, Muhsin, *Alfarabi and the Foundations of Islamic Political Philosophy* (University of Chicago Press, 2001)

Madhi, Muhsin (ed), *Philosophy of Plato and Aristotle, Alfarabi: Philosophy of Plato and Aristotle* (Cornell University Press, 2001)

Maimonides, Moses, *Mishneh Torah*

Maimonides, Moses, *The Guide of the Perplexed* (Shlomo Pines, trans, University of Chicago Press, 1963)

Melamed, Abraham, *The Philosopher-King in Medieval and Renaissance Jewish Political Thought* (State University of New York Press, 2003)

Najjar, Fauzi M, *Al-Fārābī's The Political Regime (Al-Siyāsa Al-Madaniyya also Known as the Treatise on the Principles of Beings)* (Imprimerie Catholique, Beyrouth, 1964)

Nasr, Seyyed Hossein, *An Introduction to Islamic Cosmological Doctrines* (State University of New York Press, 1993)

Qafih, Joseph (ed), *Sefer ha-mitzvot le-rabbenu mosheh ben maymon* (Mossad Harav Kook, 1971)

Sacks, Jonathan, *The Dignity of Difference: How to Avoid the Clash of Civilizations* (Continuum, 2002)

Seeskin, Kenneth (ed), *The Cambridge Companion to Maimonides* (Cambridge University Press, 2005)

Shailat, Itzhak, *The Letters and Essays of Moses Maimonides* (Shailat Publishing, 1995)

Sommer, Benjamin D, *The Bodies of God and the World of Ancient Israel* (Cambridge University Press, 2009)

Spero, Shubert, *Morality, Halakha, and the Jewish Tradition* (Ktav Publishing House/ Yeshiva University Press, 1983)

Stroumsa, Guy G, *The End of Sacrifice: Religious Transformations in Late Antiquity* (The University of Chicago Press, 2009)

Stroumsa, Sarah, 'On Maimonides and on Logic' (2014) 14 *Aleph: Historical Studies in Science and Judaism* 259

Stroumsa, Sarah, *Maimonides in His World: Portrait of a Mediterranean Thinker* (Princeton University Press, 2009)

Twersky, Isadore, *Introduction to the Code of Maimonides* (Yale University Press, 1980)

Vaksman, Nisan (ed), *Tomer Deborah* (Shoshanim, 1960)

Waardenburg, Jacques (ed), *Muslim Perceptions of Other Religions: A Historical Survey* (Oxford University Press, 1999)

Walker, Paul, *Early Philosophical Shiism: The Ismaili Neoplatonism of Abu Ya'qub al-Sijistani* (Cambridge University Press, 1993)

Walzer, Richard (ed and trans), *Al-Farabi on the Perfect State: Abū Naṣr al-Fārābī's Mabādi' ārā' ahl al-madīna al-fāḍila* (Clarendon Press, 1985)

Weiss, Raymond and Charles Butterworth (eds), *Ethical Writings of Maimonides* (Dover Publications, 1975)

# 14 The commandment of love in family law

*Dubravka Hrabar*

*If I speak in the tongues of men and of angels,*
*but have not love,*
*I am a noisy gong or a clanging cymbal.*
*And if I have prophetic powers,*
*and understand all mysteries and all knowledge,*
*and if I have all faith, so as to remove mountains,*
*but have not love,*
*I am nothing.*
*If I give away all I have,*
*and if I deliver up my body to be burned,*
*but have not love, I gain nothing.*
*Love is patient and kind;*
*love does not envy or boast;*
*it is not arrogant*
*or rude.*
*It does not insist on its own way;*
*it is not irritable or resentful;*
*it does not rejoice at wrongdoing,*
*but rejoices with the truth.*
*Love bears all things,*
*believes all things,*
*hopes all things,*
*endures all things.*
*Love never ends.*
...
*So now faith, hope, and love abide,*
*these three;*
*but the greatest of these is love.*

Hymn to Love (1 Cor 13: 1–13)

## Family and love

Family as the fundamental unit of mankind is subject to regulation in many international documents, national legal systems and academic disciplines. It is the most natural and oldest social group based on the feelings of its members towards one another. The feelings that a wife and husband, parents and children, and often other relatives feel for each other make up the cohesive force keeping the family together.[1] Feelings are the mystical answer to the sustainability of mankind. However subtle, durable, vehement, strong or threatened by the outside world, feelings are the foundation of every family. The feelings that a man and a woman develop for one another are of a special nature and will eventually lead to a decision to fully commit to one another and enter into marriage or an extramarital union. Also, the most exalted feelings of parents towards their children, which are reciprocated soon thereafter, can simply be referred to as 'love'. Love underlies all family relationships and brings its members together. A man and a woman enter into marriage guided by love, a sense of belonging and commitment. A mother and father have an unconditional love for their child, and a relentless desire to give, even at the cost of their own lives. A child's love for his or her parents goes through a transformation from complete dependence to immeasurable gratitude. Love is thus a ubiquitous ingredient of family relationships, carried over from one generation to the next. 'Love is an active power in man'.[2] Most people and families live their family lives in love, with love and for love, and only some never experience this joy and meaning of life.[3]

Love has been described in numerous works of art and literature; it appears to be the motor of human relationships (from the Trojan War, through the New Testament Epistles to the modern age); it is omnipresent and imposes itself as the meaning and purpose of life itself.

Love between family members can be found in many forms: φιλία, ἔρος and ἀγαπή. It comprises many elements: fondness, affection, altruism, requited love, commitment, emotional intimacy, friendship, passion, intimacy, personal interest, courtesy, etc.[4] Their intensity may vary or change shape over time, but the love

1 The complete answer lies in the accomplishment of unity, becoming one with another person in love. The desire for the unity of two people is the most powerful aspiration in a man. It is the fundamental passion, the force binding mankind, the clan, the family, the society; see Erich Fromm, *Umijeće ljubavi* [*The Art of Loving*] (Harper & Brothers, 1956) also available online at: <www.znakovi-vremena.net/Dokumenti/Erich_Fromm-Umjece_ljubavi.pdf> 31.

2 '*Love is an active power in man*; a power which breaks through the walls which separate man from his fellow men, which unites him with others; love makes him overcome the sense of isolation and separateness, yet it permits him to be himself, to retain his integrity. In love the paradox occurs that two beings become one and yet remain two.' Ibid 35 (italics in original).

3 Here we are referring to arranged marriages and families with members prone to violence.

4 Love is described as a complex and intense feeling of affection. In philosophy, it originally denotes an inclination towards the other (a close one, the world, God), selflessness as a tendency for one's own existence to be practically determined by the other, the alien and the different; see generally, *Hrvatska enciklopedija* (*Croatian encyclopedia*), Leksikografski zavod 6 *Miroslav Krleža,* Zagreb 710.

is still there (if it exists) as the basis of the personal relationships between family members. It is the source of all other emotions, actions, hopes and aspirations.

There is thus no doubt that love has for millennia been a binding force as a natural condition, a metaphysical force drawing people together. Law has codified love, recognising it as a human need, transposing natural feelings into legal norms.

Law as a set of legal rules, principles and institutes regulating relationships in the society, laid down rules at the time of its first written records sanctioning the role of the man in the family, ascribing value to the family as a unit of society and protecting it. Over time the legal perspective has seen many changes with regard to the rights of particular family members. Views on the need for the law to protect certain members of the family and the roles they play in the family (especially towards the end of the second millennium, when this concerned the rights of women, mothers, and children), went through many changes, resulting in the extension of various other rights (and social benefits in particular) onto the family and its members.

## Marriage – family – love – law

Family as the fundamental social group regulated by law, due to the cohesive forces it is dominated by, is in some legal systems anchored in family law as a special branch of law, and as part of the broader civil law branch in others (which is particularly the case in Western European systems). Any consideration and analysis of family law regulations and particular provisions can, therefore, provide insights into the state of social consciousness and value system of each individual society. The value system can easily be assessed from the family law provisions which reflect the relationship of the state and society with the family and govern its protection. Also worthy of consideration is the protection of the legal status of particular family members and the various types of family that (do not) enjoy legal protection. Furthermore, regulation of particular institutes of family law, both in terms of their existence and of the quality and quantity of protection, will provide answers to the questions as to whether and to what extent the family represents a value in a particular society.

Marriage is 'a basic human good',[5] a:

> special type of bond. It unites spouses in body, as well as in mind and heart, and is particularly apt for procreation and family life . . . only marriage objectively entails the assumption of obligations of permanence and exclusivity. The spouses take a vow to commit to each other their *whole* beings for their *whole* lives.[6]

5 Sherif Girgis, Ryan T Anderson and Robert P George (eds), *What is Marriage? Woman and Man: A Defense* (translated back into English from the Croatian edition: *U ime obitelji*, (Zagreb, 2015) 14; (originally: Encounter Books, 2012) (italics added).

6 Ibid 37.

Marriage is often likened to friendship. However, even though these are both social relationships between two persons, they do not possess the same social value or have the same impact on the society. The difference between the two is explained by the fact that, unlike marriage, friendship 'does not affect the general good in a structured way that requires legal recognition and regulation'.[7] However, this distinction is not suitable when comparing marriage to extramarital union. Although the purpose of marriage is usually procreation and rearing children, and this process has the best prospects in stable unions, both for the children and in the society,[8] the same goals can undoubtedly be achieved within an extramarital union. Long-term extramarital unions (short-term or occasional unions are usually not entered into with procreation in mind) are in many ways similar to marriage. So, the question is raised as to why marriage is presumably a more desirable legal institute than extramarital union, with the assumption that they share the same qualities. It is a fact that marriage has been legally regulated in all cultures through history, while extramarital union sees a rise in terms of gaining the same effects as marriage after the Second World War, with the exception of the formalities of establishment and dissolution. The justification of marriage as a legally regulated institution is found in the strong culture of marriage[9] as a desirable form of union between a man and a woman. Marriage reflects 'simple rules for simple people'[10] which force them into togetherness even when its fragility becomes evident. Marriage is, therefore, a clear and recognisable institution whose 'rules of the game' are familiar to those who intend to enter it, and the basic dominant idea is complete commitment to one another for life. Conversely, we contend that extramarital union, due to the absence of formality and clear 'rules of the game', has an aleatory quality. Marriage is a set value with defined rules and it is assumed that the spouses abide by them. This is where the role of the state as a system comes in as the one to ensure order, which makes marriage an important general good of the individual and the society as a whole. We argue that the state should not encourage legal regulation of extramarital union which would raise it to the same level as marriage[11] because this creates a doubly absurd situation – not only does this parallel institute to marriage demean its value at its root, but the partners in an extramarital union are become subject to the exact rules that they wish to avoid by not entering into marriage. It is thus practically an oxymoron.

7 Ibid 38.

8 Ibid.

9 Ibid 39.

10 Amy L Wax, 'Diverging Family Structure and "Rational" Behaviour: The Decline' in Lloyd R Cohen and Joshua D Wright (eds), *Marriage as a Disorder of Choice, Research Handbook on the Economics of Family Law* (Edward Elgar Publishing Inc, 2011) 59, 61.

11 This is the case in the latest *Family Act* of the Republic of Croatia of 2015. We believe that the legal protection should have been limited to the material effect of these communities (maintenance and property relations).

Marriage with children becomes a family. The birth or adoption of a child does not only mark the beginning of a family, but it also represents the moment at which the family gains full meaning and achieves its purpose. Family becomes the source and the end, a sturdy circle around marriage and procreation. It is a guarantee and support to children's development.[12]

It is worth observing how various family legislations respond to the call for love as the foundation of family and marriage, ie whether they do it in a precise and open manner or only modestly and reluctantly imply that love should lie at the basis of every marriage and family. It is our opinion that these two institutes should be observed as the most important and common vehicles for protecting and conveying the culture, societal values, traditions, religion and identity from one generation to the next.

Marriage is a formalised union of a woman and a man, but however much the spouses may want to be considered a family, as an even more desirable form of union, the two are simply not the same. We contend that a family comprises a wife, a husband and their offspring, meaning that children are a decisive element in assessing whether a community is a family or not. In addition, it has been said that families have been known to become extinct, which means there were no offspring. Otherwise, if marriage were equated with family, then these would be two synonymous terms, but with different, albeit similar, content. This would also open doors for the right to a family life to same-sex partners (whether or not registered) who cannot have children together.[13]

A union between a woman and a man in marriage is only possible where there is true love between the partners. Sherif Girgis et al, argue that: 'marriage involves acts that bring the spouses together in a comprehensive manner and unites them in seeking the all-encompassing spectrum of good.'[14]

However, dark clouds are gathering over the traditional concept of marriage and family. European family law, seen as a total of individual national legal systems regulating family relations, is increasingly marked with steps towards modernisation of certain institutes, constituting a serious threat to the basic natural union by way of extending family rights to individuals who cannot meet the criteria of a traditional family. It is hard to predict the direction which the development and rights (within and) of the family will take in the future, but we believe that a look

12 The importance of the family based on marriage and the influence of the family structure on the development of children has been emphasised in research carried out by some left-wing institutions; see *Family Act* of the Republic of Croatia of 2015, 42 and 43.

13 The issue of the right to a family life for same-sex, ie extramarital, unions was resolved by the European Court of Human Rights in a number of judgments. The right to a family life (Art 8 ECHR) was recognised for extramarital unions in the judgment in *Schalk and Kopf v Austria* [2010] ECHR 995 (24 June 2010), and for same-sex *de facto* unions in the judgment in *X and others v Austria* [2013] ECHR 148 (19 February 2013) and in *Gas and Dubois v France* [2010] ECHR 444 (11 March 2011).

14 Girgis, Anderson and George, above n 5, 32.

back can strengthen the struggle for traditional family values, which serve the general good.

## Love between wife and husband (in a family) in the Old and New Testament

Family law of the Western civilisation is rooted in Roman law, which in turn draws from even older writings. The impact of religions of the Mediterranean is therefore unquestionable, whether it be Judaism, Christianity or Islam. For this reason, it is worth considering the messages pertaining to love as the indisputable basis and meaning of marriage and family encountered in the writings of these religions.

**Christianity** considers love as a programme and a goal: '[a]bove all, clothe yourselves with love, which binds everything together in perfect harmony'.[15] The apostles' concept of love stems from Christ's love of all people,[16] while St Paul considers the love between wife and husband as a commandment of love in its reciprocity, drawing an analogy with the love of Christ for the Church.[17] Moreover, the apostle commands children to obey their parents, which he considers 'just', and to fathers he says: 'do not provoke your children to anger, but bring them up in the discipline and instruction of the Lord'.[18]

A compassionate heart, kindness, humility, meekness, patience and tolerance are the commandments of family life.[19] Love that is the source of these behaviours which in turn lead to love represents a cycle of sustenance of family life.

In the Gospel according to Mark, the meaning and purpose of reciprocity, dependence and a deep unity of wife and husband in marriage are very clearly indicated. It invokes Christ's command and the Book of Genesis (Genesis 2:24). When a man leaves his father and mother to join his wife,[20] he can only do it out of pure, deep love.

The Old Testament provides proof of a deep-seated principle of marital fidelity, affection and love (eg Book of Ruth, Book of Tobias).[21] Love pervades the lines of the Song of Solomon, which is dedicated to passionate love. It 'stands for human life and promotes one of its vital aspects. In its own way it emphasises the

15 St Paul's Epistle to the Colossians (3:12,14).

16 'Therefore be imitators of God, as beloved children, and live in love, as Christ loved us and gave himself up for us, a fragrant offering and sacrifice to God', St Paul's Epistle to Ephesians (5:2).

17 'He who loves his wife loves himself. For no one ever hates his own body, but he nourishes and tenderly cares for it, just as Christ does for the church . . . [e]ach of you, however, should love his wife as himself, and a wife should respect her husband' (Ephesians 5:25–33).

18 Ibid (6:4).

19 St Paul's Epistle to the Colossians (3:12).

20 'At the beginning of creation, God made them male and female. Because of this, a man should leave his father and mother and be joined together with his wife, and the two will be one flesh. So they are no longer two but one flesh.' Mark (10:6–9).

21 'Lord . . . [g]rant that she and I will be shown mercy and grow old together', Tobias (8:7).

good and the dignity of love drawing a man to a woman'[22] – the love of man is a reflection of the love of God.[23]

So, from the Old Testament to the present day the pre-Christian and Christian conception of love between a man and a woman is equated with the love of Jesus Christ for the people of Israel, ie the Church, that is to say for every man. Wife and husband united in marriage are expected by the nature of marriage to give each other endless and unconditional love, to be one, to form an unbreakable union for life,[24] and in this union to give oneself wholly to the other in fidelity.[25] Love in its essence cannot be limited or conditioned, recalled or unfaithful. If it is, then it is not love. Love is what St Paul the Apostle describes in the Epistle to the Corinthians (Hymn to Love, 1 Cor 13:1–13).

The Catholic wedding ceremony[26] also refers to love that marks the beginning of the life shared between a man and a woman, and which must persist. Several references to love are made in the ceremony, which stress its significance in marriage.[27] What is more, both the bride and the bridegroom make a promise of fidelity, love and respect in their wedding vows.[28] By exchanging wedding rings[29] they reiterate their love and fidelity.[30]

22 Translated from *Jeruzalemska Biblija* (*The Bible of Jerusalem*), *Kršćanska sadašnjost* (Zagreb, 2011) 926.

23 'for love is as strong as death . . . [r]ushing waters can't quench love; rivers can't wash it away', Song of Solomon, (8:6–7).

24 'So they are no longer two but one flesh. Therefore, humans must not pull apart what God has put together.' (Matthew 19:6.); see also Genesis (2:24).

25 Spouses 'are called to grow continually in their communion through day-to-day fidelity to their marriage promise of total mutual self-giving.' See also John Paul II, 'Apostolic exhortation', *Familiaris consortio* (22 November 1981), (1982) 19: *Acta Apostolicae Sedis* 74, 101.

26 *Rite of Marriage* renewed by a decision of the Holy Ecumenical Assembly of the Second Vatican Council, promulgated by the authority of Pope Paul VI, has been in force since 1 July 1969.

27 'My dear friends, you have come together in this church so that the Lord may seal and strengthen your love in the presence of the Church's minister and this community. Christ abundantly blesses this love' . . . [w]ill you love and honour each other as man and wife for the rest of your lives?' (English version: *The Rite of Marriage* (Catholic Book Publishing Co, 1970)), Croatian version: *Nedjeljni i blagdanski misal za narod*, 2. dopunjeno izdanje, (Zagreb: Kršćanska sadašnjost, 1992) 846; *Red slavljenja ženidbe*, 2. Tipsko izdanje (Zagreb, Kršćanska sadašnjost, 1997), no 59, 24. In the rite of marriage according to the Church of England there is a difference in the priest's questions for the man and the woman. The man is asked: 'Wilt thou love her, comfort her, honour, and keep her, in sickness and in health, and forsaking all other, keep thee only unto her, so long as ye both shall live?', and the woman is asked: 'Wilt thou obey him, and serve him, love, honour, and keep him, in sickness and in health, and forsaking all other, keep thee only unto him, so long as ye both shall live?'; see *The Book of Common Prayer and Administation of the Sacraments* . . . to the Use of the Church of England (Cambridge University Press, 1961) 177.

28 'I, *Name*, take you, *Name*, to be my wife and promise to be true to you in good times and in bad, in sickness and in health, to love you and honour you all the days of my life'.

29 The ring as the circle symbolises continuity, permanence, eternity.

30 '*Name*, take this ring as a sign of my love and fidelity'. Prior to these words, the rings are blessed by the priest with these words: 'Lord, bless these rings that you will give one another

## Love in Sharia law and Judaism

Even though the European legal systems, as mentioned above, stem from the Digest and the Code of Justinian and are rooted in Christianity, we believe it necessary to draw a comparison with some important characteristics of Islamic law and point to some relevant differences. Sharia law is unalterable[31] and applies to all its members. It is to some degree complemented by state regulations, but these in turn have to be in line with the religious law. There have been occasional attempts at codification, but they have all been unsuccessful, especially in the area of family law.[32] Some Islamic countries, however, have enacted laws regulating certain institutes such as maintenance, divorce, etc.[33] It is thought that these reformist laws primarily sought to make divorce more difficult for the husband, facilitating filing divorce petitions for the wife, prohibiting underage people from marrying, guaranteeing freedom for women, particularly in choosing a husband, and imposing boundaries on or fully banning polygamy.[34]

As regards the theme of love as a source of legal regulation of marriage, the Qur'an prescribes the duty of love for husband to wife (in addition to securing her maintenance, sustenance, clothes, dwelling and medical care).[35] The wife must respect her husband, while her own rights, especially from the Western perspective on women's rights, are substantially different to the detriment of women.

Jewish law is in many ways similar to Roman, German or canon law, stemming mostly from divine positive law.[36]According to Jewish law, marriage is a permanent union of two persons of opposite sex, which commits a man and a woman to mutual respect and love.[37]

## Love in family regulations

Judeo-Christian sources had an impact on the national regulations that have developed in the area of family relations, particularly on those that remain in force in the European countries. These influences are present in the domains of tradition

as a symbol of love and fidelity'; see *Nedjeljni i blagdanski misal za narod*, 2. dopunjeno izdanje (Zagreb: Kršćanska sadašnjost, 1992) 848; *Red slavljenja ženidbe*, 2. tipsko izdanje, (Zagreb: Kršćanska sadašnjost, 1997) 66, 27.

31 Alexander Bergmann, Murad Ferid and Dieter Henrich, *Internationales Ehe- und Kindschaftsrecht* (*International Marriage and Children's Rights*) (Verlag für Standesamtwesen GmbH, Frankfurt a M, Berlin, 2007), Religiöse Eherechte – Islam, 2.

32 Ibid 3.

33 Ibid 3.

34 'Die Hauptziele dieser Reformgesetze sind, die Erschwerung der Scheidung für den Mann, die Ermöglichung der gerichtlichen Scheidung auf Antrag der Frau, das Verbot der Kinderehe, die Garantie der Freiheit für die Frau, die bei der Parnerwahl selbst entscheiden soll; die Einschränkung oder das gänzliche Verbot der Polygamie', ibid 4.

35 Ibid 12.

36 Bergmann, Ferid and Henrich, above n 31, 173; Lieferung, Religiöse Eherecht – Juden, 45 Lieferung, 1.

37 Ibid 4.

and religion as important factors in the shaping of national family regulations. The entire Western civil law circle is marked by the influence of the Digest, which is in turn based on the remnants of Roman law. This is particularly true of the multitude of institutes, which have received many updates over the course of history (eg divorce, maintenance, custody of children, etc). However, the impact of the Old and New Testament on the family law concepts of marriage and family remains dominant.

Law is more than simply a set of regulations; it also paves the way for the society, directing its members towards desirable conduct. Law should, presumably above all, protect human rights, look out for every individual, particularly children and other dependent members of the society. Law should be entrenched in a man's consciousness by his morality and Kant's moral law; and for those bereft of such thought, law should at least provide boundaries for their behaviour.

The law of marriage focuses on the formation of marriage, its effects and dissolution. Different national regulations (found in civil codes or special family regulations) are confronted with various age-old traditions coming from religion, custom, culture and the environment. These account for the diversity of 'European family law', which is at the same time its richness.[38]

At this moment, family law is facing a challenge of relatively fast changes in the concept of family, especially with certain groups of people, but at the same time, it continues to reflect vast agreement about the traditional concept of family, desirability of marriage and the need to retain it as the only type of family. The need for a legal imperative of protection of the family was also expressed in a recent UN Resolution.[39]

Considering the ancient single source of national family systems in Europe – the Old and New Testament, as mentioned above – we will look into how the commands of love from those ancient scriptures dispersed, changed shape or disappeared in national family regulations and why these transformations took place.

The outline of a series of European laws presented here will demonstrate their differences, and show how the 'commandment of love' took different shapes. Still, all of them have preserved love in some shape or form.

**Andorra** (*Marriage Act of 1995*) imposes a duty of the spouses to live together, respect one another, be faithful, help each other morally and materially, and behave in the best interest of the family (Article 9).[40]

38 Irena Majstorović, 'Obiteljsko pravo kao različitost u jedinstvu: Europska unija i Hrvatska' in Aleksandra Korać Graovac and Irena Majstorović (eds), *Europsko obiteljsko pravo* (*European Family Law*) (Narodne novine, Zagreb, 2013) 1–24.

39 Human Rights Council adopted on 1 July 2015 the *Resolution on the Protection of the Family* (A/HRC/29/L.5).

40 Article 9, 'Die Ehegatten sind, außer wenn sie durch triftigen Grund daran gehinder sind, zur ehelichen Lebensgemeinschaft verpflichtet, und sie sind ferner verpflichtet, sich gegenseitig zu achten, einander die Treue zu bewahren, einander moralisch und materiell zu helfen und stets im Interesse der Familie tätig zu werden'; see Bergmann, Ferid and Henrich, above n 31, 173; Lieferung, 27 (Andorra).

The **Austrian** *General Civil Code* (*Allgemeines Bürgerliches Gesetzbuch* – 'ABGB') imposes a duty on the spouses to form a comprehensive union, which entails in particular cohabitation, fidelity, kindness and support.[41] So, on the one hand, the tangible, external elements of marriage (cohabitation) are present, and on the other those which can be assumed knowing the nature of a woman and a man sharing a life together (the comprehensiveness of a marital union). Kindness is a reflection of respect, and fidelity, which primarily refers to sexual fidelity, is a *condicio sine qua non* of most marriages. Fidelity can, however, be considered in a broader sense in terms of loyalty, in the same manner as support can be material (in terms of maintenance), but also moral (in sickness, mourning, etc).

**Belgium** provides for a similar content of marriage in its *Civil Code*, imposing a duty of cohabitation, mutual fidelity, provision of support and assistance.[42]

The two territories[43] of **Bosnia** and **Herzegovina** have two separate family Acts,[44] regulating spousal rights in an almost identical manner. Both Acts provide for the duty of fidelity, mutual respect and assistance.[45] The provisions regarding a mutually agreed place of residence between spouses and handling of affairs in the marital union, ie the family, imply cohabitation.

The **Bulgarian** *Family Code* connects the regulation of family relations with the principles of respect, care and assistance among family members, while the relations between the spouses are based on mutual respect, care for the family and understanding.[46]

41 *Austrian General Civil Code* 1812 (*Allgemeines Bürgerliches Gesetzbuch*) § 90(1) 'Die Ehegatten sind einander zur umfassenden ehelichen Lebensgemeinschaft, besonders zum gemeinsamen Wohnen, sowie zur Treue, zur anständigen Begegnung und zum Beistand verpflichtet', accessed on 3 February 2016, available at: <www.jusline.at/Allgemeines_Buergerliches_Gesetzbuch_(ABGB).html>.

42 *Belgium Civil Code* 1998, 'Les époux ont le devoir d'habiter ensemble; ils se doivent mutuellement fidélité, secours, assistance' accessed on 3 February 2016, available at: <www.droitbelge.be/codes.asp#civ>.

43 Federation and the Brčko District.

44 Obiteljski Zakon Federacije Bosne I Hercegovine, accessed on 3 February 2016, available at: <www.fbihvlada.gov.ba/bosanski/zakoni/2005/zakoni/25hrv.pdf and http://skupstinabd.ba/3-zakon/ba/Porodic – ni%20zakon%20Brc – ko%20Distrikta%20BiH/000%20 23–07%20Porodic – ni%20zakon%20Brc – ko%20Distrikta%20BiH.pdf>.

45 *Family Act of the Federation of Bosnia and Herzegovina*, No 35/05, 41/05, Article 30: (1) The spouses shall be equal in marriage. (2) The spouses shall be faithful to one another and provide to each other respect and assistance. (3) The spouses shall jointly decide about the place of residence. (4) The spouses shall jointly and with equal participation decide about having and rearing children, regulation of their relationship and conduct of affairs in the marriage, ie the family.

*Family Act of the Brčko District*, Art. 20: (1) The spouses shall be equal in marriage. (2) The spouses shall be faithful to one another and provide to each other respect and assistance. (3) The spouses shall jointly decide about the place of residence. (4) The spouses shall jointly and with equal participation decide about having and rearing children, regulation of their relationship and conduct of affairs in the marriage, ie the family.

46 Article 2, The family relations shall be regulated in compliance with the following principles: (7) respect, care and support between the family members, Art 14. The relations between

The **Croatian** family legislation[47] mentions the principle of solidarity in family life, the duty of mutual respect and provision of assistance to family members, and among the personal rights and duties of the spouses it mentions the duty of fidelity, mutual assistance and maintenance, respect and maintenance of harmonious marital and family relations.[48] It is interesting to note that solidarity in family life and in the family community is mentioned among the fundamental principles. However, we contend that this word should be replaced with a word with more emotional weight, such as 'devotion' or 'love'. Solidarity can have a materialistic connotation; we, therefore, do not believe it to be a dominant characteristic of family life or communication between the spouses, but rather of the relationship between the state and an individual who is in some sort of trouble.[49]

However, it should be noted that (taken from the *2003 Family Code*) in the ceremony of marriage, according to Article 19, the registrar, among other things, emphasises the 'significance of marriage, and in particular that a harmonious marriage is paramount for family life'.

The **Czech** *Civil Code*[50] contains two provisions regarding the rights and duties of the spouses, similar to the above regulations. They concern the duty of mutual respect, cohabitation, fidelity, mutual assistance, but also, interestingly enough, the duty to respect the other one's dignity (section 687).[51] Another interesting provision concerns the duty to provide information about the other spouse concerning his or her income, assets and liabilities, work, education, and other similar activities (section 688).

The **Finnish** *Marriage Act*[52] contains brief references to equality, mutual trust and work for the good of the family.

---

spouses shall be built up on the basis of mutual respect, common cares for the family and understanding. Promulgated State Gazette, No 47/23.06.2009, effective 1.10.2009, amended, SG No 74/15.09.2009, effective 1.10.2009, SG No 82/16.10.2009.

47 *Family Act,* Narodne novine, 105/2015.

48 Ibid Article 4: 'Solidarity is the basic principle of family life. All family members shall provide each other respect and assistance.' Art 31: 'The spouses shall be faithful to one another, provide assistance and material support, respect one another and maintain harmonious marital and family relations.'

49 In Chapter IV – Solidarity, of the *European Charter of Fundamental Rights,* Articles 27–38 lay down various rights of workers, such as employment, social security and social assistance, health care, environmental and consumer protection.

50 *Civil Code of the Czech Republic* (3 February 2012), available at: http://obcanskyzakonik.justice.cz/images/pdf/Civil-Code.pdf.

51 Other duties such as maintenance of the union, creating a healthy family environment and joint care of children would go beyond the 'emotional' duties of the spouses.

52 Section 2 (411/1987) 'The spouses shall be equal. In the marriage, they shall display mutual trust and together work for the good of the family'. 234/1929; amendments up to 1226/2001 included, accessed on 3 February2016, available at: <www.finlex.fi/en/laki/kaannokset/1929/en19290234.pdf>.

The simple provision of Article 212 of the **French** *Code Civil* imposes a spousal duty of mutual respect, fidelity, support and assistance.[53]

A rare provision is found in §1353 of the **German** *Civil Code*[54] providing that marriage is formed 'auf Lebenszeit', ie 'for life' or for a longer period. It also imposes the duty to live in a marital community and be responsible for one another.

The **Italian** *Civil Code*[55] imposes the spousal duties of fidelity, moral and material support, cooperation in the interest of the family and cohabitation, and the duty to contribute to meeting family needs.

The **Latvian** *Civil Code*[56] speaks of the duty of mutual fidelity, cohabitation, mutual care and joint efforts for the good of the family.

According to the *Civil Code* of **Luxemburg**[57] the spouses have to live together, with the courts having jurisdiction in the event of disagreement as to their joint residence.[58] However, no provisions pertaining to fidelity, mutual assistance and similar duties are found.

**Montenegrin** law contains a similar provision to that of the Bosnian and Herzegovinian legislation mentioned above, and to Croatian, as will be pointed out below, concerning a duty to lead a life together, mutual fidelity and respect, development and maintenance of harmonious marital and family relations.[59]

53 Les époux se doivent mutuellement respect, fidélité, secours, assistance, accessed on 4 February 2016, available at:<http://legifrance.gouv.fr/affichCodeArticle.do?cidTexte=LEGITEXT000006070721&idArticle=LEGIARTI000006422735&dateTexte=20160202>.

54 (1) Die Ehe wird auf Lebenszeit geschlossen. Die Ehegatten sind einander zur ehelichen Lebensgemeinschaft verpflichtet; sie tragen füreinander Verantwortung; accessed on 4 February 2016, available at: <http://buergerliches-gesetzbuch.net/paragraph-1353>.

55 Dal matrimonio deriva l'obbligo reciproco alla fedeltà, all'assistenza morale e materiale, alla collaborazione nell'interesse della famiglia e alla coabitazione). Entrambi i coniugi sono tenuti, ciascuno in relazione alle proprie sostanze e alla propria capacità di lavoro professionale o casalingo, a contribuire ai bisogni della famiglia, accessed on 4 February 2016, available at: <www.jus.unitn.it/cardozo/obiter_dictum/codciv/Codciv.htm>.

56 *Latvian Civil Code* s 84 Marriage creates a duty on the part of a husband and a wife to be faithful to each other, to live together, to take care of each other and to jointly ensure the welfare of their family.

57 Civil Code of Luxembourg, available at: <www.legilux.public.lu/leg/textescoordonnes/codes/code_civil/CodeCivil_PageAccueil.pdf>.

58 Article 215. (L. 4 juillet 2014) Les conjoints sont tenus de vivre ensemble. A défaut d'accord entre conjoints sur la résidence commune, la décision appartiendra au juge qui la fixera après avoir entendu les motifs invoqués par chacun des conjoints. Néanmoins, le tribunal pourra, pour des motifs légitimes, autoriser les conjoints à résider séparément. En çe cas il statuera également sur la résidence des enfants.

59 Article 40: 'The spouses shall lead a life together, be faithful to one another, provide mutual assistance, respect one another, help one another grow, maintain harmonious marital and family relations.' Službeni list Republike Crne Gore, no. 1/2007, 9.1.2007, accessed on 4 February 2016, available at: <www.sluzbenilist.me/PravniAktDetalji.aspx?tag=%7B79054F65-3C37-4FC8-912B-49704386C652%7D>.

**The Netherlands** binds the spouses to mutual fidelity, provision of assistance and support, and anything else the other spouse might need.[60]

**Polish** law binds the spouses to marital relationship, support, fidelity and collaboration for the benefit of the family (Article 23 *Polish Family and Guardianship Code*).[61]

**Portugal** (*Civil Code*, §1672) sets out the duty of mutual respect, fidelity, collaboration, support and cohabitation.[62]

Only one European country, the **Russian Federation**, mentions 'love' in its laws, ie in the general principles of the *Family Code*.[63] It reads as follows:

> 1 . . . [t]he family legislation shall proceed from the necessity to consolidate the family, to build family relations on feelings of mutual love and respect, on mutual assistance and on responsibility of all its members before the family.[64]

Mutual respect and assistance are also referred to further in the text among the rights and duties of the spouses.[65]

**Slovakia** (*Family Code*, §§ 18–20) establishes the duty of cohabitation, fidelity, respect for each other's dignity and support.[66]

**Spain** (*Civil Code*, Articles 66–68; Article 68 modified by Law 15/2005)) also prescribes the duty of respect, support, thoughtfulness, cohabitation and fidelity.[67]

**Sweden** prescribes in almost identical wording the duty of fidelity, thoughtfulness and cohabitation (*Marriage Act*, section 1, para 2).[68]

European legal documents do not deal with marriage and family in terms of regulating their source, foundations and purpose. This is understandable to a certain extent, considering that the *Charter of Fundamental Rights of the European Union (2010)*[69] in particular only systematises existing legal principles[70] and

60 Article 1:81: Spouses owe each other fidelity, assistance and support. They have a duty to provide each other with what is necessary. Accessed at: <www.dutchcivillaw.com/civilcodebook01.htm>.

61 *Polish Family and Guardianship Code*, accessed on 5 February 2016, available at: <www.coe.int/familypolicy/database>.

62 *Portugal Civil Code* 1996, §1672.

63 *The Family Code of the Russian Federation* no. 223-fz of 29 December 1995 (with the Amendments and Additions of 15 November 1997, 27 June 1998, 2 January 2000, 22 August, 28 December 2004, 3 June, 18, 29 December 2006, 21 July 2007, 30 June 2008), available at: <www.jafbase.fr/docEstEurope/RussianFamilyCode1995.pdf>.

64 Ibid Art 1.

65 Ibid Article 31. '3. The spouses shall be obliged to build their relations in the family on the basis of mutual respect and mutual assistance, to facilitate the welfare and the consolidation of the family, and to take care of their children's well-being and development.'

66 *Slovakia Family Code* 2010, §§ 18–20.

67 *Spain Civil Code* 1889, Arts 66–68; Art 68.

68 *Sweden Marriage Act* 2001, s 1, para 2.

69 *Charter of Fundamental Rights of the European Union,* OJ C 326, 26.10.2012.

70 See Siniša Rodin, 'Foreword' in Nada Bodiroga-Vukobrat and Sanja Barić, *Povelja temeljnih prava Europske unije s komentarom* (Charter of fundamental rights of the European Union with a commentary) (Organizator, Zagreb, 2002) 9.

does not enter the sphere of unification of national laws. Moreover, the European Union has limits as to the extent to which it can interfere with national family law systems,[71] so its legislation primarily concerns conflict of laws and procedural law.[72] It is thus no surprise that the Charter refers to the right to marriage and family only in Article 9,[73] which it guarantees pursuant to national regulations governing these rights, remaining at a superficial level and within the boundaries of human rights, without tackling the sensitive foundations of these rights. The European legislator, if he can be called that, seems to have 'drifted away' towards the world of some other human rights, not dealing with the original foundations of these rights and institutes, turning his glance away from the importance of the very core of the relationships such as the one between spouses.

Even though half a century older, the *Convention for the Protection of Human Rights and Fundamental Freedoms (1950)* goes along similar lines, containing an almost identical provision in Article 12, but bearing, however, one important difference – unlike the Charter, which dropped the heterosexual feature of marriage, it speaks of the right to marry and found a family as a right given to a man and a woman.[74] However, the Convention also avoids dealing with the internal relationship between husband and wife which gives its mark to marriage, nor does it speak about the foundations on which a marriage should grow and become stronger.

## Concluding remarks

The outline of legal provisions from a number of European states presented here shows great similarities between the different countries. It is interesting to note that the characteristics of marriage referred to in the various regulations can be construed as the foundations, but also the meaning and purpose of, marriage. From a legal perspective, all the presented features are both rights and duties (responsibilities) of the spouses. Among them are: cohabitation, fidelity, kindness, support, mutual respect, assistance, joint care for the family, understanding, mutual trust, joint efforts for the good of the family, a long-term union, life in a marital community, responsibility for one another, moral and material support, collaboration in the interest of the family, contribution to family needs, mutual care, joint work on securing the good of the family, development and maintenance of harmonious marital and family relations, moral and material support, conduct compatible with family interests, respect for one another's dignity, thoughtfulness.

71 Similarly see Aleksandra Korać Graovac, 'Povelja o temeljnim pravima Europske unije i obiteljsko pravo' in: Graovac and Majstorović, above n 38, 25.

72 Ibid 15.

73 *Charter of Fundamental Rights of the European Union,* OJ C 326, 26.10.2012, Art 9, 'The right to marry and the right to found a family shall be guaranteed in accordance with the national laws governing the exercise of these rights.'

74 More on this comparison but on the level of the right to marry and found a family see *Italian Civil Code*, above n 52, 39.

Love got 'stuck' in the branches of family only in Russian legislation.

In conclusion, it can be said that the multitude of expressions speaking of the need, grown into a duty, of giving oneself fully to another in marriage,[75] which cannot exist without love, can be justified in the legal perspective on rights and duties as a classical dichotomy of the legal personality of every individual. Listing marital duties, beginning with cohabitation and ending with the general expression 'the interest of the family', is much simpler than justifying the expression 'duty of love'. It is nearly impossible, because love is born and exists, or it does not. It cannot be enforced, like a debt; it would not be true. The love of the spouses can be seen in all the various forms of giving – fidelity, respect, assistance, long-term commitment, material support, and other variations, but it is not enforceable. Legislators find it easier to prescribe the 'derivatives' of love because their absence can be proved when a divorce is sought. If their absence is proved in a divorce proceeding, this means that there is no love and that the meaning of the marriage has disappeared. It can thus be concluded that the practical reasons of procedural and substantive nature have forced the legislator to choose to prescribe various reflections of marital love as duties of the spouses, implying the existence of love as indispensable for a successful marriage and family life. Consolation can be found in the fact that the affection between a woman and a man, and the decision to live together in marriage, do not depend on a legal norm, so that expressions of mutual love have no connection to the legal regulation. The content of a marriage depends on the love felt and given selflessly by a particular woman and man to one another.

## References

*Austrian General Civil Code* 1812

*Belgium Civil Code* 1998

Bergmann, Alexander, Murad Ferid and Dieter Henrich, *Internationales Ehe- und Kindschaftsrecht* (*International Marriage and Children's Rights*) (Verlag für Standesamtwesen GmbH, Frankfurt a M, Berlin, 2007)

Bodiroga-Vukobrat, Nada and Sanja Barić, *Povelja temeljnih prava Europske unije s komentarom* (Charter of Fundamental Rights of the European Union with a commentary) (Organizator, Zagreb, 2002)

75 'What does one person give to another? He gives of himself, of the most precious he has, he gives of his life. This does not necessarily mean that he sacrifices his life for the other – but that he gives him of that which is alive in him; he gives him of his joy, of his interest, of his understanding, of his knowledge, of his humour, of his sadness – of all expressions and manifestations of that which is alive in him. In thus giving of his life, he enriches the other person, he enhances the other's sense of aliveness by enhancing his own sense of aliveness. He does not give in order to receive; giving is in itself exquisite joy. But in giving he cannot help bringing something to life in the other person, and this which is brought to life reflects back to him. In true giving he can but receive that which is returned to him. By giving we make the other person a giver and we both take part in the joy of what is brought to life', Fromm, above n 1, 39.

*Book of Common Prayer and Administation of the Sacraments* (Cambridge: University Press, 1961)

*Bulgarian Family Code* Promulgated State Gazette, No 47/23.06.2009, effective 1.10.2009, amended, SG No 74/15.09.2009, effective 1.10.2009, SG No 82/ 16.10.2009

*Charter of Fundamental Rights of the European Union*, OJ C 326, 26.10.2012

*Civil Code of Luxembourg* 1998, available at: <www.legilux.public.lu/leg/textescoordonnes/codes/code_civil/CodeCivil_PageAccueil.pdf>

*Civil Code of the Czech Republic* 2012

Cohen, Lloyd R and Joshua D Wright (eds), *Marriage as a Disorder of Choice, Research Handbook on the Economics of Family Law* (Edward Elgar Publishing Inc, 2011)

*Croatian Family Act* 2015, Narodne novine, 105 of 2015

*Croatian Family Code 2003*

*Family Act of the Brčko District* (Official Gazette of BDBiH no. 23/97)

*Family Act of the Federation of Bosnia and Herzegovina*, No 35/05, 41/05

*Family Act* of the Republic of Croatia of 2015

*Finnish Marriage Act* 411 of 1987, available at: <www.finlex.fi/en/laki/kaannokset/1929/en19290234.pdf>

*French Civil Code* 2004, available at: <http://legifrance.gouv.fr/affichCodeArticle.do?cidTexte=LEGITEXT000006070721&idArticle=LEGIARTI000006422735&dateTexte=20160202>

Fromm, Erich, *Umijeće ljubavi* (*The Art of Loving*) (Harper & Brothers, 1956) also available online at: <www.znakovi-vremena.net/Dokumenti/Erich_Fromm-Umjece_ljubavi.pdf>

*Gas and Dubois v France* [2010] ECHR 444 (11 March 2011)

Girgis, Sherif, Ryan T Anderson and Robert P George (eds), *What is Marriage? Woman and Man: A Defense* (Encounter Books, 2012)

Graovac, Aleksandra Korać and Irena Majstorović (eds), *Europsko obiteljsko pravo* ('European Family Law') (Narodne novine, Zagreb, 2013)

Hrvatska enciklopedija (Croatian encyclopedia), Leksikografski zavod 6 *Miroslav Krleža*, Zagreb 710

Human Rights Council adopted on 1 July 2015 the *Resolution on the Protection of the Family* (A/HRC/29/L.5)

*Italian Civil Code* 1942, available at: <www.jus.unitn.it/cardozo/obiter_dictum/codciv/Codciv.htm>

*Jeruzalemska Biblija* (*The Bible of Jerusalem*), *Kršćanska sadašnjost* (Zagreb, 2011)

John Paul II, 'Apostolic exhortation', *Familiaris consortio* (22 November 1981), (1982) 19: *Acta Apostolicae Sedis* 74

*Latvian Civil Code* 1997

*Nedjeljni i blagdanski misal za narod*, 2. dopunjeno izdanje (Zagreb: Kršćanska sadašnjost, 1992)

Obiteljski Zakon Federacije Bosne I Hercegovine, accessed on 3 February 2016, available at: <www.fbihvlada.gov.ba/bosanski/zakoni/2005/zakoni/25hrv.pdf and http://skupstinabd.ba/3-zakon/ba/Porodic – ni%20zakon%20Brc – ko%20 Distrikta%20BiH/000%2023–07%20Porodic – ni%20zakon%20Brc – ko%20 Distrikta%20BiH.pdf>

*Polish Family and Guardianship Code* 1964

*Portugal Civil Code* 1996

*Red slavljenja ženidbe*, 2. tipsko izdanje, (Zagreb: Kršćanska sadašnjost, 1997)
*Rite of Marriage* (Catholic Book Publishing Co, 1970); Croatian version: *Nedjeljni i blagdanski misal za narod*, 2. dopunjeno izdanje, (Zagreb: Kršćanska sadašnjost, 1992)
*Russian Federation Code 1995*, (with the Amendments and Additions of 15 November 1997, 27 June 1998, 2 January 2000, 22 August, 28 December 2004, 3 June, 18, 29 December 2006, 21 July 2007, 30 June 2008)
*Schalk and Kopf v Austria* [2010] ECHR 995 (24 June 2010)
*Slovakia Family Code* 2010
Službeni list Republike Crne Gore, no. 1/2007, 9.1.2007, accessed on 4 February 2016, available at: <www.sluzbenilist.me/PravniAktDetalji.aspx?tag=%7B79054F65-3C37-4FC8-912B-49704386C652%7D>
*Spain Civil Code* 1889
*Sweden Marriage Act* 2001
*X and others v Austria* [2013] ECHR 148 (19 February 2013)

# Index

For Product Safety Concerns and Information please contact our EU representative GPSR@taylorandfrancis.com
Taylor & Francis Verlag GmbH, Kaufingerstraße 24, 80331 München, Germany

www.ingramcontent.com/pod-product-compliance
Ingram Content Group UK Ltd.
Pitfield, Milton Keynes, MK11 3LW, UK
UKHW022010180926
475701UK00003B/289
* 9 7 8 0 3 6 7 3 3 6 7 7 6 *